MW00355184

Ideology, Social Theory, and the Environment

Ideology, Social Theory, and the Environment

William D. Sunderlin

ROWMAN & LITTLEFIELD PUBLISHERS, INC.
Lanham • Boulder • New York • Oxford

ROWMAN & LITTLEFIELD PUBLISHERS, INC.

Published in the United States of America
by Rowman & Littlefield Publishers, Inc.
An Imprint of the Rowman & Littlefield Publishing Group
4720 Boston Way, Lanham, Maryland 20706
www.rowmanlittlefield.com

P.O. Box 317, Oxford OX2 9RU, United Kingdom

Copyright © 2003 by Rowman & Littlefield Publishers, Inc.

Cover Image Photo Credits: Swallowtail butterfly (Papilio ulysses) in Indonesia (Alain Compost); log extraction in Serawak, Malaysia (John Turnbull); children selling baobab fruit in Zimbabwe (Manuel Ruíz Pérez); Indah Kiat pulp and paper factory in Sumatra, Indonesia (Christian Cossalter). All photographs property of the Center for International Forestry Research (CIFOR). Used with permission.

All rights reserved. No part of this publication may be reproduced, stored in a retrieval system, or transmitted in any form or by any means, electronic, mechanical, photocopying, recording, or otherwise, without the prior permission of the publisher.

British Library Cataloguing in Publication Information Available

Library of Congress Cataloging-in-Publication Data
Sunderlin, William D.
  Ideology, social theory, and the environment / William D. Sunderlin.
    p. cm.
Includes bibliographical references and index.
  ISBN 0-7425-1969-4 (cloth : alk. paper)—ISBN 0-7425-1970-8 (paper : alk. paper)
Environmentalism. 2. Ideology. 3. Neo-Malthusianism. 4. Economic development—Environmental aspects. I. Title.
  GE195 .S86 2003
  363.7—dc21

                                                            2002004954

Printed in the United States of America

∞ ™ The paper used in this publication meets the minimum requirements of American National Standard for Information Sciences—Permanence of Paper for Printed Library Materials, ANSI/NISO Z39.48-1992.

To my father, Charles Eugene Sunderlin
And to the memory of my mother,
Sylvia Sweetman Sunderlin

Contents

	Acknowledgments	ix
	Introduction	1
Chapter 1	Ideology, Social Theory, and Paradigms	13
Chapter 2	Human Evolution and Socioenvironmental Outcomes	37
Chapter 3	Ideology and the Environment: From Paradigm Isolation to Paradigm Integration	76
Chapter 4	Competing Views on the Population-Resource Balance	108
Chapter 5	Economic Growth: For Worse or for Better?	146
Chapter 6	Toward a New Concept and Definition of Environmentalism	187
Chapter 7	Global Environmental Change and the Challenge of Paradigm Integration	207
	References	215
	Index	243
	About the Author	261

~

Acknowledgments

My first debt is to the Center for International Forestry Research (CIFOR) for granting me a sabbatical leave to write this book. I want to especially thank Jeff Sayer (former director general of CIFOR) and the center's board of trustees for recognizing the merits of this project in spite of the fact that it is not squarely focused on forestry.

I am very grateful to the following people for painstakingly reviewing the book prospectus and/or providing detailed comments on draft chapters of the book: Filomeno Aguilar, Martha Armstrong, Jill Belsky, Gilles Bergeron, Fred Buttel, Navroz Dubash, David Kaimowitz, Ed Kinane, Pieter Leroy, Jack Manno, Nancy Peluso, Manuel Ruíz Pérez, Michael Ross, Tom Rudel, and Sven Wunder. Ed Kinane spent countless hours doing a first-rate job of copyediting before I sent the draft to the publishers. At Rowman & Littlefield, Dianne Ewing, Gretchen Hanisch, April Leo, and Chrisona Schmidt were gracious, patient, and efficient in escorting me through the publishing process and in bringing my draft up to standard. I value Brooke Graves's professionalism in doing the index.

I want the following people to know how much I appreciate their various gestures of support in helping me produce this book: Arild Angelsen, Chris Barr, Neil Byron, Anne Casson, Carol Pierce Colfer, Wil de Jong, Chimère Diaw, Amy Dudley, David Edmunds, Paul Gellert, Ed Griffin-Nolan, Sri Hastuti, Zacky Irvan, Pam Jagger, Esther Katz, Budhy Kristanty, Lois Levitan, Ousseynou Ndoye, Bob Oakley, Molly Oakley, Widya Prajanthi, Sisi Ratnasari, Yahya Sampurna, Frances Seymour, Patricia Shanley, Yuni Soeripto, Gene Sunderlin, Etienne van de Walle, Gary Weinstein, and Wiwik Widyarini.

~

Introduction

Although the contrast between our civilization and that of our hunter-gatherer ancestors could scarcely be greater, we do have one thing in common—we too depend
entirely on Earth's natural systems and resources to sustain us. Unfortunately, the
expanding global economy that is driving the Dow Jones to new highs is, as currently structured, outgrowing those ecosystems. Evidence of this can be seen in
shrinking forests, eroding soils, falling water tables, collapsing fisheries, rising tem-
peratures, dying coral reefs, melting glaciers, and disappearing plant and animal
species. (Lester Brown, project director of the Worldwatch Institute, in *State of the
World 2000* [Brown et al. 2000, 4])

Since the first Earth Day was held thirty years ago, report cards on Planet Earth
have become a litany of gloomy predictions: global warming, overpopulation, pol-
luted oceans and dwindling natural resources. The arrival of the 21st century is the
perfect moment to reexamine our planet's ability to sustain mankind, and *Earth
Report 2000*, sponsored by the Competitive Enterprise Institute—"the best environmental think tank in the country," according to the *Wall Street Journal*—sets a
new standard for such an examination. In remarkably clear fashion, *Earth Report
2000* explains the key issues regarding our planet's fitness to sustain future generations. It debunks many of the myths, statistical and scientific, that have influenced
policies of the recent past. (Ronald Bailey, Competitive Enterprise Institute, *Earth
Report 2000* [Bailey 2000a])

The views expressed by representatives of the Worldwatch Institute and the
Competitive Enterprise Institute could not be more different. Dating back to
1984, the Worldwatch Institute has published millions of copies of its *State of the
World* reports that are now distributed in thirty languages around the world. The

message of the institute is starkly pessimistic: Unless rapid population growth is brought under control, and unless excessive demands on the natural resource base are halted, civilization as we know it will collapse. Ronald Bailey first mobilized a frontal attack on the Worldwatch Institute with his *The True State of the Planet* (Bailey 1995) and then followed it up, through sponsorship of the Competitive Enterprise Institute, with *Earth Report 2000* (Bailey 2000a). Its diametrically opposite, optimistic message is that not only are human beings not in excess, and resources generally plentiful and pollution overstated, but the key to improving our situation is to allow material prosperity and economic growth to flourish.

Is the chasm between these views explained merely by differences in sources of information? Is it explained by lack of sufficient drive by one of the parties in the debate to uncover the real truth? Michael Novak, in the introduction of *Earth Report 2000*, appears to espouse this perspective, criticizing the environmental movement as follows:

> Instead of reflecting first, we sometimes rush into thoughtless action. Instead of making a reflective, seriously intended, self-committing choice, we sometimes prefer to follow the line of least resistance and to drift lazily along, long-term consequences be damned. (2000, xvii)

I believe this observation is seriously off the mark. Novak fails to grasp a basic point that is the premise of this book. The differences between the views espoused by representatives of the Worldwatch Institute and the Competitive Enterprise Institute, as well as the views of other analysts commenting on the state of the environment, are often best understood as differences in ideology, not differences in access to information and in the will to know. Lester Brown and Ronald Bailey are in complete disagreement on the degree and nature of the environmental threat, as well as what to do about it, because they have entirely different mental models of how the world works. These mental models are political, economic, and ecological and tend to be built on preconceptions about the nature of economic activity, the appropriateness of government intervention in the market, the path of socioeconomic development, and the ecological consequences of industrialization and wealth accumulation, among other issues.

The point I am making is not that environmental analysts are somehow less trustworthy for being guided by their worldviews. Environmental analysts, like analysts of all stripes and like all human beings, for that matter, are inescapably motivated by deeply held preconceptions about how the world works. The point being made is that by acknowledging and shedding light on the ideological premises that form the substrate of the views of analysts, and of our own views as well, we are better positioned to make sound judgments about what makes sense, and what does not make sense, in shaping our future.

The Crucial Importance of Ideology

The argument can be taken a step further. Ultimately, understanding the nuances and implications of competing ideologies may well be just as important as monitoring social, economic, and environmental data as a basis for making cogent decisions on management of the earth's future. Ideology is crucially important not only for understanding the causes and nature of our environmental problems but also for attaining durable solutions. Why is ideology so important? There are five reasons.

First, ideology is a filter through which we view, interpret, and evaluate socioeconomic evolution. Our mental models determine how we answer such questions as: Do capitalism, industrialization, and technological development have the potential to liberate human beings from poverty and disease? If yes, why? If not, why not?

Second, ideology—particularly political and economic ideology—explains why perspectives on environmental problems can be different and why they can be utterly contradictory. An example of contradictory views is, on one hand, the belief that humans greatly exceed the carrying capacity of the earth (Brown et al. 1999; Ehrlich 1996; Myers 1998) and, on the other hand, that the world would be better off with a larger population (Simon 1996; Wattenberg 1997; Eberstadt 2000a). Another example is the belief, at one extreme, that economic growth is the cause of environmental problems (Daly 1996a,b; Douthwaite 1999; Prugh et al. 1999) and, at the other extreme, that economic growth is the solution to environmental problems (Dunn and Kinney 1996; Huber 1999; Beckerman 1996). Simply examining the environmental views, data, and technical arguments that the proponents rely on would not produce an adequate understanding of why these positions are in deep conflict. Understanding their ideological premises, whether explicit or implicit, would be far more productive.

Third, there is much at stake in what kinds of environmental views prevail, and the ideology embedded in particular views helps determine whether they will become policy or be disregarded. For example, opposition to worldwide population planning programs was formalized in United States public policy beginning in the 1980s, in part through the efforts of Julian Simon, a conservative economist and population specialist at the University of Maryland (Ahlburg 1998). Pronatalist views were well received during the Reagan (1981–1989) and Bush (1989–1993) administrations, and more recently have found favor again in George W. Bush's presidency.

Fourth, ideology—and in particular political ideology—is important in environmental debates precisely because it is unacknowledged or disguised. Political ideology is often the "hidden agenda" or the "Trojan horse" behind an environmental proposal. We may misinterpret a debate as being framed exclusively or primarily in terms of ecological worldviews, when in fact political ideals are the essence of what is being contested. Knowledge of the politics that motivates a particular idea is crucial to understanding its merits and demerits. The importance of drawing attention to ideology is often in direct proportion to its absence from the discussion.

Fifth, ideology is crucially important even when a proponent of an environmental view may not display awareness of his or her own ideology, which is often the case. The example of the competing views of Lester Brown and Ronald Bailey, above, is instructive. Bailey, of the Competitive Enterprise Institute, is self-consciously and transparently on the right of the political spectrum. Brown does not identify his political orientation in his writings, though various aspects of his arguments mark him as a centrist. We are accustomed to thinking of ideological polemics happening between representatives of the left and right. Nevertheless, polemics between the left and the center, or between the center and the right (as in the case of Brown and Bailey), are every bit as bitterly contested and as important as battles that we might label as overtly political.

Key Messages in the Book

Because competing ideologies shape our understanding of how the world works, an understanding of ideology has to be brought—deliberately, forthrightly, and systematically—to the stage of discussion about the environment. For various reasons, the term "ideology" has practically vanished from intellectual discourse despite being as important a concept now as it ever has been (Eagleton 1991). Though for some people the term "ideology" has a pejorative meaning associated with such characteristics as tendentiousness and blind devotion to a cause, other, broader, and more neutral meanings of the term are more appropriate. Rescuing the term from its negative connotations is an important project because the pejorative meaning rests on the false assumption that ideology is what "they" have and what "we" do not have. The sooner we realize that "we" all have it, the sooner we are able to fully grasp its significance. "Ideology," though tainted by negative connotations, is the best term available to describe the mental models that we all carry of how the world works, of how it ought to be, and of how it should be set right so that our fondest hopes can be realized.

In this book the term "ideology" is synonymous with "political ideology," unless otherwise specified. Nonpolitical mental models are also important to the subject matter of the book, not the least being ecological or environmental mental models. These shall be referred to later under the nomenclature of "paradigms." (See the discussion in chapter 2 on the "human exemptionalism"[1] and "new environmental" paradigms introduced by Catton and Dunlap 1978.)

Conventionally political ideologies are classified in terms of the "left," "center," and "right." In this book, I refer to (respectively) "class," "managerial," and "individualist" paradigms in accordance with the nomenclature set out by Alford and Friedland (1985).[2] The class paradigm rests on the belief that economic accumulation and class exploitation are key societal problems. Those in the managerial paradigm believe political power, policies, laws, regulations, and technological innovation govern our destiny. The individualist paradigm emphasizes the role of the individual in society, either as bearer of knowledge, culture, and beliefs, or as an economic actor. These three social theory paradigms will serve as the overarching theoretical framework for analysis and discussion.

My other key messages are the following:

- The three social theory paradigms are deeply embedded in history and the fabric of socioeconomic development and are therefore likely to persist in their broad outlines over the long term.
- Certain basic tenets in each paradigm make eminent sense, and none of the three paradigms is sufficient—in and of itself—to serve as the exclusive basis for understanding the causes of, or resolving, environmental problems.
- Through "paradigm isolation" there is a tendency to reject (whether consciously or unconsciously) the tenets of competing paradigms, no matter how strong their merits or how weak their logical conflict with certain tenets in the home paradigm.
- The class paradigm faces the strongest isolation of the three and is largely ostracized from mainstream and policy discourse, despite the fact that it plays a crucial role in understanding the causes of, and therefore in conceptualizing solutions to, environmental problems.
- A partial integration of paradigms is not only possible, but necessary. Such an effort, however, must be framed within an understanding that certain incompatibilities among the paradigms are mutually irreconcilable.

Social Theory

My analysis of ideology and paradigms is framed largely within the rubric of sociological theory. Sociologists readily recognize that the class, managerial, and individualist paradigms mentioned above tend to be associated, respectively, with the classical exemplars of sociological theory (Karl Marx, Max Weber, and Emile Durkheim) and with various contemporary extensions of classical sociological thought.

This book, however, occupies a larger theoretical "space" than sociology, and for that reason I have chosen to use the more embracing term "social theory" to describe its disciplinary framework. Given the book's focus on political ideology, it necessarily delves into the realm of political science. Moreover, attention will be given to underlying assumptions of Marxian and neoclassical economics and their connection to the three paradigms, so economics per se is part of the framework as well.

Related Literature

This is by no means the first book to examine environmental issues from the perspective of sociological paradigms and social theory. Others in this tradition are Humphrey and Buttel 1982; Dickens 1992; Redclift and Benton 1994; Harper 1996; Goldblatt 1996; Bell 1998; Barry 1999; and Humphrey et al. 2002.

The books most closely related to *Ideology, Social Theory, and the Environment* are Humphrey and Buttel (1982, 15–18), Harper (1996, 50–52), and Humphrey et al. (2002, 34–68), which ground their analyses in the classical sociological paradigms. Harper (1996) also anchors his analysis in classical economics (48–50) as well as in the contemporary extensions of sociology and economics (52–56). Humphrey et al. (2002, 34–68) draw a link between sociology and political science, labeling the Marxist tradition "radical," the Weberian tradition "managerial," and the Durkheimian tradition "conservative."[3] Harper (1996, xvi, 63, 174, 188, 272) discusses compatibilities and incompatibilities among various sociological paradigms, but paradigm isolation and integration are not a major concern of his work. Bell (1998, 145–206) gives considerable attention to environmental ideology but not to political ideology per se.

This book makes a distinctive contribution to the environmental literature by putting political ideology front and center, focusing on the three classical paradigms and their contemporary formulations, and examining in detail possibilities for achieving a degree of integration among the three paradigms. In this connection, it is important to recognize that paradigm integration of various kinds (micro-macro linkages in the United States and "agency structure" in Europe) has been one of the major preoccupations of late twentieth-century social theory (Ritzer 2000, 80–83, 359–418).

This book counters a tendency to dismiss the relevance of classical social theory in general terms (e.g., Giddens 1987, 26–29) and in relation to the environment (e.g., Goldblatt 1996, 1–13). Goldblatt correctly points out that "the theoretical legacy left to us by classical social theory has some substantial limitations both for examining the relationships between societies and their environments, and for exploring the origins of a politics of the environment" (1996, 1). Classical theories were formulated long before the onset of the environmental crisis that afflicts us at the turn of the twenty-first century. Nevertheless, I believe it is necessary to understand classical social theory for three reasons. First, it is the foundation on which modern social theory is built. Second, analysts of the environment (even nontheoretical ones) tend to be strongly influenced by various aspects of the classical social theory tradition whether they are consciously aware of it or not. Third, the classical social theory tradition is essential for defining the political spectrum (left, center, right), and these conceptual categories have considerable power for understanding the causes of environmental problems and the movements in reaction to these problems.

I believe both classical and modern social theory are essential for making sense of our environmental predicament. However, classical social theory must be actively promoted because it runs the risk of being neglected. My project is to elevate the importance of classical theory at a time when its relevance is being considerably underestimated. As explained by Buttel, "The future of environmental sociology may well lie in whether it is able to restore the 'classical project' of uniting sociological abstraction with a meaningful role in addressing moral and political issues" (2000a, 34).

What This Book Does Not Aim to Do and Does Not Accomplish

Although I examine in detail the issue of ideology, social theory, and the environment, this book should not be considered comprehensive and definitive. In giving attention to *political* ideology, I leave aside other relevant ideological genres, among them feminist, religious, and various ecological ideologies.

Despite my focus on political ideology, some readers—believing that I have not sufficiently analyzed the many political ideologies related to the environment—will be unsatisfied. For example, I touch on social ecology, eco-socialism, Marxist ecology, political ecology, conservative environmentalism, free market environmentalism, and so on, but not at a level of detail that will satisfy those seeking an in-depth understanding of these philosophies and movements. To these readers I ask forbearance and patience in understanding my goal, which is to make a strong case for the contemporary relevance and crucial importance of the three social theory paradigms as a matrix for understanding the modus vivendi of these philosophies and movements.

Some of the most heated and important debates over environmental directions occur not among proponents in different paradigms, but among those sharing the same paradigm.[4] For example, many well thought through and revealing polemics on economic growth take place entirely within the managerial paradigm. While giving attention to these within-paradigm battles, I may be perceived as giving them less attention than they deserve in terms of their intrinsic importance. But here again I ask the reader's indulgence. Please understand that my main mission is to highlight and underscore the importance of conflict among paradigms and the grounds for possible integration.

Finally, it should be noted that another possible weakness of this book is the geographic coverage of the environmental literature consulted. The "raw material" for this book is mainly the writings of North Americans, Europeans, and Australians, even though the book takes a global view of environmental problems. My reasons for being unable to include as many writers from developing countries as I would like are less linguistic (I read French, Spanish, and Indonesian) than practical. First, I was based in the United States for my library work, and developing country authors are underrepresented there. I readily acknowledge the limited scope of literature that I draw on and encourage others, perhaps with more time and money, to explore these themes using the broadest possible international literature.

My Own Background and Biases

It is fitting in a book of this kind for me to be forthright about my background and ideological leanings. I am a rural sociologist by training. Since getting my Ph.D. in 1993, I have been a professional researcher, working first at the International Center for Living Aquatic Resources Management (ICLARM) in 1993–1994 and then at the Center for International Forestry Research (CIFOR) ever since. Both of these research institutions are part of the Consultative Group on International Agricultural Research (CGIAR). Readers who know of the CGIAR will recognize that it is deeply steeped in the managerial paradigm (which I define in detail in chapter 1). Among the managerial characteristics these institutions demonstrate is considerable attention to policy (both as sources of problems and as solutions) and to the ability of technology to ameliorate social and environmental problems. The so-called Green Revolution was largely the product of the International Rice Research Institute (IRRI) and the Centro de Investigación de Maíz y Trigo (CIMMYT), two of the original GCIAR research centers.

Although I am now settled into a work environment that follows a managerial approach, my background is as an activist in the class tradition. Between 1977 and 1982, I worked as a staff member of a radical/liberal activist organization in the United States. We actively opposed the deployment of nuclear weapons, the construction of nuclear power plants, and in the early 1980s, the U.S. government's war against Nicaragua.

Given my activist and professional research background, I might be assumed to be strongly influenced by the class and managerial traditions and not the individualist paradigm. But this is not the case. For twenty years, I have been acutely aware that our social, economic, and environmental crises are partly rooted in our cultural and belief systems, and that they will never be adequately resolved without reform (if not revolutionary transformation) of these systems. This, of course, is one of the hallmarks of the individualist tradition.

What I bring to the task of writing this book is the personal conviction that all three dominant social science paradigms are integral to understanding the problematic relationship between the human species and planet earth, and indispensable to whatever solutions we devise. I am acutely aware, as well, that a simple merger of these perspectives is impossible. What is needed is astute analysis of deep conflicts among the traditions, with an eye to understanding which components of the traditions are mutually compatible and synergistic, and which are not.

Being a person who knows he is strongly influenced by all three streams of modern social theory makes me transideological, not nonideological. This is relevant in two respects. First, as I explain in the next chapter, I believe all people are ideological, by my definition of the term, irrespective of claims to the contrary. Second, I believe that raising ideology to the level of consciousness and being open to crossing ideological boundaries in critical reflection improves rather than undermines the nature of empirical inquiry. Throughout the book I will make remarks on what I believe to be true or untrue in various paradigmatic assertions. I certainly make no claims of having a monopoly on the truth, and I know I can be as wrong as the next person. However, generally speaking, I believe that being aware of my presuppostions and prejudices and why I have them raises the quality of my criticism. I follow the precept of Mohan and Kinloch, who say that "refusal to acknowledge the central role of ideology is itself an ideological act that prevents citizens from becoming full participants in their own governance" (2000, 9).

Structure of the Book

This book is structured as follows. Chapter 1 on ideology, paradigms, and social theory provides the theoretical background. It explains why ideology is marginal in the theoretical world (and why it has even been declared dead by some observers), why it is an important concept, and why analysis of ideology must be revived in order to adequately understand global environmental change. The three key paradigms of sociology (class, managerial, and individualist) are linked to three key conceptual categories in political science (radicalism, liberalism, conservatism) to form the social theory framework I employ. I argue that the tenets of all three paradigms are indispensable for understanding the social order, even though in crucial respects they contradict one another. I introduce the concept of *paradigm isolation:* the tendency of proponents of a given paradigm to elevate their tenets over and against the tenets of other paradigms. I also introduce the concept of *paradigm integration:* the tendency of proponents to embrace not only the tenets of the home paradigm but those of competing paradigms as well.

Chapter 2, on human evolution and socioenvironmental outcomes, provides a longitudinal backdrop on which I build subsequent theorizing and analysis. The stages of socioeconomic evolution, from the hunting and gathering period through the industrial age, are briefly summarized and linked to corresponding changes in environmental impacts. The key message in this chapter is that the character and scope of environmental change are closely linked to successive stages of *class* (human relations of production), *power* (founding and elaboration of the state and other large organizations), and *culture* (knowledge, values, beliefs, and traditions).

The chapter demonstrates that social and environmental outcomes cannot be understood apart from each other, that poverty and wealth are a joint phenomenon that cannot be understood apart from each other, and that although environmental literature focuses on the relationship of poverty to environmental degradation, other interactions between levels of living and environmental outcomes must also be considered. The chapter critiques the influential "Commoner-Ehrlich" equation $I = P \times A \times T$ (environmental impact = population $\times$ affluence $\times$ technology) for assuming that population, affluence, and technology are the most important variables to be considered for understanding environmental impacts.

In chapter 3, the three key ideological perspectives on the environment, corresponding to the class, managerial, and individualist paradigms in social theory, are defined, compared, and contrasted. The reasons for the existence of these three paradigms are analyzed, including who espouses them and why. The chapter then explores three types of paradigm isolation: "rejectionist," in which the tenets of a competing paradigm are wholly and explicitly rejected; "contingent," in which the tenets of a competing paradigm are subordinated to the "prime mover" logic of the home paradigm; and "implicit," in which silence indirectly expresses a position with respect to a competing paradigm. Evidence of limited paradigm integration to date is shown and discussed. The challenges to further paradigm integration are explained. I note that the class paradigm is strongly ostracized from mainstream and policy discourses, and that this is perhaps the key threat to an adequate understanding of the underlying causes of environmental problems and attaining lasting solutions.

The remainder of the book explores the problem of paradigm isolation and prospects for paradigm integration by examining ideological perspectives on three key problems: the population-resource balance (i.e., the problem of "emerging scarcities"), economic growth (i.e., "emerging excesses"), and the legitimacy of various forms of environmentalism (i.e., forms of agency in addressing emerging scarcities and excesses).

Chapter 4 begins by reviewing information on the population-resource balance. The theories of the key progenitors of modern population paradigms— Thomas Malthus, Karl Marx and Friedrich Engels, and Esther Boserup—are then summarized. Six contemporary population paradigms are identified through cross-classification of three population perspectives (neo-Malthusianism, anti-Malthusianism, and intermediate "despairing optimism") with the three social theory paradigms (class, managerial, and individualist). (Three theoretical cells are essentially vacant.) Among these six, three are dominant in modern population thought: class anti-Malthusianism, managerial neo-Malthusianism, and individualist anti-Malthusianism. Thus contemporary neo-Malthusianism essentially resides in the political center while being challenged from both left and right. The logic of isolation among these three paradigms is explained in terms of ideological interests within each of the home paradigms. Evidence of tentative steps toward integration are described, and the bases for further integration are discussed. Two formal theoretical models striving toward population paradigm integration are evaluated. They are found lacking for being insufficiently comprehensive or for being tendentious.

Analysts differ on whether economic growth is a major cause of—or a major solution to—environmental problems. Chapter 5 begins by reviewing the debate and discusses semantic issues in order to identify the substantive differences in points of view. (The "dematerialization" debate is one example of needless, politically driven obfuscation.) The views of various analysts (antigrowth, neutral, and progrowth) are cross-classified with the three social theory paradigms. I find that antigrowth dominates the left, anti- and progrowth share the political center, and progrowth dominates the right. The antigrowth posture on the left is not a foregone conclusion but rather a recent development indirectly resulting from the collapse of communism and Marxist theoreticians' embrace of environmentalism. The most vigorous and substantive debates take place within the political center. This should not distract us from the fact that the polemic is deeply political, having a great deal to do with conceptions of the appropriateness or inappropriateness of the neoclassical economic vision. Areas of paradigm incompatibility, as well as paradigm isolation and potential integration, are identified. Ecological modernization aims at paradigm integration but fails to fully resolve the underlying polarity.

Chapter 6 identifies and analyzes three *forms* of environmentalism: civic, state, and corporate. Respectively, these forms are primarily identified with the left, center, and right of the political spectrum. The state and corporate forms are recent theoretical categories that have emerged in response to the explosive growth of worldwide civic environmentalism. Their emergence forces a wholesale revision of what constitutes "environmentalism." The chapter also identifies three *modes* of environmentalism: personal, ideal, and instrumental. The personal mode involves concern over the consequences to the self of environmental degradation. The ideal mode involves concern over the worldwide consequences of environmental damage and embraces the conventional, "public goods" meaning of the term. In the instrumental mode, resolution of environmental problems is viewed not as an end in itself, but rather as a means to nonenvironmental ends. The chapter argues that framing problems in terms of the forms and modes of environmentalism can assist our understanding of how they can be resolved.

The closing chapter first summarizes the main points of the book: (1) paradigm isolation is counterproductive because it tends to lead public mobilization on environmental issues in divergent and sometimes mutually contradictory directions and therefore can paralyze or retard urgently needed public action; and (2) paradigm isolation can be understood in terms of the persistence of the ideological underpinnings that gave rise to such divisions, but it is largely unnecessary and self-defeating.

The chapter then makes the case for paradigm integration, discussing three steps toward this goal. The first step is to recognize that all of the key tenets of the social theory paradigms (empowerment of civil society and serious attention to poverty and inequality, policy and legal reform and technological innovation, cultural transformation and freeing of economic initiative) are legitimate and necessary venues for action in dealing with global environmental change. The second is to recognize that these tenets spring from frames of reference that are in certain respects mutually contradictory, but this does not mean all initiatives that spring from them are mutually contradictory. The third is to recognize that effective and durable solutions to environmental problems will be the outcome of conflicting and negotiated interests, and are therefore necessarily complex. Although paradigm integration is a necessary step toward effectively addressing global environmental problems, it is not sufficient. Durable negotiated solutions must be facilitated in a democratic setting that guarantees civil liberties and human rights and avoids repressive and militaristic solutions to regional and national-level conflicts.

Notes

1. The name first proposed was "Human Exceptionalism Paradigm" (Catton and Dunlap 1978, 41).

2. I have substituted the term "individualist" for Alford and Friedland's (1985) "pluralist." The term "pluralist" has fallen into disuse since the 1980s. Alford and Friedland (1985, 35) indicate that "individualist" is a possible synonym for "pluralist."

3. The predecessor volume used the terms "radical," "liberal," and "conservative" (Humphrey and Buttel 1982, 18–21).

4. As explained by Alford and Friedland: "The most intense conflicts usually occur between persons who share the same fundamental assumptions. In intellectual life, as in religious groups and political parties, the sharpest polemics are reserved for the heretic and the dissenter" (1985, 29). The bitterness of these battles has to do with the fact that opponents are fighting for the same niche.

CHAPTER ONE

⁓

Ideology, Social Theory, and Paradigms

[Ideas,] both when they are right and when they are wrong, are more powerful than is commonly understood. Indeed, the world is ruled by little else. Practical men, who believe themselves to be quite exempt from any intellectual influences, are usually the slaves of some defunct economist. Madmen in authority, who hear voices in the air, are distilling their frenzy from some academic scribbler of a few years back. (Keynes 1936, 383)

Ideology—the framework of ideas, beliefs, and values that structures our world-view—is a powerful force that governs our thoughts and emotions in ways that we often do not fully recognize and that may or may not be well-grounded in reality. The eminent early-twentieth-century economist John Maynard Keynes persuasively summarizes this important truth. Yet he *understates* the power of ideology in three ways. First, as we shall see in this chapter, ideas that shape our outlook do not date only "a few years back" but often more than a century back. Second, it is often not just a "defunct economist" who can influence our views. We can be swayed by a whole range of disciplines, including not just economics but also political science, sociology, anthropology, philosophy, and psychology, among others. Third, the relevance of the effect of ideology is not limited to "practical men." Ideology wields its influence on all people capable of reasoning—men, women, and children alike.

However, in saying of ideas that "the world is ruled by little else," Keynes *overstates* the importance of ideology in two ways. First, to say that little other than ideas rules the world tends to exaggerate the degree of conscious and deliberate control that humans exercise over their destiny. For example, population growth, to name just one of various socioeconomic trends, influences the course of history, but in no way is it the product of planning by world lead-ers. Second, our contemporary ideas (and beliefs and values) are the product of not only ideologues of the past but also the substratum of socioeconomic conditions and trends that shape our life circumstances. What I mean by "life circumstances" is material conditions such as level of wealth or poverty, ac-cess to employment and resources, which themselves are influenced by socio-economic trends such as rapid population growth, economic globalization, and democratization, among others. These opportunities and constraints shape our worldview just as much as ideas do, and they are strongly related to—though, crucially, not *reducible to*—the influence of ideas. It is a com-monplace of modern social science to distinguish between the material and the ideal and, in a related way, between structure and agency. This book fol-lows in that tradition.

A key aim of this book is to elevate the concept of ideology so that it receives attention in proportion to its importance in the realm of environmental studies. Ideology, as we shall see, has been neglected and in fact suppressed as a category of inquiry. Although I will argue that ideology is a crucial vantage point for un-derstanding the human condition and its relationship to environmental change, the importance of ideology must not be exaggerated, lest this project lose its credibility.

I aim to demonstrate how ideology generally, and political ideology in partic-ular, shapes dominant views on the causes of, nature of, extent of, and solutions to environmental problems. The importance of the concept requires inspired at-tention and scrutiny. Chapter 1 provides a foundation for this project by defin-ing ideology, by demonstrating its contemporary importance in spite of its virtual absence from theorizing and intellectual discourse, by conceptualizing political ideology within the framework of social theory, and by defining three ideological traditions or paradigms that will serve as the overarching theoretical framework for the rest of the book.

Ideology Defined

Ideology, in its most simple formulation, is a worldview or a mental model of how human society does and/or ought to function to support the livelihoods and/or aspirations of its members or a subgroup of its members. A more specific defini-tion is provided by van Dijk:

> ideologies may be very succinctly defined as the *basis of the social representations shared by members of a group*. This means that ideologies allow people, as group members, to organize the multitude of social beliefs about what is the case, good or bad, right or wrong, *for them*, and to act accordingly. Ideologies may also influence what is accepted as true or false, especially when such beliefs are found to be rele-vant for the group. (1998, 8)

Another definition is provided by Mohan and Kinloch:

> Ideologies are systems of evaluations that attempt to explain our experiences in understandable and logical terms. As such, they seek to stimulate and precede action; consequently, they are indispensable in dealing with human reality. They provide us with a set of comprehensible values that make life meaningful. (2000, 9)

Ideologies are inherently conflictual because they define themselves in an oppositional way among themselves.[1] Van Dijk (1998, 73) explains that "ideologies develop as a functional consequence of the conflicts of interest that emerge from goals, preferences or rights that are seen as mutually incompatible." They concern themselves with competing views on various dimensions of human activity and identity. There are political ideologies on the appropriateness of capitalism as an economic model and on the relationship of society to the state; there are racial and ethnic ideologies concerning differences among subgroups in the human community; there are gender ideologies on the respective capabilities of and relationships between the sexes; and there are environmental ideologies on the relationship of humans to their natural environment.

The concept of ideology dates back to a period of convulsive social change in eighteenth-century Europe and is often associated with views on capitalism. With the rapid development of capitalism and the associated phenomena of industrialization and urbanization in this period, class polarization became starkly evident. Many people in cities worked long hours in crowded, unsanitary, and unhealthy conditions in factories, if they were lucky enough to have a job (and many were not), while a minority of business owners benefited handsomely from this arrangement. There emerged contrasting views among theorists on a variety of topics, but no debate was so central and contentious as that concerning capitalism and whether it would ultimately bode well or ill for the human condition.

The same debate on the nature and effects of capitalism occupies a central place in social theory to this day and justifies the privileged attention to political ideology in this book.[2] I am here defining *political ideology* narrowly as the form of ideology that concerns itself primarily with capitalism and the role of the individual and the state in relation to capitalist society. In this respect political ideology refers to the left-center-right spectrum in political theory (and homologous categories in sociology and economics, as specified below). Political ideologies such as nationalism, nazism, and fascism, that are not directly concerned at the theoretical level with capitalism, are therefore not part of this narrow definition that I am applying. Eatwell provides a useful definition of political ideology, calling it *Political Ideology*

> a relatively coherent set of empirical and normative beliefs and thought, focusing on the problems of human nature, the process of history, and socio-political arrangements. . . . Depending on its relationship to the dominant value structure, an ideology can act as either a stabilizing or radical force. Political ideologies are

> essentially the product of collective thought. They are "ideal types," not to be con-
> fused with specific movements, parties or regimes which may bear their name.
> (1999, 17)

At the most general level, ideologies function to maintain dominance over other groups or to resist such dominance (van Dijk 1998, 8, 138). At a more specific level, the ideologies of dominant groups may serve to conceal or obfuscate the truth and defend the group against criticism (van Dijk 1998, 138; Eagleton 1991, 52). The ideologies of dominated groups serve to empower them and "to create solidarity, to organize struggle and to sustain opposition" (van Dijk 1998, 138). Van Dijk adds that

> both at the negative and the positive side, ideologies serve to protect interests and
> resources, whether these are unjust privileges, or minimal conditions of existence.
> More neutrally and more generally, then, ideologies simply serve groups and their
> members in the organization and management of their goals, social practices and
> their whole daily social life. (1998, 138)

Eagleton points out that ideologies tend to legitimize themselves by claiming a larger share of explained reality than they can shoulder by "universalizing" and "eternalizing" themselves. He says that "values and interests which are in fact specific to a certain place and time are projected as the values and interests of all humanity. The assumption is that if this were not so, the sectoral, self-interested nature of the ideology would loom too embarrassingly large, and so would impede its general acceptance" (Eagleton 1991, 56).

The term "ideology" as used in this book has two important characteristics. First, as implied above, it is *inclusive* in the sense of referring not just to the worldviews of dominant groups but also to those of dominated or subordinate groups. This is important because during much of its early history the term "ideology" referred to a worldview promulgated by elites dominating society. A more inclusive term is needed, and in recent decades "ideology," for better or worse, has become that term. Second—and related to the first point—the term as used here is nonpejorative and neutral. There is no a priori supposition that a particular ideology is inherently good or bad, true or false. Later in this book I will question particular claims made in the name of an ideology without necessarily calling into question the notion of ideology or the premises of the ideology itself.

The second definition is important because it combats a long-standing tendency to equate "ideology" with "distorted thinking" and "an over-simplified worldview." As pointed out by Eagleton, "there is no such thing as a presuppositionless thought and to that extent all our thinking might be said to be ideological" (1991, 3–4). Since we all have "ideology," it is necessary at the analytical and theoretical level to move beyond the common, pejorative bias that says, in the words of van Dijk, "Ours is the Truth, and Theirs is Ideology" (1998, 2).

A brief review of the etiology of "ideology" will show how its meaning changed over time. The term was coined by the French philosopher Destutt de Tracy in 1795 and referred to the general science of ideas, which aimed to clarify and improve the public mind (Scruton 1982, 213). Karl Marx and Friedrich Engels (1970) in their classic treatise *The German Ideology* (mid-1840s), used the term "ideology" to designate a distorted system of ideas and beliefs promulgated by the ruling class in capitalist society to generate support for itself. Marx and Engels used the metaphor of the camera obscura, a medieval device used to produce a reversed mirror image of a scene, to define ideology. "Just as the *camera obscura* distorts its image by inversion, so ideology distorts our ideas about society by inverting (and thus concealing) the relationships of the social structure" (Cormack 1992, 10).

In particular, Marx and Engels were aiming to challenge the prevailing Hegelian notion (espoused by a group called the Young Hegelians) that ideas have primacy in human existence. Marx and Engels believed instead that material conditions, in particular economic forces and class struggle, have primacy in determining the conditions of human existence. In "turning Hegel upside down," they sought to demonstrate that ideas are an epiphenomenon of the economic system (not the other way around) and have served to make subordinate classes acquiesce to their place in society (Morrison 1995, 44–50). Marx and Engels explain: "The ideas of the ruling class are in every epoch the ruling ideas, i.e. the class which is the ruling *material* force of society, is at the same time its ruling *intellectual* force" (1970, 64).

Throughout its history the concept of ideology has oscillated between positive and negative connotations, but pejorative meanings of the term, with significant exceptions, have tended to dominate (McLellan 1995, 1, 5). The label "false consciousness" for ideology, first used by Engels, was picked up in the work of the twentieth-century neo-Marxist theoretician Georg Lukács (Morrison 1995, 314).[3] The neo-Marxist Antonio Gramsci conceptualized ideology not in terms of coercion but rather through the more subtle workings of the "hegemony" of the state; control of intellectual life is not simply imposed by a ruling class, according to Gramsci, but is also achieved through persuasion and construction of consensus (Waters 1994, 182–83). Karl Mannheim ([1929] 1936), through his book *Ideology and Utopia*, helped broaden the concept of ideology. The book "turned the Marxist theory of ideology against the Marxists themselves" by pointing out that the political aims of the working class are just as ideological as the ideas imposed by the dominant class (Collins 1994, 94).

In the course of the second half of the twentieth century the concept of ideology tended to become more inclusive and less pejorative (van Dijk 1998, 3). However, strong strains of past exclusive and pejorative uses of the term are retained in contemporary theoretical work. Because a unified and broadly shared concept of ideology does not yet exist, confusion and incoherence continue in discussions of this topic.

A Premature Postmortem

The report of my death has been grossly exaggerated. (Mark Twain, quoted in Paine 1912, 1039)

At the turn of the millennium there is little doubt that conflicting ideologies are alive throughout the world. Poor, disenfranchised, and marginalized people are mobilizing themselves in defense of their interests and against those of the privileged and the powerful. This is evident in demonstrations, confrontations, riots, wars, and other forms of violence that are founded on class tensions. It is evident in heated debates concerning the nature of economic systems and particular policies and philosophies such as globalization, neoliberalism, removal of trade barriers and public subsidies, exchange rate reform, privatization, and labor and immigration quotas, among others. These confrontations and debates are occurring in developing countries (often in the context of economic recession and crises and subsequent structural adjustment policies) and in developed countries (often in the context of meetings of international policy bodies such as the World Bank and the World Trade Organization, or economic shocks such as fuel cost increases). Since the collapse of the Soviet Union and the ebbing of world communism in the 1990s, mobilizations of the poor are less frequently linked to armed guerrilla movements. Likewise, trade unions are no longer as visible as they once were in representing the interests of the working class. Though the modes of mobilization by and on behalf of the poor and the working class have changed, they are no less militant than they were before.

Confrontations are not limited to issues of class and the nature of the economic system. The September 11, 2001, attack on the World Trade Center and the Pentagon and the subsequent eradication of the Taliban regime in Afghanistan and the "war on terrorism" are evidence of conflict that joins class tensions with religious ideology. There are also regional/national ideological confrontations related to ethnicity and religion (e.g., the Israel–Palestine conflict in the Middle East; strife in Ireland, the Balkans, Kashmir, Indonesia), as well as conflict related to ethnicity, language, and national identity (Quebec, Spain), human rights and democracy (Cuba, China, Iraq, Burma), race (United States, Germany, Zimbabwe), violence and gun control (United States), and abortion (United States).

If ideological conflict is so much a part of our day-to-day existence in the twenty-first century, why is so little attention paid to the nature of ideology as a category of thought? To be sure, much attention is given to conflicts in and of themselves, but these conflicts are rarely framed, as they should be, in terms of ideology.

There are several reasons for the inadequacy of theoretical and analytic discussion of political conflict in the framework of ideology. One reason is that the long-embedded exclusive and pejorative connotations of "ideology" have impeded examining the concept and its manifestations in value-neutral terms. As explained by van Dijk, "The confused and often vague nature of traditional ideology studies is . . . due to the repetition and uncritical acceptance of a number of standard concepts of studies of ideology in the past. A typical example is the notion of 'false consciousness'" (1998, 313).

A second reason is the various pronouncements on the "death of ideology." This is closely related to the first reason, inasmuch as the death of ideology pronouncements are founded on the spurious logic that "Ours is the Truth, and Theirs is Ideology." Since the end of World War II, several high-visibility treatises have been published in the United States claiming that ascendant liberal democracy has essentially vanquished the opposition, in particular, Marxism (i.e., "ideology"). The tables were turned in an ironic manner; whereas Marxists criticized their opposition with the term "ideology," they were now on the receiving end of the same treatment. The first of these publications was Raymond Aron, *The Opium of the Intellectuals* (1957), the last chapter of which was entitled "End of Ideology?" Others included Daniel Bell, *The End of Ideology: On the Exhaustion of Political Ideas in the Fifties* (1960), and Francis Fukuyama, *The End of History and the Last Man* (1992).[4]

A third reason is that some theorists of the political left as well as the right have abandoned the concept of ideology. Eagleton explains that in the aftermath of the collapse of communism

> the abandonment of the notion of ideology belongs with a more pervasive political faltering by whole sections of the erstwhile revolutionary left, which in the face of a capitalism temporarily on the offensive has beaten a steady, shamefaced retreat from such "metaphysical" matters as class struggle and modes of production, revolutionary agency and the nature of the bourgeois state. (1991, xii)

In particular, Eagleton (1991, xi–xii) faults postmodernists and poststructuralists for abandoning the classical concept of ideology. Three factors motivate this abandonment: rejection of empiricist models of representation; a belief that notions of absolute truth are untenable; and a reformulation of the relations between rationality, interests and power that claims to make the concept of ideology redundant (Eagleton 1991, xi–xii).

In summary, some commentators on ideology have, in a spirit of triumphalism, assumed that the concept is no longer relevant because the ideologues (They) have supposedly receded from the stage of history. Other commentators, on the political left, perhaps in unconscious reaction to the marginalization of their past views, have turned their attention elsewhere.

Ideologies are alive and well and are engaging in pitched battle the world over, and this should give us pause to wonder what these death pronouncements are all about. What has died is not ideology but our ability to grasp the breadth and importance of the concept.

Social Theory and Three Key Paradigms

In the remainder of this chapter I will examine political ideology in the context of social theory and sociological paradigms. Social theory, for purposes of this discussion, is defined as the formalized body of intellectual thought in which political ideologies have been shaped and analyzed. Of course, social theory is much more than this because it concerns more than political ideology. Paradigms, for purposes of this discussion, will be defined as analytical representations of ideology in the realm of the social sciences.[5] Before turning our attention to the three key paradigms that form the theoretical context for this book, we will first examine the concept of "social theory" more closely.

Social Theory

Modern social theory was formed through the sweeping social changes that took place in Europe between 1750 and 1920—a period that Karl Polanyi ([1944] 1957) described as "the great transformation" (Morrison 1995, 1). The emergence of social theory constituted a changed relationship to historical time; whereas in the past European intellectuals referred to the lessons of classical antiquity, beginning with the eighteenth-century Enlightenment they were oriented toward the future (Callinocos 1999, 13). The three main concerns of modern social theory have been "(i) the political changes brought about by the French Revolution; (ii) the economic development leading to the growth of modern society and the emergence of capitalism; and (iii) the rise of individualism" (Morrison 1995, 6). As explained by Zeitlin (1997), considerable ideological debate in this period, first in relation to the eighteenth-century Enlightenment and later in relation to the legacy of Marxist thought, led to the creation of classical sociological theory.

Social theory is often considered synonymous with sociological theory, though there are important differences. Giddens explains that social theory is broader than sociology,

> dealing as it does with a whole range of issues to do with human action, social institutions and their mutual connections. But sociology, whose prime field of study is the social world brought about by the advent of modernity, has a peculiar and privileged relation to social theory. (1987, vii)

Karl Marx, Max Weber, and Emile Durkheim are the intellectual progenitors of the three main paradigms in classical sociology and of the modern extensions of these paradigms. They will thus receive privileged attention in the theoretical parameters of this book. Though sociology and these three figures are central to the subject matter of this book, it is necessary to go beyond the discipline of sociology and frame the subject matter in the larger domain of social theory. There are three reasons for extending the discussion beyond sociology. First, by the very nature of the main topic—political ideology—we need to give attention to such disciplines as political science and political economy. Second, because our political inquiry concerns perspectives on capitalism and industrialism, we need to embrace the discipline of economics. In particular, it will be necessary to compare and contrast the assumptions of Marxist and neoclassical economics. Third, it will also be useful to draw on the perspectives of other disciplines (e.g., anthropology, geography, and psychology).

Three Key Paradigms

This section defines and conceptualizes three key paradigms: "class" (associated with the left of the political spectrum), "managerial" (associated with the center), and "individualist" (associated with the right). This formulation is inspired by Alford and Friedland's *Powers of Theory: Capitalism, the State, and Democracy* (1985) and is an elaboration of an earlier article I wrote on the subject matter of this book (Sunderlin 1995a). I present the defining characteristics of each of the three paradigms (see table 1.1) below, focusing on the essential positions that unite classical exemplars and their modern followers. Note that these characteristics are "ideal types." There are many deviations from these characteristics among contemporary theorists in all three traditions.

Class Paradigm

Proponents of the class paradigm, following Marx, believe history has been shaped by one central societal process: property owners' drive to accumulate capital. They see the world in terms of two mutually antagonistic social groupings and assert that a minority of relatively well-off people prosper economically at the expense of a relatively impoverished majority. Those in the impoverished majority cannot escape being exploited by the elite minority because they have no access to independent means of support (land, machinery, etc.). They have no resources except their own labor power and must acquiesce to the conditions of work provided to them by the minority who own the means of production. The relationship between these two classes is seen as inherently conflictual.

Theorists in the class tradition tend to focus their analyses on society as a whole and on the relationship of classes in society. Consistent with the focus on class relations, the key dimension of society in the class perspective is economic. This approach is related to five conceptual components of Marx's materialist philosophy: (1) means of production, (2) forces of production, (3) relations of production, (4) modes of production, and (5) ideology as superstructure.

Means of production refers to anything in the external world that can be used to satisfy material needs, and it is the monopolization of the means of production that causes class conflict. *Forces of production* are the characteristic available techniques in any given economic era (mode of production), for example: land, tools, the plow, and methods of cultivation in the feudal period; and industrial methods, science, and machine technology in the capitalist period.

Table 1.1. Three Key Paradigms

Defining Characteristics	Key Paradigms		
	Class	Managerial	Individualist
Central societal process	Accumulation within a capitalist mode of production	Rationalization of a mode of domination in an industrializing society	Differentiation with a modernizing society
Level of analysis	Societal	Organizational	Individual
Key dimension of society	Economic (class)	Political (power)	Behavioral (culture)
Associated economic philosophy	Critical and pessimistic stance toward capitalism (Marxist economics)	Conditional support of capitalism or neutrality (e.g., Keynesian economics)	Positive and optimistic view of capitalism (e.g., neoclassical economics)
Associated modern political labels and tendencies	Left Radical Progressive	Center Liberal Moderate Technocratic	Right Conservative
Modern formulations	Neo-Marxism (Hegelian Marxism, critical theory, world systems theory, post-Marxist theory)	Analytic sociology Neo-Weberianism	Functionalism Rational choice theory

Source: Adapted from Alford and Friedland (1985), table 2, p. 16.

Relations of production refers to the type of coercive bond existing between owners of the means of production and those who provide labor in the course of production. Slavery, serfdom, and wage labor are the relations of production corresponding, respectively, to ancient, feudal, and capitalistic modes of production. *Modes of production* (ancient, feudal, and capitalistic) are the total way of life of a society as determined by its characteristic forces of production and relations of production (Morrison 1995, 315, 319–22). In the Marxist framework the mode and relations of production are the "substructure" that determines the "superstructure"—a given society's law, government, and ideas (Wallace and Wolf 1991, 90–91).

Proponents of the class paradigm tend to have a critical and pessimistic stance toward capitalism.[6] This follows logically from the view that class struggle involves the systematic oppression of those who sell their labor to the owners of the means of production. This oppression is seen as the product of inherent, structural characteristics of capitalist relations of production, and not of the capitalist's attitude per se. Marx's theory of surplus value explains that profit in the production process is proportional to workers' lack of access to the value generated by their surplus labor. Surplus labor is defined as that proportion of daily labor expenditure above and beyond what is needed to meet workers' subsistence needs (i.e., "necessary labor"). Surplus labor is said to be unpaid and therefore creates value for the capitalist that is denied to the worker. The inability of workers to obtain the full value of their work (in Marxist parlance, the "separation of labor from labor power") results from labor's lack of bargaining power over its conditions of work and from the imperative of capitalists not just to accumulate capital but to do so by reducing costs to the minimum, or risk going bankrupt in a competitive business environment. "Variable costs" (i.e., labor costs) are by definition flexible, whereas "fixed costs" (nonlabor input costs) tend not to be.

Modern proponents of the class paradigm maintain the defining characteristics of their tradition, even though many have departed substantially from the original tenets of Marxist philosophy, even abandoning the label "Marxist" altogether. One of the main changes has been a tendency to abandon the rigid economic determinism and materialism espoused by Marx and Engels and their early followers. Among the modern formulations of the class tradition are neo-Marxist philosophies such as Hegelian Marxism (Georg Lukács and Antonio Gramsci), critical theory (Jürgen Habermas and the Frankfurt School), dependency theory (André Gunder Frank) and world systems theory (Immanuel Wallerstein), and post-Marxist theory (John Roemer, G. A. Cohen, John Elster, Erik Olin Wright). Another change among some proponents has been a tendency to embrace some of the defining characteristics of the managerial or individualist paradigms. This tendency toward integration is in particular characteristic of the post-Marxist formulations (Ritzer 2000, 168). The challenges involved in achieving paradigm integration will be discussed below.

Managerial Paradigm

Proponents of the managerial paradigm focus on the fact that society has come to be dominated by the state and large corporations. Rationalization is seen as the primary characteristic of this historical trend. Through industrialization and the growth of large businesses, there has emerged a perceived need for bureaucratization, centralized management, large-scale planning, and technical sophistication for coping with the complexity of the modern world. The state is viewed as the key agent in the process of rationalization and domination of society. For this reason, proponents of the paradigm see the state as a major reference point in their analyses. Many proponents of the managerial paradigm attribute social problems to lack of elaboration of, and errors in, state governance. The essential tools for addressing social problems, for them, is improved management and legal reform. Some proponents, however, attribute social problems not to the procedural aspects of governance but to the fact of rationalization and domination in and of itself.[7]

In keeping with the theoretical postulates established by Max Weber, proponents of the managerial paradigm focus on organizations in their analysis of society. The key dimension in managerial analysis is political, focusing on power relationships among dominant and subordinate organizations, and the state is viewed as the dominant organization in society (Alford and Friedland 1985, 25, 161, 164).

Weber (who lived from 1864 to 1920) fashioned much of his theory in critical response to Marx's ideas. (Karl Marx, who lived from 1818 to 1883, had already died by the time Weber began producing his theories.) Weber rejected Marx's dialectical materialism and rigid economic determinism, believing that while economic factors are an important determinant of social structure, religious, educational, legal, and political factors are important as well (Wallace and Wolf 1991, 82; Morrison 1995, 4, 216). In contrast to Marx, Weber believed that power is fundamental rather than merely a product of the economic system (Waters 1994, 222). Moreover, Weber believed that ideas and values are not merely the product of material economic interests, but are relatively autonomous and can have profound effects on economic structures (Ritzer 2000, 27). These elements of Weber's critique of Marx are amply evident in the work of contemporary proponents of the managerial perspective.

Proponents of the managerial perspective tend to conditionally support or be neutral toward capitalism as an economic system. Such conditional support may vary from strident criticism at one extreme to effusive praise at the other. What binds these views together is a belief that capitalism has something positive to offer, though some constraint and/or reform (large or small) of the system may be required in order to temper its negative aspects. This wide spectrum of views is bounded by avoidance of the class perspective (strong opposition to capitalism as a system) and the views of some in the individualist perspective (support for unrestrained capitalism). Often proponents of the managerial view voice no opinion at all concerning capitalism, and this silence can be interpreted as neutrality, in the sense of obliviousness or in the sense of avoiding the possible controversy involved in taking a stand for or against.

This centrism can be seen clearly in Weber's ideas. In contrast to Marx, who believed that social theory should be used to promote change and eliminate economic inequalities, Weber believed that social theory should be used to search for historical truths and that theoretical concepts should be neutral and not based on value judgments (Morrison 1995, 215). Moreover, and again in contrast to Marx, Weber believed that in the transition from past to modern times, direct antagonism between the classes had diminished through market mediation of wage disputes and through legal measures allowing workers to form associations. He believed that interests of manufacturers and business executives, rather than those of workers, suffered in the course of wage disputes (Morrison 1995, 238). Weber's centrism and relative lack of identification with the interests of workers is evident in other ways. He was not greatly concerned about the lack of popular control over political elites and he showed a degree of acceptance of the universality of domination (Bottomore 1993, 17, 53).

At the theoretical level managerialists' conditional support of capitalism can be linked to the science and practice of Keynesian economics. Keynesianism, the economic doctrine associated with John Maynard Keynes (1883–1946), is the most influential twentieth-century theory of macroeconomics. It advocates active stimulation of demand through public government spending in order to promote economic growth. His theory suggests that, at various times, a capitalist economy may require considerable government intervention to assure its survival (Scruton 1982, 248–49). Institutional economics is another school of thought with a link to managerialism. Its practitioners criticize orthodox economists for overreliance on theoretical and mathematical models and advocate attention to the noneconomic, institutional environment (Bannock et al. 1998, 210). In answer to the question, Why focus on institutions? North answers, "They are the rules of the game of a society and in consequence provide the framework of incentives that shape economic, political, and social organization" (1997, 6).

The most prominent modern theorists carrying on the Weberian tradition in sociology are Ralf Dahrendorf, Lewis Coser, and Randall Collins. They are associated with "analytical sociology" (Wallace and Wolf 1991, 75, 139–74). The common ground of this school of thought is that they believe, in contrast to their contemporaries in the Marxist tradition, that social science is not necessarily value-laden and can achieve the same degree of objectivity as the natural sciences (Wallace and Wolf 1991, 77). Analytical sociologists are influenced by Marxism, but Weber is the dominant influence. Other neo-Weberians such as Nicholas Abercrombie, Stephen Hill and Bryan Turner, and Margaret Archer reject the attempts of modern theorists to reconcile the work of Marx and Weber. Their common ground is a belief that culture can be viewed as autonomous from social structure (Waters 1994, 202–4).

Individualist Paradigm
Proponents of the individualist paradigm see increasing differentiation as the central societal process. This means that the division of labor increases as industrialization proceeds and as society becomes more complex. In preindustrial times, there was relatively little economic integration among people, communities and households were relatively independent from one another, and people tended to have multiple work roles in providing household subsistence. With the onset of industrialization and urbanization, work roles have become increasingly narrow and specialized in connection with an increasingly integrated and complex economy. Some individualists see differentiation as a necessary foundation

for the process of modernization—social betterment through economic growth and increasing technological sophistication.

Individualists see the individual as the key point of reference for understanding the social order. They argue that the aggregate of individual values and preferences, rather than economic class or political power, shapes human history. It follows that social problems can be traced to cultural deficiencies: immorality, tendencies toward criminality, lack of education and religious faith, and so on.[8] The solutions to social problems are therefore often framed in terms of mass education and training, and through campaigns to increase awareness and morality.

The key classical exemplar of the individualist paradigm is Emile Durkheim (1858–1917). He viewed the division of labor as leading to functional interdependence and also to increased individual autonomy as people were freed from the bonds of tradition, family, and "collective consciousness." He claimed this process, characterized by economic individualism and anomie (absence of moral regulation), presents a threat inasmuch as it can lead to recurrent conflicts and disorders. Durkheim believed that *moral individualism* was necessary to counteract the tendency toward anomie. He defined moral individualism as "the opposite of egoism . . . not the glorification of self-interest but that of the welfare of others" (Giddens 1995, 83). Durkheim strongly opposed the utilitarian view that social progress can be achieved through the pursuit of individual self-interest. Moreover, he opposed methodological individualism, the belief that society is simply the sum of the individuals who compose it; he believed society has a separate, sui generis reality.

Durkheim, like Weber, shaped his theories partly in opposition to those of Marx. Although considered a liberal in his time, Durkheim's effect on sociology has been conservative (Ritzer 2000, 18).[9] This should come as no surprise because the key tenets of his theory are profoundly conservative. Durkheim recognized the existence of classes in society, but he believed that conditions in the modern age could lead to a situation that is—although hierarchical—nonetheless peaceful and stable (Zeitlin 1997, 330). He believed that the growing division of labor in society was leading to solidarity of interests among all classes—hence his term "organic solidarity." "Classes" in his lexicon are called "functions" and are viewed as "coordinative, cooperative, and unifying—never as conflictive" (Zeitlin 1997, 333). Durkheim viewed history as progressing from conditions of conflict and war in the feudal past to liberation from these ills through the pacific and unifying influence of industrialization. He thus argued against Marx that no fundamental restructuring of society was necessary. Industrialization would engender positive moral forces and feelings of mutual solidarity through exchange of services, reciprocity of obligations, and interdependence (Zeitlin 1997, 332, 337–38).

Proponents of the individualist tradition tend to have a positive outlook on capitalism and often voice unconditional support of this economic system. It is therefore fitting to draw attention to a convergence between the individualist outlook and the key tenets of neoclassical economics.[10] Proponents of both individualism and neoclassical economics tend to have a positive view of capitalism and the process of industrialization.[11] Just as individualism focuses analytically on the individual, so too does the science of neoclassical economics. Neoclassical economics examines the "utility maximizing behavior" of individual consumers and firms. Its mainstream practitioners turn a blind eye to assumptions involving classes, stratification, and power relations in society, deeming them theoretically irrelevant. One important discontinuity between the two philosophies must be underscored. Whereas Adam Smith and other intellectual ancestors of neoclassical economics glorified individualism, self-interest, and competition in the belief that these impulses were socially beneficial (Morrison 1995, 14–16), this is not the case for Durkheim, and it is not necessarily the case for others in the individualist tradition.

The most prominent modern formulation of the individualist paradigm is functionalism (or structural-functionalism as it is sometimes called), which was the dominant sociological theory from the mid-1940s through the mid-1960s (Ritzer 2000, 93–94). The leading theorists of functionalism were Talcott Parsons and Robert Merton. The continuity with Durkheim is clear. Functionalism's central tenet is that society has an inherent tendency toward reorganization and balance when social ills are experienced. This view of society is based on models of organic systems in the biological sciences. The belief in self-correction and a tendency toward equilibrium implies a benign and optimistic outlook on society. Structuralism can be equated with conservatism in its implication that no interference or intervention are required to achieve an optimal social outcome. This stands in sharp contrast to conflict theory (embracing the class paradigm and some proponents of the managerial paradigm). Where conflict theorists see class conflict as a defining feature of the structure of society arising out of the pursuit of economic interests, structuralists see a tendency toward unity (Wallace and Wolf 1995, 19).

Functionalism places considerable importance on values and beliefs (Wallace and Wolf 1995, 19). As Parsons explains, "A social system consists in a plurality of individual actors . . . who are motivated in terms of a tendency to the 'optimization of gratification' and whose relation to their situations, including each other, is defined and mediated in terms of a system of culturally structured and shared symbols" (1951, 5).

Parsons echoed Durkheim's belief in the beneficial outcome of the division of labor. Parsons's basic argument was that a system of stratification "is both desirable and necessary in a complex industrial society; it fills occupations effectively and keeps the entire social system functioning smoothly. Consequently, social stratification is an 'evolutionary universal' because without it a highly differentiated society cannot be maintained" (Wallace and Wolf 1995, 49).

A recent expression of the individualist paradigm is rational choice theory. Neil Smelser called it "the main item on the agenda of most social scientists in the 1990s" (Wallace and Wolf 1995, 281). This theory, which has been taken up in the disciplines of sociology, economics, and political science (where it is known as "public choice" theory), presumes that people are rational and make choices based on what they believe to be the most effective means to reach their goals (Wallace and Wolf 1995, 279–80). Proponents tend to analyze social action in terms of individual beliefs and motivations alone, to the exclusion of attention to institutions and other nonindividual factors (Wallace and Wolf 1995, 340–41).

The Political Spectrum and the Three Key Paradigms

In this chapter I draw a theoretical link between the Marxist (class) and the left/radical position on the political spectrum, the Weberian (managerial) paradigm and the center/liberal position, and the Durkheimian (individualist) paradigm and the right/conservative position. Although these links between key sociological and political science conceptual categories are intuitively obvious, they are rarely made, for three possible reasons. First, there may be a lack of cross-fertilization of ideas between sociology and political science. Second, historically, the definitions of "liberalism" and "conservatism" have been ambiguous and fluid, making it difficult to see the logic of the linkage. Third, there are contemporary distortions in the meanings of political science categories that tend to understate (if not negate) the importance of a political center and to misidentify and ostracize the political left. In this section I discuss these last two problems in an effort to solidify the association of sociological and political science concepts in the theoretical model used in this book.

Historical Fluidity of Concepts

Over the past two centuries the meanings of the terms "liberal" and "conservative" have been transformed. However, if we examine the essence of their contemporary meanings, it is clear they are now identified with the center and the right (respectively) on the political spectrum, and therefore with the managerial and individualist paradigms.

Krieger observes that despite diverse usage, a core definition for "liberalism"

> considers individuals the seat of moral value and each individual as of equal worth. Hence, the individual should be free to choose his or her own ends in life. Liberalism may be morally neutral in regard to the ends people choose for themselves, but it is not morally neutral in its view that such individual choice is desirable and must be safeguarded from unwarranted interference from the state. (1993, 538)

Roberts and Edwards say that

> classical liberalism is recognizable from the late seventeenth century onwards, most notably in England in the writing of John Locke, and parallels the development of

limited government and the removal of state restrictions on production and trade. Liberalism in this sense is strongly associated with minimal state power, government being merely an instrument for the maintenance of the social and political framework necessary for free individual action. (1991, 74)

Following these definitions, it can be supposed that liberalism is mainly associated with the individualist rather than the managerial paradigm, inasmuch as it espouses strong attention to the individual and support for unrestrained capitalism.

However, the meaning of liberalism has changed greatly and now is closely associated with the managerial paradigm (see table 1.1). In the late nineteenth and early twentieth centuries "social liberalism" emerged in Britain, France, and the United States in reaction to economic downturn and mass employment (Bellamy 1999, 31–37). Liberalism adopted the view that "government should enable democratic participation and extend health, welfare and education rights in order to encourage the development of the individual citizens, capable of rationally selecting proper goals" (Roberts and Edwards 1991, 74). In the United States, this shift in the meaning of liberalism was strongly propelled by the depression of the 1930s, the government's subsequent New Deal programs, and the emergence of Keynesian economics. The government grew in order to oversee the corporate sector and ensure that it operated in the public interest (Garry 1992, 66). Liberalism is now identified with considerable government intervention and social spending of an enabling nature (Bellamy 1999, 27). For conservative critics in the United States, the term "liberalism" has become synonymous with the pejorative term "big government spending" and with the managerial notion of a strong role for government.

Although liberalism is now associated with the political center, public awareness of this fact lags behind because of, among other reasons, lingering vestiges of the original meaning of the philosophy. Another reason for the confusion is that the relatively recent economic philosophy "neoliberalism" reverts to the original meaning of the term "liberalism," inasmuch as it promotes limited government intervention in the economy.

The meaning of "conservatism" has also changed considerably over time. The earliest meaning of conservatism involved the defense in nineteenth-century Europe of precapitalist interests and traditions (aristocracy, the monarchy, and an established church) (Krieger 1993, 183–84). In the twentieth century, the term acquired various core meanings, including resistance to utopian thinking; defense of moral obligations such as devotion to family, patriotic duty, and religion; and resistance to forcible redistribution of property (Krieger 1993, 185–86). From the mid-1940s through the mid-1970s conservatives in the United States and Europe supported a large degree of government intervention to stimulate economic production and to assure social welfare. But they have since shifted to the belief that there should be minimal government intervention (Krieger 1993, 186). Conservatism and the political right favor institutions of private property as a means of assuring political and economic liberty, and individualism over and against collectivist institutions (Krieger 1993, 791). The tendency in conservative philosophy to give privileged attention to the individual, its focus on values, and its support for relatively unrestrained capitalism mark it as being strongly associated with the individualist paradigm.

Contemporary Distortions

In contemporary politics the meanings of political labels are frequently distorted. The reasons are partly ideological and therefore relate directly to the subject matter of this book. Identifying two of these distortions will help us to better understand the conceptual linkage between the theoretical categories of sociology and political science.

The first distortion involves the apparent absence of a political center at the level of theory and discourse. For example, definitions of the terms "centrism" and "moderate" were found in only one of five political science dictionaries I consulted.[10] What explains this lack of serious theoretical attention to the nature of the political center? Perhaps it is because liberalism, given the relatively recent theoretical metamorphosis mentioned above, has not yet been clearly identified as occupying the political center between the left (radicalism) and the right (conservatism). Though this explanation might sound strange, liberals themselves have tended to reject the centrist label (Robertson 1986, 187–88). Another reason (see below) may have to do with the tendency in political discourse to identify liberalism with the left. Whatever the reasons might be, it should be clear that the political center, given its clear association with the managerial paradigm and the defining characteristics of that tradition, deserves attention as a theoretical category unto itself, distinct from "left" and "right."

The second distortion involves a pronounced tendency to stigmatize, delegitimize, and ostracize the left (i.e., the class paradigm) in conventional discourse. Ostracization is readily evident in U.S. political talk shows on television that pit a liberal commentator (labeled a representative of "the left") versus a conservative commentator (labeled a representative of "the right"). It is as if the true left (i.e., a proponent of the class paradigm) did not exist.[11] This tendency to exclude the true left from the bounds of acceptable political discourse has its basis in a long-standing, tacit understanding among liberal and conservative ideologues and theoreticians that questioning capitalism as an economic model cannot be entertained seriously. Recall (see table 1.1) that tolerance of, or dedication to, capitalism as the dominant economic model is the common ground shared by liberals (proponents of the managerial paradigm) and conservatives (proponents of the individualist paradigm).

The ostracization of the left is a practice that has deep roots. It is reflected in the etymology of the terms "left" and "right." Coined in the French revolutionary parliament in the eighteenth century, they referred to the fact that radical representatives sat to the left of the presiding officer's chair, while conservatives sat on the right (Krieger 1993, 531). The "left" and "right" designations were deliberately horizontal and egalitarian in their implications, challenging the traditional vertical "up" and "down" designations characteristic of the hierarchical mental framework of the past order (Laponce 1981, 10). Nonetheless, "left" and "right" are not arbitrary and carry connotations prejudicial to the left. In the Christian cultures of Europe, right was equated with being on the side of God, and it was associated with the notions of privilege, dominance, and sacredness. Further, prior to the end of the eighteenth century the left in all Indo-European cultures referred to the bad, negative, and evil side of things (Laponce 1981, 10, 29).

In summary, there is a logical theoretical link between the three key categories of political science and those of sociology. These links are valid in spite of an apparent lack of convergence. The liberal tradition is closely identified with the managerial paradigm; the center occupies an important theoretical position on the political spectrum worthy of more attention; the left is equated fundamentally with the class paradigm and not with the managerial paradigm (appearances to the contrary notwithstanding). Last, there is a long-standing tendency to ostracize the left (i.e., the class paradigm), which should not deter us from understanding its true identity.

From Paradigm Isolation to Paradigm Integration

Even in the prosperous democracies, troubling gaps in well-being persist. Traditional explanations like imperialism, dependency and racism are no longer adequate, and increasingly observers are concluding that the principal reason why some countries and ethnic groups are better off than others lies in cultural values that powerfully shape political, economic and social performance. (Lawrence E. Harrison and Samuel P. Huntington, *Culture Matters: How Values Shape Human Progress* [2000], dust cover)

The passage above argues, in effect, that past radical explanations of inequality (such as imperialism, dependency, and racism) are invalid and that the true cause and explanation of inequality is to be found in worldwide differences in cultural values. In the context of the foregoing discussion, this quote is readily identifiable as an exposition of contemporary conservative political ideology, and of the individualist paradigm in social theory.

The passage is also an example of what I call *paradigm isolation*, the tendency of proponents of a particular paradigm to elevate their own theoretical tenets over and against those of one or more competing paradigms. The term *theoretical tenets*, as used here, refers to the assumptions concerning "central societal process," "level of analysis," and "key dimension of society" as presented in table 1.1.

There are two basic forms of paradigm isolation (see table 1.2). In *explicit* paradigm isolation, a statement is made that explicitly rejects the tenets of one or more competing paradigms or views the tenets of one or more competing paradigms as contingent on, and subordinate to, the tenets of the home paradigm. In *implicit* paradigm isolation, a statement is framed entirely in terms of the tenets of the home domain, and no reference is made to the tenets of other paradigms. With implicit paradigm isolation it is usually unclear if such lack of reference is conscious or unconscious.

The quote from Harrison and Huntington is an example of explicit paradigm isolation. It is both rejectionist and contingent. In saying that "explanations like imperialism, dependency and racism are no longer adequate" the statement explicitly rejects arguments made in the class paradigm. It implies that cultural values are an underlying cause (or a "prime mover" in sociological terms) that influences other, subordinate factors (political, economic, social) that tend to be viewed as prime movers in other paradigms.

Paradigm isolation is a practice equally evident in statements made by proponents of all three key paradigms. The example of conservative/individualist paradigm isolation above should in no way be interpreted to mean that this practice is particularly characteristic of conservatives.

Statements that reveal paradigm isolation are examples of *the practice of being ideological.* They remind us of the definition and functions of ideology as explained earlier. When they are explicit, they tend to exhibit conflictual thinking defined in opposition to other, competing ideas. They tend to maintain or resist dominance, defend a particular group against criticism, aim at protecting a group's interests or resources, serve a group's organization and management goals, and exhibit a tendency toward universalizing and eternalizing space- and time-specific assumptions.

There is a tendency in paradigm isolation, as in ideological thinking in general, to oversimplify the real world. Paradigm isolation tends to involve "either/or" binary possibilities rather than "both/and" perspectives on the functioning of the social order. If we challenge the tendency toward paradigm isolation, it is possible to imagine that—in the real world—all of the key tenets of the

Table 1.2. Forms of Paradigm Isolation

General	Form Specific	Description
Explicit	Rejectionist	Tenets of other paradigm or paradigms explicitly rejected
Explicit	Contingent	Tenets of other paradigm or paradigms viewed as contingent on and/or subordinate to those in the home paradigm
Implicit	—	Ideas framed entirely in terms of the tenets of the home paradigm, and reference made to no other

three paradigms would have high and equal standing. It is possible to imagine that capital accumulation, rationalization of modes of domination, and role differentiation are equally relevant. It is possible to imagine that factors related to class, power, and culture are intricately related in a web of mutual causation, and that societal, organizational, and individual levels of analysis all make sense.

This is not to say that the competing views among the three key paradigms are all ill founded and illogical, and that the path to a multiparadigm integration requires only a suspension of ideological tendencies and astute analysis of causation. On the contrary, I would argue that some of the premises of the three paradigms are mutually inconsistent for readily understandable reasons and are therefore mutually irreconcilable. We cannot, for example, render compatible the claim that capitalism is the *cause* of the world's problems with the claim that it is their *solution*.

There is growing recognition among social theorists that needless polarization exists among the major classical traditions. Consequently, a major preoccupation in the discipline of sociology in the last two decades has been the search for a multiparadigm integration. Efforts at integration have been under way in the 1980s and 1990s that concern themselves mainly with particular philosophical issues and levels of analysis. Integration of agency and structure has been the dominant theme of European social theory; the main figures in this movement have been Anthony Giddens, Margaret Archer, Pierre Bourdieu, and Jürgen Habermas (Ritzer 2000, 81, 387–418). In the United States, the so-called macromicro linkage has been the central problematic; the main figures in this field have been George Ritzer, Jeffrey Alexander, Norbert Wiley, James Coleman, Allen Liska, Randall Collins, and Norbert Elias (a European) (Ritzer 2000, 80, 359–85).

Within these movements there have been efforts toward paradigm integration focused on the three classical traditions. Among the major efforts of this kind are the following. Randall Collins draws on all three traditions (and phenomenology and ethnomethodology as well), though more from Weber and Durkheim than from Marx (Ritzer 2000, 128). He emphasizes that the central ideas of Marx and Weber are complementary rather than conflictual (Collins 1994, v). Jeffrey Alexander's neofunctionalism seeks to synthesize functionalism and conflict theory and to "push functionalism to the left and reject Parsons' optimism about modernity" (Wallace and Wolf 1995, 68). Ralf Dahrendorf and Lewis Coser argue that conflict and consensus are two equally important facets of society (Wallace and Wolf 1995, 154–55; Ritzer 2000, 123).

Although significant progress has been made toward integrating parts of theories that are in needless contradiction, there are, and there will always be, certain domains in the three traditions of social theory that are in contradiction. This reflects the real-world tensions and conflicts among the interests and concerns of the proponents of various ideologies, not the failed imagination of theorists. This theme will be explored in greater detail in later chapters.

Assessing the Three-Paradigm Framework

But the most common ways in which we seek to understand the trajectories of development of modern societies have been strongly influenced—and limited—by
the context of their origin in nineteenth- and early twentieth-century Europe.
"Classical social theory" has continued to hold sway well beyond the circumstances
of its first formation. (Giddens 1987, 26)

Modern social theory, as Giddens points out, has exerted an enormous and in
some ways unjustified degree of influence on our contemporary outlook. Why
then should a book on environmental problems in the early twenty-first century
hark back to the nineteenth century and to classical social theory in forming its
frame of reference? There are three parts to the answer.

First, it is precisely because it has had great influence on us that we need to
understand well the grip that classical theory still exerts on our thoughts and
imaginations, both conscious and unconscious.

Second, as we have seen, there are contemporary extensions of classical social
theory that, although in some ways quite different from their antecedents, still share
key characteristics with those antecedents. We cannot fully understand modern social theory or political ideology without reference to classical social theory.

Third, the essences linking classical and modern theory are made relevant not
just by theorists but also by continuing real-world circumstances that inspire the
ideas. It makes complete sense that the world's poor, marginalized, and disenfranchised people tend to gravitate toward a worldview that highlights conflict
between rich and poor and that questions the prerogatives of the rich. It makes
complete sense that government officials and policy makers (among others) tend
to be immersed in the managerial/technocratic worldview. After all, one of the
functions of government is to seek policy-oriented and technocratically oriented
solutions to problems that tend to avoid the extremes of class transformation, on
one hand, and complete removal of government constraints on individual activities, on the other. It makes complete sense that the heads of corporations and
businesses vigorously promote the unfettered rights of individuals to engage in
economic activities as they see fit.

There are, of course, significant exceptions to these crude categorizations. For
example, some of the world's poor are swept up in right-wing movements of various kinds and, conversely, many of the world's most radical minds emerge from
an elite background. The point here is not to reify the social moorings of theory
but rather to point out some broad realities concerning the "material" inspirations for theory that tend to go unnoticed.

Although there are important strengths in an approach that gives prominence
to the three classical social theory paradigms and their contemporary extensions,
there is one undeniable weakness: a high degree of crude reductionism that over-
looks theoretical divergences and subtleties. One can legitimately ask why the
three categories are not subdivided into, and cross-classified by, various distinct

orientations, in keeping with what happens in the real world. The reason for maintaining our focus on the three paradigms, and for avoiding analytic proliferation and subtlety, is to ensure that we do not lose our grounding in the defining characteristics of the paradigms. The importance of maintaining this level of abstraction will be evident in later chapters.

Conclusion

Although the world is riven by conflicting and competing worldviews, surprisingly little attention is given to ideology as a theoretical category of inquiry. Among the reasons for this are the persistence of pejorative and exclusivist connotations of the concept, as well as pronouncements of the "death of ideology" connected with global political change involving the diffusion of liberal democracy and the collapse of communism. This chapter has endorsed a nonpejorative and inclusive definition of ideology which recognizes that the concept embraces all forms of consciousness, not just those deemed "false."

This chapter has formulated a theoretical framework that links political ideology to the three key paradigms of social theory. The class paradigm is associated with the left/radical position on the political spectrum and has an oppositional stance toward capitalism; the managerial paradigm is associated with the center/liberal position and exhibits conditional acceptance of capitalism; and the individualist paradigm is associated with the right/conservative position and tends to favor release of constraints on capitalist development.

Paradigm isolation is the tendency of proponents to elevate the tenets of their home paradigm over and against the tenets of other, competing paradigms. Although social theorists have attempted to bridge differences among the three paradigms, certain differences remain intractable, as they are rooted in competing material interests that cannot simply be wished away. We will see in later chapters that paradigm isolation is rooted in the views of many prominent theorists of global environmental change, and this tendency has pervasive influence on how environmental problems are perceived, defined, and addressed. Before we turn our attention to paradigm isolation in the environmental context, we must set the stage by examining the linkage between phases of socioeconomic development and patterns of global environmental change.

Notes

1. Van Dijk adds: "Conflicts of class, 'race' and gender thus pitch dominant groups against (usually) minority groups or groups with less power. These conflicts are usually about access and control over material or symbolic resources" (1998, 171).

2. Callinocos explains that "social theory is an irredeemably political form of thought. . . . It follows that some consideration of the relationship between social theories and political ideologies is unavoidable" (1999, 5).

3. "False consciousness is a term Marxists use to describe the situation where the proletariat fails to perceive what they believe to be the 'true' nature of its interests and does not develop a revolutionary class consciousness" (Abercrombie et al. 1994, 64).

4. For a useful summary of the "end of ideology" literature, see McLellan 1995, 44–55.

5. "In ordinary speech the word paradigm designates a typical example or model to be replicated or followed. This connotation is carried over into the technical use of the term introduced by the philosopher and social historian Thomas Kuhn" (Marshall 1998, 476).

6. While this is true, it is also the case that Marx and his followers tended to view capitalism as a necessary stage in the unfolding of historical progress, and an improvement on past modes of production.

7. These two types of proponents correspond, respectively, to the *functional* and *political* managerial worldviews as specified in Alford and Friedland 1985, 182–83.

8. Alford and Friedland (1985, 16) refer to "cultural (values)" as the key dimension of society in the pluralist (what I call "individualist") perspective. I substitute the terms "behavioral (culture)" for "cultural (values)" (see table 1.1) to retain the customary nomenclature when referring to the key dimensions of the three perspectives, that is, "class, power, and culture."

9. Giddens (1995, 93-107) cautions against labeling Durkheim a "conservative," pointing out that he did not argue for a return to traditional beliefs but instead advocated embracing modernity and moral individualism. This is true, but it does not negate the reasons that justify designation of Durkheim as a conservative. Durkheim viewed the culture and morality of the individual as a preeminent social force, which I view to be a hallmark of conservatism. Moreover, Durkheim's optimistic and favorable view of the development of industrial capitalism resonates well with contemporary conservatism.

10. While there is a general affinity between the individualist paradigm and neoclassical economics, this association should not be overdrawn. There are managerialists who espouse a neoclassical vision of the world. While believing in the core tenets of neoclassical theory, they are inclined to favor intervention in economic activities to safeguard the environment.

11. There are, however, important exceptions. For example, as we shall see in chapter 3, deep ecologists are individualists but they are critical of industrial development.

12. The dictionary defining the terms was Scruton 1982. The dictionaries not listing the terms were Krieger 1993, Robertson 1986, Plano et al. 1973, and Roberts and Edwards 1991.

13. Another example is Chickering's *Beyond Left and Right: Breaking the Political Stalemate* (1993), which identifies the category "liberal" with "left" and "conservative" with "right." He follows a general tendency to define as "left" not only the political center but also everything left of it. This implicitly taints centrists by association with Marxists and reinforces a tendency of centrists to distance themselves from the true left.

~

CHAPTER TWO

Human Evolution and
Socioenvironmental Outcomes

This chapter has four goals. The first is to demonstrate that contemporary environmental problems have deep historical (and even prehistorical) roots. This point is often obscured by the tendency to analyze the causes of environmental problems in terms of present or existing social conditions. The second goal is to explain environmental problems in terms of the conceptual categories of social theory (see chapter 1) and to demonstrate that all three key social theory paradigms are relevant to understanding the genealogy of contemporary environmental problems. Chapter 1 stated that class, power, and culture are (respectively) key variables in the class, managerial, and individualist social theory paradigms. This chapter will show that these variables form the bedrock of any explanation of human evolution, and of the contemporary social and environmental outcomes of this process. The third goal is to lay the groundwork for understanding that there are powerful interactive and synergistic dimensions among the domains of explanation of the three paradigms. The implication—elaborated in later chapters—is that an integral view of human evolution contradicts and undermines the logic of some forms of paradigm isolation. The fourth goal, building on the first three, is to demonstrate the perils of not taking class, power, and culture into account in understanding the origin and nature of contemporary environmental problems. This will be done through an examination of the so-called Commoner-Ehrlich equation.

By its nature, the conceptual model presented in this chapter runs the risk of overreaching its grasp and trying to be a "be-all and end-all" explanation of the origins of environmental problems. That is certainly not the intent, and the theoretical advancements proposed are in fact modest. Several clarifications and disclaimers are therefore necessary to make sure this chapter is not misunderstood.

Why?

Key social attributes of human evolution are summarized in this chapter, but with considerable economy of detail and with no claim whatsoever that all relevant variables and details are included. For example, no mention is made of changes in gender roles or of property regimes, and human energetics is used as a shorthand measure for human affluence, instead of referring to all forms of human affluence. Biophysical determinants of human evolution are considerably downplayed in the full knowledge that they are in fact important. For example, Jared Diamond (1999) has made a powerful case that regional plant-genetic endowments have influenced the course of human history. While it would certainly be possible to include more causal factors and a great deal more detail in this conceptual model, to do so would defeat its purpose, which is to summarize and highlight what I believe to be the key variables of evolutionary social change, the relationships among them, and their relationship to contemporary environmental change.

In this chapter I summarize the views of some evolutionary determinists (including the classical theorists)—people who believe all societies follow a uniform, sequential, linear path of human development. Some believe this will result in a progressive outcome that is better than where the evolutionary process began. I do not support this perspective on social evolution, and my exposition of these views should not be inferred as agreement with them.

The chapter is composed of four subsequent sections. The first builds a theoretical model of human evolution based on six causal variables (class, power, culture, population, affluence, and technology) and summarizes the contemporary social and environmental outcomes of this evolution. The second analyzes synergies among the six causal variables, and also between contemporary social and environmental outcomes. The third section criticizes the Commoner-Ehrlich equation for its inattention to class, power, and culture, and contrasts it to the theoretical model proposed in this chapter. The concluding section summarizes the chapter's main insights.

Human Evolution and Socioenvironmental Outcomes

This section first summarizes the key attributes of human evolution in terms of social theory variables (class, power, culture) and what I call "conventional" variables (population, affluence, technology). Conventional wisdom says that population, affluence, and technology are the key variables to be considered in any analysis of the causes of environmental problems.

The six variables are cross-classified in this section against Boyden's (1992, 100–104) four phases of human existence: the primeval phase (to 10,000 B.C.), the early farming phase (beginning around 10,000 B.C.), the early urban phase (beginning around 3500 B.C.), and the high energy phase (beginning at the time of the industrial revolution in A.D. 1750) (table 2.1). Key contemporary social and environmental outcomes of the process of human evolution are identified, some specified as "good" and others as "bad" (table 2.1). Various important out-comes are not discussed here, but the point of this theoretical exercise is to be synthetic and illustrative rather than comprehensive.

Boyden's (1992) ecological phases are markers of key transitions in systems of human organization that have had profound ecological consequences: the do-mestication of crop and animal species and the establishment of agriculture; the founding of cities and the rise of urban populations; and the use of fossil fuels and the onset of the industrial revolution. As we shall see, these phases correspond well to key transitions with respect to class, power, culture, population, affluence, and technology. There are some exceptions to this good fit. For example, there is little connection between the onset of early urban areas in 3500 B.C. and the emergence of the feudal mode of production. Moreover, the capitalist mode of production begins in the sixteenth century, prior to the high energy phase, though arguably there is a strong causal link between the emergence of capital-ism and the onset of the industrial revolution. These caveats aside, Boyden's (1992) phases are an appropriate framework for categorizing key transitions with respect to the social theory and conventional variables.

Class

The history of environmental change is in key respects the history of capital ac-cumulation—the ever increasing capacity of humans, over time, to transform their surroundings to produce wealth and fulfill their needs and desires. The his-tory of capital accumulation is fundamentally the history of class change through successive modes of production (MOPs). A society divided by class is one in which an elite dominates and appropriates the labor of a subordinate class; this domination and appropriation happens in order to generate wealth (among other purposes). The succession of MOPs over time is one that enables (along with other factors, as we shall see later) an ever greater capacity to transform natural resources into wealth. It should be stressed that various MOPs can coexist within ecological phases. For example, although slavery began in the early farming phase, it still exists, on a much-reduced scale, in the twenty-first century.

People in primeval society subsisted through hunting and gathering of foods. There were no classes as such—there was no systematic exploitation of one seg-ment of society by another for purposes of producing an economic surplus (i.e., production above and beyond subsistence needs).

Beginning in approximately 10,000 B.C., humans began to domesticate species of crops and animals. The establishment of agriculture enabled soci-eties to produce an economic surplus, allowing the emergence of a segment of society not involved directly in the fulfillment of subsistence needs. These are the conditions that permitted the emergence of an elite seeking to expand its wealth and control within a given society, and also over and against other so-cieties through warfare and pillage. Slavery emerged in 10,000 B.C. (Meltzer 1993a, 9) at the time of the onset of agriculture. Marx used the term "ancient

Table 2.1. Some Key Attributes of Socioeconomic Evolution and Some Social and Environmental Outcomes at the Turn of the 21st Century

Variables		Ecological Phases		
	Primeval (3,000,000 to 10,000 B.C.)	Early Farming (begins 10,000 B.C.)	Early Urban (begins 3500 B.C.)	High Energy (begins A.D. 1750)
Social theory				
Class	Classless society	Ancient mode of production begins Slavery introduced 10,000 B.C.	Feudal mode of production evident in fourth century A.D.	Capitalist mode of production begins in 18th century Colonialism and core-periphery distinctions
Power	Stateless, low complexity societies	Agricultural surplus enables establishment of complex societies	Advent of full-blown states in 3000 B.C.	Growth of states and capitalist enterprises TNCs hegemonic over states in late 20th century
Culture	Subsistence orientation	Emergence of culture of domination of humans and nature for accumulation, power, and status	Deepening and broadening of culture of early farming phase	Enlightenment, empiricism, science, individualism, consumerism, earth seen only as resource. Questioning of above begins 19th c.
Conventional				
Population	0.0007%–0.003% annual increase = 100,000–23,000-year doubling time No urban population	0.05% annual increase = 1,530-year doubling time No urban population	0.06% annual increase = 1,240-year doubling time Minute urban population	1.6% annual increase = 43-year doubling time 45% live in cities in late 20th c.

	Protohuman: 2,000 kilocalories per day	Hunters: 5,000 kilocalories/day	Early agriculturists: 12,000 kilocalories/day	Advanced agriculturists: 26,000 kilocalories/day	Industrial society: 77,000 kilocalories/day Technological society: 230,000 kilocalories/day
Affluence	Protohuman: 2,000 kilocalories per day Hunters: 5,000 kilocalories/day		Early agriculturists: 12,000 kilocalories/day	Advanced agriculturists: 26,000 kilocalories/day	Industrial society: 77,000 kilocalories/day Technological society: 230,000 kilocalories/day
Energy Technology	Fire	Fire	Fire Domestic crops Domestic animals	Fire Domestic crops Domestic animals Water Wind	Fire Domestic crops Domestic animals Water Wind Fossil fuels Nuclear and solar

Type of Outcome	Category of Outcome	
	Social	Environmental
Good	Greatly increased agricultural and industrial productivity through scientific and technological innovation in 20th century	Agricultural intensification has enabled reconversion of 16 million hectares of agricultural land to forest in developed countries
	Increased average per capita income	Drastically reduced production of chlorofluorocarbons and halons since 1986 in developed countries
	Control and elimination of certain diseases through public hygiene, education, and medical breakthroughs Increased average life-expectancy	Some air and water quality improvements through legal and technological measures in developed countries
	Achievement of demographic transition in many developed countries	Potentially reduced environmental pressure through reduced net human fertility in developed countries

Table 2.1. Some Key Attributes of Socioeconomic Evolution and Some Social and Environmental Outcomes at the Turn of the 21st Century (*Continued*)

Type of Outcome	Category of Outcome	
	Social	*Environmental*
Bad	The rate of agricultural productivity increase is slowing.	Land degradation and conversion and constraints on water supplies threaten the prospect of feeding an additional 2 billion people in next 30 years.
	2.8 billion (almost half of all people) live on less than $2 a day and 1.2 billion people (one-fifth) live on less than $1 a day.	Human activities appropriate 39% of terrestrial organic matter.
	The average income in the richest 20 countries is 37 times higher than the average in the poorest 20. The gap has doubled in 40 years.	Destruction of forests, coral reefs, and other habitats threatens loss of 7 of 22 million species in next 30 years.
	Progress in limiting mortality, controlling disease, and raising life expectancy is greatly skewed against developing countries.	Excessive release of carbon and other greenhouse gases threatens unknown changes in agriculture.
	The demographic transition is stalled in some developing countries.	Various other forms of air and water pollution present grave threats worldwide.

mode of production" to describe early agricultural civilizations that featured distinct class division between patricians and slaves acting as direct producers (Morrison 1995, 309). Slaves were a large part of the labor force in the Sumerian (Mesopotamian), Greek, Hebrew, and Roman civilizations (Meltzer 1993a). They made up a third of the population of the Greek city-states in the fifth century B.C., and perhaps half the population of early Rome (Meltzer 1993a, 65, 128). Slaves were acquired by elites largely through subjugation of other societies by wars of conquest (Meltzer 1993a). Slavery was a prominent MOP well after the early farming phase. It was, for example, the backbone of the colonial plantation economies from the sixteenth through the nineteenth centuries in the Americas (Meltzer 1993b).

The first reference to the term "feudalism" dates back to ninth-century Europe (Herlihy 1970, xiii), though the practice of feudalism probably originated several centuries earlier.[1] The definition of the term "feudalism" has been the subject of disagreement and controversy (Gould and Kolb 1964, 268–70; Prestwich 1985, 300–301). As employed here, it refers to an economic system in which a privileged elite (lords) could demand rents from subordinated producers (serfs) for which they offered little in return (Herlihy 1970, xiv–xvii). More specifically, it was a system of agricultural production in which serfs perform economic services for lords in the form of either direct labor on the lord's land or payment of tribute (in cash or in kind) from production on the serf's own land (Dobb 1964, 35, 66). The serf, unlike the slave, possesses means of production (land and tools) but, unlike a free farmer, must perform economic services for the lord (Dobb 1964, 36). Feudalism was a prominent feature of the economic systems of European states until feudalism went into a pronounced decline in the fourteenth century.[2] Among the reasons for the decline were the inefficiency of the feudal system; the need of lords for additional income; overexploitation of serfs; differentiation of the peasantry and the rise of well-to-do farmers; replacement of serfs with hired labor; the growth of trade and the money economy; population decline in the thirteenth century; and environmental deterioration on agricultural lands (Dobb 1964, 37–60).

The defining characteristic of capitalism is the existence of wage laborers (propertyless workers) whose only option to provide for their subsistence needs is to sell their labor to capitalists (owners of the means of production). Unlike serfs, wage laborers do not own their means of subsistence and, unlike both slaves and serfs, wage laborers are at least nominally free to choose a contractual work relationship with their employer. Capitalist relations of production first made their appearance in England in the late sixteenth century (Dobb 1964, 18). Thereafter they spread to various countries in Europe and the United States and propelled the industrial boom that began in the mid-eighteenth century. Capitalism has become synonymous with the unprecedented scope of economic development and accumulation of wealth that has taken place in the course of the industrial revolution through to the present day.

The growth of capitalism has meant relations of domination and submission not only at the microlevel of class, but also at the macrolevel of relationships among countries and world regions. European countries and the United States, the so-called core countries leading the process of capitalist industrial development, colonized countries of the "periphery" (in the Americas, Africa, and Asia), forcing them to support the process of capital accumulation in the core (Wallerstein 1979). While countries of the core entrenched their role as producers of industrial goods in the nineteenth century, countries of the periphery became producers of raw materials for export to core countries, as well as purchasers of manufactured goods produced in the core countries (at first textiles and then machinery and equipment). During World War II, 71 percent of all world industrial production was monopolized by just four core countries (Dickens 1998, 21). Since the end of the colonial era in the middle of the twentieth century, manufacturing and overseas trade have become less monopolized by the core than they were in the past (Dickens 1998, 67–68). However, several core countries still dominate the world economic system, and economic relations between so-called developed and developing countries remain extremely unequal.

Power

The history of environmental change is also in key respects the history of the growth of the state and other large organizations. In fact, in certain respects, the state has been so closely linked to (and in some cases synonymous with) economic elites and accumulation over the course of history, that one should rightly ask in what ways and to what extent the developments of class and power are fundamentally different. These evolutions are quite different, but in ways that are sometimes difficult to perceive.

According to Hall and Ikenberry, there are three defining characteristics of a state:

> First, the state is a set of institutions; these are manned by the state's own personnel. The state's most important institution is that of the means of violence and coercion. Second, these institutions are at the centre of a geographically bounded territory, usually referred to as a society. . . . Third, the state monopolises rule making within its territory. This tends toward the creation of a common political culture shared by citizens.[3] (1989, 1–2)

Societies in primeval times were simple and horizontal, and had relatively low complexity. States, as defined above, did not exist in the primeval ecological phase.

In the same way that the invention of agriculture and the creation of an economic surplus created the preconditions for class society, so too did it lay the groundwork for the emergence of the state. The state did not emerge instantly but rather evolved through predecessor systems of domination and collection of tribute that might be called protostates. Diamond (1999, 265–92) describes the development of the state as a transition from "egalitarianism to kleptocracy," as societies gradually evolved from the status of band, to tribe, to chiefdom, and finally to statehood. Key in this process is that agriculture allows food to be stockpiled and enables the formation of a political elite that asserts the right of taxation over food producers, evades the need to produce food directly itself, and can therefore engage in full-time political activities (Diamond 1999, 90).

The first "full-blown" state appeared in 3000 B.C. in the Middle East (Hall and Ikenberry 1989, 16; Berdan 1989, 78) in the early urban ecological phase. By 2200 B.C. several states and empires were fully developed in Mesopotamia, Egypt, Crete, the Indus Valley, and China (Berdan 1989, 78). As explained by Berdan, "Early states were supported by relatively productive and multifaceted economies. They were based on intensive agricultural production that yielded considerable and fairly reliable surpluses. These surpluses supported large, concentrated populations, often in cities, and allowed a segment of the population to pursue nonagricultural specializations such as religious offices, political positions, craft production, and trading enterprises" (1989, 80). Diamond makes the case that agglomeration of populations to 50,000 or more is strongly associated with the degree of social complexity necessary for statehood (1999, 268–69, 284). As explained by Braudel, "By the laws of a simple and inevitable political arithmetic, it seems that the vaster and more centralized the state, the greater the chance its capital had of being populous" (1979a, 527).

The modern national state—a "well-defined organization with a legitimate and continuous monopoly of violence over a defined territory" (Schwartz 1994, 10–42) and "a peculiar mix of force and right that shapes the lives of generations" (Held 1989, 51)—emerged after A.D. 1500. It exhibited a well-developed legal architecture, military prowess, and a financial system and can thus be called "a peculiar amalgam of 'lawyers, guns, and money'" (Schwartz 1994, 19). Its development in Europe is associated with the emergence of capitalism and then the industrial revolution in the high energy ecological phase. Comparative study of the modern nation-state, with the aim of understanding the hegemonic rise of Europe, concludes that it was important for the state to have an intermediate level of control over society. A despotically strong state such as China suppressed economic activity, whereas weak Indian and Islamic states were unable to support economic development. Also important were infrastructural strength and competition among politically fragmented European states (Hall and Ikenberry 1989, 22–42, 95–96).

Although always tied to the social project of capital accumulation, the state's role and function are distinct from those of ruling classes in ways that become more apparent with the turn to modernity. Braudel explains that

> the state undoubtedly encouraged capitalism and came to its rescue. But the formula can be reversed: the state also discouraged capitalism which was capable in return of

harming the interests of the state. Whether favourable or unfavourable, the modern state was one of the realities among which capitalism had to navigate, by turns helped or hindered, but often enough progressing through neutral territory. (1979b, 554)

In addition to being directly and indirectly involved in supporting the interests of privileged classes (e.g., certain forms of taxation, waging war on behalf of economic interests, and supporting scientific innovation and technology in furtherance of industrial development), states perform many social functions that are not necessarily tied to the maintenance of privilege. Among these functions are enactment of policies that redistribute or subsidize incomes, eradication and control of disease, support for public education, infrastructural development, disaster relief services, and so on. States must balance a constellation of often competing interests, and in doing so they aim to maintain the legitimacy of their rule in the eyes of elites as well as ordinary members of civil society. They seek to achieve through deeds what cannot be entirely done through might and, in so doing, maintain the conditions of stable rule over the long term. Some have claimed that these civic deeds are fundamentally aimed at mitigation of class frictions, and that thus the state is essentially a tool of elites. These arguments have receded in recent years as it has become clear—even to Marxist commentators—that states have at least a degree of autonomy from capitalist interests.[4]

In the course of the latter half of the twentieth century, important changes have taken place in the role of the state with regard to economic accumulation. In the course of the "developmentalist" period (1940s to 1970s), economic growth was organized primarily on a national basis, with governments exercising a relatively large degree of control over national enterprises. A flurry of postcolonial state building aimed at raising standards of living in developing countries. In the "globalist" period (1970s to the present), global economic integration and the growth of transnational corporations have led to a situation where the power of economic management has been relocated from nation-states to global institutions (McMichael 1996, 2, 8–10, 132).

Culture

Contemporary environmental change has everything to do with human cultural change, dating back to prehistoric times. After all, our appetite for resources reflects a degree of conscious decision making, and our decisions are the product of our ideas, beliefs, and values. In this section, I summarize the essences of cultural change as they relate to outlooks on economic accumulation and perceptions of the environment.

At the most basic level of synthesis, cultural change can be summed up as a three-stage process. First, in primeval times, human beings were oriented to subsistence and believed themselves to be at one with the natural world. Second, beginning in the early farming phase, there emerged a culture justifying domination of humans by humans and of nature by humans. This was linked to elites' pursuit of accumulation, power, and social status, and this trend has persisted until the present day. Consumption above the level of subsistence became not only acceptable but increasingly, over time, an obsessive goal not only for elites but also for the masses. Third, there have emerged (notably since the nineteenth century) a counterculture and organized movements that rebel against the domination of humans by humans (emancipation, labor, and human rights movements). Also since the nineteenth century, there have emerged a culture and movements questioning the domination of nature by humans (conservation and later environmentalism) and also consumption for the sake of consumption (voluntary simplicity and environmentalism).[5] Variants of these three-stage formulations have been presented by Harper (1996, 35–48), Earley (1997, 2–3), and Lowenthal (1990).

Milbrath (1989, 119) has described a contemporary "dominant social paradigm" (DSP) that corresponds to the second phase of cultural development described above. The DSP has six characteristics: (1) low evaluation of nature; (2) compassion only for those near and dear; (3) the assumption that risks are acceptable in order to maximize wealth; (4) there are no meaningful limits to growth; (5) contemporary society is essentially okay; and (6) markets and experts, rather than dissent, should govern politics. Many of these perspectives have their roots in values that were promulgated in the Enlightenment and the early industrial revolution: empiricism, the scientific approach, and rationalism; and belief in the goodness of individualism, self-interest, and competition.

The so-called human exemptionalist paradigm (or HEP), identified by Catton and Dunlap (1978, 42-43) can be viewed as an elaboration of the environmental characteristics of the DSP. Essentially, those who believe in the HEP exhibit four anthropocentric assumptions: (1) humans have culture and are therefore unique; (2) culture can be adapted far more rapidly than biological traits; (3) therefore human differences can be easily altered; and (4) cultural accumulation is without limit so progress can carry on indefinitely (Catton and Dunlap 1978, 42-43).

Counterposed to the HEP, and corresponding to the environmental awakening in the third cultural phase above, is the so-called new ecological paradigm, or NEP (Catton and Dunlap 1980, 34). The NEP consists of four linked assumptions: (1) while humans have exceptional characteristics (e.g., culture), that does not change the fact that they are interdependently involved in the ecosystem; (2) human interactions with nature are complex and therefore lead to unintended consequences; (3) human dependence on the biophysical environment imposes potent constraints; and (4) although human inventiveness seems to extend the limits of carrying capacity, ecological laws cannot ultimately be changed (Catton and Dunlap 1980, 34).

Population
For entirely logical reasons, it is customary to link contemporary environmental change to growth over time in human numbers. After all, there is an undeniable link between the exponential growth of human population around the time of the industrial revolution in 1750 and the dramatic changes in land use and land cover that have occurred since then.

A graph (figure 2.1) showing the growth of population on an arithmetic scale since 10,000 B.C. illustrates the long period of slow, incremental growth in the course of most of history, and the dramatic increase in human numbers in the last three centuries. In the primeval period, the average annual population increase was an infinitesimal 0.0007 to 0.003 percent per year (Vasey 1992, 192–93), implying a 100,000- to 23,000-year doubling time. There was no urban population. In the period 8000 B.C. to A.D. 1, the doubling time was 1,530 years (Weeks 1996, 30). This corresponds to a 0.05 percent annual population increase in the early farming phase.[6] There was no urban population. In the early urban ecological phase there was (by definition) the beginning of an urban population, but it was minute. Although it grew over time, it remained a very small fraction of total population until the beginning of the high energy phase.[7] In the period A.D. 1 to 1750, the doubling time was 1,240 years (Weeks 1996, 30). This corresponds to a 0.06 percent annual population increase in the early urban phase.[8] Dramatic change is evident in the high energy ecological phase: the average annual population increase has become 1.6 percent per year with a forty-three-year doubling time (Cohen 1995, 27), and the urban population is now 45 percent (Simmons 1996, 1).

The graph of arithmetic growth of human population since 10,000 B.C. gives the impression that the industrial revolution is the only pulse of rapid population growth, but that is an illusion. In fact, there were three population pulses: the first when tool making was introduced, the second when agriculture was introduced, and the third at the time of the industrial revolution (Whitmore et al. 1990, 25–26). The scale of the arithmetic graph does not allow the earlier pulses to be seen. A logarithmic graph of human population growth (figure 2.2) shows the pulse effect of tool making, agriculture, and industry. The agricultural revolution enabled human population to grow forty-fold from approximately 4 million in 10,000 B.C. to approximately 170 million in A.D. 1 (Cohen 1995, 400; Whitmore et al. 1990, 26).

One important feature of contemporary human population change is the extremely unequal rate of growth between developed and less developed countries. In the 1990s, the average annual population growth rate was 0.6 percent in high income countries and 2.0 percent in low income countries (World Bank 2000, 279). Of the projected increased population growth of 2 billion people between 2000 and 2025, 97 percent of that growth will occur in developing countries (World Bank 2001, vi).

Affluence

The history of human evolution shows a steady increase of average per capita affluence over time, if affluence is defined as the amount of energy consumed. Energy consumption closely parallels resource consumption generally. In modern times, per capita commercial energy consumption is a close analog of per capita gross domestic product (Foley 1976, 88).

Protohumans consumed only somatic energy—the energy converted by their own bodies through metabolism of digested food. (Digestion converts the photosynthetic energy in food into metabolic energy.) On a daily basis this amounted to 2,000 kilocalories (see table 2.1). With the invention of fire and tools in the primeval phase, use of extrasomatic energy sources began, and human energy consumption increased to an average of 5,000 kilocalories per day (Bennett 1976, 42).

With the introduction of ever more sophisticated extrasomatic energy converters in subsequent ecological phases, per capita energy use grew dramatically, from

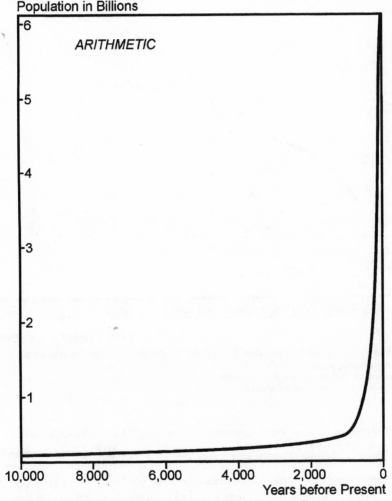

Figure 2.1. Human Population Growth from 10,000 B.C. to the Present on an Arithmetic Scale
Source: Adapted from Whitmore et al. 1990, 26.
Reprinted with permission of Cambridge University Press.

Population in Millions

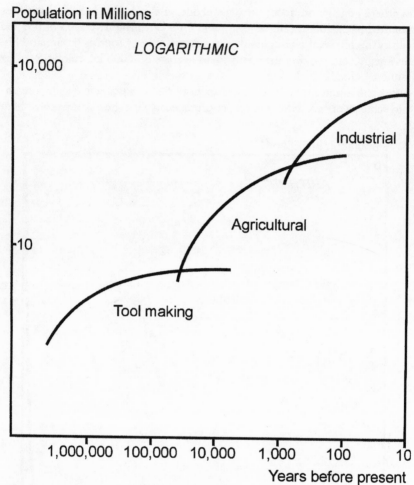

Figure 2.2. Human Population Growth from 10,000 B.C. to the Present on a Logarithmic Scale
Source: Adapted from Whitmore et al. 1990, 26.
Reprinted with permission of Cambridge University Press.

12,000 kilocalories for early agriculturalists, to 26,000 kilocalories for advanced agriculturalists, to 77,000 kilocalories in industrial society, to 230,000 kilocalories in modern technological society (Bennett 1976, 42). Between 1850 and 1995, average per capita energy use worldwide increased twenty-fold (Smil 1999, 133).

It should be stressed that, as with population growth rates, rates of energy consumption are extremely unequal between rich and poor countries. In 1990, the world annual per capita consumption of energy was 57 billion joules per year; the rates by world region were 13 billion joules in Africa, 29 billion joules in South

America, 24 billion joules in Asia, 126 billion joules in Europe, and 203 billion joules in North America (UNEP 1993, 289–93). According to Debeir et al. (1991, 134) extreme inequality of energy consumption has its origins in the early nineteenth century, when European and North American development surged forward because of their invention of converter machines that could make use of fossil fuels on an industrial scale. After World War I, large enterprises in Europe and North America monopolized most of the world's oil reserves, electrical networks, industries related to energy production, and energy distribution chains (Debeir et al. 1991, 134).

Technology

The history of human evolution is the history of technologies that are ever more efficient and powerful in transforming natural resources into usable products and services. This section, in keeping with the approach presented in the section on affluence, gives special attention to successive introductions of new energy technologies. The section adapts Simmons's (1996, 27) view of the sequential introduction of fire, animal domestication, wind, water, fossil fuels, nuclear power, and direct solar energy sources. I have added plant domestication to this model.[9]

The use of fire began as early as 1.5 million years ago (Boyden 1992, 72). Among the intentional uses of fire for early hominids were heating, lighting, nocturnal protection of communities, cooking of plant and animal foods, manipulation of plant and animal communities (e.g., flushing of animals for hunting), disinfestation, and tool making (Clark and Harris 1985, 19). The use of fire for heating enabled humans to colonize regions that would otherwise have been too cold (Simmons 1996, 38).[10] Paleolithic food gatherers doubled their use of energy when they began to use fire in food preparation (Cook 1971, 135). Cooking reduced the toxins, bacteria, and fungi in foods (Simmons 1996, 41). In the early farming phase, fire was used increasingly as a tool for land clearing and the establishment of agricultural plots.

The domestication of plant and animal species in the early farming phase was nothing short of a revolution in the energy economy of human society. As explained by Diamond,

> by selecting and growing those few species of plants and animals that we can eat, so that they consume 90 percent rather than 0.1 percent of the biomass of an acre of land, we obtain far more calories per acre. As a result, one acre can feed many more herders and farmers—typically, 10 to 100 times more—than hunter-gatherers. (1999, 88)

According to Smil (1999, 108), foraging supports on average a tenth of a person per square kilometer, whereas modern farming supports one thousand people per square kilometer. This is why, in the words of Southwick (1996, 129), "Of all human activities, agriculture has had the greatest impact, not only in stimulating rapid population growth and the development of elaborate civilizations, but also in altering the earth's land surface."

The domestication of animals enabled the increase of economic surpluses in six ways: (1) they became a major source of animal protein (meat, milk, blood), replacing wild game; (2) they provided manure as a fertilizer for agriculture, as well as other materials such as horn and hide; (3) they provided traction for plowing, processing of crops (threshing and trampling), and raising of water; (4) they enabled the cultivation of lands that would otherwise be uneconomical for farming; (5) they provided a means of transport for people and goods; and (6) they (in particular horses) provided an important logistical advantage in early warfare (Diamond 1999, 77, 88–89, 358; Smil 1999, 112; Simmons 1996, 103). Pastoral societies, depending on domesticated and semidomesticated animals, colonized areas that were marginal to agriculture and where the available cellulose—otherwise unpromising—could be used as forage for animals (Simmons 1996, 103). Prior to the use of draft animals, early farmers were confined to soils that could be plowed by digging sticks; the introduction of draft animals allowed the practice of agriculture over a wide range of soil types (Diamond 1999, 89; Boyden 1992, 147). The use of a draft animal enabled the plowing of a field three times faster than with human labor (Smil 1999, 112). Whereas humans produce only 75 watts of exertion, draft animals can produce from 500 to 700 watts of power (Simmons 1996, 93–94).

The use of water for irrigation and for powering mills was begun just prior to and during the early urban ecological phase. The development of irrigation is associated with the rapid growth of intensive agriculture and booming human populations in the Tigris-Euphrates lowlands between 4100 B.C. and 1900 B.C., in the Nile Valley between 4100 B.C. and A.D. 100, and in the Basin of Mexico between 1150 B.C. and A.D. 1519 (Whitmore et al. 1990). Irrigation greatly increased the productivity of agriculture by making it possible in areas where it might not otherwise be and by increasing the duration of the growing season. The Tigris-Euphrates valley was transformed by irrigation from a semiarid steppe to fertile cropland (Simmons 1996, 95–96).

Waterwheels, which convert the kinetic energy of running water in streams into the rotary motion of mills, were first used by the Greeks and Romans in the first century B.C. (Smil 1999, 120; Boyden 1992, 148). They did not come into wide use until the Middle Ages; by the eleventh century A.D. they were in use throughout Europe (Boyden 1992, 148).

Sail ships, which use the kinetic energy of the wind to create forward motion, have been an important means of transportation dating back thousands of years (Smil 1999, 130–31). Small sail ships were used on the Nile in the fourth millennium B.C. and were used to sail across the Mediterranean Sea in 2500 B.C. (Boyden 1992, 148). The use of wind power for turning mills is more recent. Windmills date back to Persia in the seventh century A.D. (Boyden 1992, 148). The use of windmills became common in Europe in the late twelfth century in areas that had little water power but strong winds (Smil 1999, 122–23).

As we saw in the discussion of affluence, the high energy ecological phase ex-hibits a quantum leap in the use of energy associated with the onset of the in-dustrial revolution in the mid-eighteenth century.[11] Smil explains that "by pro-viding energy flows of high power density, fossil fuels and electricity made it possible to embark on a large-scale industrialization creating a predominantly ur-ban civilization with unprecedented economic growth" (1999, 134). In ecologi-cal terms, the industrial revolution signified supplementing the use of solar en-ergy (e.g., agriculture, water, wind) with the ultimately nonrenewable stored photosynthetic energy in fossil fuels. Thus, in the course of the nineteenth and twentieth centuries, industrialized countries and those that they dominate be-came dependent on continuous supplies of fossil fuels. The use of fossil fuels in the industrial revolution is closely tied to the increasing use of metals, chemicals, machines, and plastics (Simmons 1996, 208–11).

Headrick (1990, 55–56) has identified five periods of technological develop-ment during the industrial revolution. The first period, in the last third of the eighteenth century and the beginning of the nineteenth century, involved the introduction in England of cotton mills and the boom of iron production. The second period saw the introduction of the steam engine, beginning in the middle of the nineteenth century, first for pumping and then for powering ma-chines. The third period, in the last third of the nineteenth century, features the use of steel and chemicals and the beginning of the use of electricity. In the fourth period at the beginning of the twentieth century, the internal combustion engine comes into use. And in the fifth period, after World War II, smokestack industries are replaced with the production of electronic devices and growth of services. Other energy technology developments in the twentieth century of considerable importance include jet propulsion and the use of nuclear energy for electrical power generation.

The industrialization of agriculture during the high energy phase has greatly in-creased the productivity of both land and labor by substituting mechanical power and fossil fuels for animal and human power and by introducing the use of artificial fertilizers and pesticides, as well as high-yielding plant varieties (Vasey 1992, 214–15, 245; Grübler 1994, 293, 311; Bartlett 1989, 253–55; Boyden 1992, 128). In the last century, the area of cultivated land has increased by a third, but with aver-age yields increasing fourfold due to productivity increases, total harvests have been increased sixfold (Smil 1999, 133). Grübler (1994, 304–9) has identified three pe-riods of modern agricultural development. During the period of agricultural inno-vation in England (1850–1870), complex crop rotation patterns were introduced, and fallow lands and grasslands were converted to croplands. During the period of agricultural mercantilism (mid-nineteenth century to the 1930s), large-scale agri-cultural trade and increased use of commercial fertilizer were enabled by the devel-opment of the iron and chemical industries, railway networks, refrigeration, and new methods of food preservation. During the period of agricultural industrializa-tion (1930s to the 1990s), biological innovations, new cheap factor inputs, and mechanization have produced spectacular yield increases not just in developed countries but also throughout the world.

Considerable dependence on nonrenewable fossil fuels, as well as the occasional price instability of fossil fuels and their large contribution to the problem of global warming, have motivated a search for long-term energy alternatives. Nuclear power, a highly favored option in the 1950s and 1960s, fell out of favor in the late twentieth century due to high costs and the technological challenge of radioactive waste disposal. The nuclear option has not been completely written off, in part because it produces no carbon emissions. The direct use of solar energy has received considerable attention in recent decades. There are two approaches, involving either the direct use of solar energy for residential or industrial heating or the conversion of solar energy to electricity. Although showing promise for meeting certain energy needs, most solar applications are not yet competitive with nonrenewable energy sources, and their efficiency is limited by the intermittence of solar radiation in some world regions. The greatest challenge facing either the nuclear or the solar option is the immense and growing scale of energy demand worldwide. Improvements in the efficiency of energy technologies are therefore a growing priority for meeting future energy needs.

Social Outcomes

The good news in the social outcomes of human social evolution can be summarized as follows (see table 2.1):

1. Agricultural productivity increase has been phenomenal, with average yields keeping pace with population growth. In 1995 world per capita food supplies were 18 percent higher than they were thirty years before (Alexandratos 1995, 1). In recent decades world food production increased faster than population not just in developed countries, but also in developing countries, with the exception of sub-Saharan Africa (Islam 1995, 2; Dyson 1996, xv).

2. Worldwide average per capita income has increased. Between 1965 and 1998 average incomes more than doubled in developing countries, and between 1990 and 1998 the number of people in extreme poverty fell by 78 million (World Bank 2001, v–vi).

3. There has been enormous progress in the control and elimination of major diseases. Between 1982 and 1993, annual child mortality from the five leading diseases (pneumonia, diarrhea, measles, tetanus, and whooping cough) declined (UNICEF 1994, 1). Between 1980 and 1998, the mortality rate for children under five years of age decreased from 123 per 1,000 to 75 per 1,000 worldwide (World Bank 2001, 277).

4. Average life expectancy has increased. In the last two hundred years countries now considered developed have more than doubled life expectancy from less than thirty-five to seventy years; in the three decades after World War II, life expectancy in developing countries rose from thirty-two to fifty years (Coale 1974, 48, 51).

5. The demographic transition has been achieved in many rich countries. In rich countries, the total fertility rate[12] has decreased steadily and is now at or below the level of replacement[13] in most such countries. Population growth in many of these countries will come to a stop and even reverse in coming decades, meaning decreased resource pressure from population growth in these countries. The demographic transition (change from high birth and death rates to low birth and death rates) has resulted in these countries from a complex combination of social factors (Cohen 1995, 46–75). (This topic will be examined in greater detail in chapter 4.)

The bad news in the social outcomes of human social evolution can be summarized as follows (see table 2.1):

1. The rate of agricultural productivity increase is slowing. In spite of the need to feed more than a billion additional people by the year 2020, the annual growth in cereal production is declining. At the world level, the rate of growth was approximately 2.3 percent in 1967–1982 and 1.6 percent in 1982–1994; it will be about 1.0 percent in the period 1995–2020 (Pinstrup-Andersen et al. 1999, 5, 15). Cereal production will not keep up with demand in developing countries and their imports will double in 1995–2020 (Pinstrup-Andersen et al. 1999, 5).

2. Poverty remains a colossal problem in developing countries. Almost half the world's population, 2.8 billion people, live on less than $2 per day, and 1.2 billion people, a fifth of the population, lives on less than $1 a day (World Bank 2001, 3). Although the proportion of people in poverty declined from 28 percent to 24 percent between 1987 and 1998, the absolute numbers remained the same (World Bank 2001, 23). South Asia (43.5 percent of total) and sub-Saharan Africa (24.3 percent of total) jointly compose more than two-thirds of the world's poor (World Bank 2001, 24).

3. There is a huge gulf between rich and poor countries, and it is getting wider. The average income in the richest twenty countries is thirty-seven times higher than the average in the poorest twenty, and the gap has doubled in the past forty years (World Bank 2001, 3).

4. Progress in limiting mortality and controlling disease is greatly skewed against poor countries. In 1998, the mortality rate for children under five years of age was 107 per 1,000 in low income countries, 38 per 1,000 in middle income countries, and 6 per 1,000 in high income countries (World Bank 2001, 277). In 1997 the average life expectancy at birth was 64.4 years in developing countries and 77.7 years in industrialized countries (UNDP 1999, 171). In 1993 the number of doctors per 100,000 people was 76 in developing countries and 253 in industrialized countries (UNDP 1999, 175). The disproportionate impact of AIDS in Africa threatens to nullify the gains in life expectancy in the last half-century in some countries of Africa (World Bank 2001, 4).

5. The demographic transition is stalled in many poor countries. The average annual rate of population increase has declined in poor countries from 2.3 percent in the 1980s to 2.0 percent in the 1990s (World Bank 2001, 279).

Nevertheless, this represents a doubling time of thirty-five years and, as mentioned earlier, almost all population growth in the next several decades will take place in developing countries. The factors believed by some to motivate decline in the rate of population growth (e.g., economic growth, income equality, reproductive rights, women's participation in the labor force, etc.) are not falling into place in many of the poorest developing countries.

The good news in the environmental outcomes of human social evolution can be summarized as follows (see table 2.1):

1. Agricultural intensification has enabled reforestation in rich countries. Since 1950, agricultural intensification in Europe and North America has permitted the reconversion of 16 million hectares of farmlands to forest. At the same time, population in these countries has increased by 170 million people (Grübler 1994, 324). This reforestation is good news inasmuch as it helps counter a worldwide trend toward rapid forest cover loss. Nonetheless, it should be noted that this agricultural intensification is heavily dependent on fossil fuel use and may therefore not be sustainable in the long term, that biodiversity is heavily threatened in rich countries in spite of reforestation, that there are heavy pressures on certain "old growth" forests in rich countries, and that rich country reforestation in no way compensates for rapid forest cover and biodiversity loss in poorer countries.

2. The production of ozone-depleting gases has been slowed. Since 1987, when the Montreal Protocol international agreement was signed, the production of ozone-depleting chlorofluorocarbons (CFCs) and halons has declined more than 70 percent. Nevertheless there is cause for concern because the production of these chemicals has risen in developing countries (WRI 1998, 177–79).

3. There have been important air and water quality improvements in rich countries. In recent decades, in developed countries, there has been major progress in controlling acid-forming air pollutants. Sulfur dioxide emissions in North America and Europe have declined by about 40 percent between 1980 and 1994, and there has thus been less acid rain in these world regions (WRI 1998, 181–83). Also in rich countries, there have been some encouraging though tenuous water quality improvements involving reduction of the organic load of rivers (through control of domestic sewage) and heavy metal concentrations in waters, as well as reduced water quality impact from forestry, elimination of certain highly toxic pesticides, and increased public awareness of water quality issues (Perry et al. 1996, 39).

4. Achievement of the demographic transition in rich countries has tended to reduce aggregate demand on resources. The greatly reduced rate of population growth in rich countries has averted environmental demands that would have occurred if there had been a higher rate of population growth. In view of the very high resource consumption per capita in rich countries, the implications of population decline are potentially quite significant.

The bad news in the environmental outcomes of human social evolution can be summarized as follows (see table 2.1):

1. Land degradation and conversion threaten agricultural potential. Agriculture faces the daunting task of feeding an additional 2 billion people in the next thirty years and yet, as mentioned earlier, the rate of agricultural productivity increase is on the decline. At the same time, the existing stock of agricultural land and soil is threatened by degradation, erosion, desertification, and conversion. Each year, 5–6 million hectares out of a total 1.5 billion hectares of cultivated land are lost to severe degradation; topsoil is being lost at 16 to 300 times the rate of replacement (WRI 1998, 157). Twenty-five billion tons of topsoil are being lost annually (World Bank 2000, 28). So-called marginal (arid and semiarid) lands are important for agricultural production but are threatened (Boyden 1992, 123). Annually about 8 million hectares of agricultural land are converted to nonagricultural uses (Buringh and Dudal 1987, 29–30). Increasing competition for fresh water is an important potential constraint on future agricultural yields. From 1990 to 1995, water use increased sixfold worldwide, at more than twice the rate of population increase, and there are now emerging shortages for one-third of the world's population (WRI 1998, 188–90).

2. Human activities appropriate 39 percent of terrestrial organic matter, and it is not clear if this is sustainable. In the 1980s, humans appropriated (in the sense of directly using, diverting, or reducing) 58.1 petagrams (Pg) out of a total 149.6 Pg or 39 percent of terrestrial organic matter (i.e., net primary productivity or NPP).[14] This means that 61 percent of NPP is what remains to sustain all other living species. It is not clear if this level of appropriation of NPP is sustainable in the long term (Simmons 1996, 361, 364). Human appropriation of aquatic resources is a worrisome indicator of what may lie ahead. Due to over-fishing, the yields of 35 percent of the 200 major fishery resources are decreasing, and the yields of another 25 percent are steady, but at their biological limit and vulnerable (Grainger and Garcia 1996, 31).

3. Habitat destruction is causing massive species extinction. Of the 22 million species of flora and fauna estimated to be in existence, 7 million species are under threat of extinction in the next thirty years. Three-quarters of the world's bird species are in decline and one-quarter of all mammal species are threatened (Flavin 1997, 13). The major causes of biodiversity loss are agricultural practices, deforestation, and destruction of wetlands and ocean habitats (World Bank 2000, 42). Between 1700 and 1980, 19 percent of the earth's forest cover disappeared, and through this process of deforestation, the area of agricultural land has been increased by four-and-a-half times (Richards 1990, 164). According to the FAO Forest Resources Assessment 2000, during the 1990s the rate of natural forest cover loss was 16.1 million hectares per year, and of this, 15.2 million hectares per year (94 percent) was in the tropics.

4. Global warming threatens unknown changes in agriculture. The Intergovernmental Panel on Climate Change says the global average surface temperature increased by about 0.6° C and the global average sea level rose 0.1 to 0.2 meters during the twentieth century; it claims human agency is the probable cause of

global warming (Albritton et al. 2001, 2, 4, 10). The primary source of increased atmospheric carbon dioxide (the principal suspected cause of global warming) is industrial activity, mainly in rich countries. From 1950 to 1995, the cumulative carbon emissions in developed countries were about six times larger than those in developing countries; on a per capita basis in 1995, residents of developed countries produced five times more carbon emissions than residents of developing countries (WRI 1998, 176). Among the projected adverse impacts of global warming are a reduction in potential crop yields in most tropical and subtropical regions, decreased water availability in water-scarce regions, an increase in the frequency and severity of extreme weather events, significant disruption of ecosystems, and increased risk of extinction of some vulnerable species and loss of biodiversity (Ahmad et al. 2001, 5, 6, 11). The effects of climate change are expected to fall most heavily in developing countries, where people have the least resources and capacity to adapt (Ahmad et al. 2001, 8).

5. Various forms of air and water pollution present grave threats worldwide. In addition to global warming, there are other potentially grave dangers from pollution including continued ozone layer depletion, nitrogen and sulfur emissions, and radioactive wastes. Although the production of ozone-depleting gases has been greatly reduced since 1987 (WRI 1998, 177–79), the ozone hole over the antarctic continues to grow. The doubling since 1940 of nitrogen available for uptake (through such activities as agriculture, energy production, and transport) distorts the nutrient cycle, disrupts soil chemistry, wreaks havoc in the structure of ecosystems, increases eutrophication in aquatic ecosystems, and contributes to acid rain, global warming, and ozone depletion (WRI 1998, 179–81; Smil 1997, 112–39). Although production of sulfur dioxide (a cause of acid rain) has been reduced in rich countries, emissions could triple in Asia between 1990 and 2010 (WRI 1998, 181–83). The consequences of acid rain include damage to freshwater aquatic ecosystems and killing of forests (Smil 1997, 141–69). Inappropriate management and storage of radioactive materials threaten human health and ecosystems, and increase the danger of nuclear terrorism (Simmons 1996, 371–85).

Synergistic Relationships

In this section we will examine certain interactions among the variables just described. Some, but not all possible, interactions are considered. The aim is not to be comprehensive but to describe the essences of key tendencies.

We begin by looking at interactions among the social theory variables, and then among the conventional variables, and then among the social theory and conventional variables. Synergistic interactions—those that have a tendency to reinforce each other—are of particular interest. There are three key points. First, the synergistic interactions underscore the necessity of viewing the operation of the variables as joint rather than independent phenomena. Second, the overall tendency of these synergistic interactions has been to increase human numbers and the appropriation of natural resources. Third, there are important counter-tendencies (that are called here "negative synergies"), but to date they have been strongly dominated by the positive synergies.

Synergies among social theory and conventional variables (see table 2.2) will receive more attention than synergies among social theory variables or conventional variables. The reason is that to date little attention has been paid to the former topic, whereas substantial attention has gone to the two latter topics.

The concluding section, which looks at some synergistic interactions among the social and environmental outcomes, underscores the fact that we cannot adequately understand one type of outcome without understanding the other.

Synergies among Social Theory Variables

Effect of Class on Power

Class formation and the capital accumulation process are an essential foundation enabling the emergence of social complexity and ultimately state formation. The modern state and large enterprises are in a sense the product of successive MOPs. Going back ten thousand years, external aggression and war making have united the functions of class and power. Diamond explains that "the peoples of areas with a head start on food production . . . gained a head start on the path leading to guns, germs, and steel. The result was a long series of collisions between the haves and the have-nots of history" (1999, 103).

Effect of Power on Class

From the earliest times protostates and then full-fledged states have acted in the service of surplus accumulation and thus, by extension, elite classes. States have thus had an integral role in the historical succession from ancient to feudal and capitalist modes of production. Tilly says states "operate chiefly as containers and deployers of coercive means, especially of armed force" (1992, 51) and that many modern wars have supported the aggrandizement of capitalism, among other aims. In his view, "war made states, and vice versa" (Tilly 1992, 67). As mentioned earlier, the modern "semiautonomous" state has a role in regulating the accumulation process. Although this can be viewed as a negative synergy, it can also be viewed as a positive synergy inasmuch as state regulation may serve to stabilize the process of long-term accumulation.

Effect of Class on Culture

Ideology, a key component of culture, is partly a reflection of the competing interests and unequal status of dominant and subordinate classes. The development of dominant and subordinate social and environmental paradigms was discussed earlier. The institution of slavery provides an important example of class position motivating and shaping a particular cultural outlook. Early Greek civilization provided the earliest inspiration for the ideals of democracy and freedom. Yet these high ideals did not motivate early Greek thinkers to propose liberating slaves (Meltzer 1993a, 58, 91). Slavery was clearly too important to the interests of early Greek elites to allow abolitionist thought, let alone abolitionist action. Instead, the ancient mode of production generated tacit acceptance of the practice of slavery. Another important example of the influence of class on culture is the creation of consumerism in the capitalist era. Robbins explains that "there has emerged over the past five to six centuries a distinctive culture or way of life dominated by a belief in commodity consumption as the source of well-being. This culture flowered in Western Europe, reached fruition in the United States, and spread to much of the rest of the world" (1999, 8). Manno argues that "commoditization," among other destructive effects, has stunted human imagination and creativity (2000, 142-45).

Effect of Culture on Class
Culture in turn powerfully shapes the values, beliefs, and actions of people with respect to their position in the accumulation process and the exploitation of natural resources. In the words of Braudel (1979c, 623), "Capitalism also benefits from all the support that culture provides for the solidity of the social edifice, for culture—though unequally distributed and shot through with contradictory currents—does in the end contribute the best of itself to propping up the existing order." But of course, culture does not always support the existing order. An important modern example of culture inspiring class opposition is the emergence of "cosmopolitan localism."[15] Through cosmopolitan localism, subordinated or alienated people reject the homogenization of culture and imposition of Western culture and values, and instead defend and promote local culture and values (Sachs 1992, 112).

Effect of Power on Culture
As noted earlier, states and large enterprises have had a key role in creating, maintaining, and defending (in most cases) dominant social and environmental ideologies. Schmookler (1995, 23, 28, 114, 258) explains that power shapes culture in the direction of homogeneity and has created the ethic of "tyranny over nature." There are, of course, exceptions where state ideologies actively promote values in opposition to capitalism (e.g., contemporary Cuba) or Western culture and values (e.g., the Taliban movement in Afghanistan).

Effect of Culture on Power
The mobilizations of subordinate and alienated peoples in turn has a strong effect on state ideology and action. For example, the modern environmental movement, founded in the 1970s, has been a powerful motivating factor inspiring state and corporate forms of environmentalism.[16] This issue will be examined in detail in chapter 6.

Synergies among Conventional Variables

The Effect of Population on Affluence
In some clear ways, growing human population has provided the foundation for growing average human affluence. Growing human numbers are part of what led to the establishment of agriculture and settled populations; the formation of complex societies, classes, and states; the capital accumulation process; and growing average consumption of energy over time. Of course, there are important negative synergies in this relationship, especially in modern times, where excess human numbers in relation to a particular resource base can lead to declining average affluence.

The Effect of Affluence on Population
In a reciprocal way, the growth in average energy consumption over time has been part and parcel of the process of increasing capital accumulation and appropriation of resources, which in turn has enabled the growth of larger and larger human populations (Cottrell 1955, 32; Odum 1971, 26). The advent of high energy industrial society not only provided the means to support a much larger population but also enabled a predominantly urban civilization (Smil 1999, 133–34). Here, as well, there are important negative synergies. Increasing average affluence over time has contributed to average income security in households which in turn, according to some demographers,[17] has been an important factor motivating fertility reduction and, ultimately, population growth reduction and the demographic transition.

Effect of Population on Technology
Population growth over time is strongly related to the establishment of complex, differentiated societies, the drive toward capital accumulation, and technological innovation and development. At the microlevel in agrarian settings, population pressure and land shortages induced a technological shift from swidden cultivation to sedentary, land-saving, intensive agriculture (Boserup [1965] 1993). From a general economic point of view, it can be said that higher demand for goods and services over time (linked to population size), as well as higher prices for scarce goods and services, increases incentives for innovation and technological development.

Effects of Technology on Population
Technological innovation and development (together with increasing energy use, as above) are linked to the production of an ever greater economic surplus that in turn has supported an ever greater population over time. As noted earlier, the domestication of plant and animal species beginning in 10,000 B.C. enabled substantial population growth. As part of that process, the application of irrigation technology to agriculture was related to population booms in the Tigris and Euphrates lowlands, the Egyptian Nile Valley, and the Basin of

Mexico (Whitmore et al. 1990). Developing public hygiene technologies and modern medicine combined to drive down mortality rates, which, together with stable fertility rates, meant rapid population growth. Technological development has made possible the growth of urban employment and the emergence of megacities (Grübler 1994, 317). There are, however, important negative synergies between technology and population. Economic development (associated with high technology) is claimed by some demographers to be an important precursor for attaining the demographic transition and decline in population growth rates.

Effect of Affluence on Technology

Increased capacity to consume society's economic product increases the social base for appropriation of tribute, tax, and profits. Increased tribute and tax can increase state capacity to promote technological innovation and development. Increased profits promote increased competition among owners of capital, which in turn stimulates technological innovation and development. The reader should bear in mind that enterprises (and in fact entire countries) compete on the basis of keeping wages low, and this is an important check on the long-term progression toward increased affluence.

Synergies among Social Theory and Conventional Variables

The Interaction of Class and Population

The succession of MOPs over time implies an ever larger economic surplus and this, in turn, has provided the basis for an ever larger population (see table 2.2). Conversely, population change over time has been a key factor in transitions from one form of social organization to another. This synergy is well illustrated by Diamond (1999, 88–90). Eurasian societies got a head start in the domestication of plants and animals, and their populations therefore grew much faster than those of hunter-gatherer societies. Eurasian societies were thereby able to conquer hunter-gatherer societies in two ways. First, the brute numerical advantage of food producers over hunter-gatherers conferred military advantages for the former over the latter. Second, the large number of food producers made possible the establishment of complex societies and states, which then enabled wars of conquest.

Population change was a key aspect of the collapse of feudalism and the rise of capitalism. War and plague-induced population decreases after 1300 in Europe precipitated a decline in the feudal economy. Labor scarcity was aggravated by the overexploitation of serfs, causing many to flee their lands and move to towns. The labor scarcity forced many lords to mitigate servile burdens and substitute a contractual money relationship for an obligatory one (Dobb 1964, 48–51, 70). Conversely, rapid population growth in later centuries laid the groundwork for the emergence and consolidation of capitalism. Increases in food production in

Table 2.2. Matrix of Synergies between Social Theory and Conventional Variables

Social Theory Variables	Conventional Variables		
	Population	Affluence	Technology
Class	Successive MOPs increase surplus and allow larger population.	Successive MOPs generate more surplus and enable *average* increase in affluence over time.	Successive MOPs generate ever greater drive for accumulation and for technological innovation.
	Population change is a key factor enabling class change (e.g. decline of feudalism and onset of capitalism) and accumulation through conquest.	Disposal of production via increased consumption is essential to capitalism.	New technologies are a key vehicle for transitions among MOPs, e.g., domestication and slavery.
Power	States and large organizations enable accumulation, which permits population increase.	Organizational complexity enables technological development and increased affluence.	Organizational complexity is necessary for the emergence of science and high technology.
	Growing populations enlarge the base for appropriation of tribute and profit.	Increased affluence enlarges the base for appropriation of tribute and profit, encouraging growth of state and enterprises.	Technologies increase surplus and provide the basis for increasing complexity of organizations.
Culture	Ideology justifies domination of humans and nature, facilitating accumulation and population growth.	DSP and HEP provide cultural justification for increased consumption and affluence.	DSP and HEP provide cultural inspiration for innovation and scientific discovery.
	Population growth and urbanization are linked to the production of status goods and to the DSP.	Increased affluence reinforces elite allegiance to paradigms and subordinate opposition to them.	Innovation, discovery, and "progress" reinforce belief in and allegiance to the DSP and HEP.

Europe from 1700 to 1850 sustained population increases (Grübler 1994, 305). This increased population, together with large numbers of landless peasants (resulting in England from the enclosure movement) fed growing agricultural and urban wage labor markets (Heilbroner 1993, 55–56; Foster 1999a, 59–60).

Class and Affluence

Successive MOPs have generated more economic surplus over time and have enabled average increases in affluence in the long run—average because large segments of the human population, at any given point in time, can be subject to declining affluence. Conversely, disposal of economic production via increased consumption is essential to the survival of capitalism. The scale of capitalism must grow constantly or risk economic crisis. The economist Robert Heilbroner explains:

> As economists from Adam Smith through Keynes have pointed out, a "stationary" capitalism is subject to a falling rate of profit as the investment opportunities of the system are used up. Hence, in the absence of an expansionary frontier, the investment drive slows down and a deflationary spiral of incomes and employment begins. (1974, 84)

Two caveats deserve emphasis. First, aggregate demand (economic consumption) can grow over time either through growth in the number of consumers (population increase) or increase in per capita consumption, or both. Second, given this, it is possible for levels of consumption to stagnate or decline while overall growth proceeds. This is what happened in North America and Europe after 1980 with the collapse of "Fordism." Through Fordism, in decades prior to 1980, large enterprises increased the wages of workers in order to stimulate productivity gains and demand for their products.[18] Some suggest that after the economic crises of the 1970s and 1980s, Fordism is in terminal crisis, leading to post-Fordism and so-called flexible production systems (Marshall 1998, 235). In response to declining profits after the second oil shock in 1979, rich countries decided that workers were too strong and opted to combat inflation rather than maintain levels of employment (Lipietz 1997).

Class and Technology

Successive MOPs generate an ever greater drive toward economic accumulation, competition among enterprises, and technological innovation and development. Conversely, innovation and technological development are a key vehicle for the transition from one MOP to another. For example, as explained earlier, domestication of plant and animal species and the onset of food production are closely linked to the emergence of slavery and the ancient MOP. Debeir et al. (1991) explain that energy systems and technologies are characteristic of particular MOPs and that energy systems can serve to support a social class or a state apparatus. The aim of the invention of the steam engine was to enable owners of factories to produce more, faster, and at lower cost, as well as to establish the domination of capital over labor. From an energetic perspective, the onset of capitalism signified the transition from reliance on biological energy to reliance on fossil energy (Debeir et al. 1991, 7, 87).

Power and Population
As already explained, the formation of states and large organizations has been part and parcel of the process of economic accumulation, which in turn has supported population increase over time. Schmookler (1995, 81–83) says the expansion of state power through war has often involved territorial increase to reinforce its own strength and to support a larger population. Also, as noted before, growing populations have enlarged the social base for the appropriation of tribute, tax, and profit, and this in turn has assisted the growth of states and other large organizations. Conversely, an important negative synergy is that some states in modern societies have taken a lead role in population control, recognizing that rapid and uncontrolled population growth can destabilize long-term governance.

Power and Affluence
As explained before, increased social and organizational complexity over time have been closely linked to technological innovation and development, and this in turn has been related to increased average levels of affluence. Conversely, as seen before, increased average affluence over time has enlarged the base for the appropriation of tribute, tax, and profit, and this has enabled the growth of states and other large organizations, including the so-called military-industrial complex. The Gulf War in 1991 illustrates this relationship. The United States and allied countries went to war against Iraq ostensibly to protect the sovereignty of a small oil-rich country (Kuwait) that had been invaded by Iraq. In fact, the war was waged mainly to preserve the hegemony of the United States and other core countries over oil supplies in the Middle East, and this in turn is related to high levels of average energy consumption (in effect, affluence) and fossil fuel dependence in North America and Europe.

Power and Technology
As explained earlier, social and organizational complexity are the bedrock on which scientific and technological development are built. It is no accident that the rise of the modern state was contemporaneous with the rise of modern science and the Enlightenment. As Schmookler explains:

> By setting limits upon the range of a society's possibilities, technology thereby also sets limits on its capacity to generate power. Any technological breakthrough that extends those limits escalates the struggle for power within the system of civilization. (1995, 255)

Technological innovation and development have assisted the increased economic surplus over time and in turn have motivated the increasing complexity of society and the development of the state and other large organizations. Schwartz (1994, 10–21) explains that the emergence of the modern state in Europe was originally constrained by energetic and technological limits on the capacity of kings and nobles to collect agricultural tribute. Prior to the development of mechanized transportation, grain could not be transported efficiently more than twenty miles. States therefore initially concentrated on external capital accumulation through overseas mercantile trade. Eventually, invention of the railroad and other forms of mechanized transportation made long-distance transport of agricultural yields possible. This allowed increased tribute and tax collection within European societies and the turn to internally generated and more stable state growth.

In Max Weber's scholarship, the state and large organizations are embodiments of a historical trend toward increasing rationalization, planning, and scientific calculation. Freeman and Perez (1988, 52–53) demonstrate that successive organizational styles (e.g., manufacture, the factory system, standardization, monopoly and oligopoly, multinational corporations, Fordism, the information and communications age) are linked to successive technological systems.

Culture and Population

As explained earlier, ideology has been used to justify the domination of humans over humans and of humans over nature, facilitating the emergence of successive forms of MOPs. This, in turn, has been closely linked to technological development, the growth of economic surplus, and an increasing ability over time to support larger and larger populations. It is important to recognize that in modern times, cultural change has been closely linked to fundamental shifts in the operation of the capitalist economy. Beaud (1983, 33–35) observes the simultaneous emergence of the ideal of personal freedom and economic liberalism at the dawn of capitalism. Douthwaite (1999, 301) explains that the declaration "I have a right to be myself" would have been meaningless in the eighteenth century, but in modern times a cultural emphasis on personal freedom is closely linked to economic growth.

Conversely, population growth over time is linked to cultural and ideological changes. For example, the process of urbanization led to the production of nonessential luxury and status goods (Boyden 1992, 193). Growing production of these goods is closely linked to the development of the dominant social paradigm.

Culture and Affluence

The dominant social paradigm and the human exemptionalism paradigm provided the cultural justification for increased consumption of natural resources and increased affluence over time. Conversely, increasing affluence over time has a strong reciprocal effect on culture. For example, McMichael explains that in the aftermath of colonialism

> newly independent nations responded by playing the catch-up game. . . . The pursuit of rising living standards inevitably promoted westernization in political, economic, and cultural terms, as the non-European world emulated the European enterprise. . . . Third World elites, once in power, had little choice but to industrialize. (1996, 42–43)

A different example of the effect of increased (energy) affluence on culture is provided by Beaudreau (1999). His book *Energy and the Rise and Fall of Political Economy* argues that the introduction of the use of fossil fuels in the late eighteenth century was a "shock" that led to the study of political economy by the moral philosophers, and all the myriad changes in Western society ever since.

Culture and Technology
The dominant social paradigm (DSP) and the human exemptionalist paradigm (HEP) have provided important cultural inspiration for innovation and scientific discovery during the high energy ecological phase. For example, the DSP generates the belief that risks are acceptable in order to maximize the production of wealth (Milbrath 1989, 119). This in turn affects notions of risk among scientists producing new technologies. The HEP belief that progress can carry on indefinitely is certainly a hallmark of modern science, though arguably a strong countertrend is taking shape.

Conversely, scientific innovation is a key component of cultural development and change. As explained by Goudie,

> through the controlled breeding of animals and plants humans were able, by hard work, to develop a more reliable and readily expandable source of food and thereby create a solid and secure basis for cultural advance, an advance which included civilization and the "urban revolution." (1994, 16)

In contemporary society, the material fruits of "progress" tend to reinforce belief in, and allegiance to, the DSP and the HEP. Economies of scale through assembly line production have over time driven down the costs of goods that at one time were considered luxury items and made them available to the masses. (Among many examples are the automobile and the television.) Affordability of status goods and correspondingly increased consumerism tend to encourage the belief that nature should serve to produce goods (a component of the DSP) and that cultural adaptation is without limit (a component of the HEP) (Milbrath 1989, 119; Catton and Dunlap 1978, 42–43).

Variable Pairings	Nature of Synergy
Social ⬇ Environmental	The dynamics of the capital accumulation process—*not poverty and wealth in and of themselves*—drive environmental outcomes.
Environmental ⬇ Social	Environmental destruction generates social outcomes that are patterned but indeterminate. Environmental destruction can •lead to or reinforce poverty •lead to alleviation of poverty •lead to or reinforce accumulation of wealth •lead to loss of wealth

Figure 2.3.   Matrix of Synergies among Social and Environmental Outcomes

Synergies among Social and Environmental Outcomes

This section examines some key synergies between contemporary social and environmental outcomes of human evolution, looking first at the social to environmental causal pathway, and second at the environmental to social causal pathway.

It has long been understood that there is a reciprocal relationship between human evolution and environmental outcomes, but the nature of this relationship has been poorly understood and inadequately theorized. In the late 1980s the "environment and poverty" school of thought emerged, claiming that poverty drives the process of environmental destruction, and that environmental destruction in turn reinforces the "downward spiral" of poverty. An influential document promoting this view was the so-called Bruntland Report of the World Commission on Environment and Development,[19] which claimed that

> poverty is a major cause and effect of global environmental problems. It is therefore futile to attempt to deal with environmental problems without a broader perspective that encompasses the factors underlying world poverty and international inequality. (WCED 1987, 3)

The Bruntland Report has been appropriately criticized for paying no heed to the contribution of affluence and overconsumption to environmental destruction and for proposing continued economic growth as the major remedy for coping with environmental destruction (see, e.g., Lélé 1991, 614).

A subsequent school of thought in the 1990s blames wealth, principally in the form of high resource consumption in rich countries, as the main cause of global environmental problems (see, e.g., Sachs 1993). This line of argumentation is often linked to the global warming issue and the fact that rich countries contribute the lion's share of carbon dioxide and other global greenhouse gases. Many of these claims tend to go to the opposite extreme of neglecting the contribution of poverty to environmental destruction.

A first step toward an appropriate understanding is to depolarize the "need versus greed" debate and recognize that both poverty and wealth, *at the level of physical agency*, play a key role in causing environmental destruction. The second step is to go beyond the tendency to assume that poverty and wealth are somehow independent of each other. As we have seen in this chapter, *at the level of economic structure*, poverty and wealth are an inherent and joint outcome of the economic accumulation process, dating back to the establishment of agriculture and the introduction of slavery. At this level of analysis, it makes no sense to separate poverty and wealth, as if one existed independently from the other. This pivotal point is summed up well by Gallopin et al.:

> Poverty is central to the problem of environmental degradation, but so too is wealth: Two major sources of environmental degradation can thus be distinguished: those associated with prevailing patterns of economic growth in the affluent societies (and the affluent sectors within the poor countries), and those associated with poverty. Those two types of situations . . . may differ in many ways, but are not unconnected. At a higher level of analysis, affluence and poverty are complementary sides of the prevailing pattern of economic growth at the world level, uneven growth characterized by increasing inequality and growing symmetry between rich and poor countries, and between the rich and poor sectors within many countries. (1989, 377)

There remains a strong tendency in environmental analysis to view poverty and wealth as independent and ultimate causes. Little thought is given to the fact that poverty and wealth are the product of deeply rooted and complex social phenomena. It remains poorly understood that the dynamics of the economic accumulation process—*not poverty and wealth in and of themselves*—drive environmental outcomes.

There is also much distortion in analyses of the effects of the environment on social variables. In spite of efforts at demythologizing the "poverty-environment" connection, it still holds much sway. There is a tendency to give disproportionate attention to how environmental degradation and resource depletion in developing countries reinforce poverty, but little attention to other outcomes. This formulation retains a strong grip on the scientific imagination in part because it has been the favored view of powerful international institutions such as the World Bank.

This is not to say that the "downward spiral of environment and poverty" formulation is wrong. There is much empirical evidence to suggest that, at the local level in poor countries, environmental degradation and resource depletion can either lead to poverty or reinforce preexisting poverty, thereby exacerbating environmental problems. The problem is that the formulation tells only part of the story. It is also possible for environmental destruction to lead to an alleviation of poverty or at least an amelioration of household well-being. For example, often small farmers who colonize new areas of tropical forest are leaving an unsatisfactory situation behind and are moving to an area where they believe income possibilities are better. In many cases their gamble proves to be correct and they end up being better off.

Other formulations that tend to receive comparatively little attention in environmental analysis concern the causal pathway from environmental exploitation to wealth outcomes (see figure 2.3). It is a fact of history that exploitation of natural resources is the path to prosperity for *all* people living well above the level of subsistence. This is just as true for the owner of a mining company as it is for an opera singer. In the latter case, it is not just a beautiful voice that permits the accumulation of riches but also the prosperity of the singer's clientele and their modes of accumulation, the existence of opera houses in cities (centers of high consumption of fossil fuels), international transport via airplane, and so on.

And at the theoretical level, just as for the poor, overexploitation of the environment by the rich can lead to a loss of prosperity. Such cases are few and far between, and the fact that such cases are scarce embodies a profound lesson. Why is it, for example, that owners of timber concessions the world over are able to extract tropical hardwoods at an unsustainable rate and maintain their wealth? The reason is that timber concession owners (like owners of mines, deep sea fisheries, and other exhaustible resources) convert their profits from tropical hardwoods into seed capital for enterprises outside the forest sector. Once tropical hardwoods are exhausted, they can maintain their prosperity in the agricultural plantation sector, the automotive industry, telecommunications, or whatever enterprise it might be. The lesson to be drawn is that the risks and consequences of environmental destruction fall quite differently on the poor and the rich. Far more frequently for the poor than for the rich, the implication of unwise resource management is a decline in economic well-being.

Overuse and degradation of natural resources can lead to the four outcomes with respect to well-being that are described above. It is important that environmental analysis break free of the assumption that the environment-poverty pathway is the most relevant one. The other three possibilities are clearly relevant but tend to be less researched than the environment-poverty pathway. Although all four outcomes are patterned in the sense of being typologies with a basis in empirical reality, there remains much to be known about their internal dynamics, their relative "weight" in contributing to environmental problems, and how the problems they generate can be addressed.

Addressing the Deficiencies of $I = P \times A \times T$

It has become commonplace to analyze the impact of humans on their environment in terms of the so-called Commoner-Ehrlich equation (Commoner 1971, 175–77; Commoner 1972; Ehrlich and Holdren 1971; Ehrlich et al. 1977, 720–24). The equation reads

$$I = P \times A \times T$$

where "I" is the environmental impact; "P" is population; "A" is affluence or the impact per head of population; and "T" is the effect of technology. The equation holds considerable appeal because of its elegant simplicity and persuasive focus on three variables that carry such obvious importance in relation to the environment. It has become a standard formula for analyzing the causes of environmental problems (e.g., Meadows et al. 1992, 100; Hempel 1996, 59; Harper 1996, 247–54; Goodland and Daly 1998, 131; Ekins 2000, 154–62).

Yet for all its elegance and persuasiveness, the formula embodies a serious distortion, implying that population, affluence, and technology are the most important independent variables to consider in relation to environmental change. No account is taken of the social context, which governs population growth, increasing affluence, and technological development. Silence on this matter creates the impression that these three variables act sui generis, which they clearly do not.

Figure 2.4 exhibits the logic of the Commoner-Ehrlich equation and compares it to the theoretical model presented in this chapter. This model can be

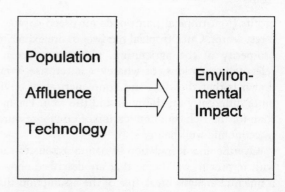

Commoner-Ehrlich model

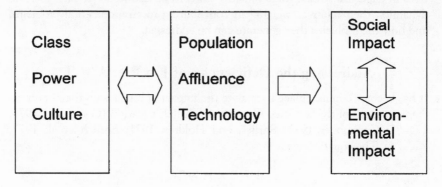

Proposed model

Figure 2.4. Commoner-Ehrlich and Proposed Models of the Social Origins of Environmental Impact

viewed as an elaboration and correction of the Commoner-Ehrlich equation. In this chapter I have demonstrated that class, power, and culture are key causal variables that influence, and are in turn influenced by, changes in population, affluence, and technology. Another key elaboration on the Commoner-Ehrlich equation is that social and environmental outcomes are considered linked and interactive. As we have seen, these links are so important that we run the risk of seriously misunderstanding the nature of environmental outcomes unless we view them jointly with the social outcomes of human evolution.

Conclusion

The social theory variables class, power, and culture are an essential foundation for understanding the effect of growing population, affluence, and technological sophistication on the environment in the course of human evolution. Increases in human population, affluence, and technological efficiency can be traced back to powerful episodic changes in the primeval, early farming, early urban, and high energy ecological phases. In the succession of phases the transformation of class relations enabled ever greater accumulation of economic surplus; increasing social complexity undergirded the emergence of the state and ever larger organizations and enterprises; and cultural change involved the ascendancy of a hegemonic ideological view justifying the exploitation of humans and nature and ever higher levels of material consumption, though with powerful modern countertendencies.

Analysis of the interactions among all six independent variables (class, power, culture, population, affluence, technology) shows the presence of synergies that reinforce the overall tendency toward growing accumulation and exploitation of natural resources over time. There are, however, potent negative synergies (e.g., the demographic transition) that demonstrate potential for slowing the rate of growth of accumulation and environmental impact in the long term.

Summary information on the key elements of contemporary social and environmental outcomes of human evolution shows that there is some good news but also considerable cause for concern. Examination of the interactions among social and environmental outcomes yields two important lessons.

First, dating from 10,000 B.C., the interaction of dominant and subordinate classes has been a key characteristic of human evolution helping to explain the nature of social and environmental outcomes. As such, it makes no sense to treat "poverty" and "wealth" as if they had an autonomous existence, detached from the dynamics of class stratification and oppression and from the process of economic accumulation.

Second, it is widely and correctly understood that environmental destruction can undermine the well-being of the poor, particularly in poor countries, and this in turn can exacerbate environmental problems in a "downward spiral." However, three other causal pathways in the linkage between environmental condition and social status have been underresearched: the possibility that environmental destruction can lead to an escape from poverty, lead to or reinforce the accumulation of wealth, and lead to a loss of wealth.

Above all, in this chapter I have tried to demonstrate and underscore the fact that all three traditions in social theory—the class, power, and cultural perspectives—are necessary for understanding contemporary environmental problems. Not only are all three perspectives indispensable in and of themselves, but also as joint, mutually dependent, and complementary perspectives. It is against this backdrop that we now turn our attention to an analysis of prominent contemporary views on the causes of, nature of, and solutions to environmental problems.

Notes

1. According to Meltzer (1993a, 204), feudalism first became evident in the Roman Empire in the fourth century A.D.

2. Though feudalism has been prominently associated with western Europe in the literature, it was also evident in early Japan and Russia (e.g., Critchley 1978, 182; Young and Arrigo 1999, 123).

3. Max Weber suggests a degree of complexity that might not take into account some early states. He defined the modern state as "composed of numerous agencies led and coordinated by the state's leadership (executive authority) that has the ability or authority to make and implement the binding rules for all the people as well as the parameters of rule making for other social organizations in a given territory, using force if necessary to have its way" (Migdal 1988, 19).

4. See, for example, Jessop 1990, 85–104.

5. Voluntary simplicity and the roots of environmentalist thought date back long before the nineteenth century but gained momentum with the onset of the industrial revolution.

6. Note that the correspondence is not precise. Weeks's (1996, 30) period is 8000 B.C. to A.D. 1, whereas the early farming period is 10,000 B.C. to 3500 B.C.

7. In 1800, a mere 2 percent of the population lived in urban areas (Simmons 1996, 1).

8. Note that the correspondence is not precise. Weeks's (1996, 30) period is A.D. 1 to 1750, whereas the early urban period is 3500 B.C. to A.D. 1750.

9. It appears that Simmons (1996) did not include plant domestication in his model because plants do not easily fit the conventional definition of a technology. Arguably, however, plant domestication is one of the most powerful energy conversion technologies ever developed.

10. Shelter and clothing also permitted colonization of places that would otherwise have been inaccessible (Goudie 1994, 14).

11. Landes (1969, 1) says three types of innovations characterize the industrial revolution: (1) substitution of machines for human effort and skill; (2) substitution of inanimate power, especially steam, for human and animal power; and (3) the use of new types of raw materials in manufacturing.

12. Average children born per woman in a reproductive lifetime at the current birth rates (Cohen 1995, 138).

13. "Replacement-level fertility means that the population will eventually neither grow nor decrease, given an assumed unchanging age pattern of death rates" (Cohen 1995, 140).

14. 1 Pg = 10^{15} grams (Simmons 1996, 364).

15. "Relocalization" is a synonymous term introduced by Mander and Goldsmith (1996, 17-19, 391–92).

16. Since the middle class has been the backbone of the environmental movement in the United States and Europe, the environmental movement is not necessarily "sub-

ordinated" or "alienated" in an economic sense. Arguably, however, the modern environmental movement is subordinated and alienated with respect to the dominant environmental paradigm (i.e., the so-called human exemptionalism paradigm). Moreover, a growing fraction of the modern environmental movement in and outside the rich countries includes poor people.

17. Some demographers dispute the causal link between modernization and fertility decline. This issue will be examined in chapter 4.

18. The aim in Fordism to increase overall wages was just one component of the Fordist philosophy. Broadly speaking, Fordism is defined as a system of production characterized by "very large-scale production units using assembly line manufacturing techniques and producing large volumes of standardized products for mass market consumption" (Dickens 1998, 165).

19. Other than WCED 1987, additional examples of "poverty and environment" writings include Durning 1989; Leonard et al. 1989; Mellor 1988; and Perrings 1989.

CHAPTER THREE

~

Ideology and the Environment: From Paradigm Isolation to Paradigm Integration

In this chapter I explain the basic elements of three contemporary ideological perspectives on the environment corresponding to the class, managerial, and individualist social theory paradigms, and I analyze tendencies among their major proponents toward paradigm isolation and integration.[1] Recall that paradigm isolation refers to the tendency to elevate the status of the "home paradigm" by criticizing a competing paradigm or paradigms (explicit and rejectionist isolation), by portraying the tenets of competitors as being extensions of and dependent on the home paradigm (explicit and contingent isolation), or by ignoring the existence of a competing paradigm (implicit isolation). Paradigm integration refers to the act of recognizing competing tenets (if not competing paradigms) as being of equal standing to those of the home paradigm and as being necessary to fully understand the causes of environmental problems and/or address them.

In this chapter I argue, first, that paradigm integration is a necessary step forward in addressing environmental problems intelligently and holistically; class, power, and culture are important dimensions of *all* environmental problems. Second, recognizing that full integration of ideologies is not possible or even desirable, the aim of paradigm integration should be the selective synthesis of the key insights of the three paradigms.

The chapter is composed of three sections and a summary. The first section describes the key elements of the class, managerial, and individualist paradigms on the environment. The second discusses examples of rejectionist, contingent, and implicit paradigm isolation. The third explains why paradigm integration is necessary, shows evidence of limited integration to date, and discusses challenges to further integration.

76

Ideological Perspectives on the Environment

Like the overarching political ideologies of which they are a part, the environmental ideologies described in this chapter are mental models that organize beliefs about what is good or bad, right or wrong. The ideologies described here are representations about the relationship between humans and the natural world—what it is, in what ways it is defective, and how it should be improved.

In a certain sense, it is misleading to view environmental ideologies as mere subsets of an overarching ideology. In recent decades issues concerning the environment have rightly acquired such high importance that "the environment" has become an integral, if not central component of modern political ideologies and related theoretical developments.[2]

This section identifies key theoretical components of the leading environmental ideologies and classifies and analyzes them as environmental paradigms. The class, managerial, and individualist "umbrellas" embrace some highly disparate tendencies (e.g., deep ecology and free market environmentalism in the individualist paradigm). While important ideological polemics occur within (not just between and among) paradigms, our concern in this chapter is to focus on the forms of antagonism and potential compatibility between and among the main environmental paradigms. Their defining characteristics are summarized in table 3.1.

Class

Proponents of the class paradigm on the environment locate the origin of environmental problems in the process of economic accumulation and antagonistic class relations. These class tensions are seen to exist within countries and also among countries. Proponents see countries of the North as prospering economically at the expense of the South, and they see this exploitation as the main factor underpinning global environmental problems. They see industrial pollution and climate change, often perceived as the main environmental problems, as the product of economic exploitation and overconsumptive lifestyles in the North. They see the South's environmental problems (tropical deforestation, land degradation, etc.) as resulting from poverty, which in turn is perceived as largely attributable to economic exploitation by the North. Statements that succinctly summarize the essence of the class paradigm on the environment appear in box 3.1.

A pervasive assumption in the class paradigm on the environment is that the process of economic accumulation is so deeply rooted and powerful that it now defies all organized attempts to minimize its adverse social and environmental effects. Thus, according to Schnaiberg's (Schnaiberg 1980; Schnaiberg and Gould 1994) "treadmill of production," the drive to accumulate wealth involves continuous increase in the use of natural resources and involves drawing ever more workers out of self-employment and into an economy that depends on expanded production. At the same time, technological development in the production process aims to replace labor with physical capital in order to increase profits and withstand competition from other producers. Governments assist both expanded accumulation and expanded consumption (through their commitment to "social security"), which leads to continuously increased consumption of natural resources and pollution. The resulting ecological disorganization reinforces socioeconomic disorganization (Schnaiberg and Gould 1994, 69).

Table 3.1. Three Key Social Theory Paradigms on the Environment

Defining characteristics	Three Key Paradigms		
	Class	Managerial	Individualist
Level of analysis	Societal	Organizational	Individual
Key dimension of society	Economic (class)	Political (power)	Behavioral (culture)
View of problem	Accumulation, class exploitation, and over-consumption (mainly in North) lead to inequality, injustice, and environmental degradation	Policy inadequacy is the main problem, with states and other organizations ultimately responsible for environmental stability	*Cultural.* Lack of knowledge and wayward culture *Free market.* Constraints on economic initiative
Proposed solutions	Activism and mass mobilization against exploitation, inequality, and injustice; restructuring of north-south relations	Diplomacy, regime-building, policy adjustment, regulation and management, economic manipulations, technological applications	*Cultural.* Education and cultural transformation *Free market.* Removal of economic constraints
Key agents of change	Countries of the south, grassroots organizations, NGOs	Government representatives (diplomats, negotiators, planners, legislators) and experts (scientists and researchers)	*Cultural.* Knowing and enlightened individuals *Free market.* Freed and enlightened enterprises
View of "sustainable development"	Tendency toward opposition	Support (managerialism is the home base of sustainable development)	Tendency toward opposition

> **Box 3.1. Some Representative Quotes by Exemplars of the Class Paradigm**
>
> This failure to prevent the increased destruction of the biosphere can be traced mainly to the logic of profit-oriented economic expansion in a finite world (Foster 1999a, 129).
>
> I am convinced that capitalism has a compulsive orientation towards growth inherent in its logic. There is in its logic no place for justice, equality, fraternity, solidarity, compassion, morality, or ethics (Sarkar 1999, 4).
>
> The political economy of the current situation is that historical capitalism is in fact in crisis precisely because it cannot find reasonable solutions to its current dilemmas, of which the inability to contain ecological destruction is a major one, if not the only one (Wallerstein 1999, 8).
>
> [Capitalism's aim] is limitless growth, or money in search of more of itself. . . . On the other hand, nature is not self-expanding (O'Connor 1998, 10).
>
> The ecosystem as we know it cannot be saved while the poor people of the South are left to make their way along the paths of a haphazard and unjust development (Athanasiou 1998, 54).
>
> Seen against the backdrop of a divided world, the excessive use of nature and its resources in the North is a principal roadblock to greater justice in the world (Sachs et al. 1998, x).
>
> Failure to challenge the treadmill of production will most assuredly produce ever-increasing ecological destruction and social inequality (Schnaiberg and Gould 1994, vii).
>
> Social justice, I think, or the increasingly global lack of it, is the most pressing of all environmental problems (Pepper 1993, xii).
>
> The "global" has been so structured, that the North . . . has all rights and no responsibility, and the South has no rights, but all responsibility (Shiva 1993, 154).
>
> The devastation of ways of life, environments, cultures, traditions and sustainable ways of answering human needs has been in the interests of conserving only one thing—the maintenance of wealth and power (Seabrook 1993, 247).
>
> Man's inhumanity to nature can be seen as a direct outcome of man's inhumanity to man (Agarwal 1990, 94).

The proposed solutions to combined socioeconomic problems (e.g., poverty and unemployment) and environmental problems are to confront class exploitation, inequality, and injustice through activism and mass mobilization against those who cause and perpetuate exploitation. Conflict is viewed as inescapable. Schnaiberg and Gould (1994, vii) say that the treadmill of production

> may be changed through the purposive mobilization of the disempowered, who must be prepared to engage in political conflicts and confrontations with established social, economic, and political hierarchies. . . . Failure to challenge the treadmill of production will most assuredly produce ever-increasing ecological destruction and social inequality

How do these 2 patterns things contribute to env prbl?

The key agents of change for betterment of the environment are grassroots and nongovernmental organizations (NGOs) and, according to many proponents, people in countries of the South opposing further exploitation.

Many (but by no means all) proponents of the class paradigm object to "sustainable development," the most common formulation of policy efforts to confront social and environmental problems. Proponents who object to sustainable development say the concept is not (as claimed) an effort to address the shortcomings of the development project in countries of the South, but rather a thinly disguised attempt by countries of the North to extend their control over the earth's natural resources and thus maintain global hegemony, economic growth, and overconsumptive lifestyles. Adams says sustainable development is "essentially reformist, calling for modification of development practice and owes little to radical ideas" (1990, 10). Hildyard charges that it is a "new wave of colonialism" (1993, 33), and Olpadwalla and Goldsmith (1992) and Seabrook (1993, 249) that it is an oppressive system of privileges. Athanasiou calls sustainable development "a suspect but redeemable project" (1998, 294), and Sachs calls it an "oxymoron" (1999, 71).

There are four main subclassifications of the class paradigm on the environment: (1) eco-Marxism (e.g., Déléage 1994; Benton 1996; O'Connor 1998; Burkett 1999; Wallerstein 1999; Foster 2000; Hughes 2000), (2) eco-socialism (e.g., Pepper 1993; Sarkar 1999), (3) social ecology (Bookchin 1996, 1999; Light 1998), and (4) political ecology (e.g., Blaikie and Brookfield 1987; Bryant and Bailey 1997; Low and Gleeson 1998).

Proponents of eco-Marxism are those most closely identified with the tradition of Marxist class analysis and dialectical materialism. Some eco-Marxists seek latent ecological insights in the writings of Marx and Engels (e.g., Burkett 1999; Foster 1999b; Foster 2000; Hughes 2000). O'Connor (1996; 1998) updates Marxist theory with his "second contradiction of capitalism." He asserts that not just exploitation of labor but also exploitation of the earth's resources will ultimately lead to a collapse of capitalism and transition to socialism.

The recent wave of eco-Marxist theory is motivated by three related setbacks experienced by Marxism in the early 1990s: (1) the collapse of communism, (2) the fact that "existing socialism" is commonly assumed to be guilty of extreme environmental mismanagement, and (3) the defection of many on the left to non-Marxist ideologies in the aftermath of these two developments. Wallerstein (1999) and Goldfrank et al. (1999) aim to update world systems theory (a distinct branch of modern Marxism) in Ecology and the World-System. Although not eco-Marxist in name, their efforts are similar to those of the eco-Marxist project.

Eco-socialist theories are similar to those of eco-Marxism but less closely tied to class analysis and dialectical materialism and more eclectic. Stretton (1976, 2, 200) faults Marxists for identifying private ownership itself—rather than its wrong distribution—as the root of evil, and he proposes a democratic socialist alternative. Grundmann (1991, 284) believes Marx's theories have theoretical power if stripped of orthodox interpretations but have their limitations. Pepper's (1993) eco-socialism draws on Marxism but also some elements of anarchism and deep ecology. Sarkar (1999, 199) sets himself apart from eco-Marxism in remarking that the chief contradiction is not between capitalism and ecology but rather between industrial society and ecology.

Social ecology (or "eco-anarchism," as it is sometimes called) views domination and hierarchy as the key negative forces in society. Thus the problem is not limited to capitalism (as in eco-Marxism), but extends to domination of people by the state, women by men, people of color by Caucasians, and so on. Social ecology strongly opposes Marxist class analysis and dialectical materialism and proposes instead "dialectical naturalism" (Bookchin 1996). Consistent with its anarchist roots, social ecology is antistate and favors radical decentralization and community-based democracy—a project that Murray Bookchin calls "libertarian municipalism" (Biehl and Bookchin 1998). Social ecology is largely identified with the writings of Bookchin, the "father" of this school of thought. There are, however, strong emerging countercurrents under the umbrella of "social ecology" (see especially Light 1998). Unlike eco-Marxism and eco-socialism, social ecology is not faced with massive theoretical revision occasioned by the fall of communism. It has always rejected communism, and ecology has been at the center of its theoretical corpus since it came into being in the 1960s.

Political ecology is a research field largely based in the premises of the class paradigm. Its two main foci are (1) analysis of the interaction of the changing environment and socioeconomy and (2) examination of the changing states of nature over time and "their contested representations under conditions of unequal power" (Blaikie 1999, 132–33). Political ecologists tend to assert that (1) environmental problems are associated with the worldwide spread of capitalism and are not simply a reflection of policy or market failures, and thus (2) there is a need for far-reaching change in political-economic processes at the local, regional, and global levels that will entail conflict and struggle (Bryant and Bailey 1997, 3). There are, however, self-identified political ecologists who dissociate themselves from the left.[3]

Beyond these broad generalities, there are no attributes of political ecology that give it greater theoretical coherence. Among the four schools of thought in the environmental class paradigm, it is the least cohesive and well-defined.[4] Blaikie calls political ecology a "capacious bandwagon" (1999, 131–32) and a wheel that is subject to continual reinvention. Indeed the school of thought has undergone three major phases. From the late 1970s to the mid-1980s, it was largely oriented to neo-Marxism and structuralism, as seen for example in Watts (1983) and Blaikie (1985) (Bryant and Bailey 1997, 14). From the late 1980s to the 1990s, political ecologists have rejected structuralist neo-Marxism in favor of a neo-Weberian, agency-oriented approach while still grounded in the left, as seen for example in Blaikie and Brookfield (1987) and Neumann and Schroeder (1995) (Bryant and Bailey 1997, 14). Beginning in the mid-1990s, political ecologists turned their attention to poststructuralism (Bryant and Bailey 1997, 1, 14; Blaikie 1999, 137, 141–44). This approach is evident in the work of Escobar (1996), Peet and Watts (1996a), and Stott and Sullivan (2000).

Eco-Marxists, eco-socialists, and social ecologists are often anthropocentric, placing their concern for the human species above that of other life forms. Among the most vocal proponents are Pepper (1993, xi), Sarkar (1999, 14), and Bookchin (1996, 71; 1999, 14–42). This position is often framed as a rejection of "biocentrism" or "ecocentrism" (i.e., the view that nonhuman life forms should have equal standing with humans), a philosophy advocated most forcefully by deep ecologists in the individualist paradigm. Political ecologists, by contrast, tend to be ecocentrists (Bryant and Bailey 1997, 15–20).

Managerial

Proponents of the managerial paradigm on the environment believe that inadequacy of government policy and of organizational structures governing the economy, technology, and society are the root cause of environmental problems. They hold states and other large, formal organizations ultimately responsible for environmental stability. Their proposed solutions for environmental problems include international diplomacy and regime building (e.g., the Montreal Protocol for the protection of the ozone layer);[5] adjustment of policies and laws at the international, national, or local level; improved regulation and management structures; manipulation of economic parameters (e.g., exchange rates, prices, subsidies); and improved application of technology.[6] The key agents of change are people in formal leadership roles such as government representatives (e.g., diplomats, negotiators, planners, and legislators) and experts (e.g., scientists and researchers). For quotes summarizing this paradigm, see box 3.2.

Despite the fact that sustainable development is a concept with no cohesive theoretical core (Adams 1990, 3), writers in the managerial tradition frequently invoke the need for sustainable development. This should come as no surprise because most definitions and book-length formulations of sustainable development embrace the key tenets of managerialism: improved government policy and management systems, change of economic incentives, improved dissemination and use of technology (see, e.g., WCED 1987; Pearce et al. 1990; Holmberg 1992; National Commission on the Environment 1993). Sustainable development is in most instances advanced as a centrist, reformist program; thus in the context of theory, the managerial paradigm is the "home base" for the concept (Sunderlin 1995b).

Who are the proponents of the managerial perspective on the environment? They cover a wide range, including those who fully embrace "the system" and also those who strongly object to it but would not be prepared to abandon it altogether. Their common ground is tolerance for capitalism, whether as supporters or as critics who choose to operate within its constraints. There are three types of proponents: (1) representatives of intergovernmental (e.g., World Bank,

Box 3.2.   Some Representative Quotes by Exemplars of the Managerial Paradigm

Adopting á central organizing principle . . . means embarking on an all-out effort to use every policy and program, every law and institution, every treaty and alliance, every tactic and strategy, every plan and course of action—to use, in short, every means to halt the destruction of the environment and to preserve and nurture our ecological system (Gore 2000, 274).

In stabilizing climate and stabilizing population, there is no substitute for leadership (Brown 2000, 20).

The time is now ripe to build the international governance structures needed to ensure that the world economy of the twenty-first century meets peoples' aspirations for a better future without destroying the natural fabric that underpins life itself (French 2000, 185).

In other words, the very constitution of the administrative apparatus in advanced industrial society emerges as an environmental problem, perhaps even the most serious of environmental problems (Torgerson 1999, 82).

All economic decisions affect the environment, and so the way to improve the environment is to change the way in which those economic decisions are made (Pearce 1998, 3).

In short, environmental reform of fiscal policy would create a world most people recognize as the one they hope their grandchildren will inherit (Roodman 1998, 27).

Strong states, in fact, may be indispensable, at least initially, for achieving a politically acceptable form of global environmental governance (Hempel 1996, xiii).

Having sustainable policies is itself a key to the long-term vision that environmental sustainability requires (May 1996, 7).

Critical threats to the Earth's habitability demand that humankind rise to the challenge of creating new and more effective systems of international environmental governance (Young 1996, 1–2).

A sustainable world would require that nations cooperate in regulating the rates of utilization of both natural resources and the natural sinks that absorb effluents (Ehrlich et al. 1995, 278).

Suppositions about responses to global environmental problems are usually framed in terms of the nation-states system; that system is seen as both the locus of causes and consequences and as the level at which appropriate policy responses must take place (Lipschutz and Conca 1993, 328).

The causes of environmental degradation frequently lie in the workings, especially the mismanagement, of the economy (Pearce and Warford 1993, 5).

The industrialized Northern countries are the main contributors to global environmental problems. . . . The main reason, of course, is the limited time horizons of the governments involved, rendering it difficult for them to take the broader view (Holmberg and Sandbrook 1992, 31).

Solutions lie in mainstream political and economic policies (Mathews 1991, 30).

If we are to avert an ecological catastrophe, we must develop a kind of global economic Keynesianism, with a significant social direction of capital flows, demand management, and technological choices (Harris 1991, 111).

> Overcoming the obstacles to sustainable development will require political vision and courage in policy and institutional change on a scale not seen in this century since the aftermath of World War II (MacNeill et al. 1991, 20).
>
> If progress in environmental policy is ever to be achieved on the international level, then the waves of political pressure and legitimation must spring from the core of national states (Mayer-Tasch 1986. 242).

World Commission on Environment and Development) and governmental (e.g., USAID, European Union) institutions, (2) representatives of nongovernmental organizations (e.g., the Worldwatch Institute, the World Resources Institute, the International Institute for Environment and Development), and (3) academic experts on topics such as international diplomacy, regime building, and "environmental governance" (e.g., Haas et al. 1993; Hempel 1996; Young et al. 1996; Young 1997) and improved management of institutions and the economy (e.g., Ostrom et al. 1993; Pearce 1998).

As we saw in chapter 1, the term "managerialism" is a label used by Alford and Friedland (1985) to designate a theoretical perspective that is closely associated with the Weberian tradition and a focus on the organizational dimension of human activities. There exists a literature functionally equivalent to theory on managerialism and the environment, but there is no such literature specifically under the rubric of "managerialism." Enteman (1993) seeks to establish the foundations of an ideology of managerialism but does not give significant attention to the issue of the environment.

Among the closest approximations of a managerial perspective on the environment are the neo-Weberian theorizings of Dryzek (1987) and Murphy (1994). Dryzek (1987) analyzes the capacities of the market, "administered systems," legal systems, and practical reasons to respond adequately to modern environmental problems. All have their strengths and weaknesses and, collectively, they are found wanting. Dryzek opts for radical decentralization, together with other forms of human organization, to furthering the goal of "ecological rationality." Murphy (1994), elaborating on Weber's concern with rationalization, asks why, if humans' distinctive quality is increasing rationalization, there is a trend toward environmental destruction. He concludes that "Weber's work helps us keep in mind that objective situations do not necessarily bring about consciousness and organized, effective action. There is no predestined symbiotic relationship lying on the horizon, just struggle to attain it" (Murphy 1994, 254).

Writings in the emerging field of ecological modernization theory (EMT) are mainstays of the managerial environmental paradigm (see, e.g., Spaargaren and Mol 1992; Mol and Sonnenfeld 2000a; Spaargaren et al. 2000; Young 2000a). As Buttel explains, "Ecological modernization is basically the extension of the practices of modern rationalism to the business enterprise and state organization in ways that lead to adaptations and restructurings that reduce resource consumption and environmental degradation" (1996, 73). In chapter 5, I will examine the issue of whether EMT in fact transcends its boundaries and embraces the class and individualist paradigms as well.

There are two books on liberalism and the environment (Wissenburg 1998; Cahn 1995), and this is important given the close theoretical link between managerialism and liberalism (see chapter 1). However, both these books apply the traditional definition of liberalism (i.e., favoring of individual rights and economic freedom) and are thus far from managerialism and liberalism (i.e., political centrism) as defined in this book. The closest thing to a theoretical construct of managerialism and the environment is the recent wave of books on environmental diplomacy and environmental governance, but none are cast in terms of social science theory.

On the whole, there has been little theorizing on managerialism (or political centrism or liberalism in the centrist sense) and the environment from a social science perspective. Why this is so is not clear, but the following might be a working hypothesis. Most proponents of the managerial perspective on the environment are involved in the structures of power (either formally or as critical outsiders) and thus are involved in "doing" rather than in theoretical social science reflection on environmental problems and solutions. Stated differently, there is no perceived need for social science reflection (as there is at the critical extremes of the class and individualist perspectives) because there is no perceived need to overhaul "the system." Reform will suffice. Moreover, many proponents of environmental managerialism, by the nature of who they are (politicians, legislators, technicians, etc.) have little contact with the world of social science, thus reinforcing a separation between practice and social science theory.

Although proponents of the managerial paradigm on the environment share the common ground of political centrism, there are sharp and divisive polemics within the paradigm. For example, the most visible and antagonistic theoretical battles for and against economic growth take place within the bounds of the managerial paradigm. (This issue will be examined in chapter 5.)

Individualist

Individual responsibility, decision making, and behavior are the themes of the individualist perspective on the environment. World environmental problems are viewed in terms of a collectivity of individual decision makers. Crucially, individuals are viewed as each having the same "weight" in the decision-making order and are not (meaningfully) stratified in terms of class and power as they are in the class and managerial paradigms. This assumption of the "universal we" is a hallmark of the individualist paradigm. However, there are two (often oppositional) divisions within the paradigm that are called here the "cultural" and

Are there overlaps o b per adisms?
—why arent they addressed, do they cause diff env problems?

"free market" traditions. See box 3.3 for statements by proponents summarizing the cultural, joint cultural-free market, and free market traditions in the individualist paradigm on the environment.

Cultural Tradition

Proponents of the cultural tradition in the individualist paradigm believe environmental problems result from a breakdown of values and norms that promote resource custodianship, and their replacement by those promoting indulgence and waste. Proposed solutions involve massive education of the public about the consequences of their wayward behavior, and through education, achieving wholesale cultural transformation that will ultimately reverse destructive patterns and safeguard the environment. The deep ecology movement is the vanguard of the cultural tradition. Among the principal writings of the movement are Devall and Sessions (1985), Devall (1988), Naess and Rothenberg (1989), and Sessions (1995). Advocates of deep ecology adamantly oppose modern, Western, technocratic culture and favor a return to traditional, even ancient values and norms. The two key norms of deep ecology involve (1) striving for self-realization through transcending the Western tradition of hedonistic ego gratification and (2) a commitment to biocentrism—the belief that "all things in the biosphere have an equal right to live and blossom and to reach their own individual forms of unfolding and self-realization" (Devall and Sessions 1985, 66–67). C. A. Bowers, a supporter of deep ecology, is the leading advocate of cultural transformation through changes in the formal educational system (Bowers 1993; Bowers 1997). The key agents of change in the cultural tradition are knowledgeable and enlightened leaders and individuals willing to accept their teachings.

Free Market Tradition

Free market proponents of environmental individualism believe that excessive government interference in the operation of the market and other forms of constraint on economic initiative (e.g., environmental laws and regulations, public and collective property rights, etc.) cause environmental problems. They believe accumulation is not the *cause* of economic deterioration (as advocated by class proponents) but is rather the *solution* to such problems. They believe environmental problems are far worse in poor countries than in rich countries, and offer this as proof that removal of constraints on economic growth and creation of wealth is the only solution to environmental problems. From this point of view, key agents of change are enlightened enterprises ("corporate environmentalists" and "eco-capitalists," discussed in chapter 6) and other unrestrained private enterprises.

Those in the free market tradition espouse a fundamentalist version of neoclassical economics. They believe government ownership and control of natural resources undermines sound management of natural resources. Well-specified

Box 3.3.   Some Representative Quotes by Exemplars of the Individualist Paradigm

Cultural

The more I search for the roots of the global environmental crisis, the more I am convinced that it is an outer manifestation of an inner crisis that is, for lack of a better word, spiritual (Gore 2000, 12).

Unless the culture of modernism is fundamentally altered, which in part means altering what students learn in public schools and universities, there will be an unending series of environmental problems (Bowers 1997, 18).

The real threats to a habitable and sustainable world in the next two centuries arise from the continuing social turmoil associated with the relatively inflexible cultural and ethnic differences among people (Starr 1997, 198).

In the twenty-first century culture will undoubtedly be one of the principal themes of sustainability, development, and governance (Arizpe 1997, 9).

In the long run, the best way the world's human and natural environments can improve is for this chapter's principles to become an integral part of the world's culture (Dunn and Kinney 1996, 243).

To the extent that human aggrandizement for the here and now comes at the expense of nonhuman nature and posterity, it is possible to view self-centered behavior—both individual and as a species—as the ultimate threat to our planet (Hempel 1996, 66).

The world environmental problem is serious, and getting steadily more so. Part of the reason is that humans have seen what they wanted to see and have deliberately blinded themselves to the less desirable consequences of their actions (Anderson 1996, 4).

[A]n "ecological unconscious" lies at the core of the psyche, there to be drawn upon as a resource for restoring us to environmental harmony (Roszak 1995, 14).

Beliefs, attitudes, and values related to material possessions and the relation of humanity and nature are often seen as lying at the root of environmental degradation (National Research Council 1992, 3).

[C]ulture has created a social system, especially in the West, that is characterized by activities, patterns of consumption, dominant assumptions, expectations and values which are not consistent with ecological sustainability and, therefore, with the survival of humankind (Boyden and Dovers 1992, 68).

Tracing them back to their root causes . . . these problems seem to be caused mainly by fundamental flaws in human nature: selfishness, greed, exploitation, power-seeking, dogmatism, intolerance and complacency (Burrows et al. 1991, 2).

It is the main point of this book that the ultimate source of all these problems is in thought itself (Bohm and Edwards 1991, x).

All these dangers (environmental crises) are caused by human intervention and it is only through changed attitudes and behaviour that they can be overcome (King and Schneider 1991, 115).

It should be fully appreciated that the significant tenets of the Deep Ecology movement are clearly and forcefully normative (Devall 1988, 23).

Cultural and Free Market

Green objectives are effectively advanced only by dispersed control, free markets, and traditional ethics, the conservative instruments for managing the problems of scarcity, dispersion, complexity, greed, growth, consumption, fecundity, and human voracity (Huber 1999, xxix).

The future of both humanity and nature rides with the new political alignment. America's conservative, free market, and libertarian forces can win only if they and the public are both informed and vigilant (Dunn and Kinney 1996, 155).

Free Market

Policy makers are facing the reality that a cleaner environment comes at an increasingly higher cost. By harnessing market forces as enviro-capitalists, we can achieve environmental ends at lower cost (Anderson & Leal 1997, 3)

People have ways to solve or minimize all major environmental problems. The single most critical factor is wealth. We must create wealth. Without wealth, neither the human nor the natural environment can improve (Dunn and Kinney 1996, 13).

---

private property rights and an unrestrained market, they argue, are essential for wise custodianship of the environment. The main proponents are Anderson and Leal (1991), founders of "free market environmentalism," and their followers (e.g., Yandle 1999). Pursuing a related project are Dunn and Kinney (1996) and Huber (1999), who have written diatribes against the left framed as conservative environmental manifestos.

The free market tradition in the individualist paradigm could not be more different from the cultural tradition. Whereas deep ecologists oppose Western values, hedonistic self-interest, and economic growth, and favor simple lifestyles and biocentrism, those in the free market tradition strongly favor Western values, unrestrained self-interest, economic growth, and high levels of material comfort and consumption; they are fervently anthropocentric. Huber, for example, notes: "We accept the traditional Judeo-Christian teaching, that man and nature are not equal. Our interests in nature are aesthetic, not moral. Our moral imperative is to put people first whenever direct choices have to be made" (1999, 204).

Despite the wide philosophical gulf often separating the cultural and free market traditions, what unites them shows their underlying theoretical unity: in both, as explained earlier, the individual is the key unit of analysis. Moreover, just as values are central to the cultural tradition, so too are they central to the free market tradition, but in a less evident way. Free market proponents believe it is through the aggregated expression of individual preferences (i.e., values) in the free market that resource shortages are avoided and environmental harmony is achieved.

Advocates of the free market tradition tend to oppose the concept of sustainable development, associating it with heavy-handed government interference in markets and with the whims of power-hungry bureaucrats. Anderson and Leal fault sustainable development's "scientific management" approach, saying it is impossible to concentrate knowledge about the environment, that it is naive to assume experts will do "what is 'right' rather than what is politically expedient" (1991, 170.) In contrast, they assert that free market environmentalism upholds the principles of ecology because it accepts that individuals are self-interested and it understands that "individuals must be relied upon for time- and space-specific information and to discover niches, just as other species in the ecosystems do" (Anderson and Leal 1991, 170). Dunn and Kinney dismiss sustainable development, saying, "the implemen-tation of the sustainability idea implies a massive bureaucracy that would be in-telligent, wise, efficient, and omnipotent—clearly, the ultimate oxymoron" (1996, 149).

The Problem of Paradigm Isolation

There is a deeply ingrained tendency among analysts of the environment to approach the issue from the perspective of just one paradigm, that is, to engage in paradigm isolation. The subsequent section on paradigm integration makes it clear that such isolation, though logical for any given paradigm, is partly unnecessary and even irrational when viewed from the joint vantage point of all three paradigms. Why is the tendency toward isolation so strong? Here are three possible explanations.

First, writers on environmental problems often represent interest groups engaged in ideological conflict. Proponents of the class paradigm often represent the economically oppressed. Proponents of the managerial paradigm are often either connected with government or in support of its overarching concerns. Some individualists, for example those in the free market tradition, side with the interests of business.

Second, analysts of environmental problems are influenced—whether knowingly or unknowingly—by the intellectual tradition within which they operate. The philosophical founders of each paradigm (Marx, Weber, Durkheim) had worldviews that are internally coherent yet in many ways mutually inconsistent. The legacy of this antagonism is experienced today. The notion of a "prime mover" in the class paradigm, for example, encourages the view that no amount of effort in policy reform or cultural change will effectively address environmental problems without prior attention to economic exploitation, inequality, and injustice. A parallel view in the managerial paradigm is that economic and cultural transformation can make no substantive progress toward environmental betterment in the absence of policy change. And last, in the individualist paradigm it is assumed that no amount of structural economic change or policy reform can meaningfully mitigate environmental problems without a prior cultural transformation and/or removal of constraints regarding the use of natural resources.

Third, environmental writers tend to undervalue the objectives of their ideological adversaries, not so much because they are viewed as unimportant but rather because to espouse these objectives would give the impression of having bought into the tenets of other paradigms. An example is the class tradition undervaluing cultural education on natural resource management, even in cases where it would be plainly useful, on the assumption that this is a conservative approach and therefore not to be taken seriously. There is a tendency within ideologies to favor a simple and easily communicable world-view over complex explanations and sophisticated plans of action. Oversimplification, unfortunately, is sometimes the price paid to gain and maintain adherents.

In this section and the subsequent one, I illustrate various forms of paradigm isolation and integration by quoting environmental writers. Two things should be understood in advance. First, isolation is not necessarily bad and the term "isolation" is not meant to be pejorative. All forms of isolation have their own logic readily understood from the vantage point of the "home" paradigm; some forms of isolation are reasonable and laudable whether viewed from the logic of the "home" paradigm or from without. Second, this exercise is in no way meant to typify particular writers as being either isolationists or integrationists. The choice of quotations is not targeted at particular writers but largely results from happenstance; most quotes are chosen because they capture in a pithy way the particular type of isolation or integration that I seek to illustrate. Moreover, the discerning reader will notice that some writers appear in both the "isolation" and "integration" sections. Most writers show tendencies in both directions.

Explicit and Rejectionist
Statements indicating explicit and rejectionist isolation often take the form of a denunciation. Statements in this mode say "the tenets and objectives of the home paradigm are the only valid ones, and those proposed by the other paradigms are only mildly helpful or irrelevant at best, dangerous at worst." The first two statements in table 3.2 (Foster 1999a, 12; Schnaiberg and Gould 1994, v) illustrate explicit rejection aimed at both opposing paradigms, dismissing as they do both managerialism and individualism. Though the quotations displayed in table 3.2 largely speak for themselves, it is helpful to put them in an interpretive context.

Class Rejection of Managerialism
The statements by Wallerstein (1999, 8), Sachs (1999, 55), Athanasiou (1998, 52) and Hildyard (1993, 33) exhibit an entrenched view among many on the left that change initiated from within or through the capitalist state cannot be either socially or environmentally productive. Many in the left maintain an instrumental view of the state, a belief that capitalist accumulation so pervades and

Table 3.2.   Examples of Explicit, Rejectionist Paradigm Isolation

Home paradigm: rejected paradigm	*Examples*
Class: managerial and individualist	Yet most current prescriptions for solving the planet's ecological problems are woefully inadequate to meet such ominous threats, since they amount to little more than calls for new international agreements, for personal restraint with regard to the growth of both population and consumption, and the adoption of a handful of so-called environmentally friendly technologies (Foster 1999a, 12).
	Environment and Society emphatically rejects these myths . . . better science will solve our environmental crises; we should educate our leaders, rather than politically confronting them (Schnaiberg and Gould 1994, v).
Class: managerial	[R]eformist legislation has built-in limits. If the measure of success is the degree to which such legislation is likely to diminish considerably the rate of global environmental degradation in say the next 10 to 20 years, I would predict that the answer is, very little (Wallerstein 1999, 8).
	Certainly, interpreting the state of the world chiefly in terms of "resources," "management" and "efficiency" may appeal to planners and economists. But it continues to promote development as a cultural mission and to shape the world in the image of the West (Sachs 1999, 55).
	It is folly to expect that changes large and significant enough to ground a new hope will grow smoothly from initiatives in the dominant institutions (Athanasiou 1998, 52).
	The global managers thus threaten to unleash a new wave of colonialism, in which the management of people—even whole societies—for the benefit of commercial interests is now justified in the name of environmental protection (Hildyard 1993, 33).
Class: individualist	My chief criticism against the cultural approach is that it uses arguments that are not only wrong but also harmful (Sarkar 1999, 239).
	Postmodernism, as well as lifestyle anarchism and deep ecology—all the prelapsarian ideologies—are significantly undermining the possibility for the reemergence of a Left. They redirect our attention away from the social question, class exploitation, and capitalism toward the self (Bookchin 1999, 141–42).
	From this perspective, it is clear that no environmental consciousness-raising can in itself alter the treadmill, all of which require us to engage in social and political conflicts with the logic of the interests that are most supportive of this economic system (Schnaiberg and Gould 1994, vii).

Table 3.2. Examples of Explicit, Rejectionist Paradigm Isolation (*Continued*)

Home paradigm: rejected paradigm	Examples
	[C]onservative interests have assembled layer upon layer of argument that insists that individualism is a necessary aspect of the human condition, a fundamental attribute of human nature. . . . [I]t is an important task of political ecology to refute this contention vigorously (Atkinson 1991, 209).
Managerial: class	If material conditions, interests, and ideas determine the efficacy of international governance systems, after all, how can regimes operate as determinants of collective outcomes in their own right? Yet this objection is not as serious as it may appear (Young 1996, 21).
Managerial: individualist	There is indeed a vast reserve of good citizenry about. But to rely on it, or on governments to stimulate it, is to waste effort. The only practical approach is to manipulate self-interest in the interests of the higher good, and in so doing continually to ask who has the right to judge the behaviour of others (Pearce 1998, 4).
	A Green might argue in response that the changes in behaviour should be voluntary, not coerced. People should be encouraged and educated to want a less materialistic and high-energy lifestyle rather than being forced to adopt one through state intervention. But this is hardly a realistic strategy in the face of the urgent crisis which presents itself today (Jacobs 1991, 128).
Individualist: class	It is not simply a matter of capitalism, as some extremists might argue (Bowers 1993, 20).
Individualist: managerial	Wealth solves the problem of scarcity with abundance. . . . They say we pursue nothing but private profit. We say they pursue nothing but bureaucratic power (Huber 1999, xxvi).
	The major reform environmental organizations have in some cases performed brilliantly, and in other cases they have compromised miserably, in their piecemeal political/economic/legal/ technological approaches to protecting the environment. By failing to take an ecocentric integrated long-range perspective, by failing to be guided by realistic visions of ecological sustainable societies, and by failing to adequately address the root causes of the ecocrisis, they have managed only to delay some of the worst of the environmental degradation (Sessions 1995, xxi).
	Attempts to maintain a sustainable habitat through the political process—whether in the form of demonstrations, working in the hallways and committee rooms of the legislature, or spiking trees—effectively preclude utilizing the full potential of the classroom to help ameliorate the crisis (Bowers 1993, 19).

> In the public's eye it is the profit-seeking big business that threatens the nation's ecological future. Yet in case after case, the real enemy of the environment has proved to be the government (Bandow 1986, 16).
>
> There are many dangers to technocratic solutions. First is the danger in believing there is a complete or acceptable solution using modern dominant ideologies and technology. The second danger is the presentation of an impression that something is being done when in fact the real problem continues (Devall and Sessions 1985, 196).

overwhelms all aspects of government in capitalist countries that no policy reform (even that motivated by outside, progressive pressure) can hope to produce constructive change.

Class Rejection of Individualism
There is a long-standing tendency in the class paradigm to either reject out of hand or to be wary of cultural arguments on the assumption that they obscure public understanding of the class perspective. This is readily evident in statements by Sarkar (1999, 239), Bookchin (1999, 141–42), Schnaiberg and Gould (1994, vii), and Atkinson (1991, 209). Skepticism toward advocacy of radical cultural change derives from the notion of the "prime mover" (i.e., cultural change is impossible without prior economic change) and from the view that the material superstructure and the state exercise hegemonic control over culture (see chapter 1).

Managerial and Individualist Rejection of Class
It is striking how infrequently writers in the managerial and individualist traditions criticize the class perspective.[7] Statements by Young (1996, 21) and Bowers (1993, 2) are exceptional. In part, this reflects the fact that the (true) left has been largely powerless in the United States and Europe in recent decades, and notably so in the aftermath of the fall of Soviet communism. In effect, the proponents of managerialism and individualism believe they can afford to ignore the class perspective. (This issue is discussed below in the section on implicit isolation.)

Managerial Rejection of Individualism
The statements by Pearce (1998, 4) and Jacobs (1991, 128) reflect the general managerial view that the individualist approach (cultural tradition) is not utterly hopeless, but rather inadequate and insufficient in comparison to the power of policy leverage or in relation to the scope of the problem.

Individualist (Cultural Tradition) Rejection of Managerialism
The statements by Sessions (1995, 21), Bowers (1993, 19), and Devall and Sessions (1985, 196) typify the deep ecology view—in common with that of the

class paradigm—that lobbying for policy change and technocratic change are merely reformist and therefore ineffectual. Moreover, deep ecology's rejection of managerialism derives from the view that the state is the spearhead of anthropocentrism and modern, Western culture.

Individualist (Free Market) Rejection of Managerialism
The statements by Huber (1999, xxvi) and Bandow (1986, 16) typify the free market individualist antipathy toward the state. This antipathy, as explained earlier, is propelled by the view that government interference constrains free enterprise and economic growth, thus blocking progress toward improved environmental custodianship by individuals and enlightened enterprises.

Explicit and Contingent
In the mind of the writer engaging in explicit and contingent isolation, the objectives and tenets of a competing paradigm may have value but are viewed as contingent on, and subordinate to, the prime mover in the home paradigm. This mode of thought is "isolation" inasmuch as it conveys the impression that the concerns of the competing paradigm will be taken care of as a matter of course by the home paradigm and thus need not receive serious attention. As above, it is useful to contextualize the examples of explicit and contingent paradigm isolation shown in table 3.3.

Class Contingent View of Managerialism
The statements by Wallerstein (1999, 8) and Athanasiou (1998, 243) say (respectively) that technology is key to both the problem and the solution. But for both writers technology is an epiphenomenon of the capitalist economy. Thus Wallerstein and Athanasiou say, in effect, that people delude themselves who focus their concerns on technology alone and not on the capitalist system.

Class Contingent View of (Cultural) Individualism
In a manner parallel to the example above, Burkett (1999, 229) and Schnaiberg and Gould (1994, 37) believe that the nature of the existing economic system defines the potential and limits for cultural change. The message here, as above, is: "change the economic system first and then secondary concerns will be dealt with as a matter of course."

Managerial Contingent View of Class
As in the case of explicit rejection, there are very few instances where proponents of the managerial paradigm express a contingent view of the class paradigm. Stokke (1991, 17) happens to be a proponent of both the class and managerial paradigms, and this explains the logic of his statement. He believes (and this is not clear from the quotation) that both a strong intervening state and

Table 3.3. Examples of Explicit, Contingent Paradigm Isolation

Home paradigm: contingent paradigm	Examples
Class: managerial	There has been an unfortunate tendency to make science and technology the enemy, whereas it is in fact capitalism that is the generic root of the problem (Wallerstein 1999, 8).
	A technological revolution is an essential part of any humane ecological transition, and this we must grant while at the same time rejecting the chorus of voices that insist that technology alone will do the job (Athanasiou 1998, 243).
Class: individualist	Ecologically informed ethics cannot thrive unless they are routinely validated, both materially and socially, by the system of production, distribution, and consumption (Burkett 1999, 229).
	However, it is equally important to recognize that environmentally aware citizens must achieve survival within socioeconomic structures that currently offer few ecologically benign occupations (Schnaiberg and Gould 1994, 37).
Managerial: class	A strong, intervening state therefore emerges as a necessary but not sufficient precondition for an ecologically sound development (Stokke 1991, 17).
Managerial: individualist	While environmental degradation is ultimately the result of aggregated individual decisions and choices, individual choices are responses to incentives, and other forms of guidance from governments (Keohane et al. 1993, 7).
Individualist: class	This tendency to produce conflict has come from our thought, from how it has evolved over the whole period of civilization (Bohm and Edwards 1991, 3).
	[B]oth overconsumption in the North and underconsumption in the South are embedded in what is rapidly consolidating as one system of natural resources. . . . I would add that ethics and values are ultimately the reference point for a new era (Arizpe 1991, 9).
	The most important root cause of these problems is human nature. Too many people, especially but not only among those in positions of power and influence, are selfish, greedy, power-seeking, and cruel. The second most important root cause is the prevalence of inappropriate economic systems, whether capitalist or collectivist (Burrows et al. 1991, 355).
Individualist: managerial	[T]he need for political action directed toward preserving wild lands, slowing the rate of pollution of land and water, and winning support for a specific piece of environmental legislation, has its roots in the environmentally destructive cultural beliefs and practices that are mostly passed on from generation to generation through the media and educational institutions (Bowers 1997, 18).

Table 3.3.   Examples of Explicit, Contingent Paradigm Isolation (*Continued*)

Home paradigm: *contingent paradigm*	*Examples*
	If an environmentally oriented policy decision is not linked to intrinsic values or ultimates, then its rationality has yet to be determined. The deep ecology movement connects rationality with a set of philosophical or religious foundations (Naess 1995a, 78).
	This does not mean that culture and the political process can ever be domains of human activity distinct from each other: the forms of politics are also grounded in cultural patterns and codes (Bowers 1993, 19).
	[E]ventual ways out of the crisis cannot be simply technological fixes, or isolated political, social and economic measures; these will have to be embedded in a (new) cultural framework (Finger 1992, 27).
	The foundations of deep ecology are the basic intuitions and experiencing of ourselves and Nature which comprise ecological consciousness. Certain outlooks on politics and public policy flow naturally from this consciousness (Devall and Sessions 1985, 65).

structural economic change between countries of the North and South are preconditions of ecologically sound development.

Managerial Contingent View of (Cultural) Individualism
The quote from Keohane et al. (1993, 7) illustrates the tendency of some writers in the managerial tradition to view state policy as shaping the cultural response to environmental degradation. The statement aims to justify a dominant role for institutions in protecting the environment.

(Cultural) Individualist Contingent View of Class
I could find no examples of a (free market) individualist contingent view of class. Given the large gulf separating the two paradigms, this is not surprising. The statements by Arizpe (1991, 9),[8] Bohm and Edwards (1991, 3), and Burrows et al. (1991, 355) illustrating a *cultural* individualist contingent view of class show that the themes and concerns of the class paradigm (conflict, inequality between North and South, inappropriate economic systems) are subordinate to culture as a prime mover.

(Cultural) Individualist Contingent View of Managerialism
I have found no examples of a (free market) individualist contingent view of managerialism and this stands to reason given the strong antistatist views of this tradi-

tion in the individualist paradigm. The examples of a cultural individualist contin-gent view of managerialism all convey that the world of politics is an extension of human culture. Naess (1995a, 78), Bowers (1993, 19), and Finger (1992, 27) go fur-ther to say policy change cannot be effective without a link to cultural change.

Implicit

Implicit paradigm isolation, like explicit paradigm isolation, involves the deval-uation of the tenets and objectives of competing paradigms. The difference is that implicit isolation is either evident from what is *not* stated in the home par-adigm or is inferred indirectly from an argument made in the home paradigm.

Most implicit isolation involves the managerialist and individualist paradigms ostracizing the class paradigm. As explained in chapter 1, the managerial and indi-vidualist paradigms define (more or less) the acceptable bounds of mainstream in-tellectual discourse inasmuch as they both assume legitimacy of the capitalist eco-nomic system, although encompassing a wide range of support or criticism. The managerial and individualist paradigms, although in certain ways displaying mutual rejection, often function as an alliance. I will explain the nature of the "managerial-individualist alliance" in greater detail in the section on paradigm integration. Im-plicit isolation against the class paradigm takes the following two forms.

First, there is a strikingly large number of writers in the managerial and indi-vidualist perspective that never refer to capitalism or to economic accumulation in their analysis of environmental problems. *The economic system is simply a given: it has no name, no permutations over time nor historical tendencies, and no essential characteristics worth discussing in relation to the environment.* This omission is noth-ing short of mind-boggling in view of the clear importance of economic accu-mulation, dating back to 10,000 B.C., in influencing changes in the landscape and resource use. This theoretical lacuna results from (1) ignorance, (2) reluc-tance to examine, much less criticize, the economic system that has showered such unprecedented prosperity on pockets of the human species, and (3) concern that criticism implies identification with the class paradigm. Writers in the class tradition are well aware of such implicit isolation. For example, Bookchin (1999, 310) explains, "The notion that capitalism is eternal compels us to stop thinking about the real social relations that constitute capitalism, just as technophobia and mysticism deflects our thinking from the growth of the market, wage labor, capital, and commodities."[9]

Second, writings in the managerial and individualist perspective sometimes assume that the managerial-individualist spectrum defines the entire relevant range of theory, thus trivializing the concerns of the class paradigm. An example is Anderson (1996), who advocates dual attention to cultural and managerial so-lutions in coping with environmental problems but gives no attention to the themes of the class position. Another example is Huber (1999), whose book im-plies that "soft green" (managerial) theory and "hard green" (free market indi-vidualist) theory defines the entire spectrum of relevant possibilities.

Implicit paradigm isolation is not limited to ostracizing the class paradigm. There are many writings from the class perspective that give scant or no attention to culture and to individual initiative. However, the class paradigm now gives far more attention to the concerns of the individualist paradigm than it did in the past. (See discussion on paradigm integration below.) In keeping with the persistence of an instrumental view of the state in the class paradigm, there are many writings from this perspective that give little or no serious attention to the tenets and objectives of the managerial paradigm. But here, also, there has been significant change in recent years and there are writers who write from a joint class-managerial perspective (e.g., Adams 1990; Low and Gleeson 1998).

Implicit paradigm isolation is also evident in managerial writings with respect to individualist concerns, and in individualist writings with respect to managerial concerns. These cases reflect the polar conflict between staunch managerialists and either deep ecologist or free market environmentalists. Overall, however, as will be evident in the following section on paradigm integration, the foundations of the managerial-individualist alliance are strong, despite their mutual antagonism.

Paradigm Integration

Given the clear relevance of class, power, and culture to environmental problems (chapter 2), meaningful and lasting solutions require dedicated attention to the central objectives of all three paradigms on the environment. Each of the following is essential: structural economic change aimed at eliminating class exploitation and the growing divide between rich and poor; profound policy change and reorientation of state priorities; and dramatic cultural transformation and engagement of individual responsibility, particularly in countries of the North, where consumerism is such a prominent intermediate cause of environmental degradation. All three objectives are necessary but none is individually sufficient to achieve lasting solutions.

It would be wrong to assume that resolution of environmental problems can be achieved optimally with proponents of the class, managerial, and individualist paradigms pursuing their respective objectives independently, complementing one another. Why? First, the proponents are in conflict with each other and this polarization—although rational from the perspective of each of the home paradigms—tends to undermine both expert and popular understanding of the causes of, and solutions to, ecological instability. Second, resolving environmental problems requires that activists, academics, theoreticians, diplomats, politicians, planners, scientists, ordinary citizens, and businesspeople cross paradigm boundaries and internalize the necessity to focus attention jointly on class, power, and culture, and not just on one of those categories alone.

Wholesale paradigm integration is surely impossible and is therefore not advocated. Why is this the case? First, there are irreconcilable ideological polarities (e.g., class paradigm proponents seeking elimination of capitalism and free market environmentalists claiming unfettered capitalist markets are the only solution). Moreover, a wholesale paradigm integration is highly unlikely, given the strength and persistence of the notion of a prime mover within each paradigm.

Partial paradigm integration, however, is feasible and desirable. Such integration begins by acknowledging that objectives lying outside the home paradigm are worthy of consideration. *Such acknowledgment is not necessarily in logical conflict with the tenets of the home paradigm.* There is only the *appearance* of logical conflict because of ingrained tendencies toward rejectionist, contingent, and implicit isolation, and as well the tendency to oversimplify reality in order to cultivate the interest of followers.

Evidence of Integration

In recent years, there have been increasing signs of paradigm integration in the literature of the three environmental paradigms. Why is this integration happening? One reason may be that continued omission of the tenets and objectives of competing paradigms can no longer be upheld. Worsening social and environmental conditions are forcing acknowledgment of the theoretical emptiness and dangers of paradigm isolation, and of the benefits of bringing all relevant perspectives to bear on an increasingly dire situation.

Figure 3.1 shows there are four points of overlap among the three key paradigms that correspond to four forms of integration: (1) class-managerial-individualist, (2) class-managerial, (2) class-individualist, and (4) managerial-individualist. Table 3.4 shows examples of paradigm integration in recent environmental literature.

Class → Managerial Integration

The statements by Bookchin (1999, 296), O'Connor (1998, 309), Low and Gleeson (1998, 213), and Sachs et al. (1998, 101) indicate the utility of the institutions of the state, even if at a minimal level (in the case of Bookchin). Among proponents of the class paradigm, there has been little analysis of the prospect for state and government policies alleviating environmental problems. This, of course, makes sense for those who believe the state is a key part of the problem, and therefore in no imaginable way a part of the solution. Two writers who have broken rank with this premise are Jacobs (1991) and Low and Gleeson (1998), who claim that a strong state is needed to overcome environmental problems. The statement by Sachs et al. (1998, 101) in their book *Greening the North: A Post-Industrial Blueprint for Ecology and Equity,* is notable for its indication of a change in orientation. Once the most strident of critics of the managerial paradigm and of the concept of sustainable development (e.g., Sachs 1991, 1993), Wolfgang Sachs, in his latest book, has become more amenable to policy solutions and even produces a plan for sustainable development in Germany. This greater openness to managerialism may result from his being faced with the task of turning radical theory into practical proposals.

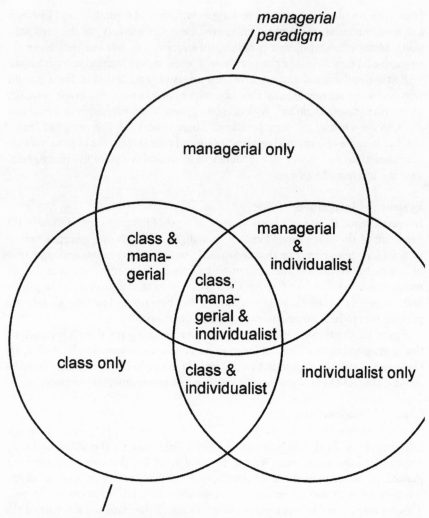

managerial
/ paradigm

managerial only

class &
mana-
gerial

managerial
&
individualist

class,
mana-
gerial &
individualist

class only

class &
individualist

individualist only

Figure 3.1. Modes of Paradigm Integration

Class → (Cultural) Individualist Integration
Many class proponents now refer to the need for cultural change. Statements indicating the importance of culture from a class perspective reflect a recent trend.
What motivates this greater openness? There are at least two reasons. First, culture is increasingly recognized as an important battleground for contested ideological allegiance in society. It fills a vacuum left by the weakness of the labor
movement. Activists in the class paradigm are reacting to the appropriation of
cultural "turf" by the deep ecology movement. Second, the role of culture in the
North's overconsumption is so obvious that it requires a more sophisticated

Table 3.4. Examples of Paradigm Integration Among Environmental Ideologies

Home paradigm: target paradigm	Examples
Class: managerial	I don't oppose centralization under any and all circumstances. But a libertarian revolutionary organization would centralize *as much as is clearly necessary and for only as long as is necessary* (Bookchin 1999, 296).
	A radical position is that renewal may not be possible without a democratic *deepening*—the "intensive" growth of democracy in the unions, in the workplace, in the community, and, above all, in the administrative apparatus of the state itself (O'Connor 1998, 309).
	The challenge of the new century, the challenge of ecological and environmental justice is nothing less than the transformation of the global institutions of governance, the reinstatement of democracy at a new level, the democratisation of both production and its regulation (Low and Gleeson 1998, 213).
	Ecological tax reform offers one of the best examples of diversion of market dynamism to environmental objectives. This is a key element in transition to a sustainable economy (Sachs et al. 1998, 101).
Class: individualist	However, despite our argument for the importance of material explanations, we believe that nonmaterial motivations . . . do have critical environmental implications. . . . World systems theory has been weak on its analyses of culture and individual agency (Goldfrank et al. 1999, 77).
	The power for change lies with the general population worldwide. If they remain uninformed, their spontaneous revolts will simply accelerate the descent into anarchy (Grimes 1999, 39).
	It is here and now that we must raise the banner of substantive rationality around which we must rally. . . . It involves not only a new social system, but new structures of knowledge (Wallerstein 1999, 10–11).
	The home perspective believes in making room for others by means of an orderly retreat; it proposes a new kind of rationality . . . for meeting the crises of justice and of nature (Sachs 1999, 87).
	An ecologically sound management of human production presumes, however, that people share a fundamental ecological ethic, however diverse its forms (Burkett 1999, 229).
	Our first step in reviving the Left, I believe, will be to reclaim the knowledge that past generations possessed and master it for ourselves. . . . Revolutionaries who are committed to this vital task must first develop their own consciousness (Bookchin 1999, 334).
	The final and most basic level of conflict may be that which is internal to yourself. Positioning yourself within the context of all

Table 3.4. Examples of Paradigm Integration among Environmental Ideologies (*Continued*)

Home paradigm: target paradigm	Examples
	these conflicts and coalitions is likely to require quite a bit of soul-searching (Schnaiberg and Gould 1994, 239).
	The task before us is, therefore, an educational one. It is to raise public awareness about the mistaken path we are following, about the impossibility of affluence and growth for all, and about the fact that there is a promising alternative. If we succeed at this task the revolution will have been won by default (Trainer 1985, 275).
Managerial: class	Any child born into the hugely consumptionist way of life so common in the industrial world will have an impact on the environment that is, on average, many times more destructive than that of a child born in the developing world (Gore 2000, 308).
	[T]he most important challenge to the NGO movement will be to build political pressure on reluctant states to support participation in or strengthening of global environmental regimes (Porter et al. 2000, 218).
	It is now becoming obvious that the widening gap between rich and poor is untenable in a world where resources are shared. In the absence of a concerted effort by the wealthy to address the problems of poverty and deprivation, building a sustainable future may not be possible (Brown and Flavin 1999, 20).
Managerial: individualist	At issue is a change in understanding and values that will support a restructuring of the global economy so that economic progress can continue (Brown and Flavin 1999, 20).
	These policies—green taxes, graded ecozoning, the precautionary polluter pays principle, and so on—would work in concert with citizen activism and personal environmental responsibility to transform the economic system. . . . The policies would need a base of popular support to be implemented, and as they were implemented they would restructure the system in ways that would reinforce the values that supported them (Prugh et al. 1999, 154–55).
	Perhaps most importantly, it is difficult to see how the economic system can be changed unless culture and values change also. In democracies fundamental reform can only occur by popular consent (whether such consent is *sufficient* is another question) and this will not be forthcoming unless attitudes and values have shifted (Jacobs 1991, 47).
Individualist: class	In short, there is a sound basis for *global* cooperation between supporters of the Deep Ecology movement and ecologically concerned people in the Third World, and also with people who try to understand and lessen poverty in those regions (Naess 1995b, 400).

> The movement is *oriented towards* the individual. If we are to hope to reverse the current trends, we have to create a common front between the individual-oriented and the system-oriented activists (Naess and Rothenberg1989, 90).

Individualist: managerial

> For the past 25 years, environmental policy in the United States and around the world has relied on command-and-control regulations. . . . Certainly, some regulation was necessary, and the environment has improved (Anderson and Leal 1997, 3).

> [S]ociety must therefore view environmental management as necessarily involving an ethical and moral code backed up by emotional force, but society must also create an economic system that makes ecological sanity economically attractive (Anderson 1996, viii).

> A central premise of this book is that only by linking community ecological values with democratic design of policies and markets can the goals of environmental governance be realized in a sustainable fashion (Hempel 1996, 8).

> The changes in some practices—like dumping toxic wastes, deforestation, depleting fisheries, and losing topsoil and ground water—require immediate attention, and this will mean utilizing the political process to enact legislation. Attempting to effect changes in these areas through the long-term process of educationally guided cultural changes would be too slow a process (Bowers 1993, 20).

> If enough citizens cultivate their own ecological consciousness and act through the political process to inform managers and government agencies of the principles of deep ecology, some significant changes in the direction of wise long-range management policies can be achieved (Devall and Sessions 1985, 158).

---

analysis by the class paradigm than has yet been delivered. But not all proponents of the class perspective view culture as an important afterthought. For Sachs (1999, 87) and Shiva et al. (1991) and Shiva (1997, 2000), culture has always been integral to understanding environmental problems. They critique the North's culture of overconsumption and the North's dismantling of diverse cultural heritages in the South that are vital to maintaining ecological stability.

Class ⟶ *(Free Market) Individualist Integration*
The class and (free market) individualist paradigms do not have much common ground and there is little scope for integration. Proponents of the class perspective sometimes endorse the utility of markets under state-controlled conditions (e.g., Lappé et al. 1998, 104–6), but this scarcely counts as integration because there remains deep misgivings about a truly *free* market.

Managerial → *Class Integration*
The statements by Gore (2000, 308) and Brown and Flavin (1999, 20) resonate with two of the main concerns of the class paradigm: northern overconsumption and the relationship of income inequality to environmental destruction. These statements do not in any way, however, constitute an emerging acceptance of the core tenets of the class paradigm. Porter et al. (2000, 218) show strong support for grassroots mobilization by NGOs, an outlook customarily identified with the class paradigm.

Managerial → *(Cultural) Individualist Integration*
The statements by Brown and Flavin (1999, 20), Prugh et al. (1999, 154–55), and Jacobs (1991, 47) indicate a relatively strong and problem-free affinity of certain managerialists for the objectives of the (cultural) individualist paradigm. This linkage is a key element in the managerial-individualist alliance.

Managerial → *(Free Market) Individualist Integration*
There is little scope for integration here, given the strong discrepancy of views on the role of the state.

(Cultural) Individualist → *Class Integration*
The statements by Naess (1995b, 400) and Naess and Rothenberg (1989, 90) express openness by deep ecologists to collaborating with activists in the class paradigm. These overtures were made in response to strong criticism of deep ecology for neglecting class politics and exploitation. However, there is as yet little evidence of a genuine link between cultural individualism and the class paradigm. Recent deep ecology writings continue to demonstrate little affinity for the tenets and objectives of the class paradigm.

(Free Market) Individualist → *Class Integration*
The deep polarization between these paradigms provides little possibility of fruitful integration.

(Cultural) Individualist → *Managerial Integration*
The statements by Anderson (1996, viii), Hempel (1996, 8), Bowers (1993, 20), and Devall and Sessions (1985, 158) are evidence of the strong possibilities for integration and for strengthening of the managerial-individualist alliance. Note Bowers's (1993, 20) assertion that policy reform is an important course of action in the near term because cultural change is a long-term process.

(Free market) Individualist → *Managerial Integration*
The quote by Anderson and Leal (1997, 3) indicates decreasing rigidity in their views over time with some slight openness to the arguments of the managerial

perspective. Yet another indication of Terry Anderson's open-mindedness is his acknowledging that common property (as compared to private property) may sometimes be justified (Anderson and Simmons 1993).

The Challenge of Further Integration

Despite visible steps toward paradigm integration, the process has barely begun when measured against the scope of possibilities. As noted above, much of this integration is happening passively, with worsening social and environmental conditions forcing proponents to consider categories of thought heretofore alien to them. Great strides in theoretical integration are possible if done proactively and consciously, recognizing the benefits such pioneering steps could yield.

In assessing prospects for further integration, note the following. First, the gravity of the income polarization and environmental degradation nexus may become so extreme as to force recognition of the concerns of the class paradigm. The international policy moves toward debt forgiveness in 1999–2000 are one possible indication of a trend in this direction.

Second, it is likely that mutual affinity of certain managerialists and cultural individualists will solidify. Policy and management change overtures will more consistently take on board the need for behavioral transformation, and, reciprocally, those calling for cultural change will more systematically seek out managerial strategies for implementing their aims.

Third, despite the ideological gulf that separates the class and cultural individualist traditions, there are grounds for closer integration. Both paradigms share an impassioned rejection of consumerism, and this offers potential for cross-fertilization of ideas. Furthermore, as noted by Buttel (1996, 60), both Marxist and Durkheimian sociologies have lent themselves to possible synthesis because they are realist (as opposed to nominalist) ontologies: both posit the existence of unmeasurable underlying (sociophysical or ecological) phenomena that operate "behind the backs" of social actors.

Fourth, many proponents of the three paradigms are promoting local-level governance as a key step toward rectifying both social and environmental problems. This trend presents a two-edged possibility. On one hand, local-level governance may become yet another stage on which long-standing ideological battles are waged because the three paradigms have different agendas in promoting local-level governance. Class proponents tend to be seeking emancipation from outside corporate exploitation; managerialists are often responding to the progressive collapse of centralized control and want more efficient modes of governance; individualists oppose perceived overbearing state control and technocracy and/or favor unconstrained economic initiative. On the other hand, the striking similarities among the three paradigms in the logic and phrasing of calls for decentralization and local-level management may encourage theoretical integration.[10]

Conclusion

This chapter began by defining the ideological parameters of the three key social theory paradigms on the environment. In the class paradigm, economic accumulation, class exploitation, and overconsumption of resources are the key causes of environmental problems, and mobilization against exploitation, inequality, and injustice are the proposed solutions. In the managerial paradigm, policy inadequacy is the main problem and adjustments in the diplomatic, legal, regulatory, and technological realms are offered as solutions. In the cultural individualist paradigm, distorted values are key and cultural change and reduced consumption are the solution; in the free market individualist paradigm, government interference is the problem and removal of this constraint, in addition to specification of individual property rights, are the solutions.

Proponents of all three paradigms engage to a greater or lesser degree in paradigm isolation. They think and act, either explicitly or implicitly, as if the tenets and objectives of competing paradigms are either wrongheaded or trivial. The fallacy and danger of paradigm isolation is evident when we realize that effective and durable solutions to environmental problems necessarily involve these three elements from all three paradigms: structural economic change and rectification of growing worldwide inequalities; considerable policy change and redirecting of state priorities; and dramatic cultural transformation and engagement of individual responsibility. This powerful truth has been lost on many environmental analysts. The silent mechanics of ideological confrontation have induced many to "throw out the baby with the bathwater"—to discard reasonable, commonsense perspectives simply because they are historically alien to the home perspective.

This chapter has noted various forms of paradigm integration by environmental analysts. These crossings of ideological boundaries fall far short of their potential, both in frequency and scope. As yet, paradigm integration appears to be a passive process occurring mainly in response to worsening global circumstances, and it is not yet proactive and creative. Future efforts at integration among the three paradigmatic traditions will be indispensable for realizing the full potential of our collective efforts to address ever graver social and environmental challenges.

Subsequent chapters on the population-resource balance, economic growth, and on what constitutes "authentic" environmentalism will deepen our understanding of the pitfalls of paradigm isolation and of the need and potential for crossing ideological boundaries.

Notes

1. This chapter builds on ideas that originally appeared in a journal article titled "Global Environmental Change, Sociology, and Paradigm Isolation" (Sunderlin 1995a).

2. This is particularly true of the class paradigm. Some of its most prominent ideologues (e.g., James O'Connor, Immanuel Wallerstein) have recently made the environ-

ment their lead concern. Note as well that former Vice President Al Gore, a key proponent of the managerial paradigm, made environmental issues his central priority.

3. Atkinson (1991, 6), for example, dismisses the importance of capitalism as an analytical resting point. In the same vein, Lipietz (1995, x, xii) says he has ceased identifying with the left and does not believe oppression necessarily stems from capitalism.

4. One indication of the confused state of political ecology concerns its relationship to ecological modernization, a major new perspective that will be examined in chapter 5. Bryant and Bailey say political ecologists are "highly sceptical" of ecological modernization theorizing. Blaikie (1999, 136–38) portrays ecological modernization theory as a rapidly growing analytical narrative within political ecology.

5. List and Rittberger define a regime as "a social institution wherein stable patterns of behaviour result from compliance with certain norms and rules, whether these are laid down in a legally binding instrument or not" (1992, 90).

6. Arguments in favor of applying technological solutions (e.g., a shift from fossil fuel to solar technologies) are a frequent hallmark of managerial arguments. What is the link between policy change and technology? Both tend to be reformist, involving deliberations in the halls of power to advance their application. Policy change and technological development are tools at the disposal of people in large, formal organizations (e.g., government, large corporations, multilateral and bilateral development banks, etc).

7. There are frequent denunciations of "the left" that are actually aimed at the liberal center. Recall from chapter 1 that there is a strong tendency on the political right to define the liberal center as the left and to virtually ignore the existence of the true political left—those in the class paradigm.

8. Lourdes Arizpe (1991, 9) as well as Matthias Finger (1992, 27) (next section) are nominally individualists insofar as they exhibit a "culture first" philosophy, but they are strongly identified with the concerns of the class paradigm.

9. In a related way O'Connor states: "Indeed, more problems have been identified, and more descriptions of these problems have been written, than one person could read and absorb in a lifetime. . . . But there is no general, systematic theory of the "whys" of ecological destruction in general and of the complex inner connections between capital accumulation and economic and ecological crisis trends and tendencies, on the one hand, and social movements and politics, on the other" (1998, 125).

10. In the class tradition, the strongest voices in support of local-level governance are Murray Bookchin, Wolfgang Sachs, and Vandana Shiva. Support for localization is not universal (e.g., O'Connor 1998, 277). Opposition to globalization is an important factor motivating localization. In the managerial tradition, the World Bank is one of various major institutions devoting much attention to the possibilities for local governance. For example, the World Bank states, "The message of this report is that new institutional responses are needed in a globalizing and localizing world. . . . Localization requires national governments to reach agreements with regions and cities through subnational institutions on issues such as sharing responsibility for raising revenues" (2000, 3). Increasing attention to localization is motivated by the de facto reality of limits to state capacity and fiscal constraints. Cultural individualists tend to favor localization on the grounds of promoting individual and community empowerment. Free market individualists favor localization on the grounds of opposition to state intervention and, in some cases, support for federalism (e.g., Anderson and Hill 1997, xiv).

CHAPTER FOUR

~

Competing Views on the Population-Resource Balance

Contemporary discussion of population and resources is frequently described as a debate between "pessimists" (or "neo-Malthusians") who believe human population tends to exceed the capacity of the earth to support it and "optimists" (or "anti-Malthusians") who see no excess of population over resources. While use of the terms "pessimist" and "optimist" in this context is superficially correct, reliance on such terms obscures the deeper truth that these pessimistic and optimistic outlooks on the population-resource balance are shaped by political ideology.

In this chapter I will make three arguments. First, I will show that the Malthusian perspective dominates the center of the political spectrum, while two versions of anti-Malthusianism spring from the left and from the right. Second, I will argue that the presence of neo-Malthusian views in the political center, and of anti-Malthusian views on the left and right, can be understood in terms of the ideological rationales of the three main social theory paradigms ("class" in association with the left, "power" in association with the center, and "culture" in association with the right). Third, although some elements of the debate are irreconcilable, there are grounds for paradigm integration, and steps in that direction are evident in the population-resource balance literature.

This chapter is structured in five parts. A section on the state of the population-resource balance summarizes knowledge on the issue, providing information on the demographic transition; the current and projected adequacy of food supplies in relation to population; the influence of land, water, and energy on the population-food equation; and the prospects for a second green revolution. The next section on the theoretical antecedents of modern population paradigms describes the influence of Thomas Malthus, Karl Marx and Friedrich

Engels, and Esther Boserup. Then a section on contemporary population paradigms describes six perspectives, focusing on three of those six that are dominant in their respective social theory paradigms, and also dominant in modern debates. A subsequent section on paradigm isolation and integration examines the logic of isolation among contemporary population paradigms; evidence of steps toward integration; speculation on the prospects for further integration; and evaluation of two formal attempts at paradigm integration. The concluding section summarizes the findings and underscores the utility of understanding the population-resource issue in ideological terms.

The State of the Population-Resource Balance

This section provides basic background information on human population growth, agricultural productivity, and environmental constraints. Its intent is to provide a backdrop against which the later presentation of theoretical and ideological views on the population-resource balance can be understood. Of course, there are pitfalls in attempting to provide "factual" information in the context of a topic that is so polemically charged. To the extent possible, in this section I strive to draw on information that is relatively well agreed-on across ideological divisions (where there are differences of opinion I flag them) or has not been subject to debate. There is remarkably little friction on much of the data I present. The debate centers instead on the *implications* of these data, given varying economic, political, and cultural premises.

In this section I draw on the writings of researchers who are situated in the "center" in two senses: (1) they are in the "managerial" middle (e.g., the United Nations Population Division, the International Food Policy Research Institute (IFPRI), the Consultative Group on International Agricultural Research (CGIAR), the World Bank, the Food and Agriculture Organization of the United Nations (FAO), the Rockefeller Foundation, etc.) and (2) they tend to situate themselves in the middle of the neo-Malthusian–anti-Malthusian divide. This should in no way be interpreted to mean that I believe "facts" tend to be more credible if they are generated by representatives of the political center. The political center and managerialism are no less ideological than the class and individualist perspectives. I cite sources from the managerial center because most data that are considered "facts" on this topic are generated by researchers and institutions that are located there.

Demographic Transition
The growth of human population has been rapid in the last several hundred years (see figure 2.1 in chapter 2) and has been explosive in the course of the twentieth century, growing from 1.6 billion in 1900 to 6.1 billion in 2000 (Bongaarts and Bulatao 1999, 515). The United Nations Population Division has made

three forecasts of world population in 2050: 7.9 billion is the low projection; 9.3 billion is the medium projection; and 10.9 billion is the high projection (United Nations Population Division 2000a, 6) (see figure 4.1). The annual rate of world population increase has slowed greatly in recent decades from the historic peak of 2.1 percent per year in 1965 (Cohen 1995, 172) to 1.2 percent per year in 2000 (United Nations Population Division 2000a, 3). The rate of annual growth is expected to continue to slow, with world population stabilizing at just over 10 billion in the year 2200, assuming the U.N. medium projection and assuming fertility reaches and remains at the replacement level (United Nations Population Division 2000b, 1).

Demographic transition theory explains initial population stability in early human history, rapid growth in the last several centuries, the current deceler-

World Population (Billions)

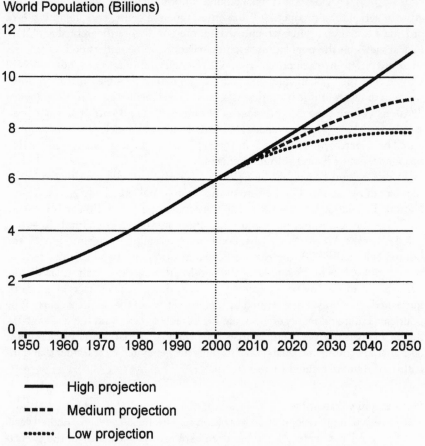

━━━━ High projection

▬ ▬ ▬ ▬ Medium projection

••••••• Low projection

Figure 4.1. World Population Size: Past Estimates and High-, Medium-, and Low-Fertility Variants, 1950–2050
Source: United Nations Population Division 2000a, 4.

ation, and projected eventual stabilization of world population. The theory holds that countries pass sequentially through three demographic stages. In stage 1, human fertility and mortality rates are both high; in stage 2, fertility and mortality both decrease, but mortality decreases earlier and faster than fertility, leading to a population boom; and in stage 3, fertility and mortality are both low and roughly equal (Demeny 1990, 46) (see figure 4.2).

Dramatic worldwide increase in average life expectancy is the main indicator of mortality decline (or the "mortality transition" as demographers call it) occurring in stage 2 of the demographic transition. The reasons for the mortality transition include medical advances (such as the invention of penicillin) that have controlled disease and epidemics; the emergence of the modern state and the role of the state in promoting hygiene (e.g., making available potable water); and creating infrastructure, transportation systems, and commerce, which in turn stabilize agricultural production and reduce the incidence of famine (Kirk 1996, 362, 368, 374).

Historic decrease in the number of births per woman is the indicator of fertility decline (or "fertility transition"), occurring in stage 2 of the demographic transition. In the classic pattern of the demographic transition, the mortality decline precipitates the process of voluntary fertility decline (Demeny 1990, 46; Kirk 1996, 379). The high number of surviving children resulting from mortality decline eventually induces parents to consciously restrict fertility. Moreover, it is often assumed that in the process of modernization, parents choose to have fewer children both because they become less advantageous (i.e., less necessary as part of a family labor force or as a form of social security in old age) and because they become more expensive (i.e., more costly to raise in terms of the parents' opportunity costs and/or finances). Among the many factors that can make

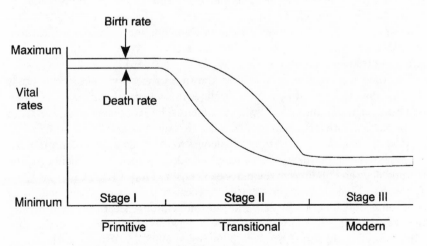

Figure 4.2. Model of the Demographic Transitions
Source: Humphrey et al. 2002, 79.

large numbers of births less advantageous and more costly, and that have encouraged or enabled reduced fertility, are (1) laws requiring a minimum age of marriage, a minimum age of employment, and compulsory schooling; (2) availability of education, especially for girls, and related delays of marriage and of first births; (3) increased employment of women outside the home; (4) cultural transformation from "children as supporters of parents" to "parents as supporters of children"; (5) government family planning programs; (6) availability of contraceptive technology; and (7) reduction of infant mortality and improvement of child welfare (Kirk 1996, 374–79).

Demographers have debated whether there is any empirical basis for the demographic transition theory. Cohen (1995, 46–47) observes that confusion has resulted from two different meanings for the term "demographic transition." One meaning equates it with "an idealized historical pattern of changes in birth, death and population growth rates." Cohen asserts that a demographic transition by this definition has indeed taken place (Cohen 1995, 46–47). All countries now called "developed" have doubled life expectancy and have reduced births per woman by half or more.

A second meaning of "demographic transition" refers to the *mechanisms* by which these changes happen. Conventional wisdom long held that social and economic development (i.e., industrialization, urbanization, education, and general modernization) induce first mortality decline and then fertility decline (Cohen 1995, 47). The "demographic transition" in this second sense has been strongly challenged. Cases have been identified where fertility decline preceded modernization, challenging the assumed causal link between social and economic development and fertility decline. A large-scale historical research project (the European Fertility Project) on transitions in Europe found, for example, that the fertility decline in France began at the time of the French Revolution, long before France could be considered developed (Coale and Watkins 1986). The same study found provincial cases in Denmark and Germany where, contrary to expectations of the theory, fertility decline occurred before rather than after the decline in infant mortality (Watkins 1986, 436).

Another challenge to demographic transition theory was posed by a study showing dramatic voluntary fertility declines in some developing countries that had been relatively untouched by development. The economies of some of these countries were either stagnant or declining (Robey et al. 1993).

How do we make sense of these challenges to the assumed mechanisms of demographic transition theory? Some have defended the theory and challenged the methodology and findings of the European Fertility Project (e.g., Chesnais 1992, 7, 346–54). Some have argued that it is necessary to go beyond the traditional focus on economic explanations and integrate cultural, ideational, and institutional explanations in a multidisciplinary understanding of causation in the transition process (e.g., Kirk 1996, 369, 379; Stokes 1995, 15–16). Some claim that not just improvements in economic welfare but also its opposite—economic hardship—can induce parents to voluntarily limit fertility. As Dyson (1996, 21) suggests, the falling global birthrate may in part be a response to constrained resources.

Controversies surrounding the validity of demographic theory should not obscure our view of a profound truth related to the first meaning of the term: the world is *in general terms* divided between rich, low fertility countries, on one hand, and poor, high fertility countries, on the other. Nearly the entire increase in world population between 2000 and 2050 will be in developing countries (figure 4.3). This is because almost all developed countries are either at or below their level of replacement fertility (2.1 births per woman), whereas many developing countries remain above (and in some cases well above) their level of replacement fertility (2.4 births per woman).[1] Fertility rates are below replacement in Europe (1.41 births per woman) and in North America (2.00); they are above replacement in Africa (5.27), Asia (2.70), Latin America and the Caribbean (2.69), and Oceania (2.41) (United Nations Population Division 2000a, 9).

Population and Food
Increases in agricultural production matched the stupendous increase of human numbers in the twentieth century. Not only that, average food prices decreased in this period. Why then are hundreds of millions of people malnourished? It is because they are poor and lack the purchasing power to get access to an adequate supply of food, despite generally low world food prices (Alexandratos 1995, 2, 8; Dyson 1994, 408). As explained by Cohen (1995, 54), the "bottom billion" are so poor that they cannot drive up the price of internationally traded food and are "economically invisible."

Although the absolute quantity of food produced has kept pace with population growth, this success may not endure. As explained in chapter 2, since 1980 there has been a steady decline in the rate of increase of agricultural production (Alexandratos 1995, 5; Islam 1995, 3; Conway 1997, 131; Pinstrup-Andersen et al. 1999, 5, 15). In order to meet projected demand, the world's farmers will have to increase grain production by 40 percent between 1995 and 2020 (Pinstrup-Andersen et al. 1999, 5) and food production by 67 percent in the next forty to fifty years (Evans 1998, 196). The challenge is particularly acute in developing countries, where rates of population growth are expected to far outstrip agricultural productivity. Grain exports from developed to developing countries will double in the period 1995 to 2020. Sub-Saharan Africa, the Middle East, South Asia, the Far East, and perhaps Latin America will become increasingly dependent on developed country exports for their food supplies (Dyson 1996, 134; Pinstrup-Andersen et al. 1999, 5). The growth of the world livestock sector magnifies the challenge because an increasing share of world grain production is being fed to animals rather than consumed directly by humans (Alexandratos 1995, 10; Islam 1995, 2; Evans 1998, 188–90). As explained by Evans (1998, 190), "The greatest problem posed by the rapid increase

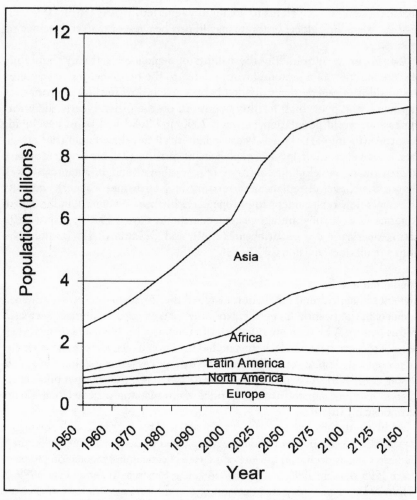

Figure 4.3. Population Growth, 1950–2150, Actual and Projected, by World Region
Source: United Nations Population Division (2000b, 41–43), tables 22 and 23. Note that the projections assume the medium-growth scenario. Data for Oceania are excluded.

in grain feeding of livestock is that grain production must not only match the increase in population but substantially exceed it to provide the requisite animal feed as well as food, thereby putting additional pressure on the resources and sustainability in agriculture."

The world regions particularly at risk of agricultural production shortfalls are sub-Saharan Africa and South Asia (Islam 1995, 1). The situation in sub-Saharan Africa is particularly grim because its per capita cereal and food production has declined rapidly (Conway 1997, 132).

Land and other Critical Resources

The capacity of world agriculture to meet future food demand partly depends on the availability of arable land. The existing area of cropland is 1.4 billion hectares (Simmons 1996, 1), and various estimates say there are from 3.0 to 3.4 billion hectares of potentially cultivable land (Evans 1998, 200). So it appears that expansion of cropland to meet increased demand is not a constraint, but this is not the case. As Evans (1998, 200) explains: "Much of the presently uncultivated area is already used for grazing livestock or is of poorer quality, too remote or subdivided to be economic, vulnerable to erosion, or cherished in its present state." Virtually all experienced agriculturists are concerned about the likely environmental costs of feeding 10 billion people (Evans 1998, 2). Recall from chapter 2 that the existing stock of agricultural land is threatened by degradation, erosion, desertification, and conversion to nonagricultural land uses. To meet increased food demand, the area of agricultural land in developing countries will have to increase from 760 million to 850 million hectares by 2010 (Alexandratos 1995, 15). The FAO projects further increases of arable land area of 30 percent in sub-Saharan Africa and Latin America, and only 4 percent in South Asia and 9 percent in the Near East and North Africa; increase of arable land will play only a minor role in increased future production (Evans 1998, 202). Even more so than in the past, agricultural intensification will have to be the mainstay of productivity growth (Alexandratos 1995, 31). The overwhelming majority of future food demand will have to be met through more efficient use of existing agricultural lands (Dyson 1996, 117). Hence the emphasis on the need for a second Green Revolution (see below).

To meet future food demand, there will have to be a substantial expansion of irrigation capacity above and beyond efficiency improvements in currently existing irrigation systems (Evans 1998, 174–75). The need for additional irrigation capacity runs up against the fact that the availability of fresh water for agriculture is increasingly constrained worldwide. In many countries, the availability of water is even more limiting than the availability of arable land (Alexandratos 1995, 18; Islam 1995, 3; Rosegrant and Sombilla 1997, 1470). The use of fossil fuels in agriculture is another potentially important constraint on future food production, both in terms of fossil fuel supply limits and also the relationship of fossil fuel combustion to greenhouse gas release and consequent effects on agriculture. Agriculture currently consumes only 5 percent of world energy, but energy may become a primary limiting factor because of its role in powering irrigation, mechanization on arable land, mineral nutrients, and other inputs (Evans 1998, 208).

The Next Green Revolution?

Agricultural experts expect there will have to be a second Green Revolution to meet the challenge of feeding as many as 10 billion people by 2050 (Conway et al. 1994; Conway 1997; Serageldin and Persley 2000). The proposed revolution, involving genetic engineering, is controversial. It has been opposed by some researchers and activists (e.g., Fowler and Mooney 1990; Dawkins 1997; Lappé and Bailey 1998; Shiva 1997; Shiva 2000) and evaluated by neutral observers (e.g., Colman 1994; Krimsky and Wrubel 1996). The core elements of the proposed revolution include the production through genetic manipulation of the following: herbicide-, disease-, and insect-resistant crops; transgenic plant products and animal species; microbial pesticides; nitrogen-fixing and frost-inhibiting bacteria; and animal growth hormones (Krimsky and Wrubel 1996).

Gordon Conway (1997, 41), president of the Rockefeller Foundation and one of the leading proponents of the next Green Revolution, says it will have to be "doubly" green in the sense of being not only highly agriculturally productive but also environmentally benign. He adds that the new technologies must be specifically targeted at developing countries because of the growing gap between demand and supply in these countries, and such technology must be developed and applied in a way that addresses the deficient purchasing power of the poor (Conway 1997, 42). Furthermore, the revolution must generate a return to high rates of agricultural productivity growth on existing Green Revolution agricultural lands (Conway 1997, 132). The daunting scale of the challenge is summed up by Evans (1998, 205): "Even for eight billion people, the *average* world yield would have to equal those of Europe and North America today, and exceed them by 25 percent to sustain ten billion."

Some leading agricultural experts have a guardedly optimistic outlook on the prospects for successful implementation of a second Green Revolution. However, most voice cautions which, when viewed collectively, make it clear that achievement of this goal is far from certain. The second Green Revolution can only succeed if there is a strong commitment to publicly funded research in both developed and developing countries (Conway et al. 1994, 13; Alexandratos 1995, 14; Evans 1998, 223). Despite this requirement, public funding for such research has been severely cut in many developed and developing countries in recent years, in part because of grain production surpluses in rich countries and because of the belief that technological breakthroughs can be summoned up as needed (Evans 1998, xii, 152). Dailey et al. (1998, 1291) warn that complacency about food production capability is based on the heady successes of the first Green Revolution, but this complacency is not justified because it ignores possible damage to, and depletion of, the ecosystem services on which future production will depend.

Can privately funded biotechnology research compensate for deficits in public research? Conway observes that "genetic engineering is a highly competitive business and inevitably, the focus of biotechnology companies has been on developed-country markets where potential sales are large, patents are well protected and the risks are lower" (1997, 159). In order to direct the benefits of biotechnology research to developing countries, where the benefits are most needed, public–private partnerships will be essential (Conway 1997, 159). Ismail Serageldin, chairman of the CGIAR (1994–2000), the network of international research centers that produced the first Green Revolution, said that "concentration of investment, science, and infrastructure in industrial countries and the lack of access to the resulting technologies are major impediments to the successful applications of modern biotechnology" (Serageldin and Persley 2000, 36).

The issue of funding aside, agricultural research leaders voice both optimism and deep concern regarding the scientific challenges involved in mobilizing revolutionary improvements in agricultural productivity (e.g., Alexandratos 1995, 1; Conway 1997, 157, 316). Vernon Ruttan, a prominent evaluator of agricultural innovation and productivity, maintains cautious optimism about the prospects for the future of agriculture. Even so, he notes that "at present there is no package of technology available to transfer to producers that can assure the sustainability of growth in agricultural production at a rate that will enable agriculture, particularly in the developing countries, to meet the demands that are being placed on it by rapid growth of population and income" (Ruttan 1995, 149–50). In a similar vein, Frederick Buttel, a rural sociologist and biotechnology analyst, claims that future agricultural productivity growth on the scale of the first Green Revolution is implausible (Buttel 1995).[2]

Theoretical Antecedents of Modern Population Ideology

Eighteenth-century Europe faced a situation strikingly similar to our current population-resource predicament. Then—as now—phenomenal population growth was taking place, and it appeared (at least to some observers) that agricultural productivity could not possibly keep pace with this rate of growth. We now know, with the benefit of hindsight, that such concerns were completely unfounded. Although hundreds of millions of people are now malnourished, their misery has little to do with deficiencies of agricultural productivity. In the course of the last two centuries, technological development in agriculture has not only kept up with population growth but in general has tended to exceed it.[3]

We now turn to the theories of Thomas Robert Malthus, Karl Marx (together with Friedrich Engels), and Esther Boserup—the three key figures shaping modern population ideology. This brief review of their arguments is important for two reasons. First, aspects of each of their theories are as compelling and provocative today as when they were first proposed. Second, a basic grounding in their views is essential for understanding the six contemporary variants of their views.

Thomas Robert Malthus
The Reverend Thomas Robert Malthus (1766–1834), an economist, is best known for his dictum that human population tends to grow exponentially whereas agricultural production only grows arithmetically. As such, he is the father of population catastrophism—the belief that there is a natural tendency for

human numbers to exceed the natural resource base. He is less well known for an equally important theory saying it is counterproductive to relieve the misery of the poor. These two theories are closely related to each other, but they are presented separately to underscore an important fact. Modern followers of Malthus espouse either the first theory ("population catastrophism") alone or population catastrophism together with the second theory ("aid restraint"). As we shall see, the difference between these two outlooks is important.

Population Catastrophism
Malthus was born in the latter half of the eighteenth century—a time when the population of England and Wales was in the process of expanding rapidly (Kates 1996, 44). As explained in chapter 2, this was also a time when tens of thousands of impoverished rural families poured into London and other European industrial centers. In 1798 Malthus wrote *An Essay on the Principle of Population, as It Affects the Future Improvement of Society*. This was the first of many editions of this book. One of its central claims was that population grows exponentially (2, 4, 8, 16, 32, 64, etc.), whereas agricultural production grows at best arithmetically (1, 2, 3, 4, 5, 6, etc.). Population, in Malthus's view, tends to exhaust available resources and can only increase through the opening of new agricultural lands and/or changes in agricultural technology. He and fellow British economist David Ricardo (1772–1823) argued that human population increases until it comes into equilibrium with capital (i.e., land and equipment) (Cohen 1995, 37).

Malthus explained that the balance between population and resources is assured by disease and starvation among the poor—what he called "positive checks." He believed that conscious avoidance of pregnancy—which he called "preventive checks"—could only be practiced by the rich, not the poor. The poor, according to Malthus, were fundamentally incapable of "moral restraint," meaning that they were unable to rationally and consciously restrict their fertility in order to avert the constraints imposed by "positive checks."

Aid Restraint
Malthus vigorously objected on principle to any actions that might alleviate the plight of the poor. Accordingly, he worked tirelessly to reform England's so-called Poor Laws so that the state would restrict its aid to the poor. A passage from the second edition of *An Essay on the Principle of Population* illustrates this conviction:

> A man who is born into a world already possessed, if he cannot get subsistence from his parents on whom he has a just demand, and if the society do not want his labour, has no claim of *right* to the smallest portion of food, and, in fact, has no business to be where he is. At nature's mighty feast there is no vacant cover for him. She tells him to be gone, and will quickly execute her own orders, if he do not work upon the compassion of some of her guests. If the guests get up and make room for him, other intruders immediately appear demanding the same favor. (Malthus 1803, 531)

Malthus believed assistance to the poor would encourage them to reproduce beyond the level that available resources allow and would therefore aggravate their plight. He believed that poverty is a product of the laws of nature and therefore not subject to alteration through human intervention.

Malthus's advocacy of aid restraint can best be understood in terms of the political role he filled during his time. His philosophy and his actions supported capitalism and the institutions of private property. His first *Essay* was a polemic against William Godwin, an English radical seeking abolition of private property, and against the Marquis de Condorcet, a representative in France's Legislative Assembly who promoted government-provided subsidies to guarantee subsistence for the poor. Malthus's ideas served as an ideological bulwark against agitation by the English working class. He is clearly at the right of the political spectrum.

Karl Marx and Friedrich Engels

Karl Marx (1818–1883) and Friedrich Engels (1820–1895) vigorously denounced the "population catastrophism" and "aid restraint" of Malthus. Malthus had passed away by the time Marx and Engels were in their prime, but they were impelled to combat his ideological legacy. Much of Marx and Engels's work was the product of their antagonism to Malthus's ideas.

Marx and Engels argued that poverty and unemployment are not in any meaningful sense manifestations of excessive numbers of human beings pressing against limited resources, but instead are structural features of capitalism essential to the accumulation of riches by ruling elites. Poor people are not in "excess," in Marx and Engels's view, in the sense of exceeding the resources that can support them, but rather in the sense that capitalism requires a "reserve army of the unemployed" to depress wages. Laborers are far more willing to accept low wages if they are competing for scarce employment, and if the penalty for not accepting low wages is to be unemployed. Capitalism's structural requirement for a "reserve army of the unemployed" was what Marx and Engels called the "law of relative surplus population." Thus, as Marx explained in *Capital*,

> the laboring population therefore produces, along with the accumulation of capital produced by it, the means by which itself is made relatively superfluous, is turned into a relative surplus-population; and it does this to an always increasing extent. This is a law of population peculiar to the capitalist mode of production; and in fact every special historic mode of production has its own special laws of population, historically valid within its limits alone. ([1867] 1967, 631–32)

For Marx and Engels unemployment is in no way a natural and—by implication—an inevitable circumstance, as Malthus would have it, but instead a historically specific and alterable condition of human existence. And likewise the level of workers' wages is not simply determined by the prevailing price of grain, as Malthus and Ricardo contended but, in Marx and Engels's view, by the struggle between capitalists and workers (Foster 1999a, 63).

Friedrich Engels advanced the argument that the availability of food during times of hunger disproves the Malthusian view. As Engels explained, "I will not accept any defense of the Malthusian theory as competent which does not begin by explaining to me, on the basis of theory itself, how a people can die of hunger from sheer abundance, and which does not bring this explanation into harmony with reason and the facts" (Meek 1971, 61–62).

The stakes in the ideological diatribe of Marx and Engels against the legacy of Malthus were high because they were attempting nothing less than to reassign blame for poverty and misery from the victim (i.e., the poor) to the perpetrator (i.e., the rich). They were trying to convince people that an apparent excess of population over resources is a mirage created by Malthus that deflects attention away from the real reasons for poverty and misery. Theirs was an uphill battle because Malthus's views represented the dominant ideology and theirs the subordinate ideology.

Esther Boserup
Esther Boserup (1910–), a Danish agricultural economist, attacks the ideas of Malthus from another point of view. Her landmark book, *The Conditions of Agricultural Growth: The Economics of Agrarian Change under Population Pressure* (Boserup [1965] 1993) contends that Thomas Malthus was fundamentally wrong in claiming that agricultural productivity determines the level of population growth. She stood Malthus's theory on its head saying that, instead, human population is an independent variable determining the capacity of agricultural production (Boserup [1965] 1993, 11–12, 14, 22, 117–18).

A key component of her theory is the insight that the fertility of soil on a given piece of land is not fixed, but instead is subject to enhancement through human intervention. This, in her view, explains why successive stages of agrarian change have involved ever higher densities of human settlement leading to increased levels of productivity on a given piece of land through the process of agricultural intensification. Thus as the density of rural population increases, we see a transition from forest fallow to bush fallow to short rotation fallow to annual cropping and finally to multicropping systems, and each of these successive stages involves the possibility of significantly greater production of food per unit area of land.

Boserup acknowledges that not all human efforts in farming lead to enhancement of the fertility of soil and that some lead to declining fertility and destruction. This occurs, she claims, because of lack of knowledge about intensification ([1965] 1993, 22). She argues, nonetheless, that there have been impressive strides toward increased agricultural productivity, notwithstanding the campaign of "neo-Malthusians" to accumulate evidence of a world headed toward destruction ([1965] 1993, 21–22). Whereas Malthusianism inherently implies a pessimistic outlook (more people = less to go around), her revolutionary philosophy implies an optimistic outlook (more people = more to go around) (Boserup [1965] 1993, 117–18).

Contemporary Population Paradigms

The theories of Thomas Malthus, Karl Marx and Friedrich Engels, and Esther Boserup have shaped contemporary population paradigms. Their roles are key because each embodies a pivotal component of the population-resource debate. Malthus underscores the issue of ultimate biological limits, Marx and Engels emphasize equity in the distribution of resources, and Boserup sheds light on human creativity and technological development under conditions of scarcity.

Malthus is the intellectual progenitor of "neo-Malthusianism," defined here as the belief that human population growth is a key problem because it tends to dangerously exceed natural resource carrying capacity, threatening malnourishment, aggravated poverty, and environmental deterioration. Unlike Malthus, neo-Malthusians encourage contraceptive practices (see Humphrey and Buttel 1982, 72), though as we shall see, this is not always the case. Marx and Engels together with Boserup are the intellectual progenitors of anti-Malthusianism, defined here as the belief that human population growth is not a key problem. Anti-Malthusians may view population growth as *a* problem but not as a *key* problem, if they view it as a problem at all. They object vigorously to the importance accorded to population growth by neo-Malthusians, and, more importantly, they criticize the logic underpinning the neo-Malthusian argument.

The "despairing optimist" population perspective sits in the middle of the neo-Malthusianism and anti-Malthusianism polarity. Lloyd Evans applies the label to himself in the following passage:

> So the young scientist, as well as the reader, must find his/her own way between the unrelieved pessimism of Paul Ehrlich and Lester Brown, the "conditional" optimism of Daniel Hillel and the unconstrained optimism of Julian Simon. Since authors owe it to their readers to declare their dispositions, I am like René Dubos, a "despairing optimist." (1998, 222)

I apply the label to like-minded scientists (e.g., Cohen 1995; Dyson 1996; Conway 1997) who believe that population-resource imbalance is a serious problem, but one that can be rectified.[4] These scientists consciously distance themselves from both the pessimism of neo-Malthusians and the optimism of certain anti-Malthusians, believing the truth lies in the middle. Despairing optimist is an important category because it describes the mind-set of a group of influential thinkers and policy makers who work in centrist international organizations such as the World Bank, FAO, and IFPRI, as well as the larger CGIAR of which it is a part.

In this section these three population perspectives are cross-classified with the three social theory paradigms to describe the range of modern population paradigms. We first take the "wide" view, examining all cells of this cross-classification matrix, and then narrow our focus to three dominant population paradigms.

The Wide View: Six Population Paradigms

Cross-classification of the three population perspectives described above (neo-Malthusian, despairing optimist, and anti-Malthusian) with the three key social theory paradigms (class, managerial, and individualist) reveals six contemporary population paradigms (see table 4.1): (1) class neo-Malthusian, (2) managerial neo-Malthusian, (3) individualist neo-Malthusian, (4) managerial despairing optimist, (5) class anti-Malthusian, and (6) individualist anti-Malthusian. Note that, for all intents and purposes, there are no proponents of the three other theoretical possibilities: "class despairing optimist," "managerial anti-Malthusian," and "individualist despairing optimist."

Each of the three social theory paradigms (class, managerial, individualist) embraces diverse views on population. There is a strong tendency among partisans in the population-resource debate to falsely conflate the neo-Malthusian/anti-Malthusian opposition with categories on the political spectrum.[5] The entire neo-Malthusian to anti-Malthusian range is encompassed in the class and individualist paradigms, whereas the managerial paradigm displays a narrower range (neo-Malthusian to despairing optimist).

In each of the three social theory categories, only one of the two population paradigms is dominant in the polemical discussions among contemporary population paradigms: (1) class anti-Malthusian in the class paradigm, (2) managerial neo-Malthusian in the managerial paradigm, and (3) individualist anti-Malthusian in the individualist paradigm. The reasons for this dominance of particular population paradigms within social theory categories are discussed below in the section on the three dominant paradigms.

Class Neo-Malthusianism

The class neo-Malthusian paradigm states that, although Thomas Malthus may have been wrong in his contempt for the poor and advocacy of withholding aid, he was right that unrestrained population growth is a problem. In the early nineteenth century, Francis Place, a disciple of utilitarian philosopher Jeremy Bentham, encouraged working people to curb their fertility, arguing that restricting their numbers could drive up wages and also resolve other problems of the working class (Ross 1998, 25). A modern echo of this argument is found in Linder (1997, 310, 313), who laments that proletarian couples are acting against their class interests by not consciously restricting their fertility. Sarkar asserts that although Malthus was wrong for blaming the poor for their poverty, his belief in diminishing returns in agricultural production and of geometrical population growth are "as good as natural laws" (1997, 130–31).

Table 4.1. Cross-classification of Social Theory Paradigms and Population Perspectives (Neo-Malthusian, "Despairing Optimist," and Anti-Malthusian)

Population Perspective	Characteristic	Key Social Theory Paradigm		
		Class	Managerial	Individualist
Neo-Malthusian (Population is a key problem)	Key logic	Though Malthus was wrong in key ways, population increase *is* harmful.	Population dangerously exceeds resources and aid *alleviates* problem.	Population dangerously exceeds resources and aid *aggravates* problem.
	Progenitor Modern proponents	Thomas Malthus Linder (1997) Sarkar (1999)	Thomas Malthus Ehrlich (1996) Myers (1998) Brown et al. (1999) Engelman et al. (2000)	Thomas Malthus Hardin (1968, 1993) Abernethy (1994) McNicoll (1998)
"Despairing optimist"	Key logic		Population-resource imbalance is a serious problem but it can be rectified.	
	Progenitor Modern proponents		René Dubos Evans (1998) Cohen (1995) Dyson (1996) Conway (1997)	
Anti-Malthusian (Population is not a key problem)	Key logic	"Surplus population" inherent to capitalism; poverty and inequality cause high fertility.		Population growth is not a problem; it is good for society in the long run.
	Progenitor Modern proponents	Marx & Engels Mamdani (1972) Murdoch (1980) Lappé & Schurman (1989) Lappé et al. (1998) Ross (1998)		Esther Boserup Simon (1996) Wattenberg (1997) Kasun (1999) CEI (1999) Eberstadt (2000b)

Managerial Neo-Malthusianism
Managerial neo-Malthusians believe that population growth tends to danger-ously exceed the earth's carrying capacity, leading to malnutrition, poverty, and environmental destruction. The linkage between population growth and en-vironmental destruction is a relatively recent theme, dating back to the mid-twentieth century. There are two characteristics of managerial neo-Malthusians that distinguish them sharply from Malthus. First, invariably they advocate pop-ulation planning and other programs aimed at restricting fertility. Second, they strongly support various forms of government aid to the poor, believing that such aid is essential for restricting fertility. Managerial neo-Malthusians agree with Malthus's "population catastrophism," but they firmly reject his philosophy of "aid restraint." The most prominent modern managerial neo-Malthusianism sup-porters are Ehrlich (1996); Myers (1991, 1998); Brown et al. (1999); and Engel-man et al. (2000). Two Washington, D.C., institutions are linked to managerial neo-Malthusianism: the Worldwatch Institute (Lester Brown, president), and Population Action International (Robert Engelman, vice president for research).

Individualist Neo-Malthusianism
Like managerial neo-Malthusians, individualist neo-Malthusians believe that population growth tends to dangerously exceed the earth's carrying capacity, leading to malnutrition, poverty, and environmental destruction. However, un-like their managerial counterparts, individualist neo-Malthusians believe that providing aid is not warranted because it aggravates the problem of excessive population growth. Proponents of individualist neo-Malthusianism are therefore authentic modern disciples of Malthus inasmuch as they espouse both "popula-tion catastrophism" and "aid restraint."

Garrett Hardin (1968), for example, in his much cited article "The Tragedy of the Commons," argued that demographic and environmental pressures are best re-solved by assigning private property rights rather than by "welfare" provisions, and through a moral transformation toward acceptance of fertility limitations. Follow-ing Malthus, Hardin (1993, 294, 302, 309) says the negative consequences of pop-ulation growth function appropriately to limit excess human fertility. Believing that aid to the poor increases fertility, he says the only form of safe foreign aid is infor-mation on birth control, and he advocates against rich countries receiving immi-grants from poor countries (Hardin 1993, 294, 305, 307). Virginia Abernethy also echoes the main messages put forward by Malthus. She implies that the fertility de-cisions of the poor are irrational (Abernethy 1994, 84–91).[6] She says development aid aggravates rapid population growth by encouraging the poor to believe that they can live at a higher level of prosperity than their local resources allow, and she therefore argues for income inequality and against income redistribution to curb fer-tility in poor countries (Abernethy 1991, 1993, 1994). Hardin (1993, 305) and Abernethy (1995) both dismiss the demographic transition theory, explaining that development accelerates rather than slows population growth.

Managerial Despairing Optimism
The hallmark of the managerial despairing optimists is the belief that the population-resource nexus is now, or is potentially, a serious problem, but that it is potentially solvable. They believe the problem should be addressed mainly through research, technological development, legal and regulatory reform, and management of the market economy. Recall that these proposed remedies are the classic tools of the managerial paradigm (see chapter 3). Proponents (e.g., Evans 1998; Cohen 1995; Dyson 1996; Conway 1997) tend to be affiliated with the international institutions that have a key formal role in addressing the population-resource issues (e.g., the World Bank, FAO, IFPRI, CGIAR).

Class Anti-Malthusianism
Following Marx and Engels, class anti-Malthusians assert that poverty and malnutrition do not result from population growth but inhere in capitalism. They stand Malthusian theory "on its head." They argue that high fertility does not cause poverty, but rather poverty (and inequality) cause high rates of fertility. The poor, they argue, need many children to increase household income and to provide social security during old age. Prominent proponents of class anti-Malthusianism include Mamdani (1972), Murdoch (1980), Lappé and Schurman (1989), Lappé et al. (1998), and Ross (1998). The Institute for Food and Development Policy in San Francisco, California, formerly directed by Frances Moore Lappé, is the most visible institutional advocate of class anti-Malthusianism.

Individualist Anti-Malthusianism
Individualist anti-Malthusians believe that population growth is not a problem and can benefit society in the long term. This is Boserup's general position although, as noted earlier, she acknowledged that population growth led to some forms of environmental destruction. Other proponents of individualist anti-Malthusianism (e.g., Simon 1981, 1996; Wattenberg 1997; Kasun 1999; Eberstadt 2000a, 2000b, 2001) differ from Boserup. They extend their optimistic outlook on human creativity and productivity beyond the realm of agriculture to all economic activities. Further, they tend to argue for free market capitalism. The Competitive Enterprise Institute (1999) in Washington, D.C., supports individualist anti-Malthusian views.

The Focused View: Three Dominant Paradigms

This section examines the three dominant modern population paradigms: class anti-Malthusianism, managerial neo-Malthusianism, and individualist anti-Malthusianism. We look at how and why these paradigms are dominant in their respective social theory categories and then explore their characteristics.

Patterns of Dominance and the Reasons for Them

Neo-Malthusianism is the dominant population paradigm in the political center (i.e., managerial paradigm), and anti-Malthusianism is dominant both on the political left (class paradigm) and the right (individualist paradigm). These three patterns of dominance are evident to people familiar with literature on the population debate.

On the left, the writings of Frances Moore Lappé and other anti-Malthusians have been disseminated and cited far more widely than those taking a leftist neo-Malthusian stance. Discussion on population in the managerial center is dominated by four neo-Malthusian figures: Lester Brown, Paul Ehrlich, Norman Myers, and Robert Engelman, and there are no notable anti-Malthusian voices at all. (Proponents of "despairing optimism" in the political center are politically powerful and visible, but recall that they deliberately refrain from taking part in the polemics.) On the right, the anti-Malthusian position of Julian Simon has towered over that of neo-Malthusian individualists, and others following him (Ben Wattenberg, Jacqueline Kasun, Nicholas Eberstadt) maintain that hegemonic viewpoint. Are these tendencies deeply rooted? I would argue that they are, though some deviations from the patterns might raise questions about the degree of rootedness.[7]

Is there any underlying logic to these patterns of dominance within each of the social theory paradigms? There is no firm empirical evidence to explain these patterns, but the following hypothetical arguments might help explain them.

Anti-Malthusian Dominance in the Class Paradigm

Dating back to the time of Marx, writers in the class perspective have been exceedingly reluctant to cede any theoretical ground to Malthus. To do so implicitly undermines the force of the argument that capitalist class oppression governs world affairs, and that food deprivation for the poor is *distributional* rather than absolute. To cede this ground, it is believed, takes attention away from the fact that famine almost always occurs in the midst of plenty. The class neo-Malthusian belief that excessive fertility undermines the bargaining power of the working class has some grounding in logic. This position, however, tends to have weak backing on the left because it implies that working-class fertility decisions are irrational and tends to contravene the argument that the poor have large numbers of children because it is economically advantageous to do so.

Neo-Malthusian Dominance in the Managerial Paradigm

We have seen that the political role of managerialism is to balance state concerns about general human welfare with the imperative of stable capitalist economic growth. From this theoretical vantage point, adherence to neo-Malthusianism (i.e., "population catastrophism") makes eminent sense. From the managerial point of view, rapid population growth and consequent famine, environmental destruction, social upheaval, political dissent, conflict, and war potentially undermine the stability of long-term governance. There are, of course, national governments that have pronatalist policies, but these are exceptional. In the last several decades, most national governments have engaged in some form of population planning.

Managerialism is the theoretical home for the strongest proponents of neo-Malthusianism in the same way that it is the home for the strongest proponents of sustainable development (see chapter 3). This is no accident. Managerial neo-Malthusianism and sustainable development are both strongly grounded in the fundamentals of managerialism: acceptance if not advocacy of government planning, acceptance or encouragement of an activist posture by developed country governments in international affairs, strong attention to policy reform, and belief in aid to alleviate social and environmental problems.

Anti-Malthusian Dominance in the Individualist Paradigm
Anti-Malthusianism and (more specifically) pronatalism are dominant in the individualist paradigm in part because these positions are consistent with the long-term structural objectives of unrestrained capitalism. Human population increase over time means a growing number of producers and consumers, leading to increased potential for profits and growth of the capitalist economy. For this reason among others, individualist anti-Malthusians are deeply concerned about a downturn in fertility and population size, particularly in the United States and countries of the West. Wattenberg explains that "modern capitalism has always been rooted in the economic fact of vigorously expanding domestic markets. That phase is ending. The ensuing turbulence will be difficult—though not impossible—to deal with" (1987, 7).

However, even if population growth experiences a downward trend, the interests of capitalism are at least partly maintained. Wattenberg says:

> Changing demographic patterns offer a split vision of the economic future. Existing businesses tend to do better when their potential customer base grows. For a while there will be plenty of extra customers coming on stream no matter what projection is used (two billion more, even under the low scenario). (1997, 63)

Individualist anti-Malthusians have other concerns related to the prospect of population decline. Wattenberg (1987) is alarmed at the prospect that fertility decline in the United States and the West would lead to loss of global hegemony of Western values and loss of U.S. control over the world political agenda. Eberstadt (1997, 2000a, 2001) voices concern about the socioeconomic consequences of a "population implosion."

If both managerialists and individualists (at least implicitly) believe in capitalism, why then does neo-Malthusianism "fit" better in the managerial paradigm and "anti-Malthusianism" in the individualist paradigm? Though the reasons are not clear, one explanation may be that managerialists tend to emphasize stability over growth, whereas individualists (and in particular free market individualists) tend to emphasize growth over stability.

One might also ask, Why did the political right support Malthusianism in Malthus's time, while now it mostly opposes Malthusianism? The answer is not clear, but one can speculate that in the eighteenth and nineteenth centuries, massive poverty, political agitation, and revolutionary movements were the primary threats to the growth of markets, whereas in the late twentieth and twenty-first centuries, slowdown in the increase of producers and consumers is a larger threat to the growth of markets.

Characteristics of the Three Dominant Paradigms

Table 4.2 displays characteristics of the three dominant population paradigms through quotes by proponents on (1) the essence of the population-resource issue, (2) the fertility behavior of the poor, (3) the consequences of rapid population growth, (4) the possibility of a second Green Revolution, and (5) solutions to rapid population growth. By comparing and contrasting views on these topics, we will gain a deeper understanding of the three paradigms.

Essence of the Issue according to Class Anti-Malthusians

As the quotes from Mamdani (1972, 14), Perelman (1996, 76), and Lappé et al. (1998, 40) illustrate, class anti-Malthusianism adheres to the Marxist anti-Malthusian tradition. The capitalist economic system is viewed as the fundamental problem, and scrutiny of that system reveals that things are not what they appear to be. "Excess population," poverty, and hunger are in no way natural but rather derive from the economic system serving capitalists. Mamdani (1972) claims that poverty and inequality cause high rates of fertility, not vice versa.

Essence of the Issue according to Managerial Neo-Malthusians

The quotes from Osborn ([1948] 1968, 44), Ehrlich (1968, xi), Engelman (1997, 48), and Brown (2000, 5) demonstrate that managerial neo-Malthusianism is consistent with Malthus's concern that population growth can exceed the resource base. However, managerial neo-Malthusians' perception of the issue differs substantially from that of Malthus. Malthus focused on the balance between the population of the poor and agricultural production, and he believed there was a tendency toward equilibrium through a *necessary and inevitable* ongoing catastrophe of famine, misery, and poverty. Managerial neo-Malthusians look beyond famine and agriculture to depletion of resources and environmental pollution, and although focusing on the poor of developing countries, they also give attention to the problem of overconsumption of resources by the rich.

Another crucial difference is that managerial neo-Malthusians believe the excess of population over resources is neither necessary nor inevitable; while there

Table 4.2. Characteristics of Main Competing Modern Population Paradigms

	Three Dominant Paradigms		
Views	*Class Anti-Malthusian*	*Managerial Neo-Malthusian*	*Individualist Anti-Malthusian*
Essence of issue	[P]eople are not poor because they have large families. Quite to the contrary: they have large families because they are poor (Mamdani 1972, 14). Unemployment and poverty cannot be reduced to natural laws; rather, they reveal fundamental flaws in capitalist society. . . . What appears as a "Malthusian problem" was, in reality, a reflection of a contradiction within capitalist society (Perelman, 1996, 76). Rapid population growth is not the root cause of hunger but is—like hunger—a consequence of social inequities that deprive the poor majority, especially poor women, of the security and economic opportunity for them to choose fewer children (Lappé et al. 1998, 40).	Shades of Malthus! He was not so far wrong when he postulated that the increase in population tends to exceed the ability of the earth to support it . . . (Osborn [1948] 1968, 44). The birth rate must be brought into balance with the death rate or mankind will breed itself into oblivion (Ehrlich, 1968, xi). Population growth at current rates challenges the planet's long-term habitability (Engelman, 1997, 48). The projected growth in population over the next half-century may more directly affect economic progress than any other single trend, exacerbating nearly all other environmental and social problems (Brown 2000, 5).	The ultimate resource is people—skilled, spirited, hopeful people—who will exert their wills and imaginations for their own benefit as well as in a spirit of faith and social concern. Inevitably they will benefit not only themselves but the poor and the rest of us as well (Simon, 1996: xxxviii). The evidence of the last hundred years suggests that rather than increasing resource scarcity, there will continue to be greater abundance even with an increasing population (Competitive Enterprise Institute 1999). The very conception of "population problems" is inherently ambiguous and arbitrary, lending itself to faulty analysis and inappropriate diagnoses (Eberstadt 2000b: 1).

Table 4.2. Characteristics of Main Competing Modern Population Paradigms (*Continued*)

Views	*Three Dominant Paradigms*		
	Class Anti-Malthusian	*Managerial Neo-Malthusian*	*Individualist Anti-Malthusian*
Fertility behavior of poor	[T]he great mass of poverty-stricken peoples of the world have large families because they are poor and *because having a large family is the economically rational decision for poor parents to make* (Murdoch 1980, 26).	[No consistent pattern of views.]	Well-off people who believe that the poor do not weigh the consequences of having more children are simply arrogant, or ignorant, or both (Simon 1996, 6). [I]t is clear that there are constraints on population growth and that families do respond rationally to these constraints (Kasun 1999, 84).
Consequences of rapid population growth	*Taking Population Seriously* (Lappé & Schurman 1989) The population is projected to stabilize . . . most likely below 11.5 billion. . . . that is within the levels that most experts estimate the earth could support (Lappé et al. (1998, 27).	Population growth generates an entire series of adverse consequences. Environments are misused and overused. Per-capita economic advance is slowed and per-capita food production stagnates. Social services are overburdened. Development generally proceeds at a slower pace (Myers1993, 152).	Population growth is a problem, but not *just* a problem. . . . We shall see that additional persons produce more than they consume in the long run. (Simon 1996, 4). [T]he statistical evidence indicates that among *developing* countries more rapid population growth may be associated with more rapid growth per capita output (Kasun 1999, 65).

Possibility of a second Green Revolution	Because the Green Revolution approach does nothing to address the insecurity that lies at the root of high birth rates—and can even heighten that insecurity—it cannot buy time while population growth slows (Lappé et al. 1998, 60).	To grow that much food, we shall need to farm all the world's current croplands as productively as Iowa's best cornfields, or three times the present world average (Myers 1998, 20).	Doomsday forecasts about population growth outstripping the food supply that take no account of these possibilities [progress in genetic engineering] surely are seriously inadequate (Simon 1996, 104).
Solutions to rapid population growth	Only in a society where resources are more or less equitably apportioned will we be able to move beyond the Malthusian politics of population to a real consideration of human reproductive rights and needs, where the desire for fewer children will be matched by a need for fewer offspring (Ross 1998, 222). To bring the human population into balance with economic resources and the environment, societies must address the extreme maldistribution of access to resources—land, jobs, food, education, and health care. That is our real challenge (Lappé et al. 1998, 40).	We can no longer afford merely to treat the symptoms of the cancer of population growth; the cancer itself must be cut out. Population control is the only answer (Ehrlich 1968, :xi). [I]t is national governments that will decide the fate of people. They allocate most of the resources, formulate population and agricultural policies, and decide how resources are distributed (Brown & Kane 1994, 212). It will take more than science and economics to solve humanity's basic predicament—it will take an ethical revolution and strong commitment (Ehrlich et al. 1995, 247).	It is wealth—not poverty—that limits family size, limits obesity, limits pollution, limits waste and inefficiency limits personal consumption. It is the rich, not the poor, who pour their wealth into green (Huber 1999, xxvi). For its part, the market economy provides restraints on its participants—restraints that prevent them from overpopulating or overinvesting or any excessive behavior detrimental to society (Kasun 1999, 94).

is an ongoing catastrophe, there are larger catastrophes on the horizon. One theme in recent neo-Malthusian literature is the possibility that certain high-fertility countries in stage 2 of the demographic transition (e.g., Ethiopia, Nigeria, and Pakistan) will revert to stage 1 (high mortality and high fertility status). This "demographic trap" is complemented by "demographic fatigue," where governments of such countries, financially and organizationally worn down by the stress of high rates of population growth, are unable to achieve the level of economic development that would enable them to reach stage 3 (Brown et al. 1999, 117–18). Other themes concerning existing or imminent catastrophe include the relationship of rapid population growth to conflict and war (Myers 1987; Myers 1993; Myers 1994; Engelman 1997, 45), "environmental refugees" and international migration (Myers 1997; Engelman 1997, 19), the global repercussions of projected agricultural production shortfall in China (Brown 1995; Brown 1996; Brown 1998a, 269), and linkage of rapid population growth to global warming (Engelman 1998), deforestation (Gardner-Outlaw and Engleman 1999), and biodiversity loss (Cincotta and Engelman 2000).

Essence of the Issue according to Individualist Anti-Malthusians
The quotes from Simon (1996, xxxviii), the Competitive Enterprise Institute (1999), and Eberstadt (2000b) are consistent with a Boserupian outlook. They believe that population pressure can ultimately be beneficial; such pressure tends to induce creativity and innovation. However, as indicated earlier, individualist anti-Malthusians have gone well beyond Boserup's focus on agricultural systems, and unlike Boserup, they tend to be messianically optimistic about the social and environmental implications of population growth.

Julian Simon pioneered the individualist anti-Malthusian argument. It says population and income increase in the development process lead to increased demand for resources and finished products, thereby increasing prices and spurring a search for alternative resources. Eventually, substitute resources are found that are cheaper, thus raising standards of living (Simon 1990, 2; Simon 1992, xi; Simon 1996, 12–13). The energy transition from wood fuel to coal and then to oil and nuclear power is offered as an example. To Simon, natural resources are not finite in the economic sense because substitutes can always be found, and per capita income is said to be likely to increase with growing population (Simon 1996, 6). Kasun (1999) builds on the arguments of Simon, emphasizing the beneficial effects of free markets while denouncing planned economies and socialism. Some individualist anti-Malthusians are anxious about an anticipated slowdown of world population growth rates. Wattenberg, who lamented a "birth dearth" in the 1980s (Wattenberg 1987), says that the U.N. revised downward forecast of future population growth will create "its own set of problems" (Wattenberg 1997, 60). Eberstadt (2000a) warns that "the specter of 'depopulation'" may lead to increased average age, increased health care problems, challenges to training a younger generation, strains on social security systems as the ratio of pensioners to members of the labor force increases, and loneliness as people have fewer and fewer blood siblings. He says an imminent population implosion threatens to "set back the progress of human development" (Eberstadt 2001).

Fertility Behavior of the Poor

Both class anti-Malthusians (e.g., Murdoch 1980, 26) and individualist anti-Malthusians (e.g., Simon 1996, 6; Kasun 1999, 84) tend to believe that the fertility decisions of the poor are rational, in the sense of being thought through and in keeping with their perception of their best interests. For both paradigms, the assertion is framed as an objection to Malthusianism. Interestingly, however, managerial neo-Malthusians are largely silent on the issue of the fertility behavior of the poor, and mentions of the matter show no consistent philosophical position. Managerial neo-Malthusians appear to have distanced themselves from Malthus's negative outlook on the behavior of the poor. There is evidence of this, for example, in Population Action International's endorsement of the position—launched at the International Conference on Population and Development held in Cairo in 1994—that all people should be free to make their own parenting choices, free of coercion (Engelman 1997, 51; Engelman et al. 2000, 5).

Consequences of Rapid Population Growth

Both class anti-Malthusians and individualist anti-Malthusians acknowledge that rapid population growth does present a problem, but they insist it is in no way *the* problem, nor an unmanageable one. The title of Lappé and Schurman's (1989) book, *Taking Population Seriously*, deliberately challenged leftists' long-standing assumption that population alarmism is only a smokescreen. But their main project is to show that inequality, poverty, and powerlessness cause rapid population growth and therefore deserve privileged attention. Individualist anti-Malthusians grudgingly (if at all) acknowledge a problem and dwell on the benefits to society they claim result from population growth (Simon 1996, 4; Kasun 1999, 65). Managerial neo-Malthusians markedly disagree. Almost invariably they portray population growth as *the* global problem, with negative repercussions experienced in all aspects of our lives (e.g., Myers 1993, 152).

Possibility of a Second Green Revolution

Class anti-Malthusians and managerial neo-Malthusians both doubt the possibility of a second Green Revolution, though their reasons are quite different. Lappé et al. (1998, 60) explain that increasing agricultural productivity alone does nothing to address the underlying causes of hunger (income insecurity, poverty, and inequality) and is therefore an inadequate course of action. Managerial neo-Malthusians imply that the challenge of raising world agricultural productivity to the level of the United States is impossible (e.g., Myers 1998, 20). This tends to underscore their point that the size of the world's population is already far too high and should be reduced. Individualist anti-Malthusians are unremittingly optimistic about the possibility of a successful second Green Revolution (e.g., Simon 1996, 104).

Solutions to Rapid Population Growth
The proposed solutions to rapid population growth, predictably, reflect the social theory paradigms in which they originate. Class anti-Malthusians believe a stable population-resource balance can only be achieved by first addressing severe income inequalities and the powerlessness of the poor (e.g., Ross 1998, 222; Lappé et al. 1998, 40). Neo-Malthusians favor aid programs aimed at fertility reduction (e.g., access to contraception and family planning services, improved education for girls, and employment opportunities for women), national and international policy decisions (e.g., follow-through on decisions made at the 1994 Cairo ICPD meeting, etc.), as well as overhauling our belief systems (e.g., Ehrlich 1968, xi; Brown and Kane 1994, 212; Ehrlich et al. 1995, 247). Individualist anti-Malthusians claim that producing wealth through the growth of capitalism and free markets will ultimately reduce high fertility rates (e.g., Huber 1999, xxvi; Kasun 1999, 94).

Paradigm Isolation and Integration

Our discussion so far has underscored the fact that modern population paradigms could not be more polarized. Whereas one group sees population growth as the problem, another sees population growth as the solution, and still another argues that the number of people is ultimately irrelevant when viewed through the perspective of equity.

The population-resource debate will surely sharpen—not abate—in coming years despite the U.N. forecast of declining population growth. Even the low growth scenario (almost 2 additional billion people by 2050) implies escalation of existing environmental challenges, and even individualist anti-Malthusians would acknowledge that agricultural scientists are still nowhere near producing revolutionary improvements in agricultural productivity. Moreover, poverty and the lack of purchasing power of the poor are colossal problems that are nowhere near to resolution.

The stakes in this ideological battle are high. Since World War II, the United States has seen major shifts in the prevailing population paradigms. From 1945 through 1974, the neo-Malthusian fertility control agenda had the upper hand in shaping policy before declining at the international level between 1974 and 1985, partly through the influence of Julian Simon (Ahlburg 1998, 317–18). From 1985 through the late 1990s, Simon's anti-Malthusian views held sway in domestic U.S. policy, while neo-Malthusianism prevailed internationally

(Ahlburg 1998, 317–18). The first major policy decision of the George W. Bush administration in January 2001 was a frontal attack against the international neo-Malthusian agenda. Bush reimposed a 1984–1993 policy that prohibits U.S. financial support for family planning organizations abroad that use funding from any other source to provide abortion counseling, referrals, or services.

Given the certainty of continued polarization, as well as the real-world consequences of population policy changes, it is useful to examine how the concepts of paradigm isolation and paradigm integration apply to the population-resource debate. This section examines the logic of paradigm isolation and provides evidence of tentative steps toward integration, before proposing a blueprint for possible theoretical integration among the three main population paradigms. The section ends with an evaluation of two formal efforts to integrate population paradigms.

The Logic of Isolation
Recall that paradigm isolation is the tendency of proponents of a given theoretical paradigm to elevate the tenets of their home paradigm either through outright rejection of the tenets of a competing paradigm, through subordination of competing tenets to the "prime mover" logic of the home paradigm, or through ignoring the tenets of competing paradigms. Each of the three main population paradigms has an underlying logic for its paradigm isolation that is summarized in table 4.3.

Class anti-Malthusians, positioned on the left and primarily motivated by allegiance to the marginalized poor, give priority attention to equity. From this vantage point, and given the reality of rampant poverty and malnutrition despite sufficient food supplies, there is little logical justification to prioritize either limiting resource use or increasing agricultural productivity. While proponents of this paradigm acknowledge that resource constraints and human potential are legitimate issues, they subordinate these factors to their overarching concern for equity and the systematic undermining of equity in a capitalist world economy.

Managerial neo-Malthusians, as centrists seeking to balance the interests of the poor and those of business, privilege the issue that appears to most directly threaten stable governance and resource management: an excess of population over resource limits. Equity and human potential are readily acknowledged as important issues, though they tend to be subordinated to the imperative of reducing the number of humans to a more manageable level.

Individualist anti-Malthusians, positioned on the right and defending and promoting capitalist enterprise and unencumbered free markets, focus on individual human potential, creativity, and productivity. They admit that equity is a problem inasmuch as poverty continues to exist and that population growth can in certain circumstances cause difficulties. However, for them, equity and resource limits are at best secondary, contingent concerns. They argue rich countries are proof that capitalist economic development will ultimately raise standards of living and lower fertility rates.

Table 4.3. Paradigm Isolation among the Three Main Modern Population Paradigms

Position on the Political Spectrum	Left	Center	Right
Paradigm	Class Anti-Malthusianism	Managerial Neo-Malthusianism	Individualist Anti-Malthusianism
Issue viewed as key	Equity	Resource Limits	Human Potential
Primary ideological motivations	Allegiance to the marginalized poor	Stable governance and resource management by balancing the interests of the poor and of business	Allegiance to capitalist enterprise and to the ideal of unencumbered markets
Nature of and reason for isolation	Proponents give limited attention to resource limits and production potential, because of sufficient existing food stocks, and inadequate and unfair distribution.	Proponents relegate issues of equity and productive capability to secondary status because of pressing urgency of environmental problems resulting from population pressure.	Proponents tend to dismiss the relevance of class and resource limits because of past promethean productivity of capitalism.

Evidence of Integration

As explained in earlier chapters, the "prime mover" logic in ideological thinking tends to lead to oversimplification of arguments and dismissal of perspectives and information that appear to challenge the tenets of the home paradigm. Proponents of an ideological position are often forced to revise and amend their worldview when confronted with facts or arguments that bring the complexity of real-life situations into full view. Table 4.4 summarizes some of the ways in which proponents of all three main population paradigms have yielded to the insights of their theoretical adversaries. As we shall see later on, this in no way amounts to capitulation or fundamental realignment of beliefs, but it does open up prospects for fruitful dialog and for ultimately crossing paradigm boundaries in meaningful ways.

Class Anti-Malthusian Acceptance of Managerial Neo-Malthusian Tenets
Foster says that "population growth is one of the most serious problems of the contemporary age" (1998, 17). Although, as indicated earlier, such statements are occasionally made by class anti-Malthusians, these acknowledgments are seldom accompanied by an in-depth discussion of the social and environmental implications of rapid population growth. One gets the distinct impression, no matter what has

been said, that the full meaning of resource limitations does not figure prominently in the minds of class anti-Malthusians. Lappé et al. (1998, 104–5) say there is a role for government in ending hunger, but only if a given government is beholden to the will of the majority and not to elites. This is a partial accommodation to managerial thinking (i.e., government and policy having an important role), but it is a contingent proposition, subject to the (unlikely) condition that the majority and not elites control the government in question.

Class Anti-Malthusian Acceptance of Individualist Anti-Malthusian Tenets
In a similar vein, Lappé et al. (1998, 104, 120, 174) state that market forces can be useful for solving hunger as long as purchasing power is widely dispersed; trade can be useful in ending hunger as long as it is directed toward meeting the interests of the poor and not the interests of elites. What is really being said is that there needs to be a wholesale transformation toward an egalitarian economic system, and only then can the arguments of the individualists (free markets and free trade) be taken seriously.

Managerial Neo-Malthusian Acceptance of Class Anti-Malthusian Tenets
Managerial neo-Malthusian writings are replete with denunciations of high levels of resource consumption in the countries of the North (e.g., Ehrlich 1968, 133; Myers 1993, 23) and calls for equity and justice and the elimination of poverty (e.g., Myers 1993, 16; Ehrlich et al. 1995, 7, 63–64; Ehrlich 1996, 28; Engelman 1997, 7, 9; Engelman et al. 2000, 3). In one striking statement Ehrlich and Ehrlich say that

> Marxists . . . are largely correct in emphasizing the importance of the political and economic dimensions of the human predicament. The world is increasingly divided between the haves and the have-nots. (1991, 250)

Despite statements that occasionally give them the appearance of being of one mind with proponents of the class perspective, managerial neo-Malthusians never question the legitimacy of capitalism. Such silence speaks volumes.

Managerial Neo-Malthusian Acceptance of Individualist Anti-Malthusian Tenets
Managerial neo-Malthusians occasionally acknowledge the stupendous advances in agricultural productivity in the twentieth century (e.g., Brown and Kane 1994, 210; Brown et al. 1999, 33). This is only a partial, backward-looking concession to the tenets of free market individualism. Managerial neo-Malthusians firmly believe that technological prometheanism in agriculture is a thing of the past, and that when all is said and done, Malthus will be shown to have been "ahead of his time" (Brown et al. 1999, 23). Other apparent concessions to individualist anti-Malthusianism tend to be forms of contingent isolation, where population-resource balance is the first order

of priority and other considerations are secondary. For example, Engelman et al., alluding to Simon, say that "it may be that *human* resources are the most important for development and prosperity, yet history and current experience demonstrate that this is most true when *natural* resources are abundant, cheap and accessible to all" (2000, 3). Another statement, following a similar logic, claims that "good policy instruments and vibrant competitive markets are crucial in converting the opportunities created by fertility decline into economic assets" (Cincotta and Engelman 1997, 20).

Individualist Anti-Malthusian Acceptance of Class Anti-Malthusian Tenets
I find no evidence of individualist anti-Malthusian acceptance of class anti-Malthusian tenets. This is a measure of how vigorously individualist anti-Malthusians reject the notions that capitalism is the fundamental problem in world affairs and that inequality must be resolved as a first order of business.

Individualist Anti-Malthusian Acceptance of Managerial Neo-Malthusian Tenets
As noted earlier, individualist anti-Malthusians occasionally acknowledge that rapid population growth can cause social and environmental problems. However, it is a pervasive belief among them that population planning programs are ineffective. Eberstadt breaks rank when he observes, "It is true that most of the developing countries reporting major fertility declines in recent decades *did* have national birth control programs in place" (2000a, 76).

Bases for Further Integration
Steps made to date toward population paradigm integration by the various proponents have been insignificant when judged against the scope of possibilities. Although some of the steps made were inspired by genuine efforts to break new ground (e.g., managerial statements on the importance of equity can be seen in that light), other steps are motivated by an attempt to bolster the "prime mover" logic of the home paradigm and border on being examples of contingent isolation.

A more genuine and useful form of integration of the three main population paradigms would have to start from the premise that each perspective contains an essential element of the complete picture. In short we must acknowledge (1) massive poverty and hunger in the midst of plenty, and their causes, in any discussion of the population resource-balance; (2) that the population-resource imbalance will reach, or has already reached, catastrophic levels, the issue of distribution notwithstanding; and (3) that human ingenuity, so prolific in the past, will continue to play an indispensable role in meeting our resource scarcity challenges.

The ideological obstacles to putting these three premises on an equal standing are formidable. *Full* population paradigm integration is out of the question because rigid and powerful (yet almost always unspoken) political loyalties make it extremely difficult to set aside the "prime mover" logic that inhibits the crossing of paradigm boundaries. Moreover, full population paradigm integration is not possible, in part because one cannot hold that population growth is both the essence of the problem and the essence of the solution.

There is, however, fertile ground for *partial* integration. First, it is possible to theorize that population is both a problem and also a solution by replacing "either-or" logic with "both-and" logic. Second, it is useful for proponents to understand the ways in which "prime mover thinking" induces them to emphasize information that favors their argument and to downplay or ignore information unfavorable to their argument. For example, managerial neo-Malthusians tend to skillfully marshal data on the absolute numbers of future additions to world population, while downplaying attention to the deceleration of growth. Conversely, individualist anti-Malthusians emphasize the deceleration of growth and pay little heed to the implications of additional billions of people. Third, and by far the most difficult, is for proponents to attempt to put aside their mind-sets and preconceived notions to attain an enhanced understanding of the problem and an effective solution. Lappé et al. recognize the magnitude of this challenge when they say, "At a time when the old 'isms' are clearly failing, many cling even more tenaciously to them" (1998, 178). Arizpe and Velázquez observe that "the population-environment debate has become deadlocked because it has become a question of taking sides instead of delving deeply into the complexity of the issues" (1994, 16).

Class and individualist anti-Malthusian proponents are separated by the widest *political* gulf, being at the extremes of the political spectrum. Nevertheless they share common ground, not only by sharing opposition to Malthusianism but also because of their tendency toward antistatism. Although the political gulf hinders meaningful reconciliation between the two paradigms, the list of "strange bedfellow" affinities is striking. Both class and individualist anti-Malthusians believe (1) the fertility decisions of the poor are rational;[8] (2) social and economic structure and not population are key;[9] (3) the racist views and eugenic programs of certain neo-Malthusians are contemptible (e.g., Ross 1998, 59–73; Kasun 1999, 212–17); and (4) state policies are a major cause of hunger (e.g., Lappé et al. 1998, 103; Eberstadt 2000b, 195).

In ending this section, I refer to a telling instance of population paradigm integration. Lappé et al. (1998, 60–61) point out that in 1986, the World Bank reached a conclusion that agreed with a principle that Lappé and her institution had championed for years. The study concluded that, given existing surplus stocks of food, a key policy step should be to redistribute purchasing power to the hungry so that they can get access to those stocks. This crossing of paradigm boundaries at the World Bank was evidently achieved not through dialog nor through expanding theoretical horizons, but rather through empirical research. Arguably, the breakthrough might have happened sooner if communication across paradigm boundaries had been more fluid and effective. For this reason, we will now turn to the work of theoreticians consciously trying to break down barriers among the main population paradigms.

Table 4.4. Evidence of Paradigm Integration Among Main Contemporary Population Paradigms

Home Paradigm	Target Paradigm	Examples of Paradigm Integration
Class anti-Malthusian	Managerial neo-Malthusian	Rapid population growth is a legitimate concern even if it is not a "prime mover."
		Government has a useful role in ending hunger if it is beholden to the will of the majority.
	Free-market anti-Malthusian	Markets can be useful for solving hunger as long as purchasing power widely dispersed.
		Trade can be useful for ending hunger as long as it is directed at meeting interests of poor and not of elites.
Managerial neo-Malthusian	Class anti-Malthusian	High consumption in North, unequal power relations, and poverty are key issues.
	Free market anti-Malthusian	Acknowledgment of agricultural prometheanism of the 20th century.
		Acknowledgment of importance of human resources.
		Acknowledgment of the utility of market incentives.
Free-market anti-Malthusian	Class anti-Malthusian	[No evidence of integration]
	Managerial neo-Malthusian	Population growth can in fact be a problem.
		Population planning programs have in fact been effective.

Theoretical Models toward Paradigm Integration

In this section I summarize and evaluate two theoretical models seeking to reconcile the seemingly irreconcilable views of adversaries in the population-resource arena. The first is a book chapter titled "Malthus and Boserup: A Dynamic Synthesis," by Ronald Demos Lee (1986). The second is a book titled *Environment, Scarcity, and Violence* by Thomas F. Homer-Dixon (1999).

Lee's point of departure is to replace "either-or" logic with "both-and" logic. His treatise begins by observing that there are two grand themes in macro-demographic theory: the Malthusian one, that population equilibrates with resources at some level mediated by technology and a conventional standard of living; and the Boserupian one, that technological change is itself spurred by increases in population. The striking association between the levels and changes in technology and population over the past million years leaves no doubt in my mind that at least one of these views is correct. But it is also possible that both are, since the two theories are not contradictory, but rather complementary. (Lee 1986, 96)

From there he proceeds to demonstrate, through a series of theoretical economic modeling exercises, that there is every reason to believe both Malthusian and Boserupian processes are at work simultaneously. Lee also takes on a provocative issue raised by the possibility of both Malthusian and Boserupian processes operating together: "If larger populations encourage more rapid technological progress, and higher technological states induce more population growth, can stationary or steady-state equilibria exist?" (1986, 96). Lee presumes that resource availability and costs would ultimately constrain growth, thus the process does not go "onward and upward forever" but rather comes to rest (1986, 128).

Cohen (1995, 38) rightly calls Lee's (1986) theoretical model "brilliant." Others have followed up with research that examines the complementarities rather than the divergences of Malthusian and Boserupian theory (e.g., Bilsborrow 1987; Marquette 1997). Colin Sage (1994, 266), referring to Lee's (1986) breakthrough, says: "Developing a fresh conceptual approach toward understanding the linkages between population and environment means exposing the ideological dimensions of the debate and overcoming the artificial antagonism between the Malthusian and Boserupian models."

Though I agree Lee's (1986) work is theoretically impressive and an important step toward paradigm synthesis, it is flawed. He has not *sufficiently* exposed the ideological dimensions of the debate. Recall his remark that "there are two grand themes in macro-demographic theory: the Malthusian one . . . and the Boserupian one" (Lee 1986, 96). This is, of course, incomplete. There are three grand themes in macrodemographic theory. We have seen in this chapter that Marx and Engels are towering figures in the population-resource debate, and their contemporary followers have mobilized a powerful critique of neo-Malthusianism. The demographic literature often presumes that Malthus and Boserup occupy the entire range of relevant theoretical debate, in the same way that some environmental theorists presume the liberal- conservative continuum encompasses the entire scope of legitimate discourse. The omission of Marx in demographic literature exemplifies the problem of implicit paradigm isolation described in chapter 3.

As mentioned earlier, any theorizing of the population-resource balance that aims to occupy the entire relevant theoretical "space" must give attention to the central concerns of the three main paradigms: equity, resource limits, and human potential. It makes no sense to debate whether scarcity leads to creative resolution (Boserup) or to a systems collapse (Malthus) without also considering that "scarcity" may often be distributional (Marx) and in no meaningful sense absolute.

Homer-Dixon's book *Environment, Scarcity, and Violence* (1999) emphasizes the need to synthesize and embrace the views of three theoretical groupings that he calls the "neo-Malthusians," the "economic optimists," and the "distributionists." (These correspond, respectively, to the managerial neo-Malthusian, individualist anti-Malthusian, and class anti-Malthusian paradigms that I identify as the main population paradigms.) From this integrated perspective, Homer-Dixon (1999) conducts empirical field research, through sixteen case studies in developing countries, on the relationship of environmental degradation and scarcity to violent conflict. Homer-Dixon (1999, 8, 15) defines and applies the concepts of "environmental scarcity" and "structural scarcity." By "environmental scarcity" he means a scarcity of renewable resources, "such as cropland, forests, river water, and fish stocks"; by "structural scarcity" he means scarcity that is "caused by a severe imbalance in the distribution of wealth and power that results in some groups in a society getting disproportionately large slices of the resource pie, whereas, others get slices that are too small to sustain their livelihoods." He finds that environmental scarcity can contribute to violence, and that in the near future such violence would probably increase because of worsening environmental scarcities in developing countries. Homer-Dixon adds that

> environmental scarcity is not sufficient, by itself, to cause violence; when it does contribute to violence, research shows, it always interacts with other political, economic, and social factors. . . . In addition, environmental scarcity's role as a cause of violence should not always be subordinated to that of political, economic, and social factors. (1999, 178–79)

Homer-Dixon says the research results enable insights on how and where environmental scarcity can cause social breakdown and violence (1999, 4–5).

At first glance, Homer-Dixon's (1999) research is a refreshingly eclectic, transideological, and pathbreaking effort shedding light on the population-resource issue. However, the book suffers from the paradigm isolation it claims it is trying to overcome. Although asserting he intends to conduct research that draws on all three population paradigms, Homer-Dixon puts the "economic optimist" paradigm squarely in the driver's seat and gives the other two paradigms a passenger role. He says "we should focus on the role of ingenuity if we want to understand the factors that determine whether societies successfully adapt to environmental scarcity" (Homer-Dixon 1999, 125). His is a strongly individualist vision, inspired by the belief that "ideas are a factor of economic production in addition to capital, labor, and land. Ideas have independent productive power" (Homer-Dixon 1999, 109).[10]

Homer-Dixon's subsequent book, titled *The Ingenuity Gap* (2000), confirms that his inquiry is fixed on the body of thought that motivates the "economic optimists." Homer-Dixon had a brilliant idea in setting out to examine the population-resource balance from the perspective of the three dominant population paradigms, but he has not done full justice to this project, giving disproportionate attention to just one of the three paradigms. Truly pioneering theory and research on the population-resource balance must not only pay attention to the central tenets of all three of the main population paradigms. Such work must also strive to overcome the tendency, evident even among conscientious theoreticians, to advance a particular paradigm in the name of open-minded eclecticism.

Conclusion

This review of the population-resource balance issue has emphasized three points. First, world population will increase by 2–5 billion people in the next half century, and almost all of this increase will occur in countries of the South. Second, world food supplies have long been adequate at the aggregate level, and hunger and malnutrition have resulted not from absolute shortages but from the inadequate purchasing power of the poor. Third, the future bodes badly because there has been a significant decline in the rate of increase of agricultural productivity since the 1980s; there is as yet no sign that a second Green Revolution can be mobilized on the scale needed; and increased food production will almost inevitably aggravate existing environmental problems.

There are three dominant population paradigms addressing these issues: (1) class anti-Malthusianism, inspired by Marx's and Engels's critique of Malthus, which emphasizes that food and resource shortages have been distributional and in no meaningful sense absolute; (2) managerial neo-Malthusianism, inspired by Malthus and promoting the view that population growth dangerously exceeds the earth's carrying capacity; and (3) individualist anti-Malthusianism, inspired by Boserup and insisting that population growth leads to a resolution of resource scarcity problems through increased application of creativity, knowledge, and technology.

This chapter has observed that paradigm isolation among these three perspectives has much less to do with pessimism and optimism per se than with political ideology. Ultimately, such politically motivated paradigm isolation obstructs our understanding of the population-resource issue. Demographic theorists and researchers are gradually realizing the perils of arguing from just one perspective, and imaginative, though also flawed, efforts have been made to integrate the various perspectives. Future efforts toward paradigm integration on the population-resource issue must carry transideological insights to new heights.

Notes

1. Replacement-level fertility stabilizes population size, given an unchanging age pattern of mortality (Cohen 1995, 140). "These levels exceed 2 because children who die before reaching the reproductive ages have to be replaced with additional births, and because the sex ratio at birth slightly exceeds one (typically 1.05 males for every female birth)" (Bongaarts and Bulatao 1999, 516).

2. Buttel's pessimistic view of the revolutionary potential of agricultural biotechnology is unchanged, particularly from the standpoints of output increase and widespread substitution for chemicals. Frederick H. Buttel, personal communication with author, February 14, 2001.

3. For example, world per capita cereal production was generally on an upward trend in the last half of the twentieth century, going from approximately 280 kg in 1950 to 371 kg in 1984. However, by 1990 per capita cereal production had declined to 360 kg (Dyson 1996, 58–59).

4. In a similar vein, Cohen (1995, 12) says, "This book is neither an alarmist tract nor a cornucopian lullaby." Dyson says, "It is hoped that the study that follows draws something from both sides of the debate, while not becoming waylaid by either extreme" (1996, 23). Conway says, "I am not a Malthusian, or even a neo-Malthusian, and I do not intend to enter the current debate on the relevance of Malthus's ideas to today's problems. But the simple fact is that by the year 2020, less than twenty-five years from now, there will be about an extra 2.5 billion people in the developing world who will require food" (1997, 15).

5. For example, Ross, in his book *The Malthus Factor* (1998), so closely identifies neo-Malthusianism with the interests of capitalism that he is unable to see that anti-Malthusianism (specifically, individualist anti-Malthusianism) is even more closely identified with the interests of free market capitalism. In spite of this, Ross's book makes an invaluable contribution by showing, in considerable detail, how Malthusianism has pervaded many of the twentieth century's reactionary tendencies, including racist and eugenics movements, the founding of population planning, the emergence of the environmental movement, cold war ideology, and opposition to land reform. Foster makes the same error: "Malthus represents the capitalist system and in this sense Malthusianism is a historic necessity of capitalism" (1998, 18). True, Malthusianism may be necessary to capitalism, but as this chapter shows, anti-Malthusianism is just as necessary to capitalism.

6. Referring to undisturbed societies, Abernethy says, "By one means or another, all peoples whose social system survives for any great length of time adjust reproduction and immigration to a sustainable level" (1993, 69). Another conclusion surfaces when she refers to people under conditions of development. In that situation, "families eagerly fill any apparently larger niche, and the extra births and consequent population growth often overshoot actual opportunity. Increase beyond a sustainable number is an ever-present threat, because human beings take their cue from the opportunity that is apparent *today*, and are easily fooled by change" (Abernethy 1994, 84–91).

7. For example, it is not so long ago (the 1970s) that Garrett Hardin, a neo-Malthusian, was far more visible than Julian Simon.

8. Stretching across a wide political gulf, Murdoch (1980, 28) cites Simon's research on the rationality of childbearing behavior.

9. This is made abundantly clear in class anti-Malthusian literature, and less so in individualist anti-Malthusian literature. Simon explains, "The social and economic structure of a country is the central factor in economic development. After this factor is recognized, we are better able to understand the unimportance of population growth and density in the short run" (1990, 2).

10. Homer-Dixon draws on the ideas of Paul Romer and "new economic growth theory" (1999, 109).

CHAPTER FIVE

~

Economic Growth:
For Worse or for Better?

It is impossible for the world economy to grow its way out of poverty and environmental degradation. In other words, *sustainable growth is impossible*. (Daly 1996a, 192)

In the long run economic growth is the surest—and probably the only—route to a general improvement in the quality of life and in the environment. (Beckerman 1996, 21)

Positions in the debate on economic growth and the environment could not be more polarized. At one extreme, antigrowth proponents (e.g., Herman Daly, above) say economic growth is the key *cause* of environmental problems. At the other extreme, progrowth proponents (e.g., Wilfred Beckerman, above) contend economic growth is the essential *solution* to environmental problems. The issue saw its heyday in the 1970s with the publication of *The Limits to Growth* report (Meadows et al. 1972) and the ensuing controversy. Since the 1970s, the harshness of the debate has been lessened through realization that certain extreme positions involved oversimplification, and also through semantic clarification, theoretical insights, and technological advancements. In spite of this, the debate is very much alive and shows no signs of abating. There is every likelihood that the global warming issue will serve as a lightning rod for further controversy concerning economic growth, and that positions will harden again in years to come. The debate remains as important as ever and it is therefore important to clarify the theoretical and ideological framework in which it is set.

This chapter makes four main arguments. First, I show that three theories (which I call "convergence theories") have had an important role in softening the hard edges of the polar positions but have not eliminated the grounds for debate. Second, I demonstrate that the debate is sure to persist because of the failure to reconcile economic growth and the environment at the world level, and also because the polarization is motivated in part by political ideology, a necessary accompaniment of capitalist civilization. Third, I make the case that ecological modernization theory—one of the three convergence theories—strives toward integration of the class, managerial, and individualist positions but fails to achieve its objective. Fourth, I make the case that one particular type of paradigm integration is a sign of hope for addressing the issue, while a particular type of paradigm isolation is a persistent cause for concern.

The chapter comprises seven subsequent sections. The second section examines different meanings of the term "growth" and provides information on growth trends in the twentieth century, as well as some forecasts of growth trends in the twenty-first century. The third section summarizes the evolution of the growth debate, looking first at the *Limits to Growth* (Meadows et al. 1972) report and its aftermath, and then at the polemic debate between neoclassical economics and ecological economics. The fourth section analyzes three convergence theories—dematerialization, the environmental Kuznets curve, and ecological modernization theory. The fifth section examines anti- and progrowth positions in terms of the class, managerial, and individualist paradigms. The sixth section documents the phenomenon of paradigm isolation among the various social theory positions on the economic growth issue. The seventh section analyzes the possibilities for paradigm integration, giving focused attention to ecological modernization theory as a vehicle for such an effort. The last section summarizes the key findings.

The attentive reader will ask why there is such a long, seemingly needless detour in this chapter before the topic of ideology and social theory is addressed in earnest in the fifth section. First, a good deal of the subject matter in the economic growth debate involves technical perspectives on the nature of economic activity, and on the relationship of production and consumption to absolute and relative resource scarcity and to pollution, among other topics. As will become evident, it is important to be grounded in the basics of these technical controversies, as well as the convergence concepts and theories they have spawned, not only because they are important in and of themselves, but also because they are related to, and in some ways disguise, the ideological and social theory content of the debate. Second, some of the most sophisticated and well-known pronouncements on the economic growth debate take place in the political center, within the boundaries of the managerial paradigm. This tends to reinforce the impression (which is largely but not entirely false) that the economic growth debate takes place beyond the bounds of political ideology.

Economic Growth in the Last Century

Before examining the trends of economic growth in the last century and related environmental developments, I will specify exactly what is meant by the term "economic growth."

Two Fundamentally Different Meanings of "Growth"

The literature on the economic growth debate offers its readers ample grounds for confusion. This is because two fundamentally dissimilar meanings are attached to the word "growth." The distinction is often not specified by the authors of these texts, even though it is crucial to understanding their arguments.

The first meaning (which I will call the "income" definition of growth) is the traditional one and refers to growth over time of per capita gross national product (or GNP).[1] GNP is a measure of the economic value of all goods and services in a given economy. The second meaning (which I will call the "throughput" definition of growth) refers to growth, over time, in the consumption of natural resources and/or energy. Throughput growth tends to be measured in physical units, for example, as tons of coal or as British thermal units (BTUs) of energy. As we saw in chapter 2, these two forms of economic growth are closely related. In the course of the last two centuries, average per capita income has grown dramatically, and this is functionally related to the exponential increase, over time, in the consumption of natural resources and energy.

If these two forms of growth are so closely related, why is it so important to distinguish one from the other? There are two reasons. First, the distinction forms the conceptual basis for understanding the core problem of the debate. More specifically, income has tended to grow in lockstep relation to throughput over time, and this has not just increased average well-being (income increase) but has also produced environmental problems (as a result of throughput increase). The distinction is also the conceptual basis for certain proposed solutions. The convergence concepts discussed later on in this chapter all essentially say that world average per capita income can and must increase, and that at the same time environmental damage can and must decrease. Some of these theories say explicitly that growth (as income) must increase while growth (as throughput) must decrease.

The divergent meanings of the term "growth" have made antagonists in the debate appear to talk past one another. For example, in the quotes at the beginning of this chapter, Daly (1996a, 192) uses the term "growth" in the "throughput" sense, whereas Beckerman (1996, 21) emphasizes the "income" meaning of "growth." The literature of the economic growth debate is rife with ambiguity, in large measure because of vagueness and inconsistency in use of the term "growth." This does not mean, however, that semantic clarity would resolve the debate. Far from it. As we shall see, there are various substantive points where antagonists clearly define their terms and arguments and confront each other head on.

With so much at stake in expressing oneself clearly, why does ambiguity in the use of the term "growth" remain widespread in the literature? Some of this lack of clarity is the result of carelessness. However, it also results, ironically, from partisans seeking not just to clarify but also to appropriate the terms of the debate. For example, Herman Daly has been the leading pioneer in forging a throughput definition of "growth" (e.g., Daly 1987, 323). In connection with this effort, Daly (Daly 1987; Daly 1990, 45; Goodland and Daly 1992, 37; Daly 1996b, 28) has argued that "growth" should be viewed as "quantitative expansion" of the economy and should be distinguished from "development," which in his view is "qualitative development" of the economy.[2] In effect, Daly has implicitly transferred the "income" or "well-being" meanings of growth to the term "development," so that "growth" would more commonly be interpreted (pejoratively) as "throughput" growth. To his credit, Herman Daly has tried to clear away some of the ambiguity by specifying a definition of the term "growth," but the various parties to the debate are still a long way from sharing a common vernacular.

Phenomenal and Uneven Growth in the Last Century

In the course of the twentieth century world population increased almost four-fold, from 1.6 billion in 1900 to 6 billion in 2000. Over the same period average income per person increased more than fourfold, from $1,500 to $6,600. The value of the gross world product[3] increased seventeen-fold, from $2.3 trillion in 1900 to $39 trillion in 1998 (Brown and Flavin 1999, 4, 10) (see figure 5.1).

This phenomenal growth has been extremely unequal in both the "income" and the "throughput" senses. According to the United Nations Development Programme's 1998 *Human Development Report* (UNDP 1998, 48–50, as seen in Porter

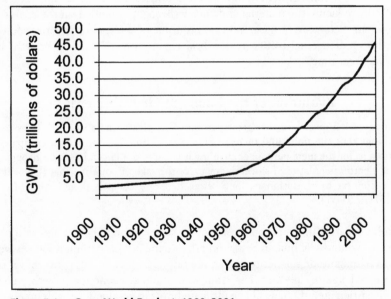

Figure 5.1.   Gross World Product, 1900–2001
Sources: The data were compiled by David Roodman at the Worldwatch Institute. The basic data are from Maddison 2001. Update data are from IMF 2001 and the U.S. Bureau of the Census 2000. Data from 1990 were converted to 2000 dollars using U.S. GDP deflator.

et al. 2000, 179), the 20 percent of world population in the highest-income coun-tries account for 86 percent of total private consumption expenditures, whereas the 20 percent of population in the poorest countries account for a mere 1.3 percent.[4] The richest fifth consume 45 percent of all meat and fish and the poorest fifth, 5 percent. The richest fifth consume 58 percent of total energy and the poorest fifth, less than 4 percent. The richest fifth have 74 percent of all telephone lines and the poorest fifth, 1.5 percent. The richest fifth consume 84 percent of all paper and the poorest fifth, 1.1 percent. The richest fifth own 87 percent of the world's vehicle fleet; the poorest fifth, less than 1 percent. When taking into account all material flows (including soil erosion, mining wastes, etc.), 45–85 metric tons of natural resources are consumed per capita annually in modern industrial economies (Porter et al. 2000, 2). In the period 1950–1995, developed countries produced ap-proximately six times more carbon dioxide emissions than developing countries (WRI 1998, 176) (see figure 5.2).

There is consensus among policy makers and scientists on the need to signif-icantly increase the income and well-being of people in developing countries. However, this global poverty alleviation mandate clearly will run up against var-ious physical constraints (see chapter 2), unless it is accompanied by changes in the way goods and services are produced and/or distributed. One of the great challenges facing human civilization in coming decades is to devise ways to achieve real income growth in developing countries, while at the same time sub-stantially reducing the material and energy throughput burden on the terrestrial ecosystem. Before we turn our attention to three of the leading theories address-ing this challenge, let us first review how the notion of "limits to growth" has evolved over time.

Evolution of the Limits to Growth Debate

If the earth must lose that great portion of its pleasantness which it owes to things that the unlimited increase of wealth and population would extirpate from it, for the mere purpose of enabling it to support a larger, but not a happier or a better population, I sincerely hope, for the sake of posterity, that they will be content to be stationary, long before necessity compels them to it. (Mill 1871, 750–51)

John Stuart Mill expressed these views a century and a quarter ago, at a time when the number of human beings and their demands on natural resources were orders of magnitude smaller than they are now. The focus of his concern was the threatened loss of "pleasantness" from unrestrained economic growth, yet he clearly anticipated there would be ultimate limits to economic growth unless the process was somehow restrained.

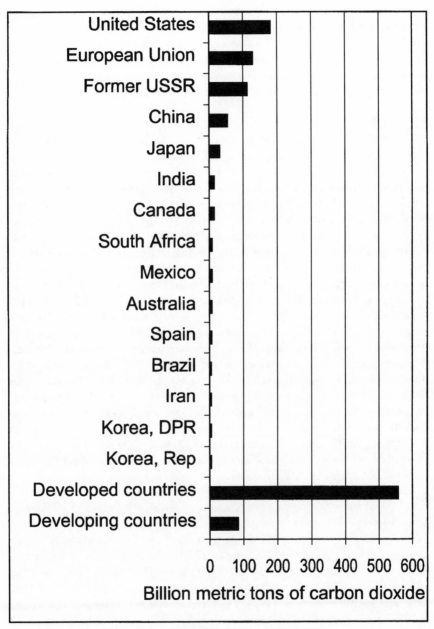

Figure 5.2. Cumulative Carbon Dioxide Emissions, 1950–1995
Source: WRI 1998, 176. Reprinted with permission.

The issue of physical limits to economic growth did not become a full-fledged and heated debate until more than a century later. In hindsight, it appears practically inevitable that a fourfold increase in human numbers, and seventeen-fold increase in economic activity would produce a controversy on whether the pace and magnitude of social and material transformations could be endured. In this section we examine the two most prominent axes of the debate.

The Limits to Growth Report

The Limits to Growth, authored by scientists at the Massachusetts Institute of Technology (Donnella Meadows, Dennis Meadows, Jørgen Randers, and William W. Behrens III; Meadows et al. 1972) is arguably the most important historical document in the controversy concerning the environmental consequences of economic growth. It was the primary catalyst for a vigorous, high-profile debate that took place in the 1970s. It was one of the main inspirations for the founding of the radical ecological ("green") movement (Eckersley 1992, 8; Dobson 1995, 35). At the turn of the twenty-first century, it remains one of the principal targets for vilification by conservative theorists who champion economic growth (e.g., Huber 1999, 5–14; Bailey 2000b, 6–11).

The Limits to Growth was a report commissioned by the Club of Rome (an international study group funded by European multinational corporations) for their Project on the Predicament of Mankind. The report and a predecessor study titled *World Dynamics* (Forrester [1971] 1973) were computer simulation models that extrapolated trends on the basis of five variables—population, food production, industrialization, pollution, and consumption of natural resources. The "limits to growth" report reached the conclusion that "if the present growth trends in world population, industrialization, pollution, food production, and resource depletion continue unchanged, the limits to growth on this planet will be reached sometime in the next one hundred years. The probable result will be a rather sudden and uncontrollable decline in both population and industrial capacity" (Meadows et al. 1972, 29).

Critics countered that the report had greatly oversimplified the state of the "real" world by relying on so few variables, had wrongly predicted resources would be exhausted, and had failed to take into account that market forces and technological innovation would ensure a plentiful supply of resources as well as limit the effects of pollution (Beckerman 1974; Kahn et al. 1976; Simon 1981; Simon and Kahn 1984; Porter and van der Linde 1995). Beckerman said that the authors and the Club of Rome "have been guilty of various flagrant errors of fact, logic, and scientific method" (1974, 242). Simon sharply condemned the report, describing it as "a fascinating example of how scientific work can be outrageously bad and yet be very influential" (1981, 286).

Twenty years after publication of the report, the authors produced a follow-up study titled *Beyond the Limits* that ran the simulation model on the basis of recent data (Meadows et al. 1992). Completely unrepentant, they claimed some crucial resource limits had already been exceeded and that "significant reductions in material and energy flows are necessary" (Meadows et al. 1992, xiv–xvi). The authors acknowledge that technological improvements have eased certain constraints, while contending that "even with the most effective technologies and the greatest economic resilience we can believe possible, if those are the only changes, the model generates scenarios of collapse" (Meadows et al. 1992, xv, 162).

One crucial difference is that the update backs away from the apocalyptic and pessimistic tone of the first report. For example, it says,

> The limits, let us be clear, are to throughput. They are speed limits, not space limits, limits to flow rates, not limits to the number of people or the amount of capital (at least not directly). To be beyond them does not mean running into an absolute brick wall. (Meadows et al. 1992, 99)

This is an important concession to a key assumption of the opposition: that people are capable of adjusting to emerging resource constraints in a creative and effective way.

Both before and after the release of *The Limits to Growth*, various other publications established the terms of the economic growth debate. These include Kenneth Boulding, "The Economics of the Coming Spaceship Earth" (1966), Herman Kahn and Anthony Wiener, *The Year 2000* (1967), E. J. Mishan, *The Costs of Economic Growth* (1967), Edward Goldsmith et al., *Blueprint for Survival* (1972), Mesarovic and Pestel, *Mankind at the Turning Point* (1974), and the "Global 2000 Study," *The Global 2000 Report to the President* (1980).

Neoclassical Economics versus Ecological Economics
For a long time, it was an article of faith in neoclassical economics that capital and labor were the essential components of the production process and that natural resources, viewed as limitless and substitutable, were superfluous. This was epitomized by Robert Solow, a leading figure in modern neoclassical theory and a Nobel laureate, who said, "If it is very easy to substitute other factors for natural resources, then there is in principle no 'problem.' The world can, in effect, get along without natural resources, so exhaustion is just an event, not a catastrophe" (1974, 11).

Ecological economics, diametrically opposed to this view, contends that natural resources are central in the production process, that their supply faces ultimate constraints, and that they should be seen as a complement to capital and labor rather than as a substitute.

Ecological Economics, a peer-review journal produced by members of the ecological economics profession, published a 1997 forum (Georgescu-Roegen versus Solow/Stiglitz) to engage in debate with their main neoclassical adversaries. Little ground was conceded by either side and the two schools of thought remain poles apart (see especially Daly 1997a; Solow 1997; Stiglitz 1997; Daly 1997b).

Some background on the differences between the two schools of thought are succinctly reviewed below to gain a better grasp of the issues at stake.

Nicholas Georgescu-Roegen (1906–1994) is one of the key intellectual progenitors of ecological economics. In his seminal book *The Entropy Law and the Economic Process* Georgescu-Roegen theorized that all economic activities are subject to the constraints of the first and second laws of thermodynamics (Georgescu-Roegen 1971).[5] The first law (also known as the principle of the conservation of matterenergy) holds that matter and energy can neither be created nor destroyed through human activities. The second law (also known as the entropy law) says that as energy is used, it is converted from a concentrated and available state ("low entropy") to a dispersed and unavailable state ("high entropy").[6] Translated into lay terms, the laws imply that "we do not produce or consume anything, we merely rearrange it" (first law), and "our rearrangement implies a continual reduction in potential for further use within the system as a whole" (second law) (Daly 1977, 109). Another implication of the two laws is that it is not possible to recycle matter with 100 percent efficiency. In concrete terms, Georgescu-Roegen said that physical laws related to matter and energy impose irrevocable bounds on the scope of human economic activities. The practical implication, as he explained, was that

> economic development through industrial abundance may be a blessing for us now and for those who will be able to enjoy it in the near future, but it is definitely against the interest of the human species as a whole, if its interest is to have a lifespan as long as is compatible with its dowry of low entropy. (Georgescu-Roegen 1973, 47)

Georgescu-Roegen was a forceful critic of neoclassical assumptions. In the 1970s Robert Solow and Joseph Stiglitz produced a new production function equation that appeared, at face value, to answer the objections of their critics. It included natural resources as a variable along with capital and labor. Georgescu-Roegen denounced this "Solow-Stiglitz variant" because it continued to assume perfect substitutability of capital for resources. He explained:

> Solow and Stiglitz could not have come out with their conjuring trick had they borne in mind, first, that any material process consists in the transformation of some materials into others (the flow elements) by some agents (the fund elements), and second, that natural resources are the very sap of the economic process. . . . The question that confronts us today is whether we are going to discover *new* sources of energy that can be safely used. (Georgescu-Roegen 1979, 98)

Almost two decades later, Solow and Stiglitz replied defiantly to the challenge posed by Georgescu-Roegen, insisting that capital can substitute for resources, and in ways both direct and indirect:

> There can be some direct substitution of capital for resource inputs, as when more precise (not necessarily more massive) machinery reduces waste, or allows the use of previously unworkable materials. But the important margin is likely to be indi-

rect, as when materials produced from renewable sources, very likely using highly capital-intensive methods, replace materials produced from nonrenewable sources. (Solow 1997, 267)

Herman Daly, a former graduate student of Georgescu-Roegen's at Vanderbilt University, is a leading figure in ecological economics. One of his main contributions has been to propose alternative economic systems that answer the challenges posed by the first and second laws of thermodynamics. His book *Toward a Steady-State Economy* proposed aiming for a world in which the physical stock of capital and the size of the human population are maintained at a certain level, and the rate of throughput is as low as possible (Daly 1973, 14). Aggregate throughput would be not just low but also constant, and it would vary according to competing uses in a market economy. A steady-state economy therefore "can develop, but cannot grow, just as the planet earth, of which it is a subsystem, can develop without growing" (Daly 1996b, 31). In arguing for a turn to a postpetroleum, solar economy, he points out the important asymmetry in the world's two sources of low-entropy energy. "The solar source is stock-abundant, but flow-limited. The terrestrial source is stock-limited, but flow-abundant (temporarily)" (Daly 1996b, 30).

Another important theme in Daly's work, and in ecological economics as a whole, has been to underscore the diametric polarity between the neoclassical and ecological economic worldview. In neoclassical models of the world, the economy is assumed to be the entire system and that nature, when considered, is a subsector of the economy. This contrasts sharply with the ecological economics view of the economy as a subset of the world ecosystem (Costanza 1991, 4–5; Martinez-Alier 1997, 17; Daly 1999, 15–16).

The debate between neoclassical economics and ecological economics on the substitutability or complementarity of resources has evolved into a debate between the merits of "weak sustainability" and "strong sustainability." Weak sustainability models draw heavily on assumptions of the substitutability of capital for resources and claim that "what matters for future generations is only the total aggregate stock of 'manmade' and 'natural' capital (and possibly other forms of capital as well), but not natural capital as such" (Neumayer 1999, 1). The essence of the strong sustainability position, on the other hand, is that because natural capital itself is nonsubstitutable, it should be preserved for future generations in addition to the total aggregate capital stock (Neumayer 1999, 1).[7]

Observers of the debate have counseled finding a middle ground between untenable extremes. Turner remarks that "it is just not helpful, or meaningful, to continue to polarize debate into total substitution versus total complementarity of man made . . . and natural capital" (1997, 300). Some writers have set out to define a reasonable middle ground,[8] but partisans of both sides appear to be just as entrenched in their views.

Three Convergence Theories

This section succinctly defines and evaluates three theories (dematerialization, the environmental Kuznets curve, and ecological modernization theory) that are premised on the possibility of reconciling income growth with decreased material and energy throughput. Before turning our attention to them, I will describe the context in which they emerged.

In the midst of the growth debate of the 1970s, it became evident to some partisans and observers that unqualified arguments (i.e., being "for" or "against" growth) were simplistic and indefensible. There emerged a consciousness of the need for greater theoretical sophistication in addressing the issue. The Club of Rome's sequel to the "limits to growth" study, entitled *Mankind at the Turning Point* (Mesarovic and Pestel 1974), is an illustration of the tendency to back away from hard-line positions and to appreciate the complexity of the issue. The authors stated, for example, that "to grow or not to grow is neither a well-defined nor a relevant question until the location, sense, and subject of growing and the growth process itself are defined" (Mesarovic and Pestel 1974, 3).[9]

Over the years, antigrowth partisans have made a conscious retreat from the absolutism of past "zero growth" campaigns. Jacobs (1991, 53–61) identified three reasons why an unqualified "zero growth" position is untenable: (1) income growth and throughput growth are not the same; (2) where renewable resources are concerned, it is not growth per se that presents a problem but rather the *rate of consumption*; and (3) world maldistribution of income must be viewed as a serious issue. Although they are strong opponents of throughput growth, ecological economists readily acknowledge and endorse the ethical imperative of income growth in developing countries. As Goodland and Daly explain, "Ecological constraints are real and more growth for the poor must be balanced by negative throughput growth for the rich. . . . Large scale transfers to the poorer countries will also be required" (1992, 38).

Some advocates of economic growth have backed away from extreme hard-line positions. The concession often takes the form of acknowledging the severity of environmental problems caused by excessive throughput growth, yet insisting that income growth is ultimately key to achieving more efficient and therefore cleaner economic production.

Since the 1970s, the growth debate has gotten more sophisticated and partisans have tended to abandon simplistic formulations of the problem. At the same time, the search for effective and durable solutions to the problems of poverty and the environment have become one of the major preoccupations of science and policy. "Sustainable development" and attention to "the quality of growth" are the two lead concepts guiding the search for "win-win" solutions to global problems. Both assume that income growth in developing countries and alleviation of environmental problems are convergent and compatible goals.

The concept of sustainable development was launched into prominence through publication of *Our Common Future* by the World Commission on Environment and Development, which defined it as "development that meets the needs of the present without compromising the ability of future generations to meet their own needs" (WCED 1987, 43). The report advocated strong economic growth worldwide while at the same time devoting much greater international policy attention than in the past to combating environmental deterioration. Reconciliation of these two goals was essentially an act of faith, based on slender evidence that energy systems and industrial technologies could be revolutionized. The report said that "sustainable development . . . requires a change in the content of growth, to make it less material- and energy-intensive and more equitable in its impact" (WCED 1987, 52). It included two chapters on how throughput might be reduced in the future.[10]

The influence of the report was considerable. In ensuing years, the concept of "sustainable development" came into wide use in research, policy, and activist circles. After publication of Our Common Future, the World Bank gave focused attention to poverty and the environment as linked and mutually reinforcing problems.[11] The Bank's 1992 World Development Report, devoted to the topic of "development and the environment," optimistically concluded that "there are strong 'win-win' opportunities that remain unexploited" (World Bank 1992, 1).

Optimistic effervescence was evident in many policy documents and analyses of the time. Concerning the possibilities introduced by the new sustainable development agenda, Ascher and Healey remarked, "Rather than trade-offs, we are blessed with complementarities" (1990, 10). At an abstract level, the emergence of the sustainable development concept can be interpreted as a willful overcoming of the contradictions of the polar positions in the growth issue. Stockdale (1989) characterizes sustainable development as being essentially a synthesis of the anti- and progrowth perspectives.

The quality of growth concept essentially says that dedicated attention to how the process of economic growth takes place can serve as a basis for mitigating or eliminating growth's adverse environmental (as well as nonenvironmental) effects. There is an implicit, retrospective critique in the quality of growth concept, which says that in the past it was wrong to suppose that attention to the quantity of growth, measured by per capita GNP, is sufficient to avert environmental problems.[12] For years, the quality of growth concept has been greatly overshadowed by sustainable development, receiving relatively cursory treatment in documents concerning the environment. This is understandable from the standpoint that the two concepts are so closely related that they are treated as synonyms or as subsets of one another (e.g., WCED 1987, 52, 364).

However the concept has been catapulted into prominence through publication of a major book by the World Bank titled The Quality of Growth (Thomas et al. 2000). Defining the concept, the authors state,

> The quality of the growth process, not just its pace, affects development outcomes—much as the quality of people's diets, not just the quantity of food, influences their health and life expectancy. . . . Complementing the pace of growth,

it refers to key aspects shaping the growth process. . . . the distribution of opportunities, the sustainability of the environment, the management of global risks, and governance. (Thomas et al. 2000, xxiv–xxv)

Just as with sustainable development, the proponents of the quality of growth concept assume optimistically, but on the basis of slender evidence, that growth and environmental improvement are fundamentally compatible goals. The authors claim that "the environmental damage and biodiversity losses from current growth patterns are frightening, but if they are addressed now, growth can achieve a better natural environment and reduce the number of poor" (Thomas et al. 2000, xxxiv).

Dematerialization, the environmental Kuznets curve, and ecological modernization theory are the product of the more hopeful intellectual climate following the antigrowth negativism of the 1970s. Their importance lies in the fact that they seek to go beyond mere wishful thinking and to provide empirical support and theoretical guidance for the project of throughput reduction. Although they focus heavily on the environment side of the poverty-environment equation, they are clearly a product of the sustainable development and quality of growth "mold" and are therefore aptly labeled "convergence theories."

Dematerialization

As a theory, dematerialization can be described as the belief that "limits to growth" can be averted through decrease over time in the material and energy content of industrial processes. Definitions of "dematerialization" by those identified with the field differ on whether it is best understood as a process or as a strategy. For example, Wernick et al. (1997, 135) define dematerialization as "the absolute or relative reduction in the quantity of materials required to serve economic functions." Ayres, on the other hand, explains that dematerialization "is, fundamentally, a strategy for achieving economic growth by continuously increasing the productivity of natural resources, in contrast to the present strategy of achieving growth by increasing the productivity of labor through the use of material capital and energy" (1998, 68). In effect, the dematerialization project embraces both of these definitions. It has a backward-looking, *descriptive* dimension that involves documenting the decline of material intensity in industrial processes; it has a forward-looking, *descriptive* dimension that involves predicting future trends; and it has a forward-looking, *prescriptive* dimension that involves trying to discover ways to intensify and accelerate dematerialization.

The evidence of dematerialization can be summarized as follows. The *proportion* (not the total amount) of carbon in the primary energy supply has decreased at the rate of 0.3 percent per year since 1860, in effect reducing the proportion by 40 percent (Ausubel 1997, 3). This process of *decarbonization* results from the fact that successive fuel regimes have a lower ratio of carbon atoms to hydrogen atoms (which are environmentally more benign) over time. The ratio of carbon to hydrogen in fuel wood is ten to one; in coal, one to one; in oil, one to two; and in natural gas, one to four (Nakicenovic 1997, 75–77). There has also been a *relative* decline in the use of physical materials, with a decline of one-third per unit of economic activity since 1970 (Wernick et al. 1997, 139). Sun and Meristo (1999) document significant decreases in the rate of increase of energy use and of carbon dioxide emission in OECD countries between 1960 and 1995 (see also Kågeson 1998). Ruth (1998) has documented dematerialization and decarbonization in the production of five metals (copper, lead, zinc, aluminum, and iron and steel) in the United States. Glyn (1995) says the impact of northern economic growth on the environment has decreased substantially since 1973 and that GDP growth is likely to diminish very substantially further because of the reduced rate of growth of the working population and projected poor productivity growth of the service sector. Among the main observed reasons for dematerialization and decarbonization are the shift over time in energy regimes; the shift in northern countries in the composition of economic activities (from primary industries, to manufacturing, and then to services); and price competition among industrial producers.

Dematerialization faces an enormous challenge if it is to contribute meaningfully to the alleviation of environmental threats. It is generally understood that material and energy intensity will have to be reduced by 90 percent if future population growth, "economic catch-up" in developing countries, and environmental limitations are taken into account (Ekins and Jacobs 1995, 40; Ayres 1998, 161). Does the evidence above indicate significant progress toward this goal? The sobering reality is that *absolute* material and energy consumption continue to increase, especially in industrialized countries (Nakicenovic 1997, 75), in spite of *relative* decreases per unit of output or declines in the rate of increase of consumption in those countries.[13] Schor observes that

> in the last half century consumption has increased dramatically in the industrialized North. The most rapid increases were during the 1950s and 1960s, the so-called "Golden Age of Capitalism." Beginning in the 1970s, the growth of GDP and consumption per capita slowed. But even so, since 1973 the average consumer in these countries found his or her consumption rising by an average of more than 2 percent per year. (1995, 68)

In the United States, absolute carbon consumption by weight increased 1.8 percent per year in the period 1950–1993, the economy is increasing physically in spite of the fact that it produced lighter products, and there are no signs of net dematerialization or of saturation of wants (Wernick et al. 1997, 138, 142, 154).

These sobering facts stand in stark contrast to optimistic declarations made by some of the pioneers of dematerialization theory and research. Jesse Ausubel says,

> after a very long preparation, our science and technology are ready also to reconcile our economy and the environment, to effect the Copernican turn. . . . We have liberated ourselves from the environment. Now it is time to liberate the environment itself. (1997, 12)

In a similar vein, Ayres (1998, 68, 161) contends that tenfold dematerialization will be feasible because consumers are not ultimately interested in goods, but rather in the services they provide. He adds that because of dematerialization (contrary to the theories of Georgescu-Roegen), there is no upper limit to the services that can be obtained from materials. Daly provides a useful corrective to this argument, pointing out that

> to the extent that "dematerialization" is just an extravagant term for increasing re-source productivity (reducing the throughput intensity of service) then by all means we should push it as far as we can. Much excellent work is done by people who use the term in this restricted sense. . . . But the notion that we can save the "growth forever" paradigm by dematerializing the economy, or "decoupling" it from resources, or substituting information for resources, is fantasy. We can surely eat lower on the food chain, but we cannot eat recipes! (1996b, 28)

Environmental Kuznets Curve
The environmental Kuznets curve (EKC) concept essentially says that environmental degradation displays an inverted-U shaped pattern over time. It is low prior to economic development, increases in the course of economic development, and then decreases when income (GDP) reaches a "turning point." The World Bank's 1992 *World Development Report* presented evidence of such an inverted-U pattern (without making reference to an "environmental Kuznets curve"), on the basis of OECD pollution data (World Bank 1992, 40–41). Panayotou (1992) responded to the World Bank analysis by suggesting that there may be an "environmental Kuznets curve" (Kågeson 1998, 6).[14] Originally proposed as a hypothesis, it became a theory for certain researchers who decided it had been (at least tentatively) validated.

The evidence presented in support of the existence of an EKC is as follows. Shafik and Bandyopadhyay (1992) found, on the basis of observations in 149 countries in the period 1960–1990, that water quality, urban sanitation, and two air pollutants conform to the EKC hypothesis, but deforestation was not significantly related to income. Panayotou (1993, as seen in Stern et al. 1996) discovered EKCs for three pollutants (SO_2, NO_x, SPM) and also for measures of deforestation. Selden and Song (1994), using pooled time-series data and cross-sectional data from thirty countries, found EKCs for four air pollutants (SO_2, NO_x, SPM, and CO) with much higher turning points than in other EKC studies. Cropper and Griffiths (1994) studied the relationship of income growth and deforestation in sixty-four countries in Latin America, Africa, and Asia in the period 1961–1991. EKCs were found in Latin America and Africa (with much higher turning points than in the Shafik and Bandyopadhyay and Panayotou's studies), but not in Asia. Grossman and Krueger (1995) seek to overcome deficiencies in past studies by relying on high quality air and water pollution data, measured by a uniform methodology, in a restricted number of countries.

They found EKCs for most of fourteen pollutants measured and conclude that "contrary to the alarmist cries of some environmental groups, we find no evidence that economic growth does unavoidable harm to the natural habitat" (Grossman and Krueger 1995, 370).

Stern et al. (1996, 1152) remark that many of the authors of EKC studies are cautious in interpreting the policy implications of their results, but that other analysts, referring to their work, have tended to ignore the qualifications. An example is Beckerman, who contends, "[T]here is clear evidence that, although economic growth usually leads to environmental deterioration in the early stages of the process, in the end the best—and probably the only—way to attain a decent environment in most countries is to become rich" (1992, 482).

In spite of the level-headed and cautious approach taken in most EKC studies, the authors came under heavy criticism in the latter half of the 1990s. Arrow et al. (1995) said the EKC argument is deficient on four grounds. First, the EKC relationships identified apply only to pollutants that have short-term costs (e.g., sulfur, particulates, fecal coliform) and not to accumulating wastes or to pollutants involving longer-term and more dispersed costs (e.g., carbon dioxide), which tend to increase with income. Second, the EKC relationship applies to some pollutants, but not to stocks of natural resources. Third, decreases of some pollutants are associated with increases of other pollutants within the same country, or transfers of pollutants to other countries. And lastly, institutional reforms leading to pollution reduction often impose a burden on the poor and on future generations.

Stern et al. (1996) make four criticisms of EKC studies. First, these studies are said to neglect the possibility of negative feedback of environmental deterioration on economic growth. Second, they tend to ignore the fact that reduced pollution in developed countries may reflect the growth of human capital and capital-intensive activities in those countries, and the increase of resource-intensive production in developing countries. Developed countries may be reducing domestic pollution because they import more goods instead of producing them domestically. Third, Stern et al. (1996) fault the quality of data used in most EKC studies. Fourth, they detect a fallacy in the assumption that world environmental conditions may improve because world mean per capita income is at the level of the turning points for certain key pollutants. They note that the great majority of people in the world are below the world mean income, not above it.[15] Therefore, according to the EKC logic, global environmental impacts will increase rather than decrease in the medium term.

Other criticisms of the EKC studies are as follows. Roberts and Grimes (1997) contend carbon intensity is declining not because of widespread economic growth, but rather because of efficiency increases in several rich countries and worse economic performance in poorer countries. Kaufmann et al. (1998) argue sulfur dioxide pollution has decreased not because of increased income but rather because of changing spatial intensity of economic activities. Suri and Chapman

(1998) say an important factor explaining the downward slope of the EKC in industrialized countries is the import of manufactured goods from industrializing countries. Torras and Boyce (1998) state the downward slope of the EKC is explained by greater equality in political power in developed countries, which gives greater influence on policy to those who bear the costs of pollution. According to de Bruyn et al. (1998), the EKC relationship estimated from panel data does not necessarily hold for specific individual countries over time. Agras and Chapman (1999) reanalyze EKC models to demonstrate that energy price is a more important variable than income. De Bruyn (2000) argues that the downward slope of the inverted U is a temporary phenomenon explained by the oil shock between 1973 and the mid-1980s, and that in its aftermath, pollution rates are once again on the rise. Cole (2000, 87) says EKCs exist only for local air pollutants. Ekins (2000) states that the EKC is not unequivocally supported for any of the environmental indicators tested in various studies.

Ecological Modernization Theory

Ecological modernization theory (EMT) was originally formulated by Joseph Huber, Martin Jänicke, and Udo Simonis in the 1980s (Cohen 1997, 108)[16] and has since been elaborated by other writers. EMT says that economic growth and ecological sustainability can be reconciled through reform of production and consumption institutions and through technological innovation (Weale 1992; Spaargaren and Mol 1992; Mol and Sonnenfeld 2000b). Hajer explains that "ecological modernisation does not call for any structural change but is, in this respect, basically a modernist and technocratic approach to the environment that suggests that there is a techno-institutional fix for present problems" (1995, 32). Authors in the EMT tradition give considerable attention to the so-called front-runner countries (Denmark, Germany, Japan, the Netherlands, and Sweden), where they perceive important environmental advancements have been made.

EMT complements scholarship on dematerialization and EKC by interpreting trends in throughput and pollution reduction in a social and institutional context. As Mol and Sonnenfeld explain, "It is not physical improvements *per se*, however, but rather social and institutional transformations which have been and still are at the core of much current scholarship on ecological modernisation" (2000b, 6). Five types of perceived transformations are the focus of the EMT project: (1) the increasing role of science and technology in alleviating environmental problems, (2) the increasing importance of markets and economic agents as vehicles for reform, (3) trends toward decentralization and consensual governance, (4) the increasing involvement of social movements in mainstream decision making, and (5) the emergence of an ideology that believes in the convergence of economic and environmental goals (Mol and Sonnenfeld 2000b, 6–7).

Supportive critics have observed various limitations of EMT, for example, that it focuses on the nation-state and gives no attention to the supranational level (Christoff 1996, 486–87), that its analysis has been largely limited to countries of the West (Blowers 1997, 854), that it gives inadequate attention to institutional and political preconditions for EMT (Leroy and van Tatenhove 2000), and that it is theoretically vague (Mol 1996, 311) and lacks identifiable postulates (Buttel 2000b, 64).[17]

Dobson (1995, 206–7) levels three other criticisms. First, he asks why "hardheaded industrialists" would be concerned about the future without pressure on them that is external to the EMT model. Second, he questions the EMT assumption that environmental protection could be a source of future economic growth, and he notes evidence that not all environmental protection measures support growth. And last, he questions the assumption that ecological modernization would confer a competitive advantage on countries that produce products that meet high environmental standards. He observes that this presupposes a world where stringent environmental standards are in force, and it is not clear how this would be achieved without radical cultural change, which lies beyond the scope of EMT.

In summary, the theories of dematerialization, the environmental Kuznets curve, and ecological modernization have three characteristics in common. First, they were propelled by the growth and environment impasse of the 1970s and were inspired by overarching convergence concepts introduced in the 1980s. Second, all three have identified potentially important grounds for hope in the form of empirical data and identification of social and institutional trends. And third, according to critics, they may have overread, misinterpreted, or exaggerated some of these grounds for hope.

Social Theory Paradigms and the Growth Debate

As we have seen up to this point, the debate on growth and the follow-up developments seem to have taken place largely outside the realm of political ideology. An important factor contributing to this impression is the fact that some of the most visible figures in the debate (e.g., Herman Daly, Lester Brown, Wilfred Beckerman, David Pearce) have framed their arguments largely in terms of the logic of the managerial paradigm. The political dimension of the debate, therefore, has been overshadowed by attention to technical themes, for example, the complementarity or substitutability of natural capital, the relative merits of "strong" and "weak" sustainability, whether tenfold dematerialization is feasible, whether there is an upper limit on the services provision of materials, and so on. We shall see in this section, however, that there are patterned arguments on the growth issue (both anti and pro) within each of the three social theory paradigms, and that an aggregated view of these patterns provides important insights on the nature of the debate.

Class Antigrowth Perspective
Whereas in years past many proponents of the class perspective tended to support economic growth uncritically, there is now almost unanimous skepticism toward,

or opposition to, growth among class perspective authors in the environmental literature. This dramatic change is explained largely by the collapse of communism in the 1990s and the recent attempt by neo-Marxists to establish their credentials in the realm of environmental theory and politics (see chapter 3). It is important to note that there is a structurally mandated "mission" of states (whether communist or capitalist) to facilitate the process of economic growth. Thus the loss of state power by socialist and communist regimes has facilitated a mass defection to the antigrowth position. Most class perspective writers on environmental issues are now "outsiders" on the process of governance who can afford to distance themselves intellectually from the accumulation imperative.

Recent class perspective criticism of economic growth is implicitly a critique of *throughput* growth, while implicitly retaining support of *income* growth for the poor and the working class. Although this is a necessary semantic distinction, it is rarely made.

Neo-Marxism and political ecology are the most prominent antigrowth voices in the class tradition. The neo-Marxists' critique of economic growth is an extension of their critique of capitalism. Neo-Marxists have always been critical of capitalist economic growth but not of economic growth per se. It has long been assumed the "first contradiction of capitalism" concerning the limits to the exploitation of labor would ultimately lead to its collapse and replacement by socialism (O'Connor 1998, 160–61, 169–70). As explained in chapter 3, O'Connor (1996; 1998) identified a "second contradiction of capitalism" concerning the limits of environmental despoliation that he believes also implies ultimate collapse of capitalist economic growth. Different from O'Connor, various other neo-Marxist theorists contend the concept of environmental limits lies latent in Marx's original writings (e.g., Foster 2000; Hughes 2000). It is important to note that although neo-Marxists oppose capitalist economic growth, they often do not call for deliberate restrictions on this growth, seeing it as a process outside human control that must run its course.

Political ecologists contend that breaching the limits of growth invokes the need to restrict northern overconsumption as a means to relieve underconsumption in the South. As Sachs explains,

> Given that the Northern consumer class occupies the available environmental space to an excessive extent, a systematic retreat from using other people's land and share of the global commons . . . is the most important step to take in the spirit of global responsibility. (1999, 173)

Like neo-Marxists, political ecologists identify deeply rooted structural inequality lying at the root of environmental problems; unlike neo-Marxists, they sometimes call for cultural transformation as a means to resolve these problems. Also unlike neo-Marxists, they do not necessarily argue that flaws in the capitalist system will lead to its collapse.

The key characteristics of the class antigrowth perspective can be summarized through quotations from some of its key proponents (box 5.1). A fundamental as-

---

Box 5.1. Quotations Illustrating Class Anti-growth Perspective:

[T]he major institutions of modern society are "addicted" to economic growth and treadmill expansion (Schnaiberg and Gould 1994, 92–93).

[O]ur most worrying global problems are directly due to an economy driven by market forces, the freedom of enterprise, the profit motive and the quest for endless economic growth (Trainer 1996, 4).

[Capitalism's aim] is limitless growth, or money in search of more of itself. . . . On the other hand, nature is not self-expanding (O'Connor 1998, 10).

To understand the "messianic religion" of consumerism, one must eventually turn to production, to the profits that are the goal of production, to the never-ending effort to ensure that there are customers in profusion (Athanasiou 1998, 43).

Capitalist economies must expand, but the ecosystem that is their host is finite by nature. It cannot tolerate the indefinite growth of any human economy, least of all one as blindly dynamic as modern capitalism (Athanasiou 1998, 300).

Without expansion, the process of accumulation must fail (Low and Gleeson 1998, 163).

Without the capitalist economy, whose grow-or-die imperative is the primary force behind the ecological crisis, citizens would be free to reconstruct their social world along ecological lines (Biehl and Bookchin 1998, 136).

Far from being a transitory phenomenon, the bio-physical limits to economic growth redefines the conditions of wealth creation for the twenty-first century (Sachs 1999, 166).

[I]n a closed space with finite resources the underconsumption of one party is the necessary condition for the overconsumption of the other party. . . . the creation of economic value has always been the art of internalizing benefits and externalizing costs. . . . who is able to retain the first while shifting the latter elsewhere is obviously a matter of power (Sachs 1999, 168).

Economic growth as we know it is like the unregulated growth of a cancer that consumes and disfigures its host as its cells reproduce without seeming limit—until the host dies (Douthwaite 1999, xii).

There has emerged over the past five to six centuries a distinctive culture or way of life dominated by a belief in commodity consumption as the source of well-being (Robbins 1999, 8).

[W]hat the industrial economy calls "growth" is really a form of theft from nature and people (Shiva 2000, 1).

---

pect of capitalism is relentless growth (Schnaiberg and Gould 1994, 92–93; O'-Connor 1998, 10; Athanasiou 1998, 300; Low and Gleeson 1998, 163; Biehl with Bookchin 1998, 136; Douthwaite 1999, xii). Capitalist economic growth is on a collision course with ultimate environmental constraints, implying grave problems and ultimate collapse of this system (Trainer 1996, 4; O'Connor 1998, 10; Athanasiou 1998, 300; Douthwaite 1999, xii; Shiva 2000, 1). Alternatively, environmental limits imply dramatic changes in the way that wealth is created and distributed (Sachs

1999, 166). Overconsumption of resources originates in capitalist overproduction and the profit system (Athanasiou 1998, 43; Robbins 1999, 8). The biophysical limits to growth have aggravated world inequality (Sachs 1999, 168).

Class Progrowth Perspective

As suggested earlier, class perspective promotion of the concept of economic growth is in the process of becoming a historical artifact in the environmental literature. (One illustrative quotation is shown in box 5.2.) It made theoretical sense to favor economic growth prior to the 1990s, when there existed strong socialist and communist states striving to industrialize and to raise standards of living. (China is a strong state and nominally a communist one, though a convincing argument can be made that its economy is in fact capitalist.) Environmental issues were then a low priority for theoreticians in the class perspective, with some notable exceptions.

Managerial Antigrowth Perspective

The main proponents of the managerial antigrowth perspective are Herman Daly and other writers in the field of ecological economics, as well as Lester Brown and other writers at the Worldwatch Institute. These proponents show a strong identification with the concept of sustainable development (e.g., Daly 1996b), and in particular with "strong sustainability" (e.g., Prugh et al. 1999, 44; Martinez-Alier 1997, 20). Writers of this persuasion are strongly grounded in the fundamentals of managerialism: they devote most of their attention to policy, regulation, adjustment of economic incentives, and technological change. We shall see later on, however, that they go well beyond the bounds of the managerial domain.

The key characteristics of the managerial antigrowth perspective can be summarized with reference to quotations from some of its main proponents (box 5.3). Economic growth is viewed as being fundamentally against the interests of social welfare (Mishan 1967, 171), and it is also fundamentally inconsistent with ecosystem stability (Meadows et al. 1972, 188; Brown 1998b, 4; Brown and Mitchell 1998, 168; Brown and Flavin 1999, 11). It is assumed that economic growth will cease perforce under the constraint of biophysical limits (Forrester [1971] 1973, 68) and that politics will also bow to this pressure (Goodland and Daly 1992, 37). Among the main solutions are to improve global planning and management (Forrester [1971] 1973, viii) and to reform economic institutions (Brown and Flavin 1999, 11; Brown 2000, 21).

Box 5.2.   Quotations Illustrating Class Pro-growth Perspective:

[W]hereas some ecocentrists might disapprove of growth *per se*, Marxists do not. In the first place they see that the 'full development of modern productive forces' is necessary before socialism can be established (Pepper 1984, 170).

Box 5.3.   Quotations Illustrating Managerial Anti-growth Perspective:

[T]he continued pursuit of economic growth by Western Societies is more likely on balance to reduce rather than increase social welfare (Mishan 1967, 171).

Every day of continued exponential growth brings the world system closer to the ultimate limits to growth. A decision to do nothing is a decision to increase the risk of collapse (Meadows et al. 1972, 188).

The challenge is to design a path for both industrial and under-developed nations through the transition from growth to a viable equilibrium (Forrester [1971] 1973, viii).

The question is only a matter of when and how growth will cease, not whether it will cease (Forrester [1971] 1973, 68).

We believe that in conflicts between biophysical realities and political realities, the latter must eventually give ground (Goodland and Daly 1992, 37).

The unfortunate reality is that the economy continues to expand, but the ecosystem on which it depends does not, creating an increasingly stressed relationship (Brown 1998b, 4).

As the world economy has expanded nearly sixfold since 1950, it has begun to outrun the capacity of the Earth to supply basic goods and services (Brown and Mitchell 1998, 168).

For us, the key limits as we approach the twenty-first century are fresh water, forests, rangelands, oceanic fisheries, biological diversity, and the global atmosphere. Will we recognize the worlds' natural limits and adjust our economies accordingly, or will we proceed to expand our ecological footprint until it is too late to turn back? (Brown and Flavin 1999, 11).

There is no middle path. The challenge is either to build an economy that is sustainable or to stay with our unsustainable economy until it declines (Brown 2000, 21).

Managerial Progrowth Perspective

The main proponents of the managerial progrowth perspective are Wilfred Beckerman, David Pearce, Robert Solow, and Joseph Stiglitz. The institutions generally identified with this point of view are the World Bank, the World Commission on Environment and Development, the United Nations Commission on Environment and Development (UNCED), and other governmental and intergovernmental bodies. Like their managerial antigrowth counterparts, they tend to be strongly identified with the concept of sustainable development (e.g., WCED 1987; World Bank 1992), and in particular with the concept of "weak sustainability" (Pearce 1998, 45–46). Beckerman (1994), however, is an exception inasmuch as he objects strongly to the concept of sustainable development.

The identifying features of the managerial progrowth position can be summarized with reference to the quotations in box 5.4. In this perspective, economic growth and ecological stability are seen as ultimately compatible goals (WCED 1987, 51; World Bank 1988, 1; Goldin and Winters 1995, 14; Beckerman 1996, 197; Thomas et al. 2000, xxxiv). Technological innovation is viewed as one of

---

Box 5.4.   Quotations Illustrating Managerial Pro-growth Perspective:

The anti-growth movement and its accompanying excessive concern with the environment not merely leads to a regressive change in the distribution of resources in the community, it also distracts attention from the real issues of choice that society has to face (Beckerman 1974, 245).

I state that natural resources will be available for the foreseeable future, that those in short supply can be replaced, and, most importantly, that technological innovation is the means by which long-range prosperity can be established (Walter 1981, 44).

Growth must be revived in developing countries because that is where the links between economic growth, the alleviation of poverty, and environmental conditions operate most directly (WCED 1987, 51).

Economic growth, the alleviation of poverty, and sound environmental management are in many cases mutually consistent objectives (World Bank 1988, 1).

We differ from the antigrowth school, however, in our belief that the limits can be avoided—that the world will not necessarily come to an end—if imaginative policies are devised and implemented (Pearce and Warford 1993, 3).

Overall, economic growth and development are perfectly consistent with environmental protection, as is trade liberalisation (Goldin and Winters 1995, 14).

[E]conomic growth is a necessary condition for proper protection of the environment. In the longer run it is probably a sufficient condition (Beckerman 1996, 197).

Experience in the developed countries shows that attaining improvements in environmental quality requires more than getting growth policies right. It requires environmental legislation and a public-sector environmental regulatory structure that comes at some cost (Weaver et al. 1997, 254).

Probably the single most important observation one can make about the economics-environment link is that if we wish to save the world's environments we can only do so by modifying and reforming the way we manage the world economy and national economies (Pearce 1998, 3).

[T]he environmental damage and biodiversity losses from current growth patterns are frightening, but if they are addressed now, growth can achieve a better natural environment and reduce the number of poor (Thomas et al. 2000, xxxiv).

---

the chief means of overcoming resource constraints (Walter 1981, 44). It is argued that overall economic growth must be maintained to alleviate poverty in developing countries (WCED 1987, 51; Thomas et al. 2000, xxxiv), and the antigrowth movement is insensitive to the needs of developing countries (Beckerman 1974, 245). Modification of government policies and economies is key in achieving compatibility between economic growth and environmental sustainability (Pearce and Warford 1993, 3; Weaver et al. 1997, 254; Pearce 1998, 3).

Individualist Antigrowth Perspective
The individualist antigrowth perspective is largely identified with the *cultural* tradition in the individualist social theory paradigm. (Recall from chapter 3 that

there is a fundamental divide between a cultural orientation and a free market orientation in the individualist paradigm.) The perspective is closely related to the deep ecology movement which, as explained earlier, takes a strong stand against high standards of living, consumerism, and industrial development; it locates both the problem and the solution in the arena of values.

The antigrowth stance of deep ecology is largely implicit rather than explicit. It is remarkable how little deep ecologists actually say about the issue of economic growth, given the depth of their antagonism toward industrial civilization. There are two possible explanations for this silence and lack of analysis. The silence may be a reaction to the stigmatization of the rigid antigrowth position in the aftermath of the debate of the 1970s. Furthermore, this silence might have been reinforced by criticism of the deep ecology movement for insensitivity to problems faced by people in developing countries (see chapter 3).

Quotations from proponents illustrate the characteristics of this perspective (box 5.5). William Catton, in his classic book *Overshoot: The Ecological Basis of Revolutionary Change*, decries the "cornucopian myth" (a euphoric belief in limitless resources) and "cargoism" (the delusion that technology will always save us from our problems). He warns that these values are leading us toward "overshoot" (or growth beyond an area's capacity, leading to die-off). Essentially, his book describes the normative context in which humans appear to be choosing to ignore the limits to growth. He strongly emphasizes the fact that civilization is precariously and carelessly dependent on nonrenewable resources (Catton 1980, 157). The necessary response is collective acknowledgment of this precariousness and of the need to abandon affluence (Catton 1980, 233). The leading voices of the deep ecology movement have views on economic growth that echo those of Catton (Naess and Rothenberg 1989, 111; Bowers 1997, 79).

Individualist Progrowth Perspective

The individualist progrowth perspective is strongly identified with the free market tradition in the individualist paradigm. Unlike their antigrowth counterparts in the cultural tradition, proponents of the individualist progrowth perspective give frequent and explicit attention to the issue. This perspective was formed largely as a backlash to the success of the environmental movement in mobilizing a large following in North America and Europe. The leading contemporary proponents are Anderson and Leal (1991), Dunn and Kinney (1996), Huber (1999), and Bailey (2000b). The key organizations promoting this perspective are the Political Economy Research Center, the Competitive Enterprise Institute, and the Cato Institute. The perspective is founded on a strong belief in the beneficial effects of unfettered capitalism, free trade, and clearly defined property rights, and in strong opposition to the concept of sustainable development and to excessive government interference in the operation of the market and private enterprise.

The essential characteristics of the perspective are summarized through quotations by its leading figures (box 5.6). High per capita income and wealth,

---

Box 5.5. Quotations Illustrating Individualist Anti-growth Perspective:

The Industrial Revolution made us precariously dependent on nature's dwindling legacy of non-renewable resources (Catton 1980, 157).

We must then ask whether we can candidly acknowledge that general affluence simply cannot last in the face of a carrying capacity deficit (Catton 1980, 233).

But the key word 'economic growth' has continued to have great importance in politics, in spite of the growing evidence that it has negative influence on contemporary quality of life in the rich industrial nations (Naess and Rothenberg 1989, 111).

[Growthmania] is a terminal condition because continued economic growth is being achieved by exploiting renewable resources at a rate that now exceeds the self-renewing characteristics of natural systems (Bowers 1997, 79).

---

attained through expansion of capitalism and free enterprise, are essential for enabling environmental improvement (Kahn et al. 1976, 1; Reilly 1990, 18; Anderson and Leal 1991, 171; Dunn and Kinney 1996, 229, 233; Huber 1999, xxvi). Freeing of constraints on market incentives (Anderson and Leal 1991, 3, 171; Huber 1999, 154) and secure private property rights (Bailey 2000b, 17) are key to improving environmental quality. Knowledge and technological innovation avert resource limitations and can function to increase resource availability (Kahn et al. 1976, 17; Simon and Steinman 1992, 117). First World countries are relatively clean and multiply resources, whereas Third World countries are relatively unclean and waste resources (Anderson and Leal 1991, 171; Dunn and Kinney 1996, 229). Without growth, those who have attained wealth risk losing it (Anderson and Leal 1991, 169).

An emerging progrowth position draws on endogenous growth theory, which has much in common with the cultural individualist tradition. It is closely related to arguments put forward by Julian Simon (see chapter 4 and the example above). Endogenous growth theory, framed as a critique of neoclassical economics, argues that ideas and innovation cannot be considered external to models of economic growth, but instead are an intrinsic part of the growth process (Romer 1990, 1994, 1996). This body of thought has become influential in the short time since its introduction, and its effect is evident in many quarters. Aghion and Howitt (1998, 151–71) state that the accumulation of intellectual capital has deflected and can continue to deflect biophysical constraints on economic activity. Barbier and Homer-Dixon say that "sufficient allocation of human capital to innovation will ensure that in the long run resource exhaustion can be postponed indefinitely, and the possibility exists of a long-run endogenous steady-state growth rate that allows per capita consumption to be sustained, and perhaps even increased, indefinitely" (1999, 145).

An aggregated view of perspectives on economic growth from a social theory perspective yields an important insight. Positions on the benefits and liabilities of economic growth run roughly parallel to views on the benefits and liabilities of capitalism as a whole. While this may be obvious at some level, it is worth emphasizing because it was not always the case. This association between views on growth and views on capitalism has been disguised by three phenomena. First, until recently, there were voices in support of unrestrained economic growth and industrialization among class paradigm proponents. Second, there is the *appearance* that anti- and progrowth stances in the managerial arena are detached from political ideology because views on the merits and demerits of capitalism go unvoiced. And third, the

---

Box 5.6. Quotations Illustrating Individualist Pro-growth Perspective:

200 years from now, we expect, almost everywhere [human beings] will be numerous, rich and in control of the forces of nature (Kahn et al. 1976, 1).

[B]ecause of the evolution of knowledge and technology, resources are increasing rather than fixed (Kahn et al. 1976, 17).

Economic expansion contributes by generating financial resources that make environmental improvements possible (Reilly 1990, 18).

[T]he environment and the market are inextricably connected in a positive rather than a negative way (Anderson and Leal 1991, 3).

In the absence of growth, those at bottom can only improve their lot by taking from those at the top (Anderson and Leal 1991, 169).

Free market environmentalism also emphasizes that economic growth and environmental quality are not incompatible. In fact, higher incomes allow us to afford more environmental quality in addition to material goods. It is no accident that less developed countries have more pollution, lower health standards, and more environmental hazards (Anderson and Leal 1991, 171).

[T]hough there are always "limits," the constraints are relaxing rather than becoming tighter (Simon and Steinman 1992, 117).

Major factors contributing to a better environment include industrialization, urbanization, the creation of new wealth, technology, cheap energy, mining, . . . and free enterprise. . . . First World nations *multiply* natural resources; Third World nations *consume* natural resources (Dunn and Kinney 1996, 229).

Free Enterprise and Capitalism Improve the Environment (Dunn and Kinney 1996, 233).

The richer we get, the farther the footprint of our wealth extends: to our children, to our neighbors, then our lands, shores, rivers, lakes, and oceans. Wealth solves the problem of scarcity with abundance (Huber 1999, xxvi).

Free markets are green because they are efficient in the economic sense of the word, the one that matters (Huber 1999, 154).

[I]t is neither technology nor economic growth that stands in the way of environmental restoration; it is more often pernicious institutional barriers, including a lack of secure property rights, corrupt governments, and a lack of education (Bailey 2000b, 17).

existence of an antigrowth stance in the individualist arena (albeit a relatively non-vocal and undertheorized one) attenuates the appearance of wholesale support for economic growth on the right side of the political spectrum.

The Anatomy Of Isolation

We have seen that the economic growth issue involves dispute of a specifically technical nature concerning whether biophysical limits to growth exist or have been breached, and whether it is possible to reconcile income growth with de-crease in material and energy throughput. The issue also involves a specifically nontechnical, political dimension. This stands to reason because, as we have seen, views on the growth issue can be classified in terms of the social theory orientations and political moorings of the proponents.

I noted earlier that some of the richest and most highly theorized parts of the debate are taking place within the bounds of the managerial paradigm, apparently free of any political motivations concerning views on the merits and demerits of capitalism. In all likelihood there are political opinions that lie behind what appear to be purely technical considerations, but it is impossible to know them, since they tend to go unacknowledged and undiscussed by the protagonists of the debate in the political center.

It is important to thoroughly understand the political dimension of the debate inasmuch as it is often a reason for the polarization of views, in addition to the technical reasons. In this section we examine the phenomenon of paradigm isolation among various proponents: the tendency to reject or downplay the significance of social theory tenets (and in some cases, technical arguments) that lie outside the home paradigm.

Table 5.1 displays quotations illustrating paradigm isolation by antigrowth proponents. In the class perspective, Sachs (1993, 13) faults the managerial assumption that environmental diplomacy can control overuse of resources and pollution, and Schor (1995, 83) downplays the significance of a values revolution, favored by cultural individualists. In the managerial perspective, Georgescu-Roegen (1973, 38) criticizes Marxism for being as bankrupt as neoclassical economics in ignoring the laws of thermodynamics, and Daly (1973, 19) and Ayres (1998, 142) dismiss assumptions that are central to the free market individualist point of view. In the individualist perspective, Naess and Rothenberg (1989, 94) refuse to accept the Marxist notion that "technical development of the means of production" (by which they mean capitalist growth) is unstoppable, and Devall and Sessions (1985, 48, 61) argue against technocratic culture and reformist environmentalism, which are rooted in the managerial center.

Table 5.2 displays quotations illustrating paradigm isolation by progrowth proponents. (No quotations are available illustrating the class progrowth perspective because it is virtually extinct.) In the managerial perspective, Pearce (1998, 114) rejects the class argument for reducing northern consumption on the basis

Table 5.1.   Examples of Paradigm Isolation by Antigrowth Proponents

Home paradigm: target paradigm	Examples
Class: managerial	Far from "protecting the earth," environmental diplomacy which works within a developmentalist frame cannot but concentrate its efforts on rationing what is left of nature. To normalize, not eliminate, global overuse and pollution of nature will be its unintended effect (Sachs 1993, 13).
Class: individualist	Public opinion has only a limited impact on social, political and economic institutions. . . . There are strong vested interests in continued economic growth (Schor 1995, 83).
Managerial: class	In Marx's famous diagram of reproduction, too, the economic process is represented as a completely circular and self-sustaining affair (Georgescu-Roegen 1973, 38).
Managerial: individualist	Also the arguments justifying inequality in wealth as necessary for savings, investment, and growth will lose their force (Daly 1973, 19).
	I know of very few cases—if any—where totally unregulated competition in the private marketplace solved an environmental problem for its own sake (Ayres 1998, 142).
Individualist: class	Within Marxist literature, the assumption is sometimes made that technical development of the means of production essentially determines all other development. . . . Those who maintain that technological development must run its course whether we like it or not are mistaken both historically and empirically (Naess and Rothenberg 1989, 94).
Individualist: managerial	[T]he deep ecological perspective leads to an uncompromising stand against the main thrust of modern, technocratic culture (Devall and Sessions 1985, 48).
	While accepting the best of reformist environmentalism, many people have sensed that something is missing. They are asking deeper questions (Devall and Sessions 1985, 61).

that it will not increase income in the south; Beckerman (1974, 248) and Weaver et al. (1997, 2) dismiss the tenets of free market individualism; and Pearce (1998, 5) argues against moralism, which is essentially the same as cultural individualism. In the individualist perspective, Huber (1999, 152) lambastes the class paradigm belief that northern wealth causes southern poverty, and Anderson and Leal (1991, 170) and Huber (1999, 145 and 155) criticize expertise and planning, which are articles of faith of managerialists working to save the environment.

Implicit isolation with respect to the class paradigm, as described in chapter 3, is strongly evident in the economic growth-environment issue. Among antigrowth

Table 5.2.   Examples of Paradigm Isolation by Pro-growth Proponents

Home paradigm: *target paradigm*	*Examples*
Class: managerial	[No examples available]
Class: individualist	[No examples available]
Managerial: class	If incomes are reduced in the North, this does nothing for the South, and is very likely to make them worse off. This is because the "lost dollar" of consumption in the North does not magically reappear in the South (Pearce 1998, 114).
Managerial: individualist	[T]he free-market system will not achieve an optimum allocation of resources to the environment (Beckerman 1974, 248).
	We are not convinced by the economic philosophy of laissez-faire that prevails in the U.S. at the end of the 21st C. We profoundly disagree with this approach to solving our problems (Weaver et al. 1997, 2).
	Intellectually justified or not, moralism will not save the world for human beings or for other species (Pearce 1998, 5).
Individualist: class	The notion that our wealth derives from—worse still, *causes*— their poverty is arrant nonsense (Huber 1999, 152).
Individualist: managerial	[It is] naive to assume experts will do what is right rather than what is politically expedient (Anderson and Leal 1991, 170).
	Central planners disdain, and so never engage, the vast reservoir of initiative and intelligence in ordinary people (Huber 1999, 145).
	So long as central planners are in primary control, the environment will never be secure (Huber 1999, 155).

advocates, the "managerial-individualist alliance" tends to come across as the only relevant spectrum of possibilities—in effect, as "the only game in town." Manifestations of this tendency appear in various ways. Dobson (1995, 75), for example, says that if technological solutions are not possible, then changes in values and morality are the only course of action left. (No account is taken of resolving inequality as a basis for addressing environmental problems.) The proponents of ecological economics, while extremely critical of neoclassical economics, have almost nothing to say about capitalism itself, in spite of its obvious relationship to the issue of growth. The capitalist economic system is for the most part simply a given, ironically, much in the same way that natural resources are simply a given for their progrowth ideological opponents. Silence on the matter of capitalism is a tacit objection to the class paradigm premise that capitalism has a complex structure that needs to be understood and that ultimately can be replaced.[18]

Possibilities for Integration

We have seen that deep division on technical issues in the economic growth debate has led to a softening of stances and the emergence of convergence concepts and theories. In parallel fashion, there has been some softening of the social theory paradigm rigidities that have been an important motivating factor in the economic growth debate. We now examine various indications of willingness to cross paradigm boundaries to see if they constitute paradigm integration: the act of putting tenets outside the home paradigm on par with those in the home paradigm. The importance of these tendencies cannot be overstated, since they represent the hope of bridging chasms that have appeared to be unbridgeable. This exploration will be done in two steps. We first look at the evidence in the general environmental literature, and then at ecological modernization theory, which consciously aims toward paradigm integration.

Evidence in the Literature

Table 5.3 displays statements by antigrowth proponents indicating examples of crossing of paradigm boundaries. These statements can be interpreted as follows.

Class → Managerial Integration
O'Connor (1998, 185) acknowledges the utility of legislation in addition to social struggle, and Douthwaite (1999, 341) asserts that although international regulation would help, it is subordinate in importance to grassroots action. As explained in chapter 3, writers in the class tradition, generally speaking, tend to be overtly dismissive of the managerial approach or give it little attention. Jacobs (1991) and Low and Gleeson (1998), however, are notable exceptions as they place high importance on a strong state for achieving environmental goals. Wolfgang Sachs, one of the most prominent class perspective critics of growth has, as indicated earlier in the book, made a transition from trenchant criticism of managerialism to implicit support of managerialism.

Class → (Cultural) Individualist Integration
Athanasiou (1998, 43), Douthwaite (1999, 336), and Sachs (1999, 186) exhibit the belief that cultural transformation is essential to dealing with environmental limits effectively. This relatively new point of view in the class paradigm runs counter to the long-standing dismissal of cultural individualist tenets.

Class → (Free Market) Individualist Integration
No examples of such integration were identified, and this is not surprising given the depth of polarization between these two perspectives.

Table 5.3.   Examples of Paradigm Integration by Antigrowth Proponents

Home paradigm: target paradigm	*Examples*
Class: managerial	While these industries can afford to unclog nature's sink, or to keep it clean, they have no incentive to do so unless they are forced by social struggles and legislation (O'Connor 1998, 185).
	[A]lthough changes in international regulations would obviously help, the only realistic way of building a sustainable world is to do so from the bottom up (Douthwaite 1999, 341).
Class: individualist	Economic expansion is an *intensive* process as well, an expansion into life, culture, and the mind (Athanasiou 1998, 43).
	The first and most important step is to reject the notion that the achievement of economic growth is a fit, proper or desirable goal for any nation. . . . The second step must be to free the moral-cultural system (Douthwaite 1999, 336).
	"How much is enough?" leads without much detour to the question "What do we want?" Sustainability in the last instance springs from a fresh inquiry into the meaning of the good life (Sachs 1999, 186).
Managerial: class	A sustainable society would not freeze into permanence the current inequitable patterns of distribution. It would certainly not permit the persistence of poverty (Meadows et al. 1992, 210).
	I have deep misgivings about economic growth per se. This is partly because the evidence is growing that economic growth (such as it is) in the western world today is benefiting only the richest people alive now, at the expense of nearly everybody else, especially the poor and the powerless in this and future generations (Ayres 1996, 117).
	Unless the needs of the poorer nations for food, sanitation, cooking fuels, and other basic requirements are being met, the world's more affluent nations can hardly expect them to contribute to solving long-term global problems such as climate change (Brown and Flavin 1999, 20).
Managerial: individualist	To preserve what is left will require major legislation and strong powers of enforcement. But one cannot hope for these without a complete break with the parochial school of economics that has paralysed the mind of all governing authorities since the industrial revolution. It will require a new vision of the purposes of life (Mishan 1967, 7).
	The final, most elusive, and most important information we need deals with human values (Meadows et al. 1972, 186).
	The alternatives will involve fundamental changes in laws, values, religious attitudes, and expectations (Forrester [1971] 1973, viii).

Some will label us antitechnology or antimarket. We are neither. We are technically trained, and we are technological enthusiasts. . . .We also respect the virtues of the market (Meadows et al. 1992:162).

In this chapter, I begin with the arguments in favor of incorporating ethical values in the calculation of economic weights for ecologically sustainable outcomes (Gupta 1996:91).

We (the authors) see the cultivation of ecological economic values and the introduction of the policies for natural capital management discussed in this book as mutually reinforcing processes (Prugh et al. 1999:156).

We need a new moral compass to guide us into the twenty-first century—a compass grounded in the principles of meeting human needs sustainably (Brown and Flavin 1999:20).

Religious groups are well positioned to warn of the dangers of making goods into gods (Gardner and Sampat 1999:58).

Individualist: class	Many supporters of Deep Ecology find common cause with and support politically oppressed peoples in many Third World nations (Devall 1988:134).
	Marxist, socialist, and anarchist perspectives can help deep ecologists explore and understand the political and social factors . . . involved in degradation of our planet (Devall 1988:137).
Individualist: managerial	The reformist response has been extremely valuable. Many parks, nature reserves and forest have been, at least temporarily, "saved" (Devall and Sessions 1985:60).

Managerial → Class Integration
Managerial antigrowth proponents can sound forceful, even strident, when arguing against income inequality and for raising standards of living in developing countries (see Meadows et al. 1992, 210; Ayres 1996, 117; Brown and Flavin 1999, 20). This is a measure of their defensiveness against frequent charges by progrowth advocates that slowing economic growth condemns people in developing countries to permanent poverty and misery. Although these statements have the "ring" of a class argument, they in no way amount to embracing the class position because they are unaccompanied by criticism of capitalism.

Managerial → (Cultural) Individualist Integration
The writings of managerial antigrowth proponents make many references to the need for cultural transformation (Mishan 1967, 7; Meadows et al. 1972, 186; Forrester [1971] 1973, viii; Gupta 1996, 91; Prugh et al. 1999, 156; Brown and Flavin 1999, 20; Gardner and Sampat 1999, 58). So regular and so strong is this refrain that it is surprising when it is *not* voiced as part of an argument on how to cope with the limits to growth. This amounts to genuine belief in the tenets

of cultural individualism, though it tends to stop short of embracing the radical rejection of modernity and the mysticism that are characteristic of the deep ecology movement. It is an indication of the "managerial-cultural individualist alliance" discussed in chapter 3.

Managerial → (Free Market) Individualist Integration
Managerial antigrowth advocates rarely indicate any support for the tenets of the free market individualist paradigm. This is not surprising since free market individualism is wholly identified with a progrowth stance, and since unrestrained expansion of markets, in the view of managerial antigrowth advocates, is synonymous with the threat posed by growth. Appreciation for the market tends to be expressed in a defensive mode (e.g., Meadows et al. 1992, 162) and presupposes constraints on the operation of the market.

(Cultural) Individualist → Class Integration
As explained in chapter 3, deep ecology theorists have expressed rhetorical support for oppressed people in developing countries, in part as a response to criticism by class proponents. Devall's statements (1988, 134, 137) are an example of such a stance. Such views do not change the fact that the tenets of the class position are largely absent from deep ecology literature.

(Cultural) Individualist → Managerial Integration
The writings of deep ecologists often express appreciation for the influence of reformist environmental activists (e.g., Devall and Sessions 1985, 60). But these gestures of appreciation for well-meaning people in the political center are overshadowed by their contempt for technocratic governance, which they see as a key cause of environmental problems.

Table 5.4 displays statements by progrowth proponents indicating examples of crossing of paradigm boundaries. These statements can be interpreted as follows.

Class → Managerial and Class → Individualist
No examples of this kind of paradigm integration were identified.

Managerial → Class
Writings by managerial progrowth advocates are replete with references to the need for economic growth in order to reduce poverty and powerlessness, particularly in developing countries (Walter 1981, 161; WCED 1987, 38; Beckerman 1996, 16). If one were to read these statements out of context, it would be easy to imagine that they are declarations made by adherents of the class paradigm. But when these statements are interpreted in context, it is clear they in no way involve embracing the tenets of the class paradigm, as they are not premised on a critique of capitalism. Progrowth advocates have deployed the growth for poverty reduction argument as an ideological weapon against the antigrowth po-

Table 5.4. Examples of Paradigm Integration by Pro-growth Proponents

Home paradigm: target paradigm	Examples
Class: managerial	[No examples available]
Class: individualist	[No examples available]
Managerial: class	In order to provide greater opportunity for the disadvantaged, it is necessary that industrial growth continue (Walter 1981:161).
	It could be argued that the distribution of power and influence lies at the heart of most environment and development challenges (WCED 1987:38).
	Stopping environmental damage often involves taking rights away from people who may be politically powerful (World Bank 1992:14).
	The alleged conflict between economic growth and the environment often reflects a conflict between the interests of the rich and poor (Beckerman 1996:16).
	In many settings policies have favored vested interests of the elite, and thus not promoted adequate investments in human capital and natural capital, which are essential for broad-based growth (Wolfensohn 2000:xiii).
Managerial: individualist	Few countries have adequately confronted the underlying causes of environmental and resource degradation—the policy distortions, market failures, and lack of knowledge about the full benefits of environmental protection and resource conservation (Thomas et al. 2000:xxxi).
Individualist: class	[W]ithout such growth the disparities among nations so regretted today would probably never be overcome, that "no growth" would consign the poor to indefinite poverty and increase the present tensions between "haves" and "have nots" (Kahn et al. 1976:4).
Individualist: managerial	Free market environmentalism emphasizes an important role for government in the enforcement of property rights (Anderson and Leal 1991:3).

sition, and they have used this weapon to good effect, putting their opposition on the defensive (see the discussion above). A relatively recent theme in World Bank literature concerns the need to challenge vested interests and abuses of power by elites (World Bank 1992, 14; Wolfensohn 2000, xiii). The statements also resemble arguments made by adherents of the class paradigm, yet they have nothing to do with the tenets of that paradigm. The World Bank is faced with having to confront corruption, collusion, and nepotism in its client countries because they operate at such a high level that they threaten national and even regional macroeconomic stability and the Bank's loan portfolios.

Managerial → (Cultural) Individualist
Managerial growth advocates rarely refer to the tenets of the cultural individualist paradigm when addressing environmental issues. One rare case is Thomas et al. (2000, xxxi) who discusses lack of knowledge as an underlying cause of environmental problems. It is likely that attention to the themes of knowledge and innovation will increase among managerialists, however, as the influence of endogenous growth theory continues to increase.

(Free Market) Individualist → Class
Free market individualists, like managerial progrowth advocates, often mobilize the growth for poverty reduction argument and for the same reason: as a weapon against the antigrowth position. An example is supplied by Kahn et al. (1976, 4). Although this argument may be heartfelt, there is a degree of opportunism in it because it tends to disguise less acceptable motivations for advocating economic growth, for example, maintenance of the relatively high standards of living of the people making these arguments.

(Free market) Individualist → Managerial
As explained earlier in the book, free market individualists disdain the tenets of managerialism and argue for strong restraints on government and regulations. They tend to be libertarian state minimalists. The example taken from Anderson and Leal (1991, 3), a rare example of affirmation toward government, is actually consistent with this view. Government is viewed as important only inasmuch as it is used to support enforcement of property rights and other goals of free market environmentalism.

Two possibilities for integration appear to be particularly promising. First, there is strong evidence of "cross-boundary" support for cultural individualism by antigrowth advocates. For writers in the class paradigm, as mentioned in chapter 3, this overture is partly inspired by the limits of possibilities for traditional approaches (mobilization of labor, revolutionary insurrection, transition to socialism, etc.), and also by turf competition in the arena of new social movements. In the case of both class and managerial antigrowth advocates, there appears to be a firm conviction that the culture of overconsumption is a key problem that must be addressed by cultural means (among others).[19] Writers in the class tradition tend to describe the problem in terms of "irrationality" and the need for a revolutionary transformation toward "rationality" (e.g., Leff 1995; Biehl with Bookchin 1998, 135; O'Connor 1998, 10; Wallerstein 1999, 10; Sachs 1999, 87).

Second, there is great utility in a theoretical approach that puts production and consumption institutions on an equal footing. A dominant assumption in the class (and particularly Marxist) tradition says that production institutions (i.e., multinational corporations, multilateral banks, the stock market, etc.) have a lead role in shaping the trajectory of economic growth; consumption institutions (i.e., consumer preferences and tastes, purchasing power, etc.) follow this lead. The assumption in individualism is just the opposite: consumption institutions lead and production institutions follow. The increasing appreciation for culture and values in the class tradition amounts to an erosion of the assumption that production institutions must be the exclusive or dominant topic of analysis. Wolfgang Sachs (1993, 1999) epitomizes this new perspective, arguing that the history of unequal power relations between rich and poor countries is one key problem (implying attention to production institutions), and excessive consumption by people in the rich countries is a related but distinct problem (implying attention to consumption institutions).

There are important themes in this area that remain largely unexplored. In his book *How Much Is Enough? The Consumer Society and the Future of the Earth* (1992), Alan T. Durning identifies three "consumption classes" in the global population—"consumers," the "middle class," and "the poor." It is potentially fruitful to integrate analysis of consumption and production classes.[20] Another promising avenue for theoretical development would be to model economic growth in terms of both the "Salter cycle"[21] and Schnaiberg's "treadmill of production." The Salter cycle postulates consumption-driven, self-sustaining economic growth, whereas the treadmill of production postulates production-driven, self-sustaining economic growth. There is reason to believe both these models describe the real world, and it may well be that the two processes reinforce each other.

Ecological Modernization Theory

Ecological modernization theory (EMT) is strongly grounded in the managerial tradition. Its central concern is the transformation of the institutional structure of the state, corporations, and civil society. Policy and legal reform, modification of economic structures and incentives, and scientific and technological advancement are the main means through which institutional transformation is to be achieved. The essence of EMT is an optimistic outlook on the possibility of resolving environmental problems through technological change (Buttel 2000a, 30). EMT is identified with a Weberian vision of rationality (e.g., Mol 1996, 307; Cohen 1997, 105) and with the concept of sustainable development (Mol and Spaargaren 1993, 438; Young 2000b, 26–27).

EMT also gives strong attention to the tenets of individualism. Belief in cultural individualism is implicit in the theory's aim of reforming not just production but also consumption institutions. EM theorists have systematically sought to build a bridge between their institutional and technological focus to theories on the role of knowledge, culture, and values. A subset of EMT writers devotes attention to Giddens's theories on "reflexive modernization," which is the belief that in modern life "social practices are constantly examined and reformed in the light of incoming information about those very practices, thus constitutively altering their character" (Giddens 1990, 38). Some EMT researchers give specific attention to culture. For example, Cohen (1998) examines how the "cultural endowments" of particular countries condition their capabilities for re-solving environmental problems. Belief in free market individualism is implicit in EMT's strong endorsement of the market mechanism as a means of achieving ecological modernization.

EM theorists appear to be comfortable taking on board the tenets of individualism, and this makes sense, given that managerialism and individualism tend to have a common affinity for the institutions of capitalism. This coalescing of perspectives bears a strong resemblance to other examples of the "managerial-individualist alliance" alluded to in this book.

But EMT has a history of antagonism toward the Marxist tradition. Joseph Huber proposed the concept of "green capitalism," a move that led to a debate with proponents of the class paradigm (Mol and Spaargaren 2000, 20). Some early documents in the EMT literature rejected Marxism outright (e.g., Spaargaren and Mol 1992). Mol explained that "the ecological modernization approach diverges from neo-Marxist social theories in that it has little interest in changing the existing relations of production or altering the capitalist mode of production" (1995, 41).

In spite of EMT's history of rejection toward the class tradition, a motion has been made to move beyond polarization and toward making EMT the standard bearer of paradigm integration on the issue of economic growth and the environment. Mol and Spaargaren acknowledge that "there is indeed considerable merit in neo-Marxist analyses of environmental conflicts," and they explain that

> mainstream EM theorists interpret capitalism neither as an essential precondition for, nor as the key obstruction to, stringent or radical environmental reform. They rather focus on redirecting and transforming "free market capitalism" in such a way that it less and less obstructs, and increasingly contributes to, the preservation of society's sustenance base in a fundamental/structural way. (2000, 23)

Although the leading theoreticians of EM have made praiseworthy strides in the direction of paradigm integration, there are four indications that they remain short of their goal. First, the stated embrace of certain aspects of neo-Marxism rings rather hollow because, in the final analysis, EM theorists' faith in merely re-forming capitalism remains unshaken and is, in fact, a cornerstone of their theory (e.g., Young 2000b, 2, 27–28).

Second, proponents of EMT misunderstand neo-Marxism on some crucial points. For example, Mol and Spaargaren say the neo-Marxist perspective is challenged by the fact that there are "decreasing *fundamental* conflicts about environmental reform programmes in industrialised countries in the late 1980s and 1990s" (2000, 23–24). This has been true, to a degree, but this ebb in conflict will not necessarily endure.[22] Moreover, this perception does not change the fact that social conflict has considerable environmental relevance in places and in ways that EM theorists give scant attention to. EM theorists have touched on the issue of social inequality in their research, yet minimally, and they apparently overlook a key issue, social inequality as a *cause* of environmental problems. Blowers appropriately observes of EMT, "What it neglects to note is that modern society is composed of very divergent interests and that inequalities of wealth and power are endemic—indeed, a natural outcome of the process of the market economy" (1997, 854).

The third weakness in EMT's integrationist overture concerns the "prime mover" problem. There are cases where the dominance of managerialism in EMT makes its presence known in unmistakable ways, and in ways that are not conducive to a balanced appreciation of other perspectives. For example, Cohen, in an article highlighting the importance of cultural endowments, says, "Because ecological modernisation is technologically intensive and demands that countries address environmental problems in strictly scientific terms, it provides little flexibility for alternative epistemologies that deviate from this narrow course" (1998, 163). Hajer asserts that ecological modernization requires "an almost unprecedented degree of trust in experts and in our political elites at the same time as this trust is continually undermined by scientific controversies and political indecision" (1995, 11). Blühdorn (2000, 211) appropriately questions this managerial extremism.

In spite of these occasional indications of paradigm rigidity, some proponents of ecological modernization theory have shown genuine interest in facing the problem of paradigm isolation related to economic growth and the environment. Buttel says that EMT "raises particularly critical issues for the field, and with modifications has significant synthetic potential for making environmental sociological theory both comprehensive and empirically useful" (2000a, 19). Time will tell if EMT can serve as an appropriate vehicle for this worthy mission.

Conclusion

After a bitter debate erupted concerning economic growth and the environment in the 1970s, the polemic has continued, but at a lower level of antagonism. There are four main reasons for attenuation of the debate. First, partial clarification of the terms of the debate made it evident that income growth must be distinguished from material and energy throughput growth, and that the main challenge is whether a decoupling is possible where the former increases while the latter decreases.[23] Second, growth opponents were forced to modify their arguments through realization that income growth in developing countries is a moral imperative. Third, the concepts of sustainable development and quality of growth generated a climate of hope; convergence between the goals of poverty alleviation and environmental improvement were simply assumed as a rhetorical act of faith. Fourth, and most important, three "convergence theories" (dematerialization, the environmental Kuznets curve, and ecological modernization theory) provided empirical findings that could be interpreted as tentative evidence of reconciliation between growth and environmental quality.

But the economic growth debate is far from resolved and will continue to be a flashpoint for conflict, for two main reasons. First, the near-term potential for decoupling of income and throughput has proven disappointing, in spite of important scientific insights and technological breakthroughs. If the ultimate goal is to dematerialize the world's economies by 90 percent, then present trends are away from this goal, not toward it. Research on dematerialization has shown a decrease in the ratio of carbon to hydrogen in the energy mix, and decreasing rates of increase of material and energy intensity per unit of economic output. But these trends will only be meaningful when and if absolute throughput declines. Research on the environmental Kuznets curve has demonstrated an apparent relationship between high income and decrease of certain pollutants, but this finding does not apply to all pollutants, may disguise increased pollution outside the national polity where the relationship is detected, and may not endure over time, among other criticisms. Research on ecological modernization has documented social and institutional changes that appear to signal the possibility of reconciling high income and low throughput, but it is not clear that a sufficient level of dematerialization can be achieved through these changes alone, and it is far from clear that these changes are replicable in other countries. The bottom line is that the economic growth debate will inevitably intensify as long as throughput growth worldwide continues to increase in defiance of natural limits.

The second reason for assured continuation of the debate is that the issues are not just technical but also ideological and closely tied to social theory traditions. We have seen that positions against and for economic growth tend to be aligned (respectively) with views against and for the institutions of capitalism. There are some important departures from this overall pattern, and there are cases where it is not clear in what ways and to what extent (if at all) political ideology influences the position of a proponent. Nevertheless, it is clear that the growth and environment debate will continue to closely mirror our overall assessment of the promethean and destructive capacities of world capitalism.

What are the grounds for hope when the issue is viewed through the perspective of possibilities for paradigm integration? While ecological modernization theory has done some important, pioneering work on how to bring together the insights of all three classical traditions in a productive way, there are some shortcomings in the effort, and much remains to be done. Beyond this observation, there are two trends— one positive and one negative—that merit particular attention.

On the positive side, not just individualists but also proponents of the class and managerial traditions are arguing for profound changes in culture, values, and modes of consumption in developed countries, where average incomes are orders of magnitude higher than they are in the poorest countries. This form of paradigm integration has the potential for gathering momentum and becoming the basis for a widely shared agenda for change. On the negative side, the contribution of the class perspective, while clearly crucial to the debate, is greatly neglected. Capitalism is now hegemonic as an economic system, and it has a clear, if ill-defined, causal role in the environmental problems we face. Yet critical reflection on capitalism as an organizing framework for the world economy and visions of alternatives remain the province of a small, alienated, and ostracized segment of the world's intellectual community.

Notes

1. "Economic growth is generally defined as an increase over time in the level of real gross national product (GNP) per capita (or, sometimes, the real level of consumption per capita)" (Pearce and Warford 1993, 42).

2. Many others have made the same distinction between "growth" and "development." See Costanza 1991, 7; Jacobs 1991, 60; Ayres 1996, 118; and Thomas et al. 2000, 2–4.

3. Gross world product is "the total of goods and services produced and consumed per person throughout the world" (Porter et al. 2000, 2). It is the aggregate of all world GDP.

4. The extreme variance in patterns of world economic growth has little to do with the resource endowments of particular countries. If anything, on average, high resource endowments in developing countries tend to be inconsistent with achieving high rates of economic growth. See in particular, Auty 1995; Sachs and Warner 1995; Ross 1999.

5. Georgescu-Roegen was not the first to propose this idea. In 1922 Frederick Soddy wrote, "The principles and ethics of human law and convention must not run counter to those of thermodynamics" (Soddy 1922, 9).

6. Georgescu-Roegen added that economic activities are also subject to the constraints of an additional fourth "law," that is, that not just energy but also matter is subject to the entropy law. On the basis of this assumption, he reacted negatively to colleagues who produced "energy theories of value" which, in his view, ignored the dissipation of matter (Cleveland and Ruth 1997, 209).

7. For other discussions of the "weak sustainability-strong sustainability" debate, see Ollikainen 1997; Pearce 1998; Prugh et al. 1999; and Ekins 2000.

8. See, for example, "Are natural capital and human-made capital substitutes or complements? Both, of course!" in Cleveland and Ruth 1997, 205–9.

9. Contemporary opponents of throughput growth often echo this point. They still find it necessary to distance themselves from naive assumptions of the past, as well as to avoid the political implications of being labeled "antigrowth." For example, Brown and Mitchell explain, "Recognizing the limits of natural systems is often seen as a call for no growth, but the issue is not growth versus no growth. The question is, What kind of growth? And where?" (1998, 170).

10. See Chapter 7, "Energy, Choices for Environment and Development," and Chapter 8 "Industry, Producing More with Less" (WCED 1987, 168–234).

11. See, for example, World Bank 1987; World Bank 1988; Schramm and Warford 1989; and Connable 1990.

12. In spite of this self-critical component of the concept, the term "quality of growth" is sometimes used to mask campaigns to promote economic growth. See, for example, Zovanyi 1998, xiii.

13. As Bunker explains, "Proponents of dematerialization have failed to recognize that absolute volume of material consumed rather than volume relative to GNP is the significant measure in ecological terms" (1996, 419).

14. The term "Kuznets curve" refers to Simon Kuznets's (1955, 1963) hypothesis that there exists an inverted-U relationship between a measure of inequality in the distribution of income and the level of income.

15. They point out appropriately that "it is the median rather than mean income that is relevant" (Stern et al. 1996, 1157).

16. See Huber 1985; Jänicke 1985; and Simonis 1990.

17. For a summary of criticisms of EMT, see Fisher and Freudenburg 2001.

18. Daly and Cobb (1989, 2) implicitly critique capitalism in their search for a "third way" between capitalism and socialism. However, their objections to capitalism are not theorized and in the end may not be substantial, since they favor private ownership of the means of production (Daly and Cobb 1989, 14). Daly and Cobb's (1989) book is a prime example of the "managerial-individualist alliance" inasmuch as it focuses on the issues of economic reform and ethical/religious transformation.

19. Wallerstein views social irrationality as a form of cognitive dissonance, where "many people want to enjoy both more trees and more material goods for themselves, and a lot of them simply segregate the two demands in their minds" (1999, 5). Managerialists tend to focus on irrationality as a form of short-sightedness. For example, Meadows et al. say that "the majority of the world's people are concerned with matters that affect only family or friends over a short period of time" (1972, 24). Brown and Flavin lament that "we live in a world that has an obsessive preoccupation with the present. . . . we are behaving as though we had no children" (1999, 20).

20. Commenting on Durning's consumption classes, Athanasiou says, "In sharp contrast to the traditional left notion of class, which focuses on ownership, and specifically, ownership of the means of production, the focus here is on eating, drinking, and driving. If ever there was a conceptual revolution, a paradigm shift, this is it" (1998, 40).

21. Salter 1960.

22. For example, in the United States, changes in environmental policy introduced by the Bush administration are provoking conflict on a scale not seen in more than a decade. In Germany, rail shipments of radioactive waste into the country have provoked civil disobedience at a level not seen in many years. Dating from 1999, meetings of world leaders on international trade issues have been greeted with mass demonstrations (some of which turned violent) by protesters opposing globalization and trade liberalization.

23. I use the term "partial" clarification to underscore the fact that continued ambiguity on the meaning of the term "growth" allows both arguments (against and for growth) to have a prolonged life without having to truly confront one another. This is a classic example of proponents of an ideology oversimplifying reality in order to gain and maintain adherents to their cause.

CHAPTER SIX

~

Toward a New Concept and Definition of Environmentalism

The environmental movement holds its place in history as the largest political cause ever undertaken by the human race. (Roszak 1995, 1)

The lead actors on the global stage—nation-states—have come to bear greatly increased responsibility for environmental protection over the twentieth century. (Frank et al. 2000, 111)

Industry, however, may have the most vital role of all. Not only does it produce much of the world's waste and pollution, but its financial resources and extraordinary capacity for innovation make it the best—if not the only—candidate to lead the rescuing cavalry. (Frankel 1998, 13)

Concern about the state of the environment has grown rapidly since the 1960s, becoming one of the main preoccupations of people around the world. At the turn of the twenty-first century, it is clear that the voices of concern are no longer limited to civil society. The quotes above summarize this state of affairs.

Environmentalism has been seen first and foremost as a people's movement, one composed of ordinary people in the civilian population. This outlook is reflected in the quote above by Roszak (1995, 1). However, environmentalism is now a cause championed by people who believe that the nation-state has a leading role in healing the planet (e.g., Frank et al. 2000, 111). It is also espoused by people who believe that corporations are the standard-bearers of ecological salvation (e.g., Frankel 1998, 13).[1]

Whereas at the dawn of the modern environmental movement many of its partisans were looked upon askance, it is now hard to find anyone who does not identify with the environmental movement on some level, whether they are ordinary citizens, members of government, or entrepreneurs. Not only that, we have arrived at a point where leadership in environmentalism is contested among representatives of civilian society, the state, and private enterprise. This rapid expansion and change in the environmental movement, as we shall see, forces a wholesale revision of what the term "environmentalism" means.

This chapter makes the following four arguments. First, from the perspective of social theory, there are three distinct forms of environmentalism that I call "civic," "state," and "corporate." Second, an adequate understanding of the meaning, possibilities, and limitations of environmentalism requires that we identify the means-ends orientations of its proponents. In other words, we need to understand in what ways environmentalism is not just an end in itself but is also a means to other, nonenvironmental ends. Third, the contested visions of what constitutes authentic and meaningful environmentalism are guided largely by political ideology and are therefore best understood as forms of paradigm isolation. And fourth, attempts to forge unity among environmentalists (e.g., "stakeholder partnerships") can benefit from analysis and reflection based in social theory and guided by the concept of paradigm integration.

The rest of this chapter is composed of six sections. The first examines the shortcomings of conventional definitions of "environmentalism" and proposes a revised one better suited to current circumstances. The second defines and discusses "civic," "state," and "corporate" forms of environmentalism. The third explores means-ends motivations and defines "personal," "ideal," and "instrumental" modes of environmentalism. The fourth describes the dynamics of paradigm isolation in the debate over what constitutes authentic environmentalism. The fifth analyzes the tentative steps taken toward "unity among environmentalists" and identifies issues that must be taken into account in order to further the goal of paradigm integration in the realm of environmentalism. A concluding section sums up the chapter.

Defining "Environmentalism"

Most definitions of "environmentalism" explicitly or implicitly assume it is a civic movement and a civic movement only, that environmentalists are motivated by the belief that humans should overcome the tendency to dominate and control nature, and that patterns of overconsumption of resources must be brought under control. For example, Cunningham et al. in *Environmental Encyclopedia* say,

> Environmentalism is the ethical and political perspective that places the health, harmony, and integrity of the natural environment at the center of human attention and concern. From this perspective human beings are viewed as part of nature rather than its overseers. (1998, 380)

Pepper in a chapter of *Modern Environmentalism* titled "Defining Environmentalism" equates environmentalism with the green movement and lists its core attributes as beliefs that "humans are part of nature," "humans are naturally cooperative," "science and technology can't be relied upon," "indiscriminate economic growth is bad," and "we must get rid of the industrial way of life" (1996, 11–13). Guha in *Environmentalism: A Global History* argues that "environmentalism must be viewed as a *social* program, a charter of action which seeks to protect cherished habitats, protest against their degradation, and prescribe less destructive technologies and lifestyles" (2000, 3).

These definitions all ring true when judged against the reality that civic movements, motivated by and large by the new ecological paradigm (NEP; see chapter 2), have pioneered the modern environmental movement.

How well do these definitions serve, however, if we judge them against Anderson and Leal's (2001) free market environmentalism or Dunn and Kinney's (1996) conservative environmentalism? They do not hold up at all. Contrary to these definitions, conceptions of environmentalism on the political right focus on the day-to-day economic decisions of individuals and enterprises rather than on grassroots political mobilization. Moreover, these conceptions are predicated on the belief that humans have a legitimate role in controlling nature, that humans are self-interested, that science and technology are key to overcoming scarcities, that economic growth and industrialization are good, and that there is no need to change lifestyles. The conventional definitions of environmentalism also do not accommodate the emerging notion of state environmentalism, which encompasses the role of state actors and governments in addressing environmental problems.

How should we deal with this radical disjuncture between definitions and forms of environmentalism? Should we, as has been done up to now, ignore those who claim they are acting in the name of environmentalism but appear not to fit the standard definition? Should free market, conservative, and state environmentalists be criticized and declared illegitimate pretenders to the name "environmentalist"?

I argue that from an analytical standpoint this would be wrong. Instead, the definition of environmentalism should be broadened to accommodate those who claim to be operating under its banner. There are three reasons for this. First, people of all persuasions have seized on the term "environmentalism" for mostly good reasons having to do with motivation to address environmental problems. (This does not negate the fact that opportunistic motivations have also been at work.) Second, people will not abandon allegiance to the term "environmentalist" no matter how passionate and well-reasoned the arguments of their adversaries, because the environment has become such an important issue. Third, and most important, broadening the definition of the term "environmentalism" is a necessary first step toward specifying core attributes of the various ideologies and activities now encompassed by the term.

"Environmentalism" is here defined as a program of action by individuals or institutions claiming to be addressing the remediation of environmental problems. Indeed, the arena of debate has become so heavily charged and adversarial that it is impossible to retain a definition of "environmentalism" based on a particular political agenda or that denotes or connotes a particular course of action toward environmental betterment. In order for the term to have any residual meaning, it must be reduced to a baseline signification referring to the stated *intent* of improving the environment.

How has it happened that people of widely disparate views have latched onto the term "environmentalism"? Decades ago, there was overt antagonism to the notion of environmentalism by people in state leadership positions and in the corporate world. However, because of the explosive growth of the environmental movement, people in positions of power have been forced to change their tune. Capitulation has meant opponents embracing "environmentalism" and defining it in their own terms. These developments respond to the sheer political force of the civic movement, as well as to changed perception of the scope and nature of environmental problems. They are now seen as global, not just national (Buttel and Taylor 1992). We are now a "risk society," where anxiety about the high level of environmental risks has become pervasive (Beck 1992).

Now virtually everyone is a supporter of environmentalism. As explained by Buttel (1992), environmentalism is socially defined and, like other ideologies, it is indeterminate and malleable.[2] To fully understand the evolution of the concept, it is best to define the term "environmentalism" as widely as possible and then specify its various forms and modes.

Forms of Environmentalism

The three forms of environmentalism described here are designations related to the sociological characteristics of its proponents. The "civic" form refers to environmentalism carried out by members of civilian society, either as individuals or as members of nongovernmental organizations (NGOs). "State" environmentalism refers to programs of environmental action put forward by aggregates of nation-states, nation-states individually, or subcomponents of nation-states. "Corporate" environmentalism refers to programs of environmental action embarked on by businesses in the private sector. This section briefly describes the origins of each form and its relationship to social theory paradigms.

Civic Environmentalism
Guha (2000, 3–4) explains that environmentalism has developed in two waves in most countries. The first wave, dating back to the late eighteenth century, is the onset of an intellectual reaction to industrialization involving pioneering thought and prophecy. The second wave, occurring in the 1960s and after, involves the formation of a popular movement and a groundswell of public support

on the basis of intellectual guidance generated by the first wave. Rachel Carson's *Silent Spring* (1962) is widely regarded as the founding event of modern environmentalism (Paehlke 1995, 261; Guha 2000, 3). Air and water pollution, the oil crises of 1973 and 1978, nuclear power generation and accidents (e.g., Three Mile Island, Pennsylvania, in 1979 and Chernobyl, Ukraine, in 1986), nuclear weapons testing, oil spills, catastrophic industrial accidents (notably the Bhopal disaster in India in 1984), tropical deforestation and biodiversity loss, ozone depletion, global warming, and violence against environmental activists have been the main issues generating millions of supporters of the environmental movement around the world.

The dominant tendency is for followers of the environmental movement to be left of center (Milbrath 1984, 89; Paehlke 1989, 6; Jacobs 1997, 14). This tendency is explained by the fact that environmental campaigns have often been civic mobilizations against the actions and interests of private enterprise and, by extension, the political right. These mobilizations have been either against governments acting in defense of corporate interests and private enterprise (e.g., the antinuclear movement) or directly against private enterprises themselves. As explained by Paehlke, "The most obvious point of similarity between environmentalism and the moderate left is their shared willingness to intervene in a market economy on behalf of values that are not economic in the usual sense—that do not promote further economic expansion" (1989, 7). There are, of course, deviations from this broad tendency. Proponents of deep ecology demonstrate an affinity for the right through their cultural individualism, in spite of the fact that they are staunchly opposed to industrialism. The wise use movement in the rural West of the United States has a strong identification with the political right (Switzer 1997, 282; Tokar 1997, xvii).

The history of civic environmentalism is replete with debate and antagonism within the movement itself over the strategies to be used against the opposition. This is a reflection of the wide range of political views encompassed in the movement. Understandably, much of the debate and antagonism occurs between representatives of the left (class orientation) and the center (managerial orientation). The analytical literature on the growth of the environmental movement gives much attention to tensions between "radicals" and "reformists," and between direct action versus legislative/lobbying strategies.[3] For some radical participants in the movement, the term "environmentalism" is so closely linked to centrism and reformism that they cannot identify with the term. One example is Dobson (1995), who argues for "ecologism" in opposition to mainstream environmentalism.

In the 1990s, defenders of corporate capitalism attacked the logic, premises, and information of the civic environmental movement (e.g., Bailey 1994; Bailey 1995; Beckerman 1996; Arnold and Gottlieb 1998a,b; Arnold 1999). Defenders of the civic environmental movement then counterattacked (e.g., Helvarg 1994; Ehrlich and Ehrlich 1996; Rowell 1996; Beder 1997; Switzer 1997; Welford

1997; and Tokar 1997). Whereas at first tensions were played out within civic environmentalism, increasingly, antagonisms are played out between the civic and corporate forms. I will examine this in detail in the section "Isolation and Polarization" below.

State Environmentalism

The term "state environmentalism" was first coined by Dietz and Kalof (1992), who measured rates of compliance of 146 nation-states with nine international environmental treaties. A follow-up study on the same data set claims that state environmentalism is a function of a country's place in the core, semiperiphery, and periphery regions of the world system (see chapter 2) (Roberts 1996). The study shows that a nation-state is more likely to be a signatory to an international environmental treaty if it has higher per capita GDP, less political repression, and less debt (Roberts 1996). Wapner (1996) has described three levels of state-level environmental action: suprastatism, statism, and substatism.

Modern state-level action to resolve environmental problems is largely a response to the civic environmental movement that sprang into existence in the 1960s. Studies in the United States have traced the connection between the pressure of citizen action groups on legislators and regulatory change at the government level (e.g., Cramer 1998). However, like its civic counterpart, state environmentalism has a long history that dates back centuries. Grove (1995, 479) says that environmentalism in the colonial period was perceived as a concern of the state rather than individuals. He shows how independent groups of scientists in the colonial period, objecting to overexploitation of resources in colonies, induced conservation policies that restricted the activities of private capital while protecting the long-term interests of the state.

State environmentalism, as defined here, relates closely to the managerial paradigm. Representatives of government who are moved to address environmental problems will logically—given the constraints of their positions—conduct their work through the political process, use the legal and legislative tools at their disposal, and appropriate funds for research and technological development where necessary. For the same reason that managerialism is undertheorized in the realm of the environment (see chapter 3), state environmentalism is not theorized.

Although not referring to the term "state environmentalism," there are writers who have analyzed the role of the state in environmental action. Proponents of world society theory (see Frank 1997; Frank 1999; Meyer et al. 1997; Frank et al. 2000) argue that environmentalism results from the diffusion of science and world-level (Weberian) rationalization. They believe that scientific analysis of environmental problems dating back to the nineteenth century generated a world-level culture that put nation-states in a leadership role in addressing those problems, and that "domestic factors" (e.g., affluence, degradation, public opinion, media coverage) are mechanisms of change rather than causal forces (Frank et al. 2000, 111).[4] Lewis (1992), a leading proponent of centrist environmentalism, advocates a strong role for the state in a "guided capitalist" model. He counsels avoiding the extremes of leftist and rightist environmentalism in addressing environmental problems.

Corporate Environmentalism

The term "corporate environmentalism" was coined by Ed Woolard, chief executive officer of the DuPont Corporation, in a speech he made in 1989 after the *Exxon Valdez* oil spill (Athanasiou 1998, 233). Corporate environmentalism, like state environmentalism, is a response to scientific discovery and confirmation of environmental problems and to civic environmental mobilization addressing these problems. Corporations at first resisted nation-state regulation of their industrial processes. They then yielded and entered into a period of reluctant compliance, leading eventually to a "beyond compliance" posture for many companies. Corporate environmentalism can be rightly viewed as window dressing and making a virtue of necessity, although arguably there is more substance to corporate environmentalism than most critics would allow.

Hoffman (2000) postulates four phases in the evolution of corporate environmentalism in the United States.[5] In the (1) "industrial environmentalism" phase (1960–1970), companies dismissed environmentalists' concerns, objected to government intervention, and handled environmental management within the firm as an operating line function. In the (2) "regulatory environmentalism" phase (1971–1981), the establishment of the U.S. Environmental Protection Agency mandated the creation of environmental health and safety departments within firms, which were viewed by firms as a necessary evil. In the (3) "environmentalism as social responsibility" phase (1982–1988), the environmental movement bore down heavily on corporations after an attempt by the Reagan administration to roll back environmental legislation. In the (4) "strategic environmentalism" phase (1989–1999), firms began to address environmental management in earnest in response not only to civic and regulatory pressure but also to economic pressure from investors, insurers, and competitors. As Hoffman explains,

> Industry began to take a proactive stance on environmental protection as it once again perceived the problem as one it could handle itself. However, unlike the situation in the period from 1960 to 1970, autonomy was not part of the corporate perception of the solution. Instead, solutions were seen as emerging from a broad range of external constituents such as environmental groups, investors, and the government. (2000, 16)

Schmidheiny's *Changing Course: A Global Business Perspective on Development and the Environment* (1992) can be considered the seminal, founding document of corporate environmentalism.[6] The book pointed a self-accusing figure at the business world and called for wholesale changes. It argued for pollution prevention and ecoefficiency, as well as "stakeholder partnerships" (collaboration with environmental groups, regulators, employees, suppliers, and other interested parties). Even more provocatively, it contended that firms must adopt full-cost pricing: financial accounting of any natural capital that is exhausted as a result of their operations (Frankel 1998, 47). The follow-up study by Schmidheiny et al., *Financing Change* (1996), is also important, exploring whether various actors in the corporate environment (leaders, investors, analysts, bankers, insurers, accountants, and raters) are in fact positive forces for environmental change.

A key realm of thought in the corporate environmental literature is whether types of environmental management activity are "win-win" (the environmental gains and the firm profits) or "win-lose" (the environment gains but at a cost to the firm's bottom line). One of the optimists is Gallarotti (1995), who argues that "win-win" is the way of the future and that "win-lose" is a myth. The pessimists include Walley and Whitehead (1994), who argue that there are some "low-lying fruit" (practically effortless win-win opportunities) that can be easily harvested, but that beyond these, most environmental gains are at a cost to the bottom line. Hoffman (2000) takes the middle position, contending the real world is one of win-lose and win-win situations. He tends to lean in an optimistic direction, however, saying that corporations will lose out in the long run if they underestimate the strategic advantages to be gained by focusing on green possibilities.

Natural Capitalism (1999), by Hawken et al., is important from the standpoint that it analyzes the capitalist economy. This is a refreshing change from the overall isolationist tendency (described in chapter 3), in which proponents of capitalism tend to take the economic system as a given and see no need to even call it by its own name, let alone examine it. Another such example is Elkington (1998), who proposes the concept of "sustainable capitalism" and the "triple bottom line" (prosperity, environmentalism, and social justice).

"Conservative environmentalism" and "free market environmentalism" (see Dunn and Kinney 1996; Huber 1999; Yandle 1999; Anderson and Leal 2001) are related to corporate environmentalism. All three have a positive view of capitalism's potential for addressing environmental problems. However, there is an important difference. A recurring theme in conservative environmentalist and free market environmentalist literature is that the severity of problems has been greatly exaggerated and distorted by radical and mainstream environmentalists and the scientific community (see especially Dunn and Kinney 1996, and Huber 1999). Most promoters of corporate environmentalism tend not to be critical of allegations made by the scientific community and civic environmentalists, instead focusing on the capacity of firms to deal with environmental problems.

Modes of Environmentalism

A "mode" of environmentalism, as I define it, refers to the means-ends motivation that underlies environmental action. The "personal" and "ideal" modes of environmentalism are those in which environmental betterment is the goal.[7] "Personal" environmentalism refers to the actions of individuals aimed at protecting themselves against a perceived environment threat. It is typified by the U.S. oppositional expression "not in my backyard" (abbreviated NIMBY). "Ideal" environmentalism is aimed at benefiting humanity as a whole and/or the biosphere. Its character is eleemosynary—motivated by generosity or compassion. It is typified by the oppositional slogan "not on planet earth" (abbreviated NOPE). It is linked to the "public goods" meaning traditionally associated with environmentalism (see table 6.1).

A debate in the literature on environmentalism helps illustrate the importance of distinguishing the personal and ideal modes. In the 1990s scholarly attention increased toward environmental movements in developing countries (e.g., Taylor 1995; Peet and Watts 1996b; Bryant and Bailey 1997; Peritore

Table 6.1. Forms and Modes of Environmentalism

| Modes | Forms | | |
	Civic	State	Corporate
Personal	"Not in my backyard"	⟶	
Ideal	"Not on planet earth"	⟶	
Instrumental	Examples	Examples	Examples
	Employment in NGO	Access to elected office	Profit, advantage or survival in green markets
	Opposition to capitalism	Maintenance of stable rule	Competition through reduction of input costs
		Balance interests of civil society and capital accumulation	Price or supply constraint response
		Diplomacy and international security	Avoidance of prosecution and fines
		Avoidance of conflict and war	Deflection of criticism
		Maintain (or rescue) legitimacy	Maintain (or rescue) legitimacy
		Response to command or coercion	

1999). Inglehart (1990, 1995) sparked a controversy claiming that environmentalism is fundamentally a postmaterialist phenomenon. He argued that environmental concern is characteristic of rich countries, where people are above the level of subsistence (i.e., "postmaterial") and therefore have the means and the time to improve their environment. Brechin and Kempton (1994) countered with empirical evidence demonstrating that, in certain respects, environmental concern is higher in developing than in developed countries, and that it is qualitatively different, being motivated by deprivation. A debate ensued pitting the defenders of the postmaterialist thesis (e.g., Kidd and Lee 1997; Abramson 1997; Lee and Kidd 1997) against opponents of the thesis (Brechin and Kempton 1997; Dunlap and Mertig 1997; Guha and Martinez-Alier 1997; Adeola 1998; Brechin 1999). A broadened and inclusive definition of environmentalism, as proposed in this chapter, embraces the types of civic environmentalism found in both rich and poor, developed and developing countries. In the final analysis, the debate is essentially about the relative "weight" of personal versus ideal forms of environmentalism in rich and poor countries.

"Instrumental" environmentalism is that in which environmental action serves as a means to a nonenvironmental end. For example, a proponent of civic environmentalism might be an employee of an environmental organization. That person, in addition to having "personal" and "ideal" motivations, might also be inspired by the instrumental goal of being employed and receiving income from that environmental organization. Another instrumental goal of participation in the environmental movement might be opposition to capitalism. Environmental movements are not just a response to the gravity of environmental problems; they have also been an opportunity for progressive movements generally speaking to redefine the way in which they confront capitalism at the time of transition from social democratic to neoliberal or neoconservative rule (Buttel 1992; Buttel and Taylor 1992). As Buttel and Taylor explain, "It seems that New Social Movements have replaced social-democratic parties and trade unions as the bulwark of opposition to conservative parties and politics" (1992, 214).

State environmentalism can be seen as motivated, in part, by instrumental goals. A politician, for example, might support an environmental agenda as a way to gain access to elected office. The president of a developing country might voice support for an environmental program foisted on it by the World Bank through a structural adjustment loan. The instrumental goal would be to maintain the conditions of stable rule by securing access to needed funds. In pursuing expanded regulation of industrial activities, a given state might be acting on a structural mandate to balance the health and safety interests of civil society against those of capital accumulation and economic growth. Other instrumental incentives at the level of the state might be diplomacy and international security, avoidance of conflict and war, legitimation (domestic and international), or response to command or coercion by a higher-level authority.

Corporate environmentalism also can be motivated, in part, by the pursuit of instrumental goals, including the search for profit, advantage, and/or survival in emerging "green" markets; interfirm competition through efficiency improvement and reduction of input costs; response to price and supply constraints; avoidance of prosecution and fines that might result if environmental laws are violated; deflecting of criticism; and maintenance (or rescuing) of legitimacy in the eyes of environmentally minded consumers (see table 6.1).

There are two observations to be made about this new framework for defining the concept of environmentalism. First, the instrumental mode should be viewed strictly as an analytic description and not as a pejorative classification. The word "instrumental," like "ideology," tends to have a pejorative connotation, but that is not the intent here. In the same way that all people are ideological, all people have instrumental motivations for participating in environmentalism.

Second, the cells of this conceptual framework have fluid, not rigid, boundaries. A person or organization acting in the name of "the environment" can be influenced by personal, ideal, and instrumental motivations all at once. Civic environmentalist organizations and their employees are sometimes fancifully imagined as motivated only by idealism. Yet environmental NGOs can be entrepreneurial in character and can be functionally similar to for-profit firms inasmuch as they contribute to economic employment, production, innovation, and technological transfer; in these organizations self-interest and opportunism coexist with commitment, loyalty, and altruism (Meyer 1995).

At the other extreme, representatives of government and leaders of corporations acting in the name of the environment are often caricatured as engaging in environmentalism exclusively for instrumental reasons. It is useful to bear in mind that people working in government or in corporations do not, in doing their work, necessarily abandon their civic status. Legislators and corporate presidents are motivated not just by the functions of government and the bottom line but also by their civic concerns as members of the human community. This point is conveyed visually by the arrows pointing to the right from the NIMBY and NOPE cells (see table 6.1). As we shall see later, this has important implications for limitations and possibilities for effective environmental action.

Isolation and Polarization

The contest over future directions of the environmental movement became bitter and high-pitched in the 1990s. The debate over left or center approaches in the civic movement was partly eclipsed by angry exchanges between partisans of the left and right. The intensity of the battle is a reflection of what is at stake: influence over growing numbers of ordinary citizens who are ever more aware of the existence of environmental problems and who are seeking convincing explanations of their causes, their extent, and what to do about them.

Social theory perspectives on what constitutes authentic environmental action help us understand the political ideologies that underlie the contested visions of civic, state, and corporate environmentalism. Table 6.2 illustrates the debate with examples of class, managerial, and individualist proponents criticizing and rejecting the environmental efforts of their opponents. Analysis of these quotations helps us acquire a deeper understanding of what motivates the partisans and the dynamics of their battle.

Class Rejection of Managerialism

The statements by Schnaiberg and Gould (1994, 55) and Hay (1994, 217–18) exemplify the belief in the class perspective that government claims to be addressing environmental problems are mere window dressing, that such efforts are mandated by the need of states to seek public legitimation, and that popular mobilization is undermined by the fact that people believe real action has been taken by the state when it has not. This is an extension of the belief that the liberal state is an instrument of capitalism (FitzSimmons et al. 1994). A related critique is that proponents of mainstream (centrist) environmentalism fail to understand that ecological degradation is inextricably connected to broader issues such as economic inequality and Third World underdevelopment (Foster 1999a, 9–10).

Class Rejection of Cultural Individualism

Proponents of the class paradigm tend to be sharply critical of "green consumerism," the notion that waste and pollution can be greatly reduced through personal lifestyle change and consumption of environmentally friendly products. Tokar's (1997, xiv) rejection of cultural individualism says that individual consumer choices tend to be overruled by corporate decisions in ways that consumers are not aware of, and that waste and pollution are not meaningfully restrained because the overriding logic of the capitalist system is to increase consumption of natural resources.

Class Rejection of Free Market Individualism

Neo-Marxists believe that corporate environmentalism is a logical impossibility because serious attention to ecological destruction would cause the capitalist system to collapse. For this reason, Wallerstein (1999, 7) believes that all stated efforts by corporations to clean up the environment are mere public relations exercises disguising deep resistance to authentic environmental management.[8]

Managerial Rejection of Class and Individualist Perspective

Lewis (1992), typifying the centrist position, rejects all forms of extreme environmentalism that interfere with organizations such as the Sierra Club and the Audubon Society, which he views as tirelessly seeking to achieve their goals through conventional political and legal channels. Lewis's (1992, 1) indictment

Table 6.2.   Quotations Demonstrating Rejection of Environmentalism Outside the Home Paradigm

Home paradigm: target paradigm	Examples
Class: managerial	Governments must *appear* to be doing something to protect the environment, mainly to appease their environmental interest groups, who can cause political troubles otherwise (Schnaiberg and Gould 1994, 55).
	[T]he state-centered processing of perceived responsibility for environment degradation represents the single major factor preventing a global response to a global crisis (Hay 1994, 217–18).
Class: cultural individualist	The concept of "green consumerism" . . . is based on the myth that environmental problems are largely the result of individual consumer choices, neglecting all the ways in which these choices are shaped and constrained by decisions made in corporate boardrooms (Tokar 1997, xiv).
Class: free-market individualist	The implementation of significant ecological measures, seriously carried out, could well serve as the coup de grâce to the viability of the capitalist world economy. Therefore, whatever the public relations stance of individual enterprises on these questions, we can expect unremitting foot-dragging on the part of capitalists in general (Wallerstein 1999, 7).
Managerial: class and individualist	In my view, many of the most committed and strident "greens" unwittingly espouse an ill-conceived doctrine that has devastating implications for the global ecosystem: so-called radical environmentalism (Lewis 1992, 1).
Free market individualist: class	Socialism now has been visibly discredited throughout the world. . . . So the radical revolutionaries have turned to environmentalism as their rallying cry and their justification for acts of eco-terrorism and defiance of democratic processes and decisionmaking (Beckerman 1996, x).
	Many environmental leaders from the political Left owe their orientation to writings and philosophies of Karl Marx. From Marx, they got hatred of free enterprise along with skepticism about the ability of individuals to make decisions beneficial to the societies in which they live (Dunn and Kinney 1996, 3).
Free market individualist: managerial	When these institutional modifications are dissected, the "beguiling simplicity and apparent self-evident meaning" of sustainable development are replaced with the reality of political controls to discipline the citizens (Anderson and Leal 2001, 162).
	Predicting catastrophe is a good way of getting money to continue your research and showing what a compassionate scientist you are (Beckerman 1996, 6).

of "radical environmentalism" is leveled at deep ecologists (i.e., cultural individualists) as well as class proponents.

Free Market Individualist Rejection of Class
The statement by Beckerman (1996, x) exemplifies the free market individualist view that neo-Marxists have opportunistically seized on and exploited the environmental issue to propagate a worldview that has already proven to be unviable. A related view is that environmentalism of the kind advocated by Marxists directly threatens capitalism and the tenets of individualism (Dunn and Kinney 1996, 3).

Free Market Individualist Rejection of Managerialism
Free market individualists deeply distrust the concept of sustainable development, believing it implies government interference in markets and loss of individual economic freedoms (Anderson and Leal 2001, 162). Beckerman (1996, 6) attacks managerialists from another angle, saying that scientists opportunistically exaggerate environmental dangers in order to create an income stream for themselves. In a related way, Arnold (1999) launches a diatribe against the institutional foundations of civic environmentalism in his book *Undue Influence: Wealthy Foundations, Grant Driven Environmental Groups, and Zealous Bureaucrats That Control Your Future.*

Certain positions taken by the left and right in the United States, observed jointly, illustrate a contradiction and weaknesses in the arguments made. Polemicists of each side tend to portray their adversaries as having the upper hand in the battle for hearts and minds. For example, commentators on the left make the case that corporate activism has successfully undermined civic environmentalism by manipulating government and the popular will and by convincing the public that environmental problems will be adequately addressed outside of the political sphere (Beder 1997, 15, 25, 233, 234, 237; Tokar 1997, xii–xvi). Commentators on the right make the case that the left has achieved superiority through a powerful and well-funded coalition of left-leaning scientists, regulators, and lawyers who have dominated the educational system and the major media (Beckerman 1996, xi; Dunn and Kinney 1996, 117, 153–54; Huber 1999, xvi, xxvii, xxx). Of course, both positions cannot be entirely correct, and this mirror-image argumentation yields an important message. There remains much to be contested because in fact people have not been won over, and the government remains a multifaceted, complex entity that embraces a wide array of interests across the political spectrum. Switzer observes that "overall . . . neither the business community nor the grassroots movements that make up the environmental opposition have been able to dramatically change the direction of environmental policy" (1997, 284).

Political ideology is an appropriate frame of reference for understanding adversarial positions on what constitutes authentic environmentalism. I concur with Pepper, who says, "A study of the history of 'green' ideas about the relationship between society and nature . . . reveals that these ideas are, and always have been, part of deeper *ideological* debates" (1996, 2). While this point may seem obvious, its importance cannot be overstated because some have claimed that environmentalism must transcend the politics of left and right. For example, Paehlke has argued that "a full development of environmental ideas—an environmental ideology—becomes possible only when environmentalism is seen as neither "left" nor "right" (1989, 3).[9] My argument is that transcendence of political ideology is not possible or even necessarily desirable. Paradigm integration involves drawing on the best ideas that all paradigms have to offer.

Toward Unity among Environmentalists?

In his book *Toward Unity among Environmentalists*, Norton (1991) issued a call to overcome the differences among various tendencies. Typifying the time in which this plea was made, the book argues for reconciling positions within civic environmentalism. This aim is as worthy now as it was then, but as this chapter makes clear, the scope of the challenge is broader than it was in the early 1990s. Achieving unity now implies building bridges of cooperation among civic, state, and corporate forms of environmentalism, and it presupposes integration among the social theory paradigms that these forms represent. As we have seen in past chapters, this is a daunting if not impossible challenge, given the degree of polarization of interests. However, partial integration is not only possible but ultimately necessary.

We have seen in this chapter evidence of the antagonism and mistrust that characterize the overall relationship among some representatives of the three forms of environmentalism. However, against this backdrop of mutual hostility and contempt, pioneering efforts have been made to bridge these differences. Dating back to the early 1990s, there are examples of grassroots environmental organizations working with government, government organizations collaborating with industry, NGOs forging links with industry, and in some cases, all three working together. These multistakeholder partnerships (MSPs) are still fairly rare, but interest in them has grown rapidly in the last decade (Covey and Brown 2001, 2; Hemmati 2002, 11).

At the international level, the United Nations Commission on Sustainable Development has become a notable example of multi-stakeholder engagement (Hemmati 2002, 4). In the United States, the most renowned partnership has been the landmark 1991 agreement between the Environmental Defense Fund (EDF) and McDonald's restaurants to produce waste reduction strategies in the fast-food chain. Although EDF was criticized for "selling out," its initiative paved the way for similar NGO-corporate partnerships (Frankel 1998, 70). Other examples of partnerships include the NGO Cultural Survival working with Ben and Jerry's and The Body Shop to produce green products from the rain forest

(Mirvis 1994, 91), and the World Wide Fund for Nature (WWF) collaborating with the World Bank on a range of environmental projects. Collaborations between government and industries ("public/private partnerships") have been implemented in various countries to reward businesses that meet or exceed regulatory targets (Frankel 1998, 72). An example of a multistakeholder partnership is adaptive and collaborative management in forestry, which brings together all stakeholders (forest communities and their organizations, environmental NGOs, government, and businesses) in forested areas facing conflict over resource use and environmental degradation.[10]

Why have these partnerships come into being? In general, the reasons have to do with partners recognizing a new benefit from collaboration. For example, in fisheries comanagement in developing countries, organizations of artisanal fishers can provide local knowledge and management functions that the government itself cannot supply, while government partners can provide police functions and regulatory capacity that the fishers' organizations could not mobilize on their own (Sunderlin and Gorospe 1997). The U.S. Agency for International Development (USAID) and the World Bank have increasingly turned to funding developing country environmental NGOs instead of developing country governments due to the failure of top-down approaches in the public sector. Also, the debt crisis of the 1980s and structural adjustment have restricted government activities (Meyer 1995, 1277). In developing countries, NGOs benefit from a working relationship with government because they can have influence on policy they would not otherwise have (Bebbington and Farrington 1993, 202).

Can partnerships serve as an effective basis for fulfilling the goals of environmentalism? Environmental partnerships are still in their infancy and there has not yet been sufficient empirical research to draw any broad conclusions about whether such arrangements can function well to address environmental problems.[11] Nevertheless, research has been done providing useful preliminary insights on both positive and negative developments concerning MSPs. On the negative side, Hemmati (2002, 6) remarks that there is a widening split between NGOs that engage in multistakeholder collaboration and those that do not. According to Covey and Brown (2001, 2), "many civil society actors remain skeptical about the potential for positive social gain through cooperation with business organizations." Concerning collaboration between the World Bank and NGOs, Covey (1998) remarks that the long-standing culture in the Bank remains a strong force favoring the status quo (p. 84), critical NGOs perceive that NGO and community collaboration is merely a tool to facilitate Bank project completion (p. 89), and that NGO collaboration serves as a tool for the Bank to blunt strong advocacy (p. 106). Poncelet (2001a) conducted ethnographic research on four partnerships in Europe and the United States and found a strong tendency to minimize and diffuse conflict. According to Poncelet (2001a), these nonconfrontational practices, in turn, risk delegitimizing conflictual approaches and producing a retreat from radical thought and innovative solutions to environmental problems. MSPs typically have little decision-making authority (Dubash et al. 2001, 18), and this can understandably deflate views on their utility.

On the positive side, Covey and Brown (2001, 7) argue that a model of collaboration that they call "critical cooperation" is likely to lead to sustained constructive engagement. They remark that—even under adversarial conditions—"Critical cooperation in the form of interest-based negotiation is possible when the parties recognize that they can influence each other's well-being. The parties do not have to be equal in power—but they do have to recognize each other as capable of imposing significant costs or providing significant benefits." An in-depth report evaluating the World Commission on Dams (WCD) resonates with this outlook. The WCD, initiated in 1997 by the World Bank and the World Conservation Union (IUCN) in response to growing protests at dam sites around the world, overcame political divisions to produce a consensus report that was, by and large, well received by its widely diverging constituencies (Dubash et al. 2001, 15-18). One of the important ingredients in this success was that—different from previous commissions of its kind—the WCD had broad representation, including pro-dam lobbyists and anti-dam protesters, rather than limiting itself to a broad middle ground (Dubash et al. 2001, 4, 9).

I anticipate that the potential for effective partnerships depends on the three following theoretical questions. These are by no means the only relevant questions to ask, but I propose that they are among the most urgent to be addressed and researched.

1. *Can civic environmentalism maintain and build on its leadership role?* We have seen that contemporary state and corporate environmentalism have come into being and have been shaped by the strong advocacy role they played in civil society. The primary voice of environmentalism resides in civil society, and this makes sense at the theoretical level because personal and ideal motives are relatively free to express themselves in the civic realm, whereas their expression tends to be subject to structural restraints (i.e., influenced by competing or subverting goals in the work setting) in the state and corporate realms. The strength of civic environmentalism vis-à-vis government and the business sector may depend on the extent to which it can mitigate internal conflicts, reconcile the adversarial differences among radicals and reformists, and form coalitions that bridge these ideological and strategic divergences.

2. *Given that overconsumption in rich countries is a crucial problem and that it is sustained not just by consumption but also by production institutions, to what extent can environmentalists of all forms coalesce and give joint attention to these twin forces underlying environmental problems?* It is futile and pointless for class proponents to insist that excessive use of resources results only from the dynamics of production in the capitalist economic system; they must recognize that there is a strong cultural dimension to overconsumption that has taken on a life of its own and is susceptible to change.

It is just as futile and pointless for cultural individualists to insist that lifestyle change and recycling, in and of themselves, can adequately address the urgency of environmental problems; they need to acknowledge that there are powerful economic and political forces at work that favor increased consumption and that are endemic to capitalism. This logic necessarily involves cross-paradigm linkages.

3. *Are the incentives that motivate state and corporate environmentalism (see table 6.1) appropriate to overcome the tendency of capitalist enterprises to maximize material and energy throughput, pollute, and promote overconsumption?* At the level of the individual firm, there is conclusive evidence that a business can reduce raw material use, operate more cleanly, encourage less consumption by making a durable product or by other means, and still make a profit. The crucial issue, however, is whether these kinds of changes can happen at the level of the aggregate world economy. Does the capitalist system collapse if it is genuinely ecologized as some claim (e.g., Wallerstein 1999, 7), or do individual capitalists and therefore the system as a whole stand to gain through a greening of the economy, as others claim (e.g., Hawken et al. 1999, xiii)? These basic questions are not resolved and require far more research attention than they have thus far received.

Conclusion

This chapter defines environmentalism as a program of action by individuals or institutions claiming to be addressing the remediation of environmental problems. This broadened definition intends to supplant the outmoded view that only members of civil society engage in environmentalism. State and corporate actors take part as well. We need to move beyond the tendency to view "environmentalism" as contested terrain. It is best to adjust the breadth of the term to the size of the growing bandwagon and to analyze the characteristics of those claiming to be environmentalists with a wider array of conceptual tools.

A revised concept of environmentalism recognizes that there are civic, state, and corporate forms, and that there are personal, ideal, and instrumental modes. It is common to view civic environmentalism in terms of personal and ideal motivations, though instrumental logic is invariably at work as well. State and corporate environmental initiatives are often dismissed for being guided by instrumental logic, though this logic is not necessarily at variance with the goal of solving environmental problems, and though personal and ideal motivations are invariably at work as well. Appreciation of the complex structure of incentives involved in all three forms enriches our understanding of the possibilities and limitations of environmental action.

The environmental literature documents growing antagonism within the environmental movement, especially between representatives of civic and corporate environmentalism. The deep polarization among segments of the environmental community is best understood and interpreted with reference to political ideology and social theory paradigms.

Since the early 1990s, there have been attempts by members of civil society, government, and industry to surmount these deeply ingrained tensions and to form partnerships in specific projects. It is as yet too early to know if these are merely well-meaning but ultimately futile gestures, or if they are concrete steps toward "on-the-ground" paradigm integration leading to a resolution of environmental problems.

In the meantime, fruitful areas of inquiry would involve understanding to what extent civic environmentalism can maintain its leadership standing, whether consumption and production can be joined as objects of attention, and whether incentives motivating environmentalism in state and corporate settings can serve the goal of healing the earth.

Notes

1. Other examples include the following. "Like it or not, the responsibility for ensuring a sustainable world falls largely on the shoulders of the world's enterprises, the economic engines of the future" (Hart 1997, 76). "As we move into the third millennium, we are embarking on a global cultural revolution. Business, much more than governments or nongovernmental organizations, will be in the driving seat" (Elkington 1998, 3).

2. Eckersley makes the related observation that "the label *Green* is an extraordinarily elastic one that has been applied to, or appropriated by, all manner of environmental and political positions" (1992, 8).

3. The same literature also analyzes tensions between conservation and preservation, between "deep" and "shallow" ecology, and between ecocentric and anthropocentric perspectives. See especially Eckersley (1992) concerning the ecocentric-anthropocentric opposition and its political ramifications.

4. Buttel (2000c) counters this view, arguing that they do not sufficiently appreciate the power of social movements, and they falsely view transferring scientific rationality from the global level to the nation-state in conflict-free terms.

5. Frankel (1998) documents the emergence of corporate environmentalism in three phases: (1) the reaction of industries to publication of *Silent Spring*, (2) the aftermath of the Bhopal disaster, and (3) Beyond Compliance. See also Hoffman's (1997) history of environmentalism titled *From Heresy to Dogma: An Institutional History of Corporate Environmentalism.*

6. Other literature in the area of corporate environmentalism includes Choucri 1991; Stead and Stead 1992; Brown et al. 1993; Shrivastava 1996; Menon and Menon 1997; Roome 1998; Nattrass and Altomare 1999; Freeman et al. 2000; Prakash 2000; and Fineman 2000.

7. What I call the "personal" mode corresponds with Stern and Dietz's (1994) "egoistic" value orientation, and what I call the "ideal" mode combines their "social-altruistic" and "biospheric" value orientations.

8. See Greer and Bruno's (1996) accusation that corporate environmentalism is merely "greenwash."

9. See also Friberg and Hettne (1985), who propose a nondeterministic model of environmental action that avoids the left and the right, and Stead and Stead (1992, x), who argue that "if humankind is to evolve toward a more ecologically safe economic system, it

must recognize that protecting the Earth is an issue that transcends traditional left-right politics."

10. The Center for International Forestry Research (CIFOR) is conducting research on "adaptive and collaborative management" in Brazil, Bolivia, Cameroon, Zimbabwe, Malawi, Ghana, Indonesia, Nepal, the Philippines, and Kyrgyzstan.

11. Poncelet (2001b) has also done research on the change of subjective understanding of participants in environmental partnerships. Margoluis et al. (2000) have conducted useful research on the effectiveness of alliances for biodiversity conservation. The research focuses mostly on alliances among NGOs.

∼

CHAPTER SEVEN

Global Environmental Change and the Challenge of Paradigm Integration

A Race to the Finish

At the turn of the twenty-first century there is a growing body of evidence that environmental problems loom large in our future. Among the most persuasive and compelling forms of evidence are data on global warming and its consequences, the threat of continued ozone depletion, the proliferation of nuclear wastes and weapons, and the degradation of soils, sources of fresh water, and biodiversity. No less a catastrophe is the linked phenomenon of an ever widening gap between rich and poor.

Yet at the same time, worldwide concern about environmental threats has never been greater, and the mobilization to avert further ecological damage is evident in all walks of life: in daily conversations, on television and in films, in school curricula, in religious sermons, in government edicts, in newspaper and magazine advertisements, in the pronouncements of businesses. An optimist might conclude that the rapidly growing mobilization will surely overtake and defeat the threat. A pessimist will tend to conclude that no matter how rapid the expansion of civic, governmental, and business sentiment, it pales against the size of the looming disasters and that the basis for hope is slim, at best.

Someone attuned to the finer points of the issue would observe the following. More important than the speed and scope of the mobilization is its quality, sophistication, and capacity to cope with ideological diversity and division. The worldwide debate has entered a vitriolic and highly polarized phase. In the United States, for example, President George W. Bush decided in 2001 to favor unhindered economic growth and to pull out of the Kyoto Protocol on global warming, leading to considerable dissent in that country and around the globe.

Comparable decisions have been made by other world leaders. Some world leaders of government and industry deny the reality of environmental threats and press on with high levels of material and energy throughput, no matter what the cost. Divergent political ideologies underlie sharply differing views on whether a threat exists at all, as well as on the gravity of the threat and how to address it, assuming it exists.

An optimist would say—and there is a degree of truth in this—that differing and contradictory political philosophies confer valuable dynamism and creativity to the deliberations on how to address environmental problems. "Let a thousand flowers blossom," as one critical reader told me upon seeing a proposal for this book. A realist would point out—quite correctly—that it is useless to suppose that all parties to the debate can be persuaded to set aside their differences and construct a transideological paradigm. Divergent political philosophies will last at least as long as world capitalism imposes an uneven distribution of economic and environmental benefits and risks on the world's population.

A concerned outlook—which motivated the writing of this book—observes the following. The thoughts, writings, and actions of many environmental experts tend to be weighted toward, if not confined to, the tenets and beliefs of one of the three classical traditions of social theory. Yet clearly the tenets of all three paradigms are not only relevant but crucial to a more complete understanding of the nature of the problems and threats we face, and how to resolve them. Given how high the stakes are, can we afford to mobilize against environmental problems on the basis of shallow and incomplete theory, and be guided by modes of thought that have a built-in tendency toward divisiveness and parochialism? I think not. We must make every effort to understand and transcend those ideological differences and blind spots in order to maximize the possibilities of confronting environmental problems in a timely and effective manner. A review of some of the main messages in the book underscores this point.

Some Key Messages

Political ideology is something that we all have, not just our political opponents and not just partisans of the left and the right, but partisans of the center as well. Political ideologies of the left, center, and right are analogues of the class, managerial, and individualist traditions in classical social theory. The central tenets of all three paradigms are key to understanding the social and environmental outcomes of human evolution.

We can best understand both the good and the bad social and environmental outcomes of human evolution through attention to

- the emergence of class stratification at the dawn of agriculture and how successive modes of production have underpinned dramatic advances in the appropriation of nature

- the power of the state in urban agglomerations and how this underlies social complexity, large organizations, warfare, and rationalization of production
- the modification of human culture through time, and how this bears directly on the degree and quality of environmental transformation

The interactions among changes in class, power, and culture over time underlie modern trends toward explosive population growth, dramatic increases in average per capita energy use and affluence, increasing sophistication of technology, and corresponding impact on the environment.

It is vital that we acknowledge and understand the diversity of ideological and social theory perspectives on the causes of and solutions to environmental problems; they all embody a part of the truth, in spite of weaknesses and fallacies within each perspective, and in spite of apparent or real contradictions among them. Proponents of the three traditions tend to elevate their "home" perspective and either downplay or entirely dismiss the tenets of competing perspectives, through processes called implicit, contingent, or rejectionist isolation.

Political ideologies that guide approaches to addressing environmental problems tend to oversimplify reality. The "prime mover" logic requires casting away complexities that appear to conflict with tenets of the home paradigm or challenge their pride of place. This oversimplification has the benefit of assisting the process of recruiting and maintaining adherents to a cause through easily interpretable messages, but it imposes a high cost in terms of diminished effectiveness of environmental campaigns.

There is evidence of greater crossing of paradigm boundaries in environmental writings in recent years. These boundary crossings are largely unconscious and respond in part to worsening social and environmental conditions. In the class perspective environmental literature there is growing (though still slight) attention to the possibility of achieving gains through state channels and policy change and serious consideration to the need for cultural change. Some writers entertain the notion of market instruments serving a useful purpose. In managerial environmental writings, there is visible growth in attention to inequality and injustice, as well as to the need to achieve through market mechanisms what regulation and command-and-control systems have not. The complementarity of policy and cultural change is a long-standing theme indicative of a "managerial-individualist alliance." Cultural individualist writings voice concern for developing country poverty, but in a defensive way, and show appreciation for the importance of policy reform, but from a condescending point of view. Free market individualists writing on environmental matters show little tendency to yield ground to their theoretical adversaries and are the most insular among the perspectives.

At the aggregate level, there is clear evidence of a greater tendency to cross paradigm boundaries, though such open-mindedness and creativity remains far short of what could be achieved. One of the main messages of this book is that generating unity and a sense of common purpose in addressing environmental problems will require not only the courage to break with deeply entrenched modes of thought but conscious and deliberate action in doing so.

Examples of forward-looking attempts to transcend paradigm boundaries were examined in the case study chapters concerning the population-resource balance, economic growth, and environmentalism. Though bold and pathbreaking, some of these initiatives demonstrate important deficiencies. Lee's (1986) "Malthus and Boserup" synthesis deftly combines managerial and individualist perspectives on population growth but ignores Marx, a key contributor to the debate. Homer-Dixon's (1999) aggregated theory of population dynamics claims to give attention to all three traditions, but in the final analysis leans heavily on a individualist perspective. Some ecological modernization theorists aim to synthesize the insights of all three classical traditions, but this effort is encumbered by an outlook deeply rooted in managerialism. Through environmental partnerships, representatives of civil society, government, and/or business are beginning to forge alliances. These efforts are few and far between and are at an early stage. It is not yet possible to say if they hold promise as a means for crossing paradigm boundaries and addressing environmental problems.

Truly pathbreaking efforts at paradigm integration not only have to overcome a tendency to impose a prime mover logic on alternative models but must strive to give serious attention to the tenets of the class paradigm. One of the main messages of this book is that paradigm isolation against the class perspective is the most pronounced and dangerous of all. I do not advance a "prime mover" argument in favor of the class paradigm but rather recognize a crucial and often ignored fact. The tenets of the class paradigm face systematic and deeply ingrained hostility in the "official" forums of world decision making, in spite of the fact that attention to these tenets is absolutely essential to any viable solution. There is one good reason for this ostracization. Socialist and communist governments have been, for the most part, unpromising models of social and environmental improvement. But there is also a bad reason for exclusion of the class perspective. It challenges like no other perspective the logic of an economic system that gives free reign to the forces of greed and encourages consumption well beyond the level of need.

Selecting the Best, Discarding the Rest

In the course of the last decade, powerful arguments have been made for "moving beyond left and right" and for pursuing a "third way" (Giddens 1994; Giddens 1998; Giddens 2000). This philosophy is commendable to the extent that it seeks to move beyond ideological conflict into more productive paths of deliberation and social organization.

Giddens's approach, however, embodies important deficiencies. Implementation of Giddens's "third way" ideas yields a quasi-centrist model of social organization that accommodates itself with the status quo. As Hall (1998) explains, the third way advocates a politics without adversaries and ends up accepting the world as it is instead of attempting to transform it. Government leaders acting in the name of the third way are aligned with the interests of multinational corporations, neoliberalism, and globalization, and are thus at odds with the left. As Faux (1999, 74, 75) observes, the third way tends to be silent about the unequal distribution of wealth and power, and is a "rationalization for political compromise between left and right in which the left moves closer to the right." Ryan charges that the third way "rests on the assumption that the ownership of the means of production is not the central issue in politics" (1999, 78). Giddens's approach, although aiming consciously toward integrating what is best in all three classical traditions, ends up neutralizing some important perspectives.

The message of this book is different. Rather than dismiss or try to neutralize ideology, we should raise its profile and consciously examine the ways its various manifestations do or do not work in our collective interests. Rather than move beyond left and right, we should strive to build models of social organization that select the best features of all three social theory traditions and discard the rest.

It is far beyond the scope of this book to propose such a model. However, there are some elementary points of consideration that might serve as a useful point of departure for those who might embark on such a project. Table 7.1 displays some of the basic strengths and deficiencies of the positions of the key social theory paradigms as they apply to efforts at resolving environmental problems.

Strengths of the Class Position

Proponents of the class tradition argue convincingly that there are flaws in the capitalist economic system that are key to understanding environmental problems, yet these flaws tend to be systematically ignored by the custodians and defenders of the system. Class proponents emphasize the role of inequality and injustice in generating environmental problems, and from this standpoint, they are correct in indicating that there is no meaningful universal "we." The interests of one class are pitted against those of others, and unless we consciously come to terms with this fact, we cannot make much progress in resolving environmental problems.

Weaknesses of the Class Position

The credibility of the class perspective has been deeply compromised by the fact that socialist and communist countries have tended to be statist, nondemocratic, and environmentally destructive. Some theorists of the class tradition are striving to overcome this legacy with attention to democratic principles and with serious analysis of environmental problems. The class perspective has (with just a few exceptions) tended to underestimate possibilities for achieving environmental improvement through influence on the capitalist state.

Table 7.1.   Strong and Weak Aspects of Paradigm Positions

| | Paradigm Positions | |
Paradigm	Strengths	Weaknesses
Class	Addresses flaws of the capitalist system that are key to understanding environmental problems	Socialist and communist regimes have tended to be statist, nondemocratic, and environmentally destructive.
	Human beings *are* unequal and in this sense there is no universal "we."	The paradigm has tended to ignore possibilities for influencing the capitalist state.
Managerial	Policy and technological change are pivotal for addressing environmental problems.	States have acted in the service of elite interests and have promoted mass consumption.
	States and corporations are susceptible to increased legitimation and market pressure from consumers.	
Individualist	Profound changes in resource use are unimaginable without profound cultural change.	It makes no sense to think of humans only in atomistic terms.
		Cultural change is not a sufficient strategy.
	Markets can yield positive social and environmental results.	
		Capitalism is a cause of unprecedented threats to humans and the planet.

Strengths of the Managerial Position

Without a doubt, policy and technological change can have beneficial effects in alleviating environmental problems, even if such measures do not get to the root of the problem. Some sophisticated proponents of the managerial view understand that the state is a heterogeneous entity responding to many contradictory forces, and that states do not in every instance answer to the imperative of capital accumulation. The interests of the state are, in effect, contested terrain. They argue convincingly that states and corporations are susceptible to increased legitimation and market pressures from consumers as environmental problems worsen. Instrumental environmentalism is surely not the whole solution, but just as surely, it must be part of the solution.

Weaknesses of the Managerial Position

One weakness stands out above all others and is the opposite of the class position's overly instrumental view of the modern state. Many proponents of managerialism ignore or underestimate the extent to which most modern states have acted to serve elite interests and promote mass consumption. Such naivete has led to considerable waste of time, producing environmental initiatives that fail because they take no account of these constraints.

Strengths of the Individualist Position

Beyond a shadow of a doubt, profound cultural changes will have to occur, mainly in rich countries, if environmental threats are to be addressed adequately. Cultural individualists are correct that overconsumption and misuse of resources are deeply tied to systems of value and belief. Free market individualists have demonstrated conclusively that the market mechanism and innovation can yield positive social and environmental results in attempts to address resource scarcities and pollution.

Weaknesses of the Individualist Position

Individualists (both cultural and free market) tend to think in terms of the "universal we," and this is a myth. For many cultural individualists, radical transformation of belief systems and reduction of consumption are not only necessary but *sufficient* strategies for action, and this is at odds with what we know to be the case. Free market environmentalists tend to greatly overestimate the "magic of the market" and ignore the fact that benefits tend to be achieved within well-defined constraints (Kuttner 1996). Moreover, the free market environmental strategy tends to minimize the severity of environmental problems, largely because strong belief in the free enterprise system tends to blind its proponents to its defects. While providing some undeniable benefits in social and environmental terms, capitalism is also the cause of unprecedented threats to human well-being and the health of the planet.

Emancipation in the Nineteenth and Twenty-First Centuries

A series of analogies can be drawn between the campaign to abolish slavery in the nineteenth century and the movement to avert environmental catastrophe at the beginning of the twenty-first century.

Both slavery and our present patterns of resource use are founded on cognitive dissonance. Past civilizations—dating from the time of ancient Greece through the nineteenth century and modern world—formally espoused belief in democracy and equality among human beings and yet, somehow, permitted the institution of slavery to flourish. In the same way, at the turn of the twenty-first century, governments around the world and their citizenries have backed the concept of sustainable development, and yet indications are that abuse of the ecosphere is growing, not diminishing.

The institution of slavery was dissolved through the resistance of slaves and a militant campaign that held morality high as a guiding principle. Yet values and principles alone did not dismantle the evil institution. World capitalism had evolved in such a way that wage labor came to be more efficient than human bondage for generating economic surplus. In a similar way, the environmental movement is guided by personal, ideal, and instrumental motivations. People have been moved to action because personal risks have reached an unacceptable level, because there is widespread perception of the immorality that ecological desecration imposes on powerless people, on future generations, and on other species, and because environmentalism serves certain important, though little-recognized, ends in contemporary capitalism. And beyond this, there are other important processes at work that support environmental goals. World population growth will in all probability level off in the middle of the twenty-first century, and some tentative steps have been made in the direction of dematerialization.

Can these conscious and unconscious processes jointly avert ever greater environmental catastrophes? An optimist would put faith in world population trends and the evidence of dematerialization, viewing them as a hopeful turn of events as civilization approaches a precipice. A better-informed person would see that continued absolute growth of material and energy throughput will likely put considerable strain on resource availability and on the capacity of the globe to absorb pollutants, no matter how rapidly population slows and no matter how soon strides are made in the direction of absolute throughput reduction.

We must conclude, therefore, that conscious and deliberate mobilization is necessary to bring to an end the enslavement of nature. This will perforce involve continued efforts to lift the burden of human oppression because, as we have seen, highly unequal world incomes are at the core of our environmental problems. Ideas and ideologies need to be brought to the realm of reflection, action, and preemptive planning because mere reaction to ecological crises will not be enough. Worldwide deliberations on the fate of the planet will be carried out to an ever greater extent in democratic polities, unless the path of history reverses itself. This is a condition to be cherished and defended, because it improves the chances that all voices will be heard, not just those that have enough power and income to sit at the negotiating table. Democratic institutions will also assist in avoiding repressive and militaristic solutions to regional and national-level resource conflicts. The more democratic the decision making, the more disparate and conflicting the views will be. This underscores the need for maintaining open minds in listening to our adversaries and in reflecting thoughtfully on the ideas and motivations that we bring to these negotiations.

References

Abercrombie, Nicholas, Stephen Hill, and Bryan S. Turner. 1994. *The Penguin Dictionary of Sociology*. 3d ed. London: Penguin.

Abernethy, Virginia. 1991. "Comment: The 'One World' Thesis as an Obstacle to Environmental Preservation." In *Resources, Environment, and Population: Present Knowledge, Future Options*, edited by K. Davis and M. Bernstam, 323–28. New York: Oxford University Press.

———. 1993. *Population Politics: The Choices That Shape Our Future*. New York: Plenum.

———. 1994. "Optimism and Overpopulation." *Atlantic Monthly* 274, no. 6: 84–91.

———. 1995. "Editorial: The Demographic Transition Model: A Ghost Story." *Population and Environment* 17, no. 1: 3–6.

Abramson, Paul R. 1997. "Postmaterialism and Environmentalism: A Comment on an Analysis and a Reappraisal." *Social Science Quarterly* 78, no. 1: 21–23.

Adams, William Mark. 1990. *Green Development: Environment and Sustainability in the Third World*. London: Routledge.

Adeola, Francis O. 1998. "Cross-National Environmentalism Differentials: Empirical Evidence from Core and Noncore Nations." *Society and Natural Resources* 11, no. 4: 339–64.

Agarwal, Anil. 1990. "The North-South Perspective: Alienation or Interdependence." *Ambio* 19, no. 2: 94–96.

Aghion, Philippe, and Peter Howitt. 1998. *Endogenous Growth Theory*. Cambridge: MIT Press.

Agras, Jean, and Duane Chapman. 1999. "A Dynamic Approach to the Environmental Kuznets Curve Hypothesis." *Ecological Economics* 28: 267–77.

Ahlburg, Dennis A. 1998. "Julian Simon and the Population Growth Debate." *Population and Development Review* 24, no. 2: 317–27.

Ahmad, Q. K., et al. 2001. "Summary for Policymakers. Climate Change 2001: Impacts, Adaptation, and Vulnerability. A Report of Working Group II of the Intergovernmental Panel on Climate Change." N.p., n.d.

215

Albritton, Daniel L., et al. 2001. "Summary for Policymakers: A Report of Working Group I of the Intergovernmental Panel on Climate Change." N.p., n.d.

Alexandratos, Nikos. 1995. World Agriculture: Towards 2010. An FAO Study. Chichester, N.Y.: Wiley.

Alford, Robert R., and Roger Friedland. 1985. Powers of Theory: Capitalism, the State, and Democracy. Cambridge: Cambridge University Press.

Anderson, E. N. 1996. Ecologies of the Heart: Emotion, Belief, and the Environment. New York: Oxford University Press.

Anderson, Terry L., and Donald R. Leal. 1991. Free Market Environmentalism. Boulder: Westview.

————. 1997. Enviro-Capitalists: Doing Good While Doing Well. Lanham, Md.: Rowman & Littlefield.

————. 2001. Free Market Environmentalism. Rev. ed. New York: Palgrave.

Anderson, Terry L., and Randy T. Simmons, ed. 1993. The Political Economy of Customs and Culture: Informal Solutions to the Commons Problem. Lanham, Md.: Rowman & Littlefield.

Arizpe, Lourdes. 1991. "A Global Perspective to Build a Sustainable Future." Development 3–4: 7–10.

Arizpe, Lourdes, ed. 1997. Las dimensiones culturales del cambio global: Una perspectiva antropológica. Cuernavaca, Mexico: Centro Regional de Investigaciones Multidisciplinarias, Universidad Nacional Autónoma de México.

Arizpe, Lourdes, and Margarita Velázquez. 1994. "The Social Dimension of Population." In Population and Environment: Rethinking the Debate, edited by Lourdes Arizpe, M. Priscilla Stone, and David C. Major, 15–40. Boulder: Westview.

Arnold, Ron. 1999. Undue Influence: Wealthy Foundations, Grant Driven Environmental Groups, and Zealous Bureaucrats That Control Your Future. Bellvue, Wash.: Free Enterprise Press/Merrill Press.

Arnold, Ron, and Alan L. Gottlieb. 1998a. Ecology Wars: Environmentalism as If People Mattered. Bellevue, Wash.: Free Enterprise Press/Merrill Press.

————. 1998b. Trashing the Economy: How Runaway Environmentalism Is Wrecking America. Bellevue, Wash.: Free Enterprise Press/Merrill Press.

Aron, Raymond. [1955] 1957. The Opium of the Intellectuals. London: Secker & Warburg.

Arrow, Kenneth, Bert Bolin, Robert Costanza, Partha Dasgupta, Carl Folke, C. S. Holling, Bengt-Owe Jansson, Simon Levin, Karl-Göran Mäler, Charles Perrings, and David Pimentel. 1995. "Economic Growth, Carrying Capacity, and the Environment." Science 268, no. 5210: 520–21.

Ascher, William, and Robert Healy. 1990. Natural Resource Policymaking in Developing Countries. Durham, N.C.: Duke University Press.

Athanasiou, Tom. 1998. Divided Planet: The Ecology of Rich and Poor. 2d ed. Athens: University of Georgia Press.

Atkinson, Adrian. 1991. Principles of Political Ecology. London: Belhaven.

Ausubel, Jesse H. 1997. "The Liberation of the Environment." In Technical Trajectories and the Human Environment, edited by Jesse H. Ausubel and H. Dale Langford, 1–13. Washington, D.C.: National Academy Press.

Auty, Richard M. 1995. Patterns of Development: Resources, Policy, and Economic Growth. London: Edward Arnold.

Ayres, Robert U. 1996. "Limits to the Growth Paradigm." Ecological Economics 19: 117–34.

Ayres, Robert U. 1998. *Turning Point: The End of the Growth Paradigm*. New York: St. Martin's.

Bailey, Ronald. 1994. *Ecoscam: The False Prophets of Ecological Apocalypse*. New York: St. Martin's.

———. 2000a. *Earth Report 2000: Revisiting the True State of the Planet*. New York: McGraw-Hill.

———. 2000b. "The Progress Explosion: Permanently Escaping the Malthusian Trap." In *Earth Report 2000: Revisiting the True State of the Planet*, edited by Ronald Bailey, 1–21. New York: McGraw-Hill.

Bailey, Ronald, ed. 1995. *The True State of the Planet*. New York: Free Press.

Bandow, Doug. 1986. "A New Approach for Protecting the Environment." In *Protecting the Environment: A Free Market Strategy*, edited by Doug Bandow, 1–18. Washington, D.C.: Heritage Foundation.

Bannock, Graham, R. E. Baxter, and Evan Davis. 1998. *The Penguin Dictionary of Economics*. 6th ed. London: Penguin.

Barbier, Edward B., and Thomas F. Homer-Dixon. 1999. "Resource Scarcity and Innovation: Can Poor Countries Attain Endogenous Growth?" *Ambio* 28, no. 1: 144–47.

Barry, John. 1999. *Environment and Social Theory*. London: Routledge.

Bartlett, Peggy. 1989. "Industrial Agriculture." In *Economic Anthropology*, edited by Stuart Plattner, 253–91. Stanford, Calif.: Stanford University Press.

Beaud, Michel. 1983. *A History of Capitalism, 1500–1980*. New York: Monthly Review Press.

Beaudreau, Bernard C. 1999. *Energy and the Rise and Fall of Political Economy*. Westport, Conn.: Greenwood.

Bebbington, Anthony, and John Farrington. 1993. "Governments, NGOs, and Agricultural Development: Perspectives on Changing Inter-Organisational Relationships." *Journal of Development Studies* 29, no. 2: 199–219.

Beck, Ulrich. 1992. *Risk Society: Towards a New Modernity*. London: Sage.

Beckerman, Wilfred. 1974. *In Defence of Economic Growth*. London: Jonathan Cape.

———. 1992. "Economic Growth and the Environment: Whose Growth? Whose Environment?" *World Development* 20, no. 4: 481–96.

———. 1994. "'Sustainable Development': Is It a Useful Concept?" *Environmental Values* 3: 191–209.

———. 1996. *Through Green-Colored Glasses: Environmentalism Reconsidered*. Washington, D.C.: Cato Institute.

Beder, Sharon. 1997. *Global Spin: The Corporate Assault on Environmentalism*. Devon, U.K.: Green; White River Junction, Vt.: Chelsea Green.

Bell, Daniel. 1960. *The End of Ideology: On the Exhaustion of Political Ideas in the Fifties*. Glencoe, Ill.: Free Press.

Bell, Michael Mayerfeld. 1998. *An Invitation to Environmental Sociology*. Thousand Oaks, Calif.: Pine Forge.

Bellamy, Richard. 1999. "Liberalism." In *Contemporary Political Ideologies*, edited by Roger Eatwell and Anthony Wright, 23–50. 2d ed. London: Pinter.

Bennett, John W. 1976. *The Ecological Transition: Cultural Anthropology and Human Adaptation*. Oxford: Pergamon.

Benton, Ted, ed. 1996. *The Greening of Marxism*. New York: Guilford.

Berdan, Frances F. 1989. "Trade and Markets in Precapitalist States." In *Economic Anthropology*, edited by Stuart Plattner, 78–107. Stanford, Calif.: Stanford University Press.

Biehl, Janet, with Murray Bookchin. 1998. *The Politics of Social Ecology: Libertarian Municipalism*. Montreal: Black Rose.

Bilsborrow, Richard E. 1987. "Population Pressures and Agricultural Development in Developing Countries: A Conceptual Framework and Recent Evidence." *World Development* 15, no. 2: 183–203.

Blaikie, Piers. 1985. *The Politics of Soil Erosion in Developing Countries*. London: Longman.

———. 1999. "A Review of Political Ecology: Issues, Epistemology, and Analytical Narratives." *Zeitschrift für Wirtschaftsgeographie* 43, no. 3–4: 131–47.

Blaikie, Piers, and Harold Brookfield. 1987. *Land Degradation and Society*. London: Methuen.

Blowers, Andrew. 1997. "Environmental Policy: Ecological Modernisation or the Risk Society?" *Urban Studies* 34, no. 5–6: 845–71.

Blühdorn, Ingolfur. 2000. "Ecological Modernization and Post-Ecologist Politics." In *Environment and Global Modernity*, edited by Gert Spaargaren, Arthur P.J. Mol, and Frederick H. Buttel, 209–28. London: Sage.

Bohm, David, and Mark Edwards. 1991. *Changing Consciousness: Exploring the Hidden Source of the Social, Political, and Environmental Crises Facing our World*. New York: HarperCollins.

Bongaarts, John. 1996. "Population Pressure and the Food Supply System in the Developing World." *Population and Development Review* 22, no. 3: 483–503.

Bongaarts, John, and Rodolfo A. Bulatao. 1999. "Completing the Demographic Transition." *Population and Development Review* 25, no. 3: 515–29.

Bookchin, 1996. Murray. *The Philosophy of Social Ecology: Essays on Dialectical Naturalism*. Montreal: Black Rose.

———. 1999. *Anarchism, Marxism, and the Future of the Left: Interviews and Essays, 1993–1998*. Edinburgh: A. K. Press.

Boserup, Esther. [1965] 1993. *The Conditions of Agricultural Growth: The Economics of Agrarian Change under Population Pressure*. London: Earthscan.

Bottomore, Tom. 1993. *Political Sociology*. 2d ed. Minneapolis: University of Minnesota Press.

Boulding, Kenneth E. 1966. "The Economics of the Coming Spaceship Earth." In *Environmental Quality in a Growing Economy*, edited by H. Jarrett, 3–14. Baltimore: Johns Hopkins University Press.

Bowers, C. A. 1993. *Education, Cultural Myths, and the Ecological Crisis: Toward Deep Changes*. Albany: State University of New York Press.

———. 1997. *The Culture of Denial: Why the Environmental Movement Needs a Strategy for Reforming Universities and Public Schools*. Albany: State University of New York Press.

Boyden, Stephen. 1992. *Biohistory: The Interplay between Human Society and the Biosphere: Past and Present*. Man and the Biosphere Series, vol. 8. Paris: UNESCO: Parthenon.

Boyden, Stephen, and Stephen Dovers. 1992. "Natural-Resource Consumption and Its Environmental Impacts in the Western World: Impacts of Increasing Per Capita Consumption." *Ambio* 21, no. 1: 63–69.

Bradshaw, York W., and Michael Wallace. 1996. *Global Inequalities*. Thousand Oaks, Calif.: Pine Forge, 1996.

Braudel, Fernand. 1979a. *Civilization and Capitalism, 15th–18th Century*. Vol. 1, *The Structures of Everyday Life: The Limits of the Possible*. New York: Harper & Row.

———. 1979b. *Civilization and Capitalism, 15th–18th Century.* Vol. 2, *The Wheels of Commerce.* New York: Harper & Row.

———. 1979c. *Civilization and Capitalism, 15th–18th Century.* Vol. 3, *The Perspective of the World.* New York: Harper & Row.

Brechin, Steven R. 1999. "Objective Problems, Subjective Values, and Global Environmentalism: Evaluating the Postmaterialist Argument and Challenging a New Explanation." *Social Science Quarterly* 80, no. 4: 793–809.

Brechin, Steven R., and Willett Kempton. 1994. "Global Environmentalism: A Challenge to the Postmaterialism Thesis?" *Social Science Quarterly* 75, no. 2: 245–69.

———. 1997. "Beyond Postmaterialist Values: National versus Individual Explanations of Global Environmentalism." *Social Science Quarterly* 78, no. 1: 16–20.

Brown, Halina Szejnwald, et al. 1993. *Corporate Environmentalism in a Global Economy.* Westport, Conn.: Quorum.

Brown, Lester R. 1995. *Who Will Feed China: Wake-Up Call for a Small Planet.* New York: Norton.

———. 1996. *Tough Choices: Facing the Challenge of Food Security.* New York: Norton.

———. 1998a. "Facing Nature's Limits." In *Population and Global Security,* edited by Nicholas Polunin, 251–70. Cambridge: Cambridge University Press.

———. 1998b. "The Future of Growth." In *State of the World 1998: A Worldwatch Institute Report on Progress toward a Sustainable Society,* edited by Lester R. Brown et al., 3–20. New York: Norton.

———. 2000. "Challenges of the New Century." In *State of the World 2000: A Worldwatch Institute Report on Progress toward a Sustainable Society,* edited by Lester R. Brown, Christopher Flavin, and Hilary French, 3–21. New York: Norton.

Brown, Lester R., and Christopher Flavin. 1999. "A New Economy for a New Century." In *State of the World 1999: A Worldwatch Institute Report on Progress toward a Sustainable Society,* edited by Lester R. Brown, Christopher Flavin, and Hilary French, 3–21. New York: Norton.

Brown, Lester R., Gary Gardner, and Brian Halweil. 1999. *Beyond Malthus: Nineteen Dimensions of the Population Challenge.* New York: Norton.

Brown, Lester R., and Hal Kane. 1994. *Full House: Reassessing the Earth's Population Carrying Capacity.* New York: Norton.

Brown, Lester R., and Jennifer Mitchell. 1998. "Building a New Economy." In *State of the World 1998: A Worldwatch Institute Report on Progress toward a Sustainable Society,* edited by Lester R. Brown et al., 168–87. New York: Norton.

Brown, Lester R., Christopher Flavin, and Hilary French, eds. 2000. *State of the World 2000: A Worldwatch Institute Report on Progress toward a Sustainable Society.* New York: Norton.

Bryant, Raymond L., and Sinéad Bailey. 1997. *Third World Political Ecology.* London: Routledge.

Bunker, Stephen G. 1996. "Raw Material and the Global Economy: Oversights and Distortions in Industrial Ecology." *Society and Natural Resources* 9, no. 4: 419–29.

Buringh, P., and R. Dudal. 1987. "Agricultural Land Use in Space and Time." In *Land Transformation in Agriculture,* edited by M. G. Wolman and F. G. A. Fournier, 9–43. New York: Wiley.

Burkett, Paul. 1999. *Marx and Nature: A Red and Green Perspective.* New York: St. Martin's.

Burrows, Brian, Alan Mayne, and Dr. Paul Newbury. 1991. *Into the 21st Century: A Handbook for a Sustainable Future.* Twickenham, U.K.: Adamantine.

Buttel, Frederick H. 1992. "Environmentalization: Origins, Processes, and Implications for Rural Social Change." *Rural Sociology* 57, no. 1: 1–27.

———. 1995. "Biotechnology: An Epoch-Making Technology?" In *The Biotechnology Revolution*, edited by Martin Fransman, Gerd Junne, and Annemieke Roobeek, 25–45. Oxford: Blackwell.

———. 1996. "Environmental and Resource Sociology: Theoretical Issues and Opportunities for Synthesis." *Rural Sociology* 61, no. 1: 56–76.

———. 2000a. "Classical Theory and Contemporary Environmental Sociology: Some Reflections on the Antecedents and Prospects for Reflexive Modernization Theories in the Study of Environment and Society." In *Environment and Global Modernity*, edited by Gert Spaargaren, Arthur P.J. Mol, and Frederick H. Buttel, 17–39. London: Sage.

———. 2000b. "Ecological Modernization as Social Theory." *GeoForum* 31: 57–65.

———. 2000c. "World Society, the Nation-State, and Environmental Protection: Comment on Frank, Hironaka, and Schofer." *American Sociological Review* 65, no. 1: 117–21.

Buttel, Frederick H., and Peter J. Taylor. 1992. "Environmental Sociology and Global Environmental Change: A Critical Assessment." *Society and Natural Resources* 5, no. 3: 211–30.

Cahn, Matthew Alan. 1995. *Environmental Deceptions: The Tension between Liberalism and Environmental Policymaking in the United States*. Albany: State University of New York Press.

Callinocos, Alex. 1999. *Social Theory: A Historical Introduction*. Washington Square: New York University Press.

Carson, Rachel. 1962. *Silent Spring*. Boston: Houghton Mifflin.

Catton, William R., Jr. *Overshoot: The Ecological Basis of Revolutionary Change*. Urbana: University of Illinois Press, 1980.

Catton, William R., and Riley E. Dunlap. 1978. "Environmental Sociology: A New Paradigm." *American Sociologist* 13: 41–49.

———. 1980. "A New Ecological Paradigm for Post-Exuberant Sociology." *American Behavioral Scientist* 24, no. 1: 15–47.

Chesnais, J. C. 1992. *The Demographic Transition: Stages, Patterns and Economic Implications*. Oxford: Clarendon.

Chickering, A. Lawrence. 1993. *Beyond Left and Right: Breaking the Political Stalemate*. San Francisco: Institute for Contemporary Studies.

Choucri, Nazli. 1991. "The Global Environment and Multinational Corporations." *Technology Review* 94, no. 3: 52–59.

Christoff, Peter. 1996. "Ecological Modernisation, Ecological Modernities." *Environmental Politics* 5, no. 3: 476–500.

Cincotta, Richard P., and Robert Engelman. 1997. "Economics and Rapid Change: The Influence of Population Growth." Occasional Paper 3. Washington, D.C.: Population Action International.

———. 2000. *Nature's Place: Human Population and the Future of Biological Diversity*. Washington, D.C.: Population Action International.

Clark, J. D., and J. W. K. Harris. 1985. "Fire and Its Roles in Early Hominid Lifeways." *African Archeological Review* 3: 3–27.

Cleveland, Cutler J., and Matthias Ruth. 1997. "When, Where, and by How Much Do Biophysical Limits Constrain the Economic Process? A Survey of Nicholas Georgescu-

Roegen's Contribution to Ecological Economics." *Ecological Economics* 22, no. 3: 203–23.

Coale, Ansley J. 1974. "The History of the Human Population." *Scientific American* 231, no. 3: 41–51.

Coale, Ansley, and Susan Cotts Watkins, eds. 1986. *The Decline of Fertility in Europe.* Princeton, N.J.: Princeton University Press.

Cohen, Joel E. 1995. *How Many People Can the Earth Support?* New York: Norton.

Cohen, Maurie J. 1997. "Risk Society and Ecological Modernisation." *Futures* 29, no. 2: 105–19.

———. 1998. "Science and the Environment: Assessing Cultural Capacity for Ecological Modernization." *Public Understanding of Science* 7, no. 2: 149–67.

Cole, Matthew A. 2000. *Trade Liberalisation, Economic Growth, and the Environment.* Cheltenham, U.K.: Edward Elgar.

Collins, Randall. 1994. *Four Sociological Traditions.* New York: Oxford University Press.

Colman, David. 1994. "Biotechnology and Agriculture." In *Ethics and Biotechnology,* edited by Anthony Dyson and John Harris, 33–46. London: Routledge.

Commoner, Barry. 1971. *The Closing Circle: Nature, Man, and Technology.* New York: Knopf.

———. 1972. "The Environmental Cost of Economic Growth." In *Energy, Economic Growth, and the Environment,* edited by Sam H. Schurr, 30–65. Baltimore: Johns Hopkins University Press.

Competitive Enterprise Institute. 1999. "Issue Brief: Population." <www.cei.org/EBBReader.asp?ID=739> (February 5, 2001).

Connable, Barber B. 1990. "Development and the Environment: A Global Balance." *International Environmental Affairs* 2, no. 1: 3–13.

Conway, Gordon. 1997. *The Doubly Green Revolution: Food for All in the 21st Century.* Ithaca, N.Y.: Cornell University Press.

Conway, Gordon R., Uma Lele, Jim Peacock, and Marin Piñeiro. 1994. *Sustainable Agriculture for a Food Secure World.* Washington, D.C.: Consultative Group on International Agricultural Research. Stockholm, Sweden: Swedish Agency for Research and Cooperation with Developing Countries.

Cook, Earl F. 1971. "The Flow of Energy in an Industrial Society." *Scientific American* 225, no. 3 (1971): 134–44.

Cormack, Mike. 1992. *Ideology.* Ann Arbor, Mich.: University of Michigan Press.

Costanza, Robert, ed. 1991. *Ecological Economics: The Science and Management of Sustainability.* New York: Columbia University Press.

Cottrell, Fred. 1955. *Energy and Society: The Relation between Energy, Social Change, and Economic Development.* Westport, Conn.: Greenwood.

Covey, Jane G. 1998. "Is Critical Cooperation Possible? Influencing the World Bank through Operational Collaboration and Policy Dialogue." In *The Struggle for Accountability: The World Bank, NGOs, and Grassroots Movements,* edited by Jonathan A. Fox and L. David Brown, 81-119. Cambridge: MIT Press.

Covey, Jane, and L. David Brown. 2001. "Critical Cooperation: An Alternative Form of Civil Society-Business Engagement." *IDR Reports* 17, no. 1: 1–18.

Cramer, Philip F. 1998. *Deep Environmental Politics: The Role of Radical Environmentalism in Crafting American Environmental Policy.* Westport, Conn.: Praeger.

Critchley, John S. 1978. *Feudalism.* London: George Allen & Unwin.

Cropper, Maureen, and Charles Griffiths. 1994. "The Interaction of Population Growth and Environmental Quality." *American Economic Review* 84, no. 2: 250–54.

Cunningham, William P., Terence H. Cooper, Eville Gorham, and Malcolm T. Hepworth. 1998. *Environmental Encyclopedia.* Detroit, Mich.: Gale.

Dailey, Gretchen, Partha Dasgupta, Bert Bolin, Pierre Crosson, Jacques du Guerney, Paul Ehrlich, Carl Folke, Ann Mari Jansson, Bengt-Owe Jansson, Nils Kautsky, Ann Kinzig, Simon Levin, Karl-Göran Mäler, Per Pinstrup-Andersen, Domenico Siniscalco, and Brian Walker. 1998. "Food Production, Population Growth, and the Environment." *Science* 281: 1291–92.

Daly, Herman E. 1973. Introduction to *Toward a Steady-State Economy,* edited by Herman E. Daly, 1–29. San Francisco: Freeman.

———. 1977. "The Steady-State Economy: What, Why, and How." In *The Sustainable Society,* edited by Dennis Clark Pirages, 107–30. New York: Praeger.

———. 1987. "The Economic Growth Debate: What Some Economists Have Learned but Many Have Not." *Journal of Environmental Economics and Management* 14, no. 4: 323–36.

———. 1990. "Sustainable Growth: An Impossibility Theorem." *Development* 3–4: 45–47.

———. 1996a. "Sustainable Growth? No Thank You." In *The Case Against the Global Economy,* edited by Jerry Mander and Edward Goldsmith, 192–96. San Francisco: Sierra Club Books.

———. 1996b. *Beyond Growth: The Economics of Sustainable Development.* Boston: Beacon.

———. 1997a. "Georgescu-Roegen versus Solow/Stiglitz." *Ecological Economics* 22, no. 3: 261–66.

———. 1997b. "Reply to Solow/Stiglitz." *Ecological Economics* 22, no. 3: 271–73.

———. 1999. *Ecological Economics and the Ecology of Economics: Essays in Criticism.* Cheltenham, U.K.: Edward Elgar.

Daly, Herman E., and John B. Cobb Jr. 1989. *For the Common Good: Redirecting the Economy toward Community, the Environment, and a Sustainable Future.* Boston: Beacon.

Dawkins, Kristin. 1997. *Gene Wars: The Politics of Biotechnology.* New York: Seven Stories.

Debeir, Jean-Claude, Jean-Paul Deléage, and Daniel Hémery. 1991. *In the Servitude of Power: Energy and Civilization through the Ages.* London: Zed.

De Bruyn, Sander M. 2000. *Economic Growth and the Environment: An Empirical Analysis.* Dordrecht: Kluwer.

De Bruyn, S. M., J. C. J. M. van den Bergh, and J. B. Opschoor. 1988. "Economic Growth and Emissions: Reconsidering the Empirical Basis of Environmental Kuznets Curves." *Ecological Economics* 25: 161–75.

Déléage, Jean-Paul. 1994. "Eco-Marxist Critique of Political Economy." In *Is Capitalism Sustainable: Political Economy and the Politics of Ecology,* edited by Martin O'Connor, 37–52. New York: Guilford.

Demeny, Paul. 1990. "Population." In *The Earth as Transformed by Human Action: Global and Regional Changes in the Biosphere over the Past 300 Years,* edited by B. L. Turner II, William C. Clark, Robert W. Kates, John F. Richards, Jessica T. Mathews, and William B. Meyer, 41–54. Cambridge: Cambridge University Press.

Devall, Bill. 1988. *Simple in Means, Rich in Ends: Practicing Deep Ecology.* Salt Lake City: Peregrine Smith.

Devall, Bill, and George Sessions. 1985. *Deep Ecology: Living As If Nature Mattered.* Salt Lake City: Gibbs Smith.

Diamond, Jared. 1999. *Guns, Germs, and Steel: The Fates of Human Societies*. New York: Norton.

Dickens, Peter. 1992. *Society and Nature: Towards a Green Social Theory*. Philadelphia: Temple University Press.

———. 1998. *Global Shift: Transforming the World Economy*. New York: Guilford.

Dietz, Thomas, and Linda Kalof. 1992. "Environmentalism among Nation-States." *Social Indicators Research* 26, no. 4: 353–66.

Dobb, Maurice. 1964. *Studies in the Development of Capitalism*. New York: International Publishers.

Dobson, Andrew. 1995. *Green Political Thought*. 2d ed. London: Routledge.

Douthwaite, Richard. 1999. *The Growth Illusion: How Economic Growth Has Enriched the Few, Impoverished the Many, and Endangered the Planet*. Gabriola Island, B.C.: New Society.

Dryzek, John S. 1987. *Rational Ecology: Environment and Political Economy*. Oxford: Basil Blackwell.

Dubash, Navroz K., Mairi Dupar, Smitu Kothari, and Tundu Lissu. 2001. *A Watershed in Global Governance? An Independent Assessment of the World Commission on Dams*. Executive Summary. Washington, D.C.: World Resources Institute, Lokayan, and Lawyers' Environmental Action Team.

Dunlap, Riley E., and Angela G. Mertig. 1995. "Global Concern for the Environment: Is Affluence a Prerequisite?" *Journal of Social Issues* 51: 121–37.

———. 1997. "Global Environmental Concern: An Anomaly for Postmaterialism." *Social Science Quarterly* 78, no. 1: 24–29.

Dunn, James R., and John E. Kinney. 1996. *Conservative Environmentalism: Reassessing the Means, Redefining the Ends*. Westport, Conn.: Quorum.

Durning, Alan B. 1989. "Poverty and the Environment: Reversing the Downward Spiral." Worldwatch Paper no. 92. Washington, D.C.: Worldwatch Institute.

Durning, Alan Thein. 1992. *How Much Is Enough: The Consumer Society and the Future of the Earth*. New York: Norton.

Dyson, Tim. 1994. "Population Growth and Food Production: Recent Global and Regional Trends." *Population and Development Review* 20, no. 2: 397–411.

———. 1996. *Population and Food: Global Trends and Future Prospects*. London: Routledge.

Eagleton, Terry. 1991. *Ideology: An Introduction*. London: Verso.

Earley, Jay. 1997. *Transforming Human Culture: Social Evolution and the Planetary Crisis*. Albany: State University of New York Press.

Eatwell, Roger. 1999. "Introduction: What Are Political Ideologies?" In *Contemporary Political Ideologies*, edited by Roger Eatwell and Anthony Wright, 1–22. 2d ed. London: Pinter.

Eberstadt, Nicholas. 2000a. "World Population Prospects for the Twenty-First Century: The Specter of "Depopulation"? In *Earth Report 2000: Revisiting the True State of the Planet*, edited by Ronald Bailey, 63–84. New York: McGraw-Hill.

———. 2000b. *Prosperous Paupers and Other Population Problems*. New Brunswick, N.J.: Transaction.

———. 2001. "Population Implosion." *Foreign Policy*. March-April. <www.foreignpolicy.com/issue_marapr_2001/eberstadt.html> (December 18, 2001).

Eckersley, Robyn. 1992. *Environmentalism and Political Theory: Toward an Ecocentric Approach*. Albany: State University of New York Press.

Ehrlich, Paul R. 1968. *The Population Bomb*. New York: Ballantine.

———. 1996. "Population and Environmental Destruction." In *Meeting the Challenges of Population, Environment, and Resources: The Costs of Inaction*, edited by Henry W. Kendall, Kenneth J. Arrow, Norman E. Borlaug, Paul R. Ehrlich, Joshua Lederberg, José I. Vargas, Robert T. Watson, and Edward O. Wilson, 27–28. Environmentally Sustainable Development Proceedings Series no. 14. Washington, D.C.: World Bank.

Ehrlich, Paul R., and Anne H. Ehrlich. 1991. *Healing the Planet: Strategies for Resolving the Environmental Crisis*. Reading, Mass.: Addison-Wesley.

———. 1996. *Betrayal of Science and Reason: How Anti-Environmental Rhetoric Threatens Our Future*. Washington, D.C.: Island.

Ehrlich, Paul R., Anne H. Ehrlich, and Gretchen C. Daily. 1995. *The Stork and the Plow: The Equity Answer to the Human Dilemma*. New York: Putnam's.

Ehrlich, Paul, Anne Ehrlich, and John Holdren. 1977. *Ecoscience: Population, Resources, Environment*. San Francisco: Freeman.

Ehrlich, Paul R., and John P. Holdren. 1971. "Impact of Population Growth." *Science* 171: 1212–17.

Ekins, Paul. 2000. *Economic Growth and Environmental Sustainability: The Prospects for Green Growth*. London: Routledge.

Ekins, Paul, and Michael Jacobs. 1995. "Environmental Sustainability and the Growth of GDP: Conditions for Compatibility." In *The North, the South, and the Environment: Ecological Constraints and the Global Economy*, edited by V. Bhaskar and Andrew Glyn, 9–46. New York: St. Martin's.

Elkington, John. 1998. *Cannibals with Forks: The Triple Bottom Line of 21st Century Business*. Gabriola Island, B.C.: New Society.

Engelman, Robert. 1997. *Why Population Matters*. Washington, D.C.: Population Action International.

———. 1998. *Profiles in Carbon: An Update on Population, Consumption, and Carbon Dioxide Emissions*. Washington, D.C.: Population Action International.

Engelman, Robert, Richard P. Cincotta, Bonnie Dye, Tom Gardner-Outlaw, and Jennifer Wisnewski. 2000. *People in the Balance: Population and Natural Resources at the Turn of the Millennium*. Washington, D.C.: Population Action International.

England, Richard W. 2000. "Natural Capital and the Theory of Economic Growth." *Ecological Economics* 34: 425–31.

Enteman, Willard F. 1993. *Managerialism: The Emergence of a New Ideology*. Madison: University of Wisconsin Press.

Escobar, Arturo. 1996. "Constructing Nature: Elements for a Poststructural Political Ecology." In *Liberation Ecologies: Environment, Development, Social Movements*, edited by Richard Peet and Michael Watts, 46–68. London: Routledge.

Evans, L. T. 1998. *Feeding the Ten Billion: Plants and Population Growth*. Cambridge: Cambridge University Press.

FAO. 2001. *Forest Resources Assessment 2000*. Rome: Food and Agriculture Organization of the United Nations. <www.fao.org/forestry/fo/fra/index.jsp> (July 10, 2001).

Faux, Jeff. 1999. "Lost on the Third Way." *Dissent* 46, no. 2: 67–76.

Fineman, Stephen, ed. 2000. *The Business of Greening*. London: Routledge.

Finger, Mathias. 1992. "New Horizons for Peace Research: The Global Environment." In *Perspectives on Environmental Conflict and International Relations*, edited by Jyrki Käkönen, 5–30. London: Pinter.

Fisher, Dana R., and William R. Freudenburg. 2001. "Ecological Modernization and Its Critics: Assessing the Past and Looking toward the Future." *Society and Natural Resources* 14, no. 8: 701–9.

FitzSimmons, Margaret, Joseph Glaser, Roberto Monte Mor, Stephanie Pincetl, and Sudhir Chella Rajan. 1994. "Environmentalism and the Liberal State." In *Is Capitalism Sustainable? Political Economy and the Politics of Ecology*, edited by Martin O'Connor, 198–216. New York: Guilford.

Flavin, Christopher. 1997. "The Legacy of Rio." In *State of the World 1997*, edited by Lester R. Brown, Christopher Flavin, and Hilary French, 3–22. New York: Norton.

Foley, Gerald. 1976. *The Energy Question*. Harmondsworth, U.K.: Penguin.

Forrester, Jay W. [1971] 1973. *World Dynamics*. 2d ed. Cambridge, Mass.: Wright-Allen.

Foster, John Bellamy. 1998. "Malthus' *Essay on Population* at Age 200: A Marxian View." *Monthly Review* 50, no. 7: 1–18.

———. 1999a. *The Vulnerable Planet: A Short Economic History of the Environment*. New York: Monthly Review.

———. 1999b. "Marx's Theory of Metabolic Rift: Classical Foundations for Environmental Sociology." *American Journal of Sociology* 105, no. 2: 366–405.

———. 2000. *Marx's Ecology: Materialism and Nature*. New York: Monthly Review Press.

Fowler, Cary, and Pat Mooney. 1990. *Shattering: Food, Politics, and the Loss of Genetic Diversity*. Tucson: University of Arizona Press.

Frank, David John. 1997. "Science, Nature, and the Globalization of the Environment, 1870–1990." *Social Forces* 76, no. 2: 409–35.

———. 1999. "The Social Bases of Environmental Treaty Ratification, 1900–1990." *Sociological Inquiry* 69, no. 4: 523–50.

Frank, David John, Ann Hironaka, and Evan Chofer. 2000. "The Nation-State and the Natural Environment over the Twentieth Century." *American Sociological Review* 65, no. 1: 96–116.

Frankel, Carl. 1998. *In Earth's Company: Business, Environment, and the Challenge of Sustainability*. Gabriola Island, B.C: New Society.

Freeman, C., and C. Perez. 1988. "Structural Crises of Adjustment, Business Cycles, and Investment Behavior." In *Technical Change and Economic Theory*, edited by G. Dosi, C. Freeman, R. Nelson, G. Silverberg, and L. Soete, 38–66. London: Pinter.

Freeman, R. Edward, Jessica Pierce, and Richard Dodd. 2000. *Environmentalism and the New Logic of Business*. Oxford: Oxford University Press.

French, Hilary. 2000. "Coping with Ecological Globalization." In *State of the World 2000: A Worldwatch Institute Report on Progress toward a Sustainable Society*, edited by Lester R. Brown, Christopher Flavin, and Hilary French, 184–202. New York: Norton.

Friberg, Mats, and Björn Hettne. 1985. "The Greening of the World: Towards a Non-Deterministic Model of Global Processes." In *Development as Social Transformation: Reflections on the Global Problematique*, edited by Herb Addo et al., 204–70. Boulder: Westview.

Fukuyama, Francis. 1992. *The End of History and the Last Man*. New York: Free Press.

Gallarotti, Guilio M. 1995. "It Pays to Be Green: The Managerial Incentive Structure and Environmentally Sound Strategies." *Columbia Journal of World Business* 30, no. 4: 38–57.

Gallopin, Gilberto C., Pablo Gutman, and Hector Maletta. 1989. "Global Impoverishment, Sustainable Development, and the Environment: A Conceptual Approach." *International Social Science Journal* 41, no. 3: 375–97.

Gardner, Gary, and Payal Sampat. 1999. "Forging a Sustainable Materials Economy." In *State of the World 1999: A Worldwatch Institute Report on Progress toward a Sustainable Society*, edited by Lester R. Brown et al., 41–59. New York: Norton.

Gardner-Outlaw, Tom, and Robert Engelman. 1999. *Forest Futures: Population, Consumption, and Wood Resources*. Washington, D.C.: Population Action International.

Garry, Patrick M. 1992. *Liberalism and American Identity*. Kent, Ohio: Kent State University Press.

Georgescu-Roegen, Nicholas. 1971. *The Entropy Law and the Economic Process*. Cambridge: Harvard University Press.

———. 1973. "The Entropy Law and the Economic Problem." In *Toward a Steady-State Economy*, edited by Herman E. Daly, 37–49. San Francisco: Freeman.

———. 1979. "Comments on Papers by Daly and Stiglitz." In *Scarcity and Growth Reconsidered*, edited by V. Kerry Smith, 95–105. Baltimore: Resources for the Future/Johns Hopkins University Press, 1979.

Giddens, Anthony. 1987. *Social Theory and Modern Sociology*. Stanford, Calif.: Stanford University Press.

———. 1990. *The Consequences of Modernity*. Stanford, Calif.: Stanford University Press.

———. 1994. *The Third Way: The Renewal of Social Democracy*. Cambridge, U.K.: Polity.

———. 1995. *Politics, Sociology, and Social Theory*. Stanford, Calif.: Stanford University Press.

———. 1998. *Beyond Left and Right: The Future of Radical Politics*. Stanford, Calif.: Stanford University Press.

———. 2000. *The Third Way and Its Critics*. Cambridge, U.K.: Polity.

Global 2000 Study. 1980. *The Global 2000 Report to the President: Entering the Twenty-First Century*. Washington, D.C.: U.S. Government Printing Office. Prepared by the Council on Environmental Quality and the Department of State, Gerald Barney, study director.

Glyn, Andrew. 1995. "Northern Growth and Environmental Constraints." In *The North, the South, and the Environment: Ecological Constraints and the Global Economy*, edited by V. Bhaskar and Andrew Glyn, 47–67. New York: St. Martin's.

Goldblatt, David. 1996. *Social Theory and the Environment*. Boulder: Westview.

Goldfrank, Walter L., David Goodman, and Andrew Szasz, eds. 1999. *Ecology and the World-System*. Westport, Conn.: Greenwood.

Goldin, Ian, and L. Alan Winters. 1995. "Economic Policies for Sustainable Development." In *The Economics of Sustainable Development*, edited by Ian Goldin and L. Alan Winters, 1–15. Cambridge: Cambridge University Press.

Goldsmith, E., R. Allen, M. Allaby, J. Davoll, and S. Lawrence. 1972. *Blueprint for Survival*. Harmondsworth, U.K.: Penguin.

Goodland, Robert, and Herman E. Daly. 1992. "Three Steps Towards Global Environmental Sustainability." *Development* 2: 35–41.

———. 1998. "Imperatives for Environmental Sustainability: Decrease Overconsumption and Stabilize Population." In *Population and Global Security*, edited by Nicholas Polunin, 117–32. Cambridge: Cambridge University Press.

Gore, Al. 2000. *Earth in the Balance: Ecology and the Human Spirit*. 2d ed. Boston: Houghton Mifflin.

Goudie, Andrew. 1994. *The Human Impact on the Natural Environment*. 4th ed. Cambridge: MIT Press.

Gould, Julius, and William L. Kolb. 1964. *A Dictionary of the Social Sciences*. New York: Free Press.

Grainger, R. J. R., and S. M. Garcia. 1996. *Chronicles of Marine Fishery Landings (1950–1994): Trends Analysis and Fisheries Potential*. FAO Fisheries Technical Paper no. 359. Rome: Food and Agriculture Organization of the United Nations.

Greer, Jed, and Kenny Bruno. 1996. *Greenwash: The Reality behind Corporate Environmentalism*. Penang, Malaysia: Third World Network.

Grimes, Peter E. 1999. "The Horsemen and the Killing Fields: The Final Contradiction of Capitalism." In *Ecology and the World-System*, edited by Walter L. Goldfrank, David Goodman, and Andrew Szasz, 13–42. Westport, Conn.: Greenwood.

Grossman, Gene M., and Alan B. Krueger. 1995. "Economic Growth and the Environment." *Quarterly Journal of Economics* 110, no. 2: 353–77.

Grove, Richard H. 1995. *Green Imperialism: Colonial Expansion, Tropical Island Edens, and the Origins of Environmentalism*. Cambridge: Cambridge University Press.

Grübler, Arnulf. 1994. "Technology." In *Changes in Land Use and Land Cover: A Global Perspective*, edited by William B. Meyer and B. L. Turner II, 287–328. Cambridge: Cambridge University Press.

Grundmann, Reiner. 1991. *Marxism and Ecology*. Oxford: Clarendon.

Guha, Ramachandra. 2000. *Environmentalism: A Global History*. New York: Longman.

Guha, Ramachandra, and J. Martinez-Alier. 1997. *Varieties of Environmentalism: Essays North and South*. London: Earthscan.

Gupta, Anil. 1996. "Social and Ethical Dimensions of Ecological Economics." In *Getting Down to Earth: Practical Applications of Ecological Economics*, edited by Robert Costanza, Olman Segura, and Juan Martinez-Alier, 91–116. Washington, D.C.: Island.

Haas, Peter M., Robert O. Keohane, and Marc A. Levy, eds. 1993. *Institutions for the Earth: Sources of Effective International Environmental Protection*. Cambridge: MIT Press.

Hajer, Maarten A. 1995. *The Politics of Environmental Discourse: Ecological Modernisation and the Policy Process*. Oxford: Clarendon; New York: Oxford University Press.

Hall, John A., and G. John Ikenberry. 1989. *The State*. Minneapolis: University of Minnesota Press.

Hall, Stuart. 1998. "The Great Moving Nowhere Show." *Marxism Today*, November-December 1998, 9–14.

Hardin, Garrett. 1968. "The Tragedy of the Commons." *Science* 162: 1243–48.

———. 1993. *Living within Limits: Ecology, Economics, and Population Taboos*. New York: Oxford University Press.

Harper, Charles L. 1996. *Environment and Society: Human Perspectives on Environmental Issues*. Upper Saddle River, N.J.: Prentice-Hall.

Harris, Jonathan M. 1991. "Global Institutions and Ecological Crisis." *World Development* 19, no. 1: 111–22.

Harrison, Lawrence E., and Samuel P. Huntington. 2000. *Culture Matters: How Values Shape Human Progress*. New York: Basic.

Hart, Stuart. 1997. "Beyond Greening: Strategies for a Sustainable World." *Harvard Business Review*, January-February, 66–76.

Hawken, Paul, Amory Lovins, and L. Hunter Lovins. 1999. *Natural Capitalism: Creating the Next Industrial Revolution*. Boston: Little, Brown.

Hay, Colin. 1994. "Environmental Security and State Legitimacy." In *Is Capitalism Sustainable? Political Economy and the Politics of Ecology*, edited by Martin O'Connor, 217–31. New York: Guilford.

Headrick, Daniel R. 1990. "Technological Change." In *The Earth as Transformed by Human Action: Global and Regional Changes in the Biosphere over the Past 300 Years*, edited by B. L. Turner II, William C. Clark, Robert W. Kates, John F. Richards, Jessica T. Mathews, and William B. Meyer, 55–67. Cambridge: Cambridge University Press.

Heilbroner, Robert. 1974. *An Inquiry into the Human Prospect*. New York: Norton.

———. 1993. *The Making of Economic Society*. Englewood Cliffs, N.J.: Prentice-Hall.

Held, David. 1989. *Political Theory and the Modern State: Essays on State, Power, and Democracy*. Stanford, Calif.: Stanford University Press.

Helvarg, David. 1994. *The War against the Greens: The "Wise-Use" Movement, the New Right, and Anti-Environmental Violence*. San Francisco: Sierra Club Books.

Hemmati, Minu. 2002. *Multi-Stakeholder Processes for Governance and Sustainability*. London: Earthscan.

Hempel, Lamont C. 1996. *Environmental Governance: The Global Challenge*. Washington, D.C.: Island.

Herlihy, David, ed. 1970. *The History of Feudalism*. New York: Harper & Row.

Hildyard, Nicholas. 1993. "Foxes in Charge of the Chickens." In *Global Ecology: A New Arena of Political Conflict*, edited by Wolfgang Sachs, 22–35. London: Zed; Halifax, N.S.: Fernwood.

Hoffman, Andrew J. 1997. *From Heresy to Dogma: An Institutional History of Corporate Environmentalism*. San Francisco: New Lexington Press.

———. 2000. *Competitive Environmental Strategy: A Guide to the Changing Business Landscape*. Washington, D.C: Island.

Holmberg, Johan, and Richard Sandbrook. 1992. "Sustainable Development: What Is to Be Done?" In *Making Development Sustainable: Redefining Institutions, Policy, and Economics*, edited by Johan Holmberg, 19–38. Washington, D.C.: Island.

Holmberg, Johan, ed. 1992. *Making Development Sustainable: Redefining Institutions, Policy, and Economics*. Washington, D.C.: Island.

Homer-Dixon, Thomas F. 1999. *Environment, Scarcity, and Violence*. Princeton, N.J.: Princeton University Press.

———. 2000. *The Ingenuity Gap*. New York: Knopf.

Huber, Joseph. 1985. *Die Regenbogengesellschaft: Ökologie and Sozialpolitik*. Frankfurt am Main: Fischer Verlag.

Huber, Peter. 1999. *Hard Green: Saving the Environment from the Environmentalists: A Conservative Manifesto*. New York: Basic.

Hughes, Jonathan. 2000. *Ecology and Historical Materialism*. Cambridge: Cambridge University Press.

Humphrey, Craig R., and Frederick H. Buttel. 1982. *Environment, Energy, and Society*. Belmont, Calif.: Wadsworth.

Humphrey, Craig R., Tammy L. Lewis, and Frederick H. Buttel. 2002. *Environment, Energy, and Society: A New Synthesis*. Belmont, Calif.: Wadsworth/Thomas Learning.

IMF. 2001. *World Economic Outlook Database*. Washington, D.C.: International Monetary Fund. <www.imf.org/external/pubs/ft/weo/2000/02/data> (January 26, 2002).

Inglehart, Ronald. 1990. *Cultural Shift in Advanced Industrial Society*. Princeton, N.J.: Princeton University Press.

———. 1995. "Public Support for Environmental Protection: Objective Problems and Subjective Values in 43 Societies." *PS: Political Science and Politics* 28, no. 1: 57–72.

Islam, Nurul. 1995. "Overview." In *Population and Food in the Early Twenty-First Century: Meeting Future Food Demand of an Increasing Population*, edited by Nurul Islam, 1–4. Washington, D.C.: International Food Policy Research Institute.

Jacobs, Michael. 1991. *The Green Economy: Environment, Sustainable Development, and the Politics of the Future*. London: Pluto.

———. 1997. "Introduction: The New Politics of the Environment." In *Greening the Millennium? The New Politics of the Environment*, edited by Michael Jacobs, 1–17. Oxford: Blackwell.

Jänicke, Martin. 1985. *Preventive Environmental Policy as Ecological Modernisation and Structural Policy*. Berlin: WZB.

Jessop, Bob. 1990. *State Theory: Putting Capitalist States in Their Place*. University Park: Pennsylvania State University Press.

Kågeson, Per. 1998. *Growth versus the Environment: Is There a Trade-off?* Dordrecht: Kluwer Academic.

Kahn, Herman, and Anthony J. Wiener. 1967. *The Year 2000: A Framework for Speculation on the Next 33 Years*. New York: Macmillan.

Kahn, Herman, William Brown, and Leon Martel, with the staff of the Hudson Institute. 1976. *The Next 200 Years: A Scenario for America and the World*. New York: Morrow.

Kasun, Jacqueline. 1999. *The War against Population: The Economics and Ideology of World Population Control*. Rev. ed. San Francisco: Ignatius.

Kates, Robert W. 1996. "Population, Technology, and the Human Environment: A Threat through Time." *Daedalus* 125, no. 3: 43–71.

Kaufmann, Robert K., Brynhildur Davidsdottir, Sophie Garnham, and Peter Pauly. 1998. "The Determinants of Atmospheric SO_2 Concentrations: Reconsidering the Environmental Kuznets Curve." *Ecological Economics* 25: 209–20.

Keohane, Robert O., Peter M. Haas, and Marc A. Levy. 1993. "The Effectiveness of International Environmental Institutions." In *Institutions for the Earth: Sources of Effective International Environmental Protection*, edited by Peter M. Haas, Robert O. Keohane, and Marc A. Levy, 3–24. Cambridge: MIT Press.

Keynes, John Maynard. 1936. *The General Theory of Employment, Interest, and Money*. New York: Harcourt, Brace.

Kidd, Quentin, and Aie-Rie Lee. 1997. "Postmaterialist Values and the Environment: A Critique and Reappraisal." *Social Science Quarterly* 78, no. 1: 1–15.

King, Alexander, and Bertrand Schneider. 1991. *The First Global Revolution: A Report by the Council of the Club of Rome*. New York: Pantheon.

Kirk, Dudley. 1996. "Demographic Transition Theory." *Population Studies* 50, no. 3: 361–87.

Krieger, Joel. *The Oxford Companion to Politics of the World*. New York: Oxford University Press, 1993.

Krimsky, Sheldon, and Roger P. Wrubel. 1996. *Agricultural Biotechnology and the Environment: Science, Policy, and Social Issues*. Urbana: University of Illinois Press.

Kuttner, Robert. 1996. *Everything for Sale: The Virtues and Limit of Markets*. Chicago: University of Chicago Press.

Kuznets, Simon. 1955. "Economic Growth and Income Inequality." *American Economic Review* 49, no. 1: 1–28.

———. 1963. "Quantitative Aspects of the Economic Growth of Nations, 8: The Distribution of Income by Size." *Economic Development and Cultural Change* 11, no. 2, pt. 7: 1–80.

Landes, David S. 1969. *The Unbound Prometheus: Technological Change and Industrial Development in Western Europe from 1750 to the Present.* London: Cambridge University Press.

Laponce, J. A. 1981. *Left and Right: The Topography of Political Perceptions.* Toronto: University of Toronto Press.

Lappé, Frances Moore, and Rachel Schurman. 1989. *Taking Population Seriously.* London: Earthscan.

Lappé, Frances Moore, Joseph Collins, and Peter Rosset, with Luis Esparza. 1998. *World Hunger: 12 Myths.* 2d ed. New York: Grove.

Lappé, Marc, and Britt Bailey. 1998. *Against the Grain: Biotechnology and the Corporate Takeover of Your Food.* Monroe, Me.: Common Courage.

Lee, Aie-Rie, and Quentin Kidd. 1997. "More on Postmaterialist Values and the Environment." *Social Science Quarterly* 78, no. 1: 36–43.

Lee, Ronald Demos. 1986. "Malthus and Boserup: A Dynamic Synthesis." In *The State of Population Theory: Forward from Malthus,* edited by David Coleman and Roger Schofield, 96–130. Oxford: Basil Blackwell.

Leff, Enrique. 1995. *Green Production: Toward an Environmental Rationality.* New York: Guilford.

Lélé, Sharachchandra M. 1991. "Sustainable Development: A Critical Review." *World Development* 19, no. 6: 607–21.

Leonard, H. Jeffrey et al. 1989. *Environment and the Poor: Development Strategies for a Common Agenda.* New Brunswick, N.J.: Transaction.

Leroy, Pieter, and Jan van Tatenhove. 2000. "Political Modernization Theory and Environmental Politics." In *Environment and Global Modernity,* edited by Gert Spaargaren, Arthur P.J. Mol, and Frederick H. Buttel, 187–208. London: Sage.

Lewis, Martin W. 1992. *Green Delusions: An Environmentalist Critique of Radical Environmentalism.* Durham, N.C.: Duke University Press.

Light, Andrew. 1998. "Bookchin as/and Social Ecology." In *Social Ecology after Bookchin,* edited by Andrew Light, 1–23. New York: Guilford.

Linder, Marc. 1997. *The Dilemmas of Laissez-Faire Population Policy in Capitalist Societies: When the Invisible Hand Controls Reproduction.* Westport, Conn.: Greenwood.

Lipietz, Alain. 1995. *Green Hopes: The Future of Political Ecology.* Cambridge, U.K.: Polity.

———. 1997. "Developments and Alternatives: Hopes for Post-Fordism." In *Environment, Technology, and Economic Growth,* edited by Andrew Tylecote and Jan van der Straaten, 206–25. Cheltenham, U.K.: Edward Elgar.

Lipschutz, Ronnie D., and Ken Conca. 1993. "The Implications of Global Ecological Interdependence." In *The State and Social Power in Global Environmental Politics,* edited by Ronnie D. Lipschutz and Ken Conca, 327–43. New York: Columbia University Press.

List, Marin, and Volker Rittberger. 1992. "Regime Theory and International Environmental Management." In *The International Politics of the Environment,* edited by Andrew Hurrell and Benedict Kingsbury, 85–109. Oxford: Oxford University Press.

Lomborg, Bjørn. 2001. *The Skeptical Environmentalist: Measuring the Real State of the World.* Cambridge: Cambridge University Press.

Low, Nicholas, and Brendan Gleeson. 1998. *Justice, Society, and Nature: An Exploration of Political Ecology.* London: Routledge.

Lowenthal, David. 1990. "Awareness of Human Impacts: Changing Attitudes and Emphases." In *The Earth as Transformed by Human Action: Global and Regional Changes in* the Biosphere over the Past 300 Years, edited by B. L. Turner II, William C. Clark, Robert W. Kates, John F. Richards, Jessica T. Mathews, and William B. Meyer, 121–35. Cambridge: Cambridge University Press.

MacNeill, Jim, Pieter Winsemius, and Taizo Yakushiji. 1991. Beyond Interdependence: The Meshing of the World's Economy and the Earth's Ecology. Oxford: Oxford University Press.

Maddison, Angus. 2001. The World Economy: A Millennial Perspective. Paris: Organization for Economic Cooperation and Development.

Malthus, Thomas Robert. 1803. An Essay on the Principle of Population. London: T. Bensley.

Mamdani, Mahmood. 1972. The Myth of Population Control: Family, Caste, and Class in an Indian Village. New York: Monthly Review Press.

Mander, Jerry, and Edward Goldsmith. 1996. The Case against the Global Economy and for a Turn toward the Local. San Francisco: Sierra Club Books.

Mannheim, Karl. [1929] 1936. Ideology and Utopia. New York: Harcourt.

Manno, Jack P. 2000. Privileged Goods: Commoditization and Its Impact on Environment and Society. Boca Raton, La.: Lewis.

Margoluis, Richard, Cheryl Margoluis, Katrina Brandon, and Nick Salafsky. 2000. In Good Company: Effective Alliances for Conservation. Washington, D.C.: Biodiversity Support Program.

Marquette, Catherine. 1997. "Turning but Not Toppling Malthus: Boserupian Theory on Population and the Environment Relationships." Working Paper no. 16. Bergen, Norway: Chr. Michelsen Institute.

Marshall, Gordon, ed. 1998. A Dictionary of Sociology. Oxford: Oxford University Press.

Martinez-Alier, Joan. 1997. "Ecological Economics and Environmental Policy: A Southern European View." In Environment, Technology, and Economic Growth, edited by Andrew Tylecote and Jan van der Straaten, 15–38. Cheltenham, U.K.: Edward Elgar.

Marx, Karl. [1867] 1967. Capital. Vol. 1. New York: International Publishers.

Marx, Karl, and Friedrich Engels. 1970. The German Ideology, Part One. Edited with an introduction by C. J. Arthur. 1st ed. New York: International Publishers.

Mathews, Jessica Tuchman, ed. 1991. Preserving the Global Environment: The Challenge of Shared Leadership. New York: Norton.

May, Peter J. 1996. "Rethinking Intergovernmental Environmental Management." In Environmental Management and Governance: Intergovernmental Approaches to Hazards and Sustainability, edited by Peter J. May, Raymond J. Burby, Neil J. Ericksen, John W. Handmer, Jennifer E. Dixon, Sarah Michaels, and D. Ingle Smith, 1–17. London: Routledge.

Mayer-Tasch, P. C. 1986. "International Environmental Policy as a Challenge to the National State." Ambio 15, no. 4: 240–43.

McLellan, David. 1995. Ideology. 2d ed. Minneapolis: University of Minnesota Press.

McMichael, Philip. 1996. Development and Social Change: A Global Perspective. Thousand Oaks, Calif.: Pine Forge.

McNicoll, Geoffrey. 1998. "Malthus for the Twenty-First Century." Population and Development Review 24, no. 2: 309–16.

Meadows, Donella H., Dennis L. Meadows, and Jørgen Randers. 1992. Beyond the Limits: Confronting Global Collapse, Envisioning a Sustainable Future. Post Mills, Vt.: Chelsea Green.

Meadows, Donella H., Dennis L. Meadows, Jørgen Randers, and William W. Behrens III. 1972. The Limits to Growth: A Report for the Club of Rome's Project on the Predicament of Mankind. New York: New American Library.

Meek, Ronald L. 1971. *Marx and Engels on the Population Bomb*. Berkeley, Calif.: Ramparts.

Mellor, John. 1988. "The Intertwining of Environmental Problems and Poverty." *Environment* 30, no. 9: 8–13.

Meltzer, Milton. 1993a. *Slavery: A World History*. Bk. 1. New York: Da Capo.

———. 1993b. *Slavery: A World History*. Bk. 2. New York: Da Capo.

Menon, Ajay, and Anil Menon. 1997. "Enviropreneurial Marketing Strategy: The Emergence of Corporate Environmentalism as Market Strategy." *Journal of Marketing* 61, no. 1: 51–67.

Mesarovic, Mihajlo, and Eduard Pestel. 1974. *Mankind at the Turning Point: The Second Report to the Club of Rome*. New York: Dutton.

Meyer, Carrie A. 1995. "Opportunism and NGOs: Entrepreneurship and Green North-South Transfers." *World Development* 23, no. 8: 1277–89.

Meyer, John W., David John Frank, Ann Hironaka, Evan Schofer, and Nancy Brandon Tuma. 1997. "The Structuring of a World Environmental Regime, 1870–1990." *International Organization* 51, no. 4: 623–51.

Migdal, Joel S. 1988. *Strong Societies and Weak States: State-Society Relations and State Capabilities in the Third World*. Princeton, N.J.: Princeton University Press.

Milbrath, Lester W. 1984. *Environmentalists: Vanguard for a New Society*. Albany: State University of New York Press.

———. 1989. *Envisioning a Sustainable Society: Learning Our Way Out*. Albany, N.Y.: State University of New York Press.

Mill, John Stuart. 1871. *Principles of Political Economy*. London: Longmans, Green.

Mirvis, Philip H. 1994. "Environmentalism in Progressive Businesses." *Journal of Organizational Change and Management* 7, no. 4: 82–100.

Mishan, E. J. 1967. *The Costs of Economic Growth*. London: Staples.

Mohan, Raj P., and Graham C. Kinloch. 2000. "Ideology, Myths, and Social Science." In *Ideology and the Social Sciences*, edited by Graham C. Kinloch and Raj P. Mohan, 7–17. Westport, Conn.: Greenwood.

Mol, Arthur, P.J. 1995. *The Refinement of Production: Ecological Modernization Theory and the Chemical Industry*. Utrecht: Van Arkel.

———. 1996. "Ecological Modernisation and Institutional Reflexivity: Environmental Reform in the Late Modern Age." *Environmental Politics* 5, no. 2: 302–23.

Mol, Arthur P.J., and David A. Sonnenfeld, eds. 2000a. *Ecological Modernisation around the World: Perspectives and Critical Debates*. London: Frank Cass.

Mol, Arthur, P.J., and David A. Sonnenfeld. 2000b. "Ecological Modernisation around the World: An Introduction." In *Ecological Modernisation around the World: Perspectives and Critical Debates*, edited by Arthur P.J. Mol and David A. Sonnenfeld, 3–14. London: Frank Cass.

Mol, Arthur P.J., and Gert Spaargaren. 1993. "Environment, Modernity, and the Risk-Society: The Apocalyptic Horizon of Environmental Reform." *International Sociology* 8, no. 4: 431–59.

———. 2000. "Ecological Modernisation Theory in Debate: A Review." In *Ecological Modernisation around the World: Perspectives and Critical Debates*, edited by Arthur P.J. Mol and David A. Sonnenfeld, 17–49. London: Frank Cass.

Morrison, Ken. 1995. *Marx, Durkheim, Weber: Formations of Modern Social Thought*. London: Sage.

Murdoch, William W. 1980. *The Poverty of Nations: The Political Economy of Hunger and Population*. Baltimore: Johns Hopkins University Press.

Murphy, Raymond. 1994. *Rationality and Nature: A Sociological Inquiry into a Changing Relationship*. Boulder: Westview.

Myers, Norman. 1987. "Population, Environment and Conflict." *Environmental Conservation* 14: 15–22.

———. 1991. *Population, Resources, and the Environment: The Critical Challenges*. New York: United Nation Population Fund.

———. 1993. *Ultimate Security: The Environmental Basis of Political Stability*. New York: Norton.

———. 1994. "Population Growth: Its Contribution to Conflict over Land and Other Natural Resources." In *Environment and Population Change*, edited by Basia Zaba and John Clarke, 101–14. Liège, Belgium: Derouaux Ordina Editions.

———. 1997. "Environmental Refugees." *Population and Environment* 19, no. 2: 167–82.

———. 1998. "Global Population and Emergent Pressures." In *Population and Global Security*, edited by Nicholas Polunin, 17–46. Cambridge: Cambridge University Press.

Naess, Arne. 1995a. "The Deep Ecological Movement: Some Philosophical Aspects." In *Deep Ecology for the 21st Century: Readings on the Philosophy and Practice of the New Environmentalism*, edited by George Sessions, 64–84. Boston: Shambhala.

———. 1995b. "The Third World, Wilderness, and Deep Ecology." In *Deep Ecology for the 21st Century: Readings on the Philosophy and Practice of the New Environmentalism*, edited by George Sessions, 397–407. Boston: Shambhala.

Naess, Arne, and David Rothenberg. 1989. *Ecology, Community, and Lifestyle: Outline of an Ecosophy*. Cambridge: Cambridge University Press.

Nakicenovic, Nebojsa. 1997. "Freeing Energy from Carbon." In *Technical Trajectories and the Human Environment*, edited by Jesse H. Ausubel and H. Dale Langford, 74–88. Washington, D.C.: National Academy Press.

National Commission on the Environment. 1993. *Choosing a Sustainable Future*. Washington, D.C.: Island.

National Research Council. 1992. *Global Environmental Change: Understanding the Human Dimensions*. Washington, D.C.: National Academy Press.

Nattrass, Brian, and Mary Altomare. 1999. *The Natural Step for Business: Wealth, Ecology, and the Evolutionary Corporation*. Gabriola Island, B.C.: New Society.

Neumann, R. P., and R. A. Schroeder, eds. 1995. "Manifest Ecological Destinies." *Antipode*, special issue, 27: 321–428.

Neumayer, Eric. 1999. *Weak versus Strong Sustainability: Exploring the Limits of Two Opposing Paradigms*. Cheltenham, U.K.: Edward Elgar.

North, Douglass C. 1997. Prologue to *The Frontiers of the New Institutional Economics*, edited by John N. Drobak and John V.C. Nye, 3–12. San Diego, Calif.: Academic Press.

Norton, Bryan G. 1991. *Toward Unity among Environmentalists*. New York: Oxford University Press.

Novak, Michael. 2000. "Introduction: Thinking Clearly." In *Earth Report 2000: Revisiting the True State of the Planet*, edited by Ronald Bailey, xvii–xix. New York: McGraw-Hill.

O'Connor, James. 1996. "The Second Contradiction of Capitalism." In *The Greening of Marxism*, edited by Ted Benton, 197–221. New York: Guilford.

———. 1998. *Natural Causes: Essays in Ecological Marxism*. New York: Guilford.

Odum, Howard T. 1971. *Environment, Power, and Society*. New York: Wiley-Interscience.

Ollikainen, Markku. 1997. "Sustainable Development from the Viewpoint of Ethics and Economics." In *Environment, Technology and Economic Growth*, edited by Andrew Tylecote and Jan van der Straaten, 39–54. Cheltenham, U.K.: Edward Elgar.

Olpadwalla, Porus, and William W. Goldsmith. 1992. "The Sustainability of Privilege: Reflections on the Environment, the Third World City, and Poverty." *World Development* 20, no. 4: 627–40.

Osborn, Fairfield. [1948] 1968. *Our Plundered Planet*. New York: Pyramid.

Ostrom, Elinor, Larry Schroeder, and Susan Wynne. 1993. *Institutional Incentives and Sustainable Development: Infrastructure Policies in Perspective*. Boulder, Colo.: Westview.

Paehlke, Robert C. 1989. *Environmentalism and the Future of Progressive Politics*. New Haven, Conn.: Yale University Press.

———. 1995. *Conservation and Environmentalism*. New York: Garland.

Paine, Albert Bigelow. 1912. *Mark Twain: A Biography*. Vol. 2. New York: Harper & Brothers.

Panayotou, Theodore. 1992. "Environmental Kuznets Curve: Empirical Tests and Policy Implications." Unpublished paper.

———. 1993. "Empirical Tests and Policy Analysis of Environmental Degradation at Different Stages of Economic Development." Working Paper no. WP 238. Technology and Employment Programme. Geneva: International Labor Office.

Parsons, Talcott. 1951. *The Social System*. New York: Free Press.

Pearce, David. 1998. *Economics and Environment: Essays on Ecological Economics and Sustainable Development*. Cheltenham, U.K.: Edward Elgar.

Pearce, David, Edward Barbier, and Anil Markandya. 1990. *Sustainable Development: Economics and Environment in the Third World*. London: Earthscan.

Pearce, David W., and Jeremy J. Warford. 1993. *World without End: Economics, Environment, and Sustainable Development*. New York: Oxford University Press.

Peet, Richard, and Michael Watts. 1996a. "Liberation Ecology: Development, Sustainability, and Environment in an Age of Market Triumphalism." In *Liberation Ecologies: Environment, Development, Social Movements*, edited by Richard Peet and Michael Watts, 1–45. London: Routledge.

———, eds. 1996b. *Liberation Ecologies: Environment, Development, Social Movements*. London: Routledge.

Pepper, David. 1984. *The Roots of Modern Environmentalism*. London: Croon Helm.

———. 1993. *Eco-Socialism: From Deep Ecology to Social Justice*. London: Routledge.

———. 1996. *Modern Environmentalism: An Introduction*. London: Routledge.

Perelman, Michael. 1996. "Marx and Resource Scarcity." In *The Greening of Marxism*, edited by Ted Benton, 64–80. New York: Guilford.

Peritore, N. Patrick. 1999. *Third World Environmentalism: Case Studies from the Global South*. Gainesville: University Press of Florida.

Perrings, Charles. 1989. "An Optimal Path to Extinction? Poverty and Degradation in the Open Agrarian Economy." *Journal of Development Economics* 30, no. 1: 1–24.

Perry, James, Elizabeth Vanderklein, and John Lemons. 1996. *Water Quality: Management of a Resource*. Cambridge: Blackwell.

Pinstrup-Andersen, Per, Rajul Pandya-Lorch, and Mark W. Rosegrant. 1999. *World Food Prospects: Critical Issues for the Early Twenty-First Century*. 2020 Vision Food Policy Report. Washington, D.C.: International Food Policy Research Institute.

Plano, Jack C., Milton Greenberg, Roy Olton, and Robert E. Riggs. 1973. *Political Science Dictionary*. Hinsdale, Ill.: Dryden.

Polanyi, Karl. [1944] 1957. *The Great Transformation: The Political and Economic Origins of Our Time*. Boston: Beacon.

Poncelet, Eric C. 2001a. "'A Kiss Here and a Kiss There': Conflict and Collaboration in Environmental Partnerships." *Environmental Management* 27, no. 1: 13–25.

———. 2001b. "Personal Transformation in Multistakeholder Environmental Partnerships." *Policy Sciences* 34, no. 3–4: 273–301.

Porter, Gareth, Janet Welsh Brown, and Pamela S. Chasek. 2000. *Global Environmental Politics*. 3d ed. Boulder: Westview.

Porter, M. E., and C. van der Linde. 1995. "Towards a New Conception of the Environment-Competitiveness Relationship." *Journal of Economic Perspectives* 9, no. 4: 97–118.

Prakash, Aseem. 2000. *Greening the Firm: The Politics of Corporate Environmentalism*. Cambridge: Cambridge University Press.

Prestwich, Michael C. 1985. "Feudalism." In *The Social Sciences Encyclopaedia*, edited by Adam Kuper and Jessica Kuper, 300–301. London: Routledge & Keegan Paul.

Prugh, Thomas, with Robert Costanza, John H. Cumberland, Herman E. Daly, Robert Goodland, and Richard B. Norgaard. 1999. *Natural Capital and Human Economic Survival*. 2d ed. Boca Raton, Fla.: Lewis.

Redclift, Michael, and Ted Benton, eds. 1994. *Social Theory and the Global Environment*. London: Routledge.

Reilly, William K. 1990. "The Green Thumb of Capitalism: The Environmental Benefits of Sustainable Growth." *Policy Review* 54: 16–21.

Richards, John F. 1990. "Land Transformation." In *The Earth as Transformed by Human Action*, edited by B. L. Turner II, William C. Clark, Robert W. Kates, John F. Richards, Jessica T. Mathews, and W. B. Meyer, 163–78. Cambridge: Cambridge University Press.

Ritzer, George. 2000. *Modern Sociological Theory*. 5th ed. Boston: McGraw-Hill.

Robbins, Richard H. 1999. *Global Problems and the Culture of Capitalism*. Boston: Allyn & Bacon.

Roberts, Geoffrey, and Alistair Edwards. 1991. *A New Dictionary of Political Analysis*. London: Edward Arnold.

Roberts, J. Timmons. 1996. "Predicting Participation in Environmental Treaties: A World-Systems Analysis." *Sociological Inquiry* 66, no. 1: 38–57.

Roberts, J. Timmons, and Peter E. Grimes. 1997. "Carbon Intensity and Economic Development 1962–91: A Brief Exploration of the Environmental Kuznets Curve." *World Development* 25, no. 2: 191–98.

Robertson, David. 1986. *The Penguin Dictionary of Politics*. London: Penguin.

Robey, Bryant, Shea O. Rutstein, and Leo Morris. 1993. "The Fertility Decline in Developing Countries." *Scientific American* 269: 60–67.

Romer, Paul M. 1990. "Endogenous Technological Change." *Journal of Political Economy* 98, no. 5: S71–S102.

———. 1994. "The Origins of Endogenous Growth." *Journal of Economic Perspectives* 8, no. 1: 3–22.

———. 1996. "Why, Indeed, in America? Theory, History, and the Origins of Modern Economic Growth." *American Economic Review* 86, no. 2: 202–6.

Roodman, David Malin. 1998. *The Natural Wealth of Nations: Harnessing the Market for the Environment*. New York: Norton.

Roome, Nigel J. 1998. "Introduction: Sustainable Development and the Industrial Firm." In *Sustainability Strategies for Industry: The Future of Corporate Practice*, edited by Nigel J. Roome, 1–23. Washington, D.C.: Island.

Rosegrant, Mark W., and Mercedita A. Sombilla. 1997. "Critical Issues Suggested by Trends in Food, Population, and the Environment to Year 2020." *American Journal of Agricultural Economics* 79, no. 5: 1467–70.

Ross, Eric B. 1998. *The Malthus Factor: Poverty, Politics, and Population in Capitalist Development*. London: Zed.

Ross, Michael L. 1999. "The Political Economy of the Resource Curse." *World Politics* 51, no. 2: 297–322.

Roszak, Theodore. 1995. "Where Psyche Meets Gaia." In *Ecopsychology*, edited by Theodore Roszak, Mary E. Gomes, and Allen D. Kanner, 1–20. San Francisco: Sierra Club Books.

Rowell, Andrew. 1996. *Green Backlash: Global Subversion of the Environmental Movement*. London: Routledge.

Ruth, Matthias. 1998. "Dematerialization in Five U.S. Metals Sectors: Implications for Energy Use and CO_2 Emissions." *Resources Policy* 24, no. 1: 1–18.

Ruttan, Vernon W. 1995. "Population Growth, Environmental Change, and Innovation: Implications for Sustainable Growth in Agriculture." In *Population and Land Use in Developing Countries: Report of a Workshop*, edited by Carole L. Jolly and Barbara Boyle Torrey, 124–56. Washington, D.C.: National Academy Press.

Ryan, Alan. 1999. "Britain: Recycling the Third Way." *Dissent* 46, no. 2: 77-80.

Sachs, Jeffrey D., and Andrew M. Warner. 1995. "Natural Resource Abundance and Economic Growth." Development Discussion Paper no. 517a. Cambridge: Harvard Institute for International Development.

Sachs, Wolfgang. 1991. "Environment and Development: The Story of a Dangerous Liaison." *Ecologist* 21, no. 6: 252–57.

———. 1992. "One World." In *The Development Dictionary*, edited by Wolfgang Sachs, 102–15. London: Zed.

———. 1993. "Global Ecology and the Shadow of Development." In *Global Ecology: A New Arena of Political Conflict*, edited by Wolfgang Sachs, 3–21. London: Zed; Halifax, N.S.: Fernwood.

———. 1999. *Planet Dialectics: Explorations in Environment and Development*. Halifax, N.S.: Fernwood; Johannesburg: Witwatersrand University Press; London: Zed.

Sachs, Wolfgang, Reinhard Loske, Manfred Linz et al. 1998. *Greening the North: A Post-Industrial Blueprint for Ecology and Equity*. London: Zed.

Sage, Colin. 1994. "Population and Income." In *Changes in Land Use and Land Cover: A Global Perspective*, edited by William B. Meyer and B. L. Turner II, 263–85. Cambridge: Cambridge University Press.

Salter, W. E. B. 1960. *Productivity and Technical Change*. Cambridge: Cambridge University Press.

Sarkar, Saral. 1999. *Eco-Socialism or Eco-Capitalism? A Critical Analysis of Humanity's Fundamental Choices*. London: Zed.

Schmidheiny, Stephan. 1992. *Changing Course: A Global Business Perspective on Development and the Environment*. Cambridge: MIT Press.

Schmidheiny, Stephan, Federico Zorraquín, with the World Business Council for Sustainable Development. 1996. *Financing Change: The Financial Community, Eco-Efficiency, and Sustainable Development*. Cambridge: MIT Press, 1996.

Schmookler, Andrew Bard. 1995. *The Parable of the Tribes: The Problem of Power in Social Evolution*. 2d ed. Albany: State University of New York Press.

Schnaiberg, Allan. 1980. *The Environment: From Surplus to Scarcity*. New York: Oxford University Press.

Schnaiberg, Allan, and Kenneth Alan Gould. 1994. *Environment and Society: The Enduring Conflict*. New York: St. Martin's.

Schor, Juliet B. 1995. "Can the North Stop Consumption Growth? Escaping the Cycle of Work and Spend." In *The North, the South, and the Environment: Ecological Constraints and the Global Economy*, edited by V. Bhaskar and Andrew Glyn, 68–84. New York: St. Martin's.

Schramm, Gunter, and Jeremy J. Warford, eds. 1989. *Environmental Management and Economic Development*. A World Bank Publication. Baltimore: Johns Hopkins University Press.

Schwartz, Herman M. 1994. *States versus Markets: History, Geography, and the Development of the International Political Economy*. New York: St. Martin's.

Scoones, I. 1999. "New Ecology and the Social Sciences: What Prospects for a Fruitful Engagement?" *Annual Review of Anthropology* 28: 479–507.

Scruton, Roger. 1982. *A Dictionary of Political Thought*. New York: Hill & Wang.

Seabrook, Jeremy. 1993. *Victims of Development: Resistance and Alternatives*. London: Verso.

Selden, Thomas M., and Daqing Song. 1994. "Environmental Quality and Development: Is There a Kuznets Curve for Air Pollution Emissions?" *Journal of Environmental Economics and Management* 27: 147–62.

Serageldin, Ismail, and G. J. Persley. 2000. *Promethean Science: Agricultural Biotechnology, the Environment, and the Poor*. Washington, D.C.: Consultative Group on International Agricultural Research.

Sessions, George. 1995. Preface to *Deep Ecology for the 21st Century: Readings on the Philosophy and Practice of the New Environmentalism*, edited by George Sessions, ix–xxviii. Boston: Shambhala.

Shafik, Nemat, and Sushenjit Bandyopadhyay. 1992. "Economic Growth and Environmental Quality: Time Series and Cross-Country Evidence." World Bank Research Paper WPS 904. Washington, D.C.: World Bank.

Shiva, Vandana. 1993. "The Greening of the Global Reach." In *Global Ecology: A New Arena of Political Conflict*, edited by Wolfgang Sachs, 149–56. London: Zed; Halifax, N.S.: Fernwood.

———. 1997. *Biopiracy: The Plunder of Nature and Knowledge*. Boston: South End.

———. 2000. *Stolen Harvest: The Hijacking of the Global Food Supply*. Boston: South End.

Shiva, Vandana, Patrick Anderson, Heffa Schücking, Andrew Gray, Larry Lohmann, and David Cooper. 1991. *Biodiversity: Social and Ecological Perspectives*. London: Zed; Penang, Malaysia: World Rainforest Movement.

Shrivastava, Paul. 1996. *Greening Business: Profiting the Corporation and the Environment*. Cincinnati: Thomson Executive Press.

Simmons, I. G. 1996. *Changing the Face of the Earth: Culture, Environment, History*. Cambridge, Mass.: Blackwell.

Simon, Julian L. 1981. *The Ultimate Resource*. Princeton, N.J.: Princeton University Press.

———. 1990. *Population Matters: People, Resources, Environment, and Immigration*. New Brunswick, N.J.: Transaction.

———, ed. 1992. *Population and Development in Poor Countries: Selected Essays*. Princeton, N.J.: Princeton University Press.

————. 1996. *The Ultimate Resource 2*. Princeton, N.J.: Princeton University Press.

Simon, Julian L., and Herman Kahn. 1984. *The Resourceful Earth*. Oxford: Basil Blackwell.

Simon, Julian L., with Gunter Steinman. 1992. "Population, Natural Resources, and the Long-Run Standard of Living." In *Population and Development in Poor Countries: Selected Essays*, edited by Julian L. Simon, 89–121. Princeton, N.J.: Princeton University Press.

Simonis, Udo. 1990. *Beyond Growth: Elements of Sustainable Development*. Berlin: Edition Sigma, WZB.

Smil, Vaclav. 1997. *Cycles of Life: Civilization and the Biosphere*. New York: Scientific American Library.

————. 1999. *Energies: An Illustrated Guide to the Biosphere and Civilization*. Cambridge: MIT Press.

Soddy, Frederick. 1922. *Cartesian Economics: The Bearing of Physical Science upon State Stewardship*. London: Hendersons.

Solow, Robert M. 1974. "The Economics of Resources or the Resources of Economics." *American Economic Review* 64, no. 2: 1–14.

————. 1997. "Reply: Georgescu-Roegen versus Solow/Stiglitz." *Ecological Economics* 22, no. 3: 267–68.

Southwick, Charles H. 1996. *Global Ecology in Human Perspective*. New York: Oxford University Press.

Spaargaren, Gert, and Arthur P.J. Mol. 1992. "Sociology, Environment, and Modernity: Ecological Modernization as a Theory of Social Change." *Society and Natural Resources* 5, no. 4: 323–44.

Spaargaren, Gert, Arthur P.J. Mol, and Frederick H. Buttel, eds. 2000. *Environment and Global Modernity*. London: Sage.

Starr, Chauncey. 1997. "Sustaining the Human Environment: The Next Two Hundred Years." In *Technical Trajectories and the Human Environment*, edited by Jesse H. Ausubel and H. Dale Langford, 185–98. Washington, D.C.: National Academy Press.

Stead, W. Edward, and Jean Garner Stead. 1992. *Management for a Small Planet: Strategic Decision Making and the Environment*. Newbury Park, Calif.: Sage.

Stern, David I., Michael S. Compton, and Edward B. Barbier. 1996. "Economic Growth and Environmental Degradation: The Environmental Kuznets Curve and Sustainable Development." *World Development* 24, no. 7: 1151–60.

Stern, Paul C., and Thomas Dietz. 1994. "The Value Basis of Environmental Concern." *Journal of Social Issues* 50, no. 3: 65–84.

Stiglitz, Joseph E. 1997. "Reply: Georgescu-Roegen versus Solow/Stiglitz." *Ecological Economics* 22, no. 3: 269–70.

Stockdale, Jerry. 1989. "Pro-Growth, Limits to Growth, and a Sustainable Development Synthesis." *Society and Natural Resources* 2, no. 3: 163–76.

Stokes, C. Shannon. 1995. "Explaining the Demographic Transition: Institutional Factors in Fertility Decline." *Rural Sociology* 60, no. 1: 1–22.

Stokke, Olav. 1991. "Sustainable Development: A Multi-Faceted Challenge." In *Sustainable Development*, edited by Olav Stokke, 8–31. London: Frank Cass.

Stott, Philip, and Sian Sullivan, eds. 2000. *Political Ecology: Science, Myth, and Power*. London: Edward Arnold; New York: Oxford University Press.

Stretton, Hugh. *Capitalism, Socialism, and the Environment*. 1976. Cambridge: Cambridge University Press.

Sun, J. W., and T. Meristo. 1999. "Measurement of Dematerialization/Materialization: A Case Analysis of Energy Saving and Decarbonization in OECD Countries, 1960–95." *Technological Forecasting and Social Change* 60, no. 3: 275–94.

Sunderlin, William D. 1995a. "Global Environmental Change, Sociology, and Paradigm Isolation." *Global Environmental Change* 5, no. 3: 211–20.

———. 1995b. "Managerialism and the Conceptual Limits of Sustainable Development." *Society and Natural Resources* 8, no. 6: 481–92.

Sunderlin, William D., and Maharlina Luz G. Gorospe. 1997. "Fishers' Organizations and Modes of Co-Management: The Case of San Miguel Bay, Philippines." *Human Organization* 56, no. 3: 333–43.

Suri, Vivek, and Duane Chapman. 1998. "Economic Growth, Trade, and Energy: Implications for the Environmental Kuznets Curve." *Ecological Economics* 25: 195–208.

Switzer, Jacqueline Vaughn. 1997. *Green Backlash: The History and Politics of Environmental Opposition in the U.S.* Boulder: Lynne Rienner.

Taylor, Bron Raymond, ed. 1995. *Ecological Resistance Movements: The Global Emergence of Radical and Popular Environmentalism.* Albany: State University of New York Press.

Thomas, Vinod, Mansoor Dailami, Ashok Dhareshwar, Daniel Kaufmann, Nalin Kishor, Ramón Lopez, and Yan Wang. 2000. *The Quality of Growth.* Oxford: Oxford University Press.

Tilly, Charles. 1992. *Coercion, Capital, and European States: AD 990–1992.* Cambridge, Mass.: Blackwell.

Tokar, Brian. 1997. *Earth for Sale: Reclaiming Ecology in the Age of Corporate Greenwash.* Boston: South End.

Torgerson, Douglas. 1999. *The Promise of Green Politics.* Durham, N.C.: Duke University Press.

Torras, Mariano, and James K. Boyce. 1998. "Income, Inequality, and Pollution: A Reassessment of the Environmental Kuznets Curve." *Ecological Economics* 25: 147–60.

Trainer, F. E. 1985. *Abandon Affluence.* Totowa, N.J.: Zed.

Trainer, Ted. 1996. *Towards a Sustainable Economy: The Need for Fundamental Change.* Oxford: Jon Carpenter; Sydney: Envirobook.

Turner, R. Kerry. 1997. "Georgescu-Roegen versus Solow/Stiglitz: An Individualistic and Interdisciplinary Perspective." *Ecological Economics* 22, no. 3: 299–302.

UNDP [United Nations Development Program]. 1998. *Human Development Report 1998.* New York: Oxford University Press.

———. 1999. *Human Development Report 1999.* New York: Oxford University Press.

UNEP [United Nations Environment Program]. 1993. *Environmental Report, 1993–94.* Oxford: Blackwell.

UNICEF [United Nations International Children's Fund]. 1994. *The State of the World's Children 1994.* Oxford: Oxford University Press.

United Nations Population Division. 2000a. *World Population Prospects: The 2000 Revision.* Vol. 1, *Comprehensive Tables.* New York: United Nations.

———. 2000b. *Long-Range World Population Projections: Based on the 1998 Revision.* New York: United Nations.

U.S. Bureau of the Census. 2000. *International Data Base.* Updated May 10. <www.census.gov/ipc/www/idbnew.html> (January 26, 2002).

Van Dijk, Teun A. 1998. *Ideology: A Multidisciplinary Approach.* London: Sage.

Vasey, Daniel E. 1992. *An Ecological History of Agriculture: 10,000 B.C.–A.D. 1000.* Ames: Iowa State University Press.

Wallace, Ruth A., and Alison Wolf. [1980] 1991. *Contemporary Sociological Theory: Continuing the Classical Tradition.* 3d ed. Englewood Cliffs, N.J.: Prentice-Hall.

——. [1980] 1995. *Contemporary Sociological Theory: Continuing the Classical Tradition.* 4th ed. Englewood Cliffs, N.J.: Prentice-Hall.

Wallerstein, Immanuel. 1979. *The Capitalist World Economy.* Cambridge: Cambridge University Press.

——. 1999. "Ecology and Capitalist Cost of Production: No Exit." In *Ecology and the World-System,* edited by Walter L. Goldfrank, David Goodman, and Andrew Szasz, 3–11. Westport, Conn.: Greenwood.

Walley, Noah, and Bradley Whitehead. 1994. "It's Not Easy Being Green." *Harvard Business Review* 72: 46–52.

Walter, Edward. 1981. *The Immorality of Limiting Growth.* Albany: State University of New York Press.

Wapner, Paul. 1996. *Environmental Activism and World Civic Politics.* Albany: State University of New York Press.

Waters, Malcolm. 1994. *Modern Sociological Theory.* London: Sage.

Watkins, Susan Cotts. 1986. Conclusion to *The Decline of Fertility in Europe,* edited by Ansley Coale and Susan Cotts Watkins, 420–49. Princeton, N.J.: Princeton University Press.

Wattenberg, Ben J. 1987. *The Birth Dearth.* New York: Pharos.

——. 1997. "The Population Explosion Is Over." *New York Times Magazine,* November 23, 60–63.

Watts, Michael. 1983. *Silent Violence: Food, Famine, and Peasantry in Northern Nigeria.* Berkeley: University of California Press.

WCED [World Commission on Environment and Development]. 1987. *Our Common Future.* Oxford: Oxford University Press.

Weale, Albert. 1992. *The New Politics of Pollution.* Manchester: Manchester University Press.

Weaver, James H., Michael T. Rock, and Kenneth Kusterer. 1997. *Achieving Broad-Based Sustainable Development: Governance, Environment, and Growth with Equity.* West Hartford, Conn.: Kumarian.

Weeks, John R. 1996. *Population: An Introduction to Concepts and Issues.* 6th ed. Belmont, Calif.: Wadsworth.

Welford, Richard. 1997. "Introduction: What Are We Doing to the World?" In *Hijacking Environmentalism: Corporate Responses to Sustainable Development,* edited by Richard Welford, 3–15. London: Earthscan.

Wernick, Iddo K., Robert Herman, Shekhar Govind, and Jesse H. Ausubel. 1997. "Materialization and Dematerialization: Measures and Trends." In *Technical Trajectories and the Human Environment,* edited by Jesse H. Ausubel and H. Dale Langford, 135–56. Washington, D.C.: National Academy Press.

Whitmore, Thomas M., B. L. Turner II, Douglas L. Johnson, Robert W. Kates, and Thomas R. Gottschang. 1990. "Long-Term Population Change." In *The Earth as Transformed by Human Action: Global and Regional Changes in the Biosphere over the Past 300 Years,* edited by B. L. Turner II, William C. Clark, Robert W. Kates, John F. Richards, Jessica T. Mathews, and William B. Meyer, 25–54. Cambridge: Cambridge University Press.

Wissenburg, Marcel. 1998. *Green Liberalism: The Free and the Green Society.* London: UCL Press, 1998.

Wolfensohn, James. 2000. Foreword to *The Quality of Growth*, by Vinod Thomas, Mansoor Dailami, Ashok Dhareshwar, Daniel Kaufmann, Nalin Kishor, Ramón Lopez, and Yan Wang, xiii–xv. Oxford: Oxford University Press.

World Bank. 1987. *Environment, Growth, and Development*. Report no. 14. Washington, D.C.: World Bank Development Committee. Prepared by Jeremy J. Warford.

———. 1988. *Environment and Development: Implementing the World Bank's New Policies*. Report no. 17. Washington, D.C.: World Bank Development Committee. Prepared by Jeremy J. Warford and Richard Ackermann.

———. 1992. *World Development Report 1992: Development and the Environment*. Oxford: Oxford University Press.

———. 2000. *Entering the 21st Century: World Development Report 1999/2000*. Oxford: Oxford University Press.

———. 2001. *World Development Report 2000/2001: Attacking Poverty*. Oxford: Oxford University Press.

WRI [World Resources Institute]. 1998. *World Resources 1998–99: A Guide to the Global Environment*. New York: Oxford University Press. A joint publication by the World Resources Institute, the United Nations Environment Program, the United Nations Development Program, and the World Bank.

Yandle, Bruce, ed. 1999. *The Market Meets the Environment: Economic Analysis of Environmental Policy*. Lanham, Md.: Rowman & Littlefield.

Young, Oran R. 1996. "The Effectiveness of International Governance Systems." In *Global Environmental Change and International Governance*, edited by Oran R. Young, George J. Demko, and Kilaparti Ramakrishna, 1–27. Hanover, N.H.: University Press of New England.

Young, Oran R., ed. 1997. *Global Governance: Drawing Insights from the Environmental Experience*. Cambridge: MIT Press.

Young, Oran R., George J. Demko, and Kilaparti Ramakrishna, eds. 1996. *Global Environmental Change and International Governance*. Hanover, N.H.: University Press of New England.

Young, Stephen C. 2000a. *The Emergence of Ecological Modernisation: Integrating the Environment and the Economy*. London: Routledge.

———. 2000b. "Introduction: The Origins and Evolving Nature of Ecological Modernisation." In *The Emergence of Ecological Modernisation: Integrating the Environment and the Economy*, edited by Stephen C. Young, 1–39. London: Routledge.

Young, T. R., and Bruce A. Arrigo. 1999. *The Dictionary of Critical Social Science*. Boulder: Westview.

Zeitlin, Irving M. 1997. *Ideology and the Development of Sociological Theory*. 6th ed. Upper Saddle River, N.J.: Prentice-Hall.

Zovanyi, Gabor. 1998. *Growth Management for a Sustainable Future: Ecological Sustainability as the New Growth Management Focus for the 21st Century*. Westport, Conn.: Praeger.

Index

Abercrombie, Nicholas, 25
Abernethy, Virginia, 124
abortion, 18
acid rain, 56, 58
activism, 8. *See also* mobilization
Adams, William Mark, 80
affluence, 10; class and, 64; culture and,
63, 66–67; definition, 48; effects on
technology, 62; environmental change
and, 48–51; human evolution and, 38,
41; interactions with other social
theory variables, 63, 72, 73; measures
of, 38; population and, 61; power and,
65; resource exploitation for, 70; rich-
poor gap, 69; technology and, 62. *See
also* wealth
Afghanistan, 18
Aghion, Philippe, 170
Agras, Jean, 162
agricultural intensification, 56, 115, 120
agricultural productivity, 53, 134;
diminishing returns, 122; increase rate,
117, 118, 143; increases in, 54, 55, 57,
113, 116; neo-Malthusian view of, 137;
population growth and, 120; second
Green Revolution in, 115–16, 133–34,
143

agriculture, 39, 45; cultivated land area,
53, 57; development of, 53–54;
environmental change and, 51–52;
feudalism, 43; land availability, 115;
land degradation, 57, 115; livestock
production, 113–14; population growth
and, 61–62
aid restraint, 118–19, 124. *See also*
poverty
AIDS, 55
air quality, 56, 58, 160
Alexander, Jeffrey, 33
Alford, Robert R., 4, 21, 84
analytical sociology, 25
Anderson, Terry L., 88, 89, 97, 104, 105;
affirmation of government, 180; free
market environmentalism, 189;
progrowth view, 169, 173
animals: domestication of, 39, 51, 52, 61,
64; livestock, 113–14
anomie, 26
anthropocentrism, 82, 88
anti-Malthusianism, 10, 108, 128, 132; of
Boserup, 120, 121; class (*see* class anti-
Malthusianism); individualist (*see*
individualist anti-Malthusianism); of
Marx and Engels, 119–20, 121, 128;

political schism in, 139; popularity of, 134; as U.S. policy, 134
Archer, Margaret, 25, 33
Arizpe, Lourdes, 139
Arnold, Ron, 200
Aron, Raymond, 19
Arrow, Kenneth, 161
Ascher, William, 157
Athanasiou, Tom, 80, 90, 94, 175
Atkinson, Adrian, 93
Ausubel, Jesse, 159
autonomy: individual, 26; of state, 46, 59
Ayres, Robert U., 158, 160, 172

Bailey, Ronald, 2, 4, 169
Bandow, Doug, 94
Bandyopadhyay, Sushenjit, 160
Barbier, Edward B., 170
Beaud, Michel, 66
Beaudreau, Bernard C., 67
Beckerman, Wilfred, 148, 152, 161; on environmental exaggeration, 200; on free market individualism, 173; on neo-Marxist environmentalism, 200; progrowth view, 167
behavior, individual, 85, 105
beliefs. See values
Bell, Daniel, 19
Bell, Michael Mayerfeld, 6
Ben & Jerry's, 201
Bentham, Jeremy, 122
Berdan, Frances F., 45
biases, 8–9
biocentrism, 82, 86
biodiversity, 56, 57, 132
Blaikie, Piers, 81
Blowers, Andrew, 183
Blühdorn, Ingolfur, 183
Body Shop, The, 201
Bohm, David, 96
Bookchin, Murray, 81, 82, 93, 97; integrationalist statements, 99
Boserup, Esther, 10, 109, 117, 143; population paradigms, 120, 121, 125
bottom line, triple, 194
Boulding, Kenneth, 153
Bourdieu, Pierre, 33

Bowers, C. A., 86, 93, 97, 104
Boyce, James K., 162
Boyden, Stephen, 38–39
Braudel, Fernand, 45, 60
Brechin, Stephen R., 196
Brookfield, Harold, 81
Brown, L. David, 202, 203
Brown, Lester, 2, 4, 104, 121; antigrowth stance, 166; neo-Malthusianism, 124, 126, 128
Bruntland Report, 69
bureaucracy, 89. See also governments; state
Burkett, Paul, 94
Burrows, Brian, 96
Bush, George W., 3, 135, 207
Buttel, Frederick H., 6, 84; on agricultural productivity, 117; on classical social theory, 7; on ecological modernization theory, 183; on environmentalism, 190; on social movements, 196; on sociology synthesis, 105

camera obscura, 17
capital, 153; intellectual, 170; as resource substitute, 154–55
capital accumulation, 39, 44; culture and, 46; distribution of, 80; as environmental problem cause, 77, 86, 106; as environmental problem solution, 86; in social evolution, 97; population growth and, 65; private ownership, 80; socioeconomic disorganization from, 77–78; state formation and, 59; state's role in, 45
capitalism, 3, 15; acceptance of, 97, 137; as beneficial, 169, 213; class paradigm view of, 22–23, 35; conservative view of, 30; consumption increases in, 198, 203–4; contradictions of, 80, 164; criticism of, 164, 177, 178, 184–85, 186n18, 210, 211; as defining social process, 21; as deleterious, 213; development of, 20, 43–44; in ecological modernization theory, 182; economic growth views and, 170–71, 184; energy technology and, 65; environmentalism antagonism

with, 191–92; examination of, 194; green, 182; growth needs, 64, 165; individualist paradigm view of, 26–27, 35; industrial revolution and, 39; inequality in, 208 (see also inequality); Malthusianism and, 144n5; managerial paradigm view of, 24, 35, 82, 84; Marxist analysis of, 119; neo-Marxist view of, 164; opposition to, 60, 196; oppression from, 107n3; population growth and, 126–28; questioning, 30; state and, 45, 212; structure of, 174; surplus population use, 119; sustainable, 194; threats to, 200, 204; wage laborers in, 43

carbon dioxide emissions, 150, 151, 159

carbon emissions, 58

carrying capacity, 1–2, 3, 108, 124, 214

Carson, Rachel, 191

Cato Institute, 169

Catton, William R., 4, 47, 169

Center for International Forestry Research (CIFOR), 8

center/liberal, 29, 30; economic growth views, 11, 147; environmentalism and, 191; Malthusian perspective, 108; managerial paradigm alignment with, 28, 35, 85, 136; neo-Malthusianism, 126, 136; power association with, 108; state environmentalism, 11

centrism, 30

Centro de Investigación de Maíz y Trigo (CIMMYT), 8

CGIAR. See Consultative Group on International Agricultural Research

Chapman, Duane, 161, 162

children, 111–12. See also fertility rates; population growth

CIFOR (Center for International Forestry Research), 8

CIMMYT (Centro de Investigación de Maíz y Trigo), 8

civic environmentalism, 11, 188, 190–92; corporate environmentalism tensions, 191–92; institutional foundations of, 200; leadership role, 203, 205; strategies used, 191

civil liberties, 12

class, 9, 26, 27, 39–44; affluence and, 63, 64; association with left, 108; culture and, 59–60; environmental change and, 39–44, 209; formation, 59, 208; human evolution and, 40–41; importance of, 73; interaction with population, 62, 64; interactions with other social theory variables, 63, 72, 73; Marxist analysis of, 80, 81; population and, 62–64; power and, 59; slavery and, 39, 43; as social theory variable, 37, 38; technology and, 63, 64–65

class anti-Malthusianism, 10, 122, 123, 125–26, 143; equity issues, 135; exemplary statements, 129–31; issue framing, 128; paradigm integration in, 136–37; population growth views, 133; on second Green Revolution, 133

class conflict, 21, 27, 59, 211; environmental problems and, 77; inevitability of, 79; oppression and, 22–23; reduction, 24

class paradigm, 4–5, 21–23, 35; antigrowth view, 163–66; anti-Malthusianism, 126 (see also class anti-Malthusianism); contingent view of individualism, 94, 95; contingent view of managerialism, 94, 95; dismissal of, 10, 93, 97, 182; eco-Marxism, 80; in economic growth debate, 184–85; eco-socialism, 80; environment in, 106n2; environmental, 77–82; identification with, 97; individualist integration, 100–103, 175, 176, 179; isolation of, 10; managerial integration, 99, 101, 175, 176, 179; paradigm integration in, 209; political ecology, 80; production/consumption institutions in, 180–81; progrowth view, 166; recognition of, 105; rejection of individualism, 91–92, 93, 198, 199; rejection of managerialism, 90–91, 93, 198, 199; rejectionist paradigm isolation, 90–93; social ecology, 80; strengths and weaknesses of, 211–12; tenets of, 106, 210

class polarization, 15
climate, 51; global warming, 57–58, 69, 132, 146
Club of Rome, 152, 156
cognitive dissonance, 213
Cohen, G. A., 23
Cohen, Joel E., 112, 113, 141
Cohen, Maurie J., 181, 183
Cole, Matthew A., 162
Coleman, James, 33
collaborations, 201–3
Collins, Randall, 25, 33
collusion, 179
colonialism, 67, 80
commoditization, 60
Commoner-Ehrlich equation, 10, 37; critique of, 38, 71–72
communism, 18, 211; collapse of, 80, 81, 164
competition, 27, 47, 64; price, 159; wage rate in, 62
Competitive Enterprise Institute, 1–2, 125, 132, 169
Condorcet, Marquis de, 119
conflict, 33, 182–83; ideological basis of, 18–19; minimizing, 202–3
conflictual thinking, 32
consensus, 17, 33
conservatism, 9; definitions, 28, 29–30; Durkheim and, 26, 36n9; individualist paradigm and, 27. See also right/conservative
conservative environmentalism, 189, 194
Consultative Group on International Agricultural Research (CGIAR), 8, 116–17, 121
consumerism, 60, 98; green, 198; rejection of, 105
consumption, 47, 60; absolute, 159; aggregate, 64; attention to, 205; culture of, 180; distinction from power relations, 181; of energy (see energy consumption); expenditure inequality, 149–50; forces promoting, 213; full-cost accounting for, 194; increase in, 148, 198; institutions, 162;

overconsumption (see overconsumption); rate of, 69, 150, 156; reducing, 106; by rich countries, 69, 103, 104, 137
consumption classes, 181
contraception, 121
Conway, Gordon, 116
corporate environmentalism, 11, 86, 187–88, 190, 193–94; civic environmentalism tensions, 191–92; instrumental goals in, 197; motivations for, 204; in United States, 193; as window dressing, 198; win-win and win-lose theories, 194
corruption, 179
Coser, Lewis, 25, 33
cosmopolitan localism, 60
cost reduction, 23
countries: developing (see developing countries); economic relationship inequities, 44; rich-poor gap, 55
Covey, Jane G., 202, 203
criticism, defense against, 16
Cropper, Maureen, 160
cultural adaptation, 67
cultural individualism. See individualist paradigm
Cultural Survival, 201
cultural tradition. See deep ecology; see also individualist paradigm
cultural transformation, 86, 89, 98, 164; children's role, 112; environment and, 209; environmental standards and, 163; implementation of, 105; need for, 100, 106, 175, 177, 213; rationality in, 180; time needed for, 104
culture, 9, 96, 101; affluence and, 63, 66–67; association with right, 108; class and, 59–60; class paradigm view of, 100, 103; in ecological modernization theory, 181–82; environmental change and, 46–47, 209; human evolution and, 40–41; interactions with other social theory variables, 63, 72, 73; politics and, 97, 108; population and, 63, 66; power and, 60; social structure and, 25; as

social theory variable, 37, 38;
technology and, 63, 67
Cunningham, William P., 188

Dahrendorf, Ralf, 25, 33
Dailey, Gretchen, 116
Daly, Herman E., 148–49, 155, 156, 160;
antigrowth view, 166, 172
de Bruyn, Sander M., 162
de Tracy, Destutt, 17
Debeir, Jean-Claude, 64
debt forgiveness, 105
decarbonization, 158–59
decentralization, 81, 84, 105, 162
decision making, 46, 162, 214; individual,
85
deep ecology, 81, 86, 88; antigrowth view,
169; class paradigm and, 104; class
position in, 178; cultural individualism
in, 191; culture in, 100; ecocentrism
in, 82; paradigm isolation in, 93–94
deforestation, 57, 132, 160
dematerialization, 11, 147, 156, 158–60,
183; progress in, 184, 214
democracy, 18, 213; community-based, 81;
liberal, 19
demographic transition, 55–56, 61,
109–13; definitions, 112; mechanisms
of, 112; preconditions for, 62; rejection
of, 124; reversion from, 132
determinism, 23, 24
Devall, Bill, 86, 93, 104, 172
developing countries: agricultural
productivity, 113; agricultural
technologies for, 116; climate change
effects in, 58; deep ecology support for,
178; demographic transition in, 112;
environmental movement in, 195–96;
import dependency, 113; income
growth in, 156, 183; insensitivity to,
169; population growth in, 48, 56, 143;
production types, 161
development, 149, 185n2; sustainable (see
sustainable development)
developmentalist period, 46
dialectical materialism, 21–23, 24, 80, 81
dialectical naturalism, 81

Diamond, Jared, 38, 45, 51; on class, 59, 62
Dietz, Thomas, 192
differentiation, 25–26, 61
diplomacy, 82, 85
diseases: control of, 54, 55, 111; as
population check, 118
Dobson, Andrew, 163, 174, 191
dominant social paradigm (DSP), 47, 63;
development of, 66; innovation and,
67; Malthusian, 120
domination, 25, 39; in capitalism, 44; of
humans, 47, 62; justifications for, 46,
66–67; of nature, 47, 188; as negative
force, 81; by state/corporations, 23, 24;
of states/countries, 44
Douthwaite, Richard, 66, 175
Dryzek, John S., 84
DSP. See dominant social paradigm
Dubos, René, 121
Dunlap, Riley E., 4, 47
Dunn, James R., 88, 89, 169, 189
Durkheim, Emile, 5, 26; intellectual
legacy of, 20, 89
Durning, Alan T., 181
Dyson, Tim, 113

Eagleton, Terry, 16, 19
Earley, Jay, 47
Eatwell, Roger, 15
Eberstadt, Nicholas, 127, 132
eco-anarchism. See social ecology
eco-capitalists, 86
ecocentrism, 82
ecological economics, 153–55, 166, 174
ecological modernization theory (EMT),
11, 84–85, 147, 156, 162–63, 181–83;
cultural individualism in, 181;
managerial paradigm dominance, 183;
paradigm integration by, 147, 184;
political ecology and, 107n4
ecologism, 191
ecology, types of, 7
eco-Marxism, 80
economic activity composition, 159
economic change, 98
economic growth, 3, 11, 146–47;
antigrowth views, 146, 158, 163–70;

capitalist, 165; convergence theories, 146, 156–63, 183; debate re (see economic growth debate); decoupling income and throughput, 183, 184; deep ecology view of, 169; definitions, 148–49, 185n1; dematerialization (see dematerialization); ecological sustainability and, 162; environmental degradation feedback in, 156–57, 161; as environmental problem cause, 88, 146; as environmental problem solution, 69, 88, 146; environmental restoration and, 156–57; ideas/innovation in, 170; in last century, 149–50; limits to (see economic growth limits); models, 181; pattern variance in, 185n4; polarization re, 11, 146; in population-resource balance, 135; progrowth views, 166–72; in social theory paradigms, 163–72; state's role in, 25, 164; throughput decrease and, 156. See also income growth; throughput growth

economic growth debate, 183–84; clarity of terminology, 148–49, 183; factual controversies, 147; growth types in, 148; ideology in, 147, 163, 184; literature underlying, 152–53; managerial paradigm in, 85, 163, 172; neoclassical versus ecological economics views, 155; Our Common Growth report, 156–57; political dimension of, 172; position softening in, 156, 175, 185n9; The Quality of Growth study, 157–58; zero-growth views, 156

economic growth limits, 150, 152; Beyond the Limits study, 152; ecological economics view, 153–55; The Limits to Growth report, 146, 152–53; Mankind at the Turning Point study, 156; neoclassical economics view, 153–55

economic surplus, 39, 44, 214; animal domestication and, 52; food stockpiles, 45; increases in, 64; population growth and, 62; state's role re, 59; technology and, 61

economics, 5, 6, 21; ecological, 153–55; global, 44, 46; Keynesian, 25; neoclassical (see neoclassical economics); as reform vehicle, 162; state and, 46; thermodynamic laws and, 154–55

economy: free market, 103; as given, 97; government intervention in, 25, 29, 78, 86, 94, 106; intervention by civic mobilization, 191; role in world ecosystem, 155; steady-state, 155, 170

eco-socialism, 7, 80, 80–81

education, 26, 86, 90; fertility rates and, 112; lack of knowledge, 180

Edwards, Alistair, 28

Edwards, Mark, 96

Ehrlich, Anne, 137

Ehrlich, Paul, 121, 124, 128, 137; neo-Malthusianism, 126, 137

Ekins, Paul, 162

Elias, Norbert, 33

elites, 39, 44, 59; power abuses by, 179; state and, 46, 213. See also class

Elkington, John, 194

Elster, John, 23

empiricism, 47

EMT. See ecological modernization theory

endogenous growth theory, 170, 180

energetics, human, 38

energy consumption, 48–50, 53; in agriculture, 115; increase in, 54, 61, 148; rates, 50–51, 159

energy regimes, 159

energy sources: asymmetry in, 155; carbon supply, 158–59; somatic, 48–49

energy technology, 41, 51, 52; alternatives, 54; class and, 64–65; development of, 52–53; fossil fuels, 53, 65

Engelman, Robert, 124, 126, 128, 138

Engels, Friedrich, 10, 17, 117; on aid restraint, 119; ecological interpretations of, 80; on hunger, 120; on population catastrophism, 119, 141; population paradigms, 121; population-resource balance and, 108–9

Enteman, Willard F., 84

environment, 69; carrying capacity, 1–2, 3, 108, 124, 214; concern re, 187; cultural transformation and, 209; effect on social outcomes, 70; human impact on, 71–72; ideological perspectives on, 10; prognostications re, 1–2; social theory paradigms for understanding, 8 (*see also* social theory paradigms); throughput burden, 150

environmental change: linkage to class, power, and culture, 9, 37, 39–46, 209; social context of, 71; socioeconomy and, 81; variables in, 71–72 (*see also* Commoner-Ehrlich equation)

Environmental Defense Fund, 201

environmental degradation/destruction: cause-effect relationships, 69–71, 73; connection to other issues, 198; economic growth and, 156–57, 161; necessity of decrease, 148; pattern of, 160; population growth and, 124 (*see also* population growth; population-resource balance); poverty and, 69, 77, 157

environmental ideologies, 6, 77–89

environmental Kuznets curve (EKC), 147, 156, 160–62, 183

environmental management, 2, 3

environmental movement, 60, 74–75n16, 187–88; backlash against, 169; in developing countries, 195–96; growth of, 190; motivations for, 214; problems spawning, 191 (*see also* environmental problems); radical, 152; state responses to, 192. *See also* environmentalism

environmental outcomes, 70, 208–9; linkage to social outcomes, 9, 68–72

environmental paradigms, 4. *See also* social theory paradigms

environmental problems, 2; addressing, 35; behavioral causes of, 86; capitalist causes of, 81; causes of, 5, 37, 69, 107n9; change agents, 78, 80, 82, 86; class conflict causes, 77, 106; class/power/culture dimensions of, 76; cultural endowments and, 182; definition of, 35; dematerialization

and, 159–60; discourse range re, 97; evidence of, 207; food production's role in, 143; historical roots, 37; inequality causes of, 164, 183; literature re, 5–6, 7–8, 84–85; overconsumption causes of, 203–4; paradigms' insufficiency re, 5; perspective diversity re, 35, 209; policy/structural causes of, 82; poverty and, 69, 77, 157; remediation of, 190 (*see also* environmental solutions; environmentalism); resolution as means to nonenvironmental ends, 11; from second Green Revolution, 116; severity of, 2, 156, 194, 200; state handling of, 207–8 (*see also* state environmentalism); technology as cause of, 94; from throughput growth, 148; understanding, 6, 73, 98. *See also* environmental degradation/destruction

environmental scarcity, 142

environmental solutions, 78, 98; capitalist, 194; change mechanisms, 192–93; class paradigm views, 79, 89, 106, 211; complexity of, 12; ecological modernization theory for, 162–63; education, 86; effect on capitalism, 198; individual, 204; individualist paradigm views, 86, 89, 106; local-level governance, 105; managerial paradigm views, 89, 106; militaristic, 12; perspective diversity on, 209; possibility of, 207; synthesis needed for, 106; system reform, 85; technological, 94, 107n6, 162, 181, 212

environmental studies, ideological inquiry in, 14

environmentalism, 47, 60, 187; authentic, 188, 198, 200; conservative, 7; definitions, 188–90, 196, 204; development of, 190–91; extreme, 198; forms of, 10, 11, 188, 190–94, 204; free market, 7; ideologies in, 198–201, 200–201; leadership in, 188; means-end orientations in, 188, 194–97, 204; modes of, 11, 194–97, 204;

motivations in, 195, 197; paradigm integration in, 201–4; partnerships in, 201–4, 205, 210; polarization within, 201, 204; political alignment in, 189, 191, 193, 197, 200–201; postmaterialism in, 196; as social responsibility, 193; unity in, 201–4
equity. *See* inequality
Escobar, Arturo, 82
ethnicity as conflict basis, 18
European Fertility Project, 112
European Union, 84
Evans, Lloyd T., 113, 115, 116, 121
evolution: social (*see* social evolution); socioeconomic, 3, 9, 40–42
evolutionary determinism, 38
excesses, emerging, 10
exploitation: combating, 79, 80, 98; inevitability of, 21; of labor, 164; by North, 77. *See also* inequality
extinctions, 57

false consciousness, 17, 19, 36n3
famine, 111, 118, 126
FAO, 121
Faux, Jeff, 211
fertility rates, 111, 134; excess, 124; factors affecting, 112–13; poverty and, 125, 133, 139; replacement-level, 113, 144n1. *See also* population growth
feudalism, 43, 62, 74n1, 74n2
Finger, Mathias, 96, 97
fire, 51
fisheries, 57
Flavin, Christopher, 104
food stockpiles, 45
food supplies, 108
forces of production, 21
Fordism, 64, 75n18
fossil fuels, 53, 67; agriculture and, 115; dependence on, 54
Foster, John Bellamy, 136
Frank, André Gunder, 23
free market environmentalism, 86, 88–89, 189, 194; antipathy to state, 94; deficiencies in, 213

free market individualism. *See* individualist paradigm
freedom, personal, 66
Freeman, C., 66
French Revolution, 20
Friedland, Roger, 4, 21, 84
Fukuyama, Francis, 19
functionalism, 27, 33

Gallarotti, Giulio M., 194
Gallopin, Gilberto C., 69
gases, 56, 58
genetic engineering, 115–16, 116–17
Georgescu-Roegen, Nicholas, 153–54, 160, 172
Giddens, Anthony, 20, 33, 181, 210–11; on classical social theory, 34
Gleeson, Brendan, 99, 175
global warming. *See* climate
globalist period, 46
globalization, 107n10
Glyn, Andrew, 159
GNP (gross national product), 148
Godwin, William, 119
Goldblatt, David, 6
Goldfrank, Walter L., 80
Goldsmith, William W., 80
Goodland, Robert, 156
Gore, Albert, 104
Goudie, Andrew, 67
Gould, Kenneth Alan, 93, 94, 198
governance: consensual, 162; environmental, 85; errors in, 23; local-level, 105, 107n10; technocratic, 178
governments: economic intervention by, 25, 29, 78, 86, 94, 106; industry collaboration with, 202; market intervention by, 89; opposition to intervention by, 169; roles of, 29, 34; undermining of, 126. *See also* state
Gramsci, Antonio, 17, 23
Green Revolution, 108; need for second, 115, 115–17
Griffiths, Charles, 160
Grimes, Peter E., 161
gross national product (GNP), 148

gross world product, 149
Grossman, Gene M., 160
Grove, Richard H., 192
growth: definitions, 147, 149; economic
(*see* economic growth); income (*see*
income growth); quality of, 156,
157–58, 183; sustainable, 146 (*see also*
sustainable development); throughput
(*see* throughput growth)
Grübler, Arnulf, 53
Grundmann, Reiner, 80
guerrilla movements, 18
Guha, Ramachandra, 189, 190
Gulf War, 65
gun control, 18

Habermas, Jürgen, 23, 33
habitat destruction, 57
Hajer, Maarten A., 162, 183
Hall, John A., 44
Hall, Stuart, 210
Hardin, Garrett, 124
Harper, Charles L., 6, 47
Harrison, Lawrence E., 31, 32
Hawken, Paul, 194
Headrick, Daniel R., 53
Healey, Robert, 157
Heilbroner, Robert, 64
Hemmati, Minu, 202
Hempel, Lamont C., 104
HEP. *See* human exemptionalist paradigm
hierarchy, 81
Hildyard, Nicholas, 80, 90
Hill, Stephen, 25
Hillel, Daniel, 121
Hoffman, Andrew J., 193, 194
Homer-Dixon, Thomas F., 140, 141–42,
170, 210
Howitt, Peter, 170
Huber, Joseph, 162, 182
Huber, Peter, 88, 94, 97; progrowth view,
169, 173
human exemptionalist paradigm (HEP), 4,
47, 63, 66, 67
human potential, 138, 141, 142
human rights, 12, 18

human social evolution. *See* social
evolution
Humphrey, Craig R., 6
hunger and malnutrition, 120, 135, 137;
causes of, 128, 133, 138, 139, 143. *See
also* population-resource balance
Huntington, Samuel P., 31, 32

ICLARM (International Center for
Living Aquatic Resources
Management), 8
ideal environmentalism, 11, 194–96, 204
ideological conflicts, 18, 89; bases of,
18–19; mechanisms of, 106;
transcending, 210–11
ideological differences, 2, 3
ideology: awareness of, 4, 9; as category of
thought, 18–19, 208; choosing features
of, 211; class and, 59; concept of, 19,
35; conflicts among (*see* ideological
conflicts); definitions, 4, 14–17;
development of, 15; dominance and,
15–16; economic-ecological
convergence in, 162; empowerment
from, 16; environmental, 6, 77–89; in
environmentalism, 188, 200–201;
etymology, 17; examination of, 214;
hidden, 3–4; importance of, 3–4, 9, 14;
legitimation of, 16; nonpolitical, 7;
pejorative nature of term, 16–17,
18–19, 35; polarization from, 147;
population-resource balance and, 108;
power of, 13; primacy of, 6, 17; social
theory paradigms and (*see* social theory
paradigms); state and, 60; as
superstructure, 21; types of, 15
IFPRI, 121
Ikenberry, G. John, 44
income: increases, 125, 149; inequality,
104, 124, 156, 177, 198, 214;
necessity of increase, 148; per-capita
increases, 54, 132, 148; rich-poor gap,
55, 105, 137, 207; security, 61; world
mean, 161
income distribution, 165; inequality of,
149–50, 156

income growth, 148, 156, 183; support of,
164; throughput decrease and, 156,
172
income polarization, 105
individual: as analysis unit, 88; in
conservatism, 30; environmentalism
by, 190, 198; in liberalism, 28–29; roles
of, 5, 15
individualism, 20, 26, 47
individualist anti-Malthusianism, 10, 122,
123, 125, 143; exemplary statements,
129–31; issue framing, 132–33;
paradigm integration, 137–38; on
population issues, 133, 135; on second
Green Revolution, 134
individualist paradigm, 4, 5, 8, 12n2, 21,
25–28, 35; antigrowth view, 168–69,
170; anti-Malthusianism, 127–28 (see
also individualist anti-Malthusianism);
characteristics of, 22; class integration,
102–3, 104, 178–80; conservative
alignment of, 30; contingent view of
class paradigm, 95, 96; contingent
view of managerialism, 95–97; cultural
tradition within, 86–88, 106, 168–69,
180; environmental, 78, 85–89; free
market tradition within, 86, 88–89,
106, 180, 182; liberal alignment of, 29;
managerial alliance with, 97;
managerial integration, 103, 104,
178–80; paradigm integration in, 209;
production/consumption institutions
in, 180–81; progrowth view, 169–72;
rejection of class paradigm, 92, 93;
rejection of class perspective, 199, 200;
rejection of managerialism, 92–93,
93–94, 199, 200; rejectionist paradigm
isolation, 90–94; strengths and
weaknesses of, 212–13; view of
capitalism, 97
industrial environmentalism, 193
industrial revolution, 53, 74n11
industrialization, 3, 15, 25; core countries,
44; Durkheim on, 26; energy
technology for, 53; reactions to, 190
inequality, 135, 141, 208; biophysical
growth limits and, 166; class paradigm

view of, 211; in countries' economic
relationships, 44; distributional, 126;
in ecological modernization theory,
182–83; as environmental problem
cause, 164, 183; explanations of, 31
income, 104, 124, 156, 177, 198, 214
income distribution, 149–50, 156;
resource distribution, 121; structural,
164
inflation, 64
information, 89; access to, 2
Inglehart, Ronald, 196
Institute for Food and Development
Policy, 125
institutions, 25, 96; centrist, 121;
consumption, 162, 180–81; economic,
166; population-resource issues, 125;
production, 180–81; transformation of,
181
instrumental environmentalism, 11,
196–97, 204, 212
instrumental logic, 204
intellectual traditions, 89
Intergovernmental Panel on Climate
Change, 57
International Center for Living Aquatic
Resources Management (ICLARM), 8
International Conference on Population
and Development, 133
International Institute for Environment
and Development, 84
International Rice Research Institute
(IRRI), 8
irrationality, 180, 186n19
IRRI (International Rice Research
Institute), 8
irrigation, 52, 61, 115

Jacobs, Michael, 93, 99, 104, 156, 175
Jänicke, Martin, 162

Kahn, Herman, 153, 180
Kalof, Linda, 192
Kasun, Jacqueline, 132
Kaufmann, Robert K., 161
Kempton, Willett, 196
Keohane, Robert O., 96

Keynes, John Maynard, 13, 25
Keynesianism, 25, 29
Kinloch, Graham C., 9, 15
Kinney, John E., 88, 89, 169, 189
Krieger, Joel, 28
Krueger, Alan B., 160
Kyoto Protocol, 207

labor: appropriation of, 39; bargaining power, 23, 126; division of, 25–26, 27; exploitation of, 164; for production expansion, 77, 153; productivity, 53, 158; replacement of, 78; sale of, 43; supply, 23, 62, 119
language as conflict basis, 18
Lappé, Francis Moore, 125, 126, 128, 133; on government's role, 137; paradigm integration and isolation, 139
leaders and leadership, 86, 188
Leal, Donald R., 88, 89, 104; affirmation of government, 180; free market environmentalism, 189; progrowth view, 169, 173
Lee, Ronald Demos, 140–41, 210
left/radical: antigrowth posture, 11; anti-Malthusianism, 108, 126; attacks on, 88, 107n7; civic environmentalism, 11; class anti-Malthusianism, 136; class association with, 108; class paradigm alignment with, 28, 35; environmental movement and, 191; liberalism and, 30; political ecology and, 81; stigmatization of, 30–31; view of state, 90, 93
Lewis, Martin W., 193, 198
liberalism, 9; definitions, 28–29, 85; environment and, 85; managerialism and, 85; social, 29. See also center/liberal
libertarian municipalism, 81
libertarian state minimalism, 180
life circumstances, 14
life expectancy, 54, 55, 111
Linder, Marc, 122
Liska, Allen, 33
Locke, John, 28
logic, instrumental, 204

Low, Nicholas, 99, 175
Lowenthal, David, 47
Lukács, Georg, 17, 23

macrodemographic theory, 141
macro-micro linkage, 33
Malthus, Thomas, 10, 108, 117–19, 122; influence of, 121, 143
Malthusianism, 117–19; complementarity with Boserupian theory, 141; fertility behavior of poor, 133; inversion of, 120, 125. See also anti-Malthusianism; neo-Malthusianism
Mamdani, Mahmood, 125, 128
management, need for, 23–24
managerial neo-Malthusianism, 10, 122–27, 143; capitalism in, 137; exemplary statements, 129–31; issue framing, 128; paradigm integration, 136–38; population issues, 133, 135; on second Green Revolution, 133–34
managerial paradigm, 4, 5, 21, 23–25, 35; antigrowth view, 166–67; characteristics of, 22; class integration, 102, 176, 177, 178–79; contingent view of class paradigm, 94–96; contingent view of individualism, 95, 96; cultural individualist view in, 180; ecological modernization theory (see ecological modernization theory); in economic growth debate, 85, 163, 172; environmental, 78, 82–85; individualist alliance with, 97; individualist integration, 102, 104, 176, 177–80; liberal alignment of, 29; neo-Malthusianism, 126–27 (see also managerial neo-Malthusianism; neo-Malthusianism); paradigm integration in, 209; progrowth view, 167–68; proponents, 82, 84; rejection of class paradigm, 92, 93; rejection of class perspective, 198–200; rejection of individualism, 93, 198–200; rejectionist paradigm isolation, 90–94; in state environmentalism, 192; strengths and weaknesses of, 212–13; tenets of, 82, 106; tools of, 125; view of capitalism, 97

managerialism, 84, 166; liberalism and, 85; neo-Malthusianism, 127
Mannheim, Karl, 17
Manno, Jack P., 60
Marx, Karl, 5, 10, 17, 24, 117; on aid restraint, 119; on capitalism, 21–22, 36n6; ecological interpretations of, 80–81, 164; intellectual legacy of, 20, 89; on population catastrophism, 119, 141; population paradigms, 121; population-resource balance and, 108; use of social theory, 24; Weber's theories and, 33
Marxism, 23, 172, 182. See also neo-Marxism
material conditions, 17
materialist philosophy, 21, 23
McMichael, Philip, 67
means of production, 21, 43
mental models, 2, 4, 14. See also ideology
Meristo, T., 159
Merton, Roger, 27
Mesarovic, Mihaljo, 153
Milbrath, Lester W., 47
military-industrial complex, 65
Mill, John Stuart, 150
Mishan, E. J., 153
mobilization, 60, 79, 106; civic, 191; contradictory, 11; for environmental solutions, 207; modes of, 18; need for, 214; by NGOs, 104
modernization, 26; fertility transition and, 111; market mechanism for, 182; reflexive, 181
modes of production, 21, 22, 208; class change through, 39; slavery, 39, 43; state's role in change of, 59
Mohan, Raj P., 9, 15
Mol, Arthur P. J., 162, 182
Montreal Protocol, 56, 82
moral individualism, 26
moralism, 173
morality, 26
mortality, 55, 62, 111; child, 54
motivations, individual, 28. See also environmentalism

MSPs (multistakeholder partnerships), 201–4
multistakeholder partnerships (MSPs), 201–4
Murdoch, William W., 125
Murphy, Raymond, 84
Myers, Norman, 124, 126

Naess, Arne, 86, 97, 104, 172
national identity, 18
nations. See countries; see also state
natural resources. See resources
negotiation, 12
neoclassical economics, 27, 36n10, 86, 88, 153–55; critiques of, 170
neofunctionalism, 33
neo-Malthusianism, 10, 108, 121; class, 122, 123; critiques of, 141; fertility control, 134; individualist, 122, 123, 124; international influence of, 134–35; managerial (see managerial neo-Malthusianism); popularity of, 134–35
neo-Marxism, 81, 164, 182; corporate environmentalism and, 198
NEP. See new ecological paradigm
nepotism, 179
net primary productivity (NPP), 57
Neumann, R. P., 81
new ecological paradigm (NEP), 4, 47, 189
NGOs. See nongovernmental organizations
nitrogen availability, 58
nongovernmental organizations (NGOs), 80, 197, 202; corporate partnerships, 201; environmentalism by, 190; managerial paradigm adherence, 84
North, Douglass C., 25
Norton, Bryan G., 201
Novak, Michael, 2
NPP (net primary productivity), 57
nuclear power, 54, 58

objectivity, 25
O'Connor, James, 80, 99, 164, 175

Olpadwalla, Porus, 80
ontologies, realist, 105
optimism, 2, 108, 120, 207, 214; in
    corporate environmentalism, 194; in
    dematerialization, 159–60; despairing,
    10, 121, 123; grounds for, 163; re
    human creativity, 125, 132, 138;
    ideology and, 143; managerial
    despairing, 122, 125; in sustainable
    development theories, 157
organizational styles, 66
Osborn, Fairfield, 128
overconsumption, 103, 104, 106, 128,
    164, 166; forces promoting, 203–4;
    values underlying, 213
oversimplification, 32–33, 90, 99; from
    extreme positions, 146; from prime
    mover logic, 136, 209

Paehlke, Robert C., 191, 201
Panayotou, Theodore, 160
paradigm integration, 5, 6, 8, 9, 10,
    98–105; application of, 12; complete,
    98–99, 208; deficient, 210–11; by
    ecological modernization theory,
    181–83; in economic growth debate,
    11, 147, 175–83, 184–85; efforts
    toward, 33; empirical data for, 183; in
    environmentalism, 188, 201–4, 205;
    evidence of, 99–105; forms of, 99, 100;
    grounds for, 108; ideology
    transcendence and, 201; increases in,
    209–10; initiatives arising from, 12;
    logic replacement, 140; necessity of,
    76, 99; partial, 139; population
    paradigms, 136–40; population-
    resource balance views, 109; in post-
    Marxist formulations, 23; sustainable
    development and, 157; tenet
    coexistence in, 11–12, 32–33, 99;
    theoretical, 105
paradigm isolation, 5, 6, 9, 35, 76, 209;
    against class paradigm, 210;
    contingent, 10, 32, 76, 94–97, 138,
    209; economic growth issue, 147,
    172–74; in environmentalism, 188,

197–201, 204; exemplary statements,
    91–93, 95–96; explicit, 31–32, 76,
    90–97; implicit, 10, 32, 76, 97–98,
    141, 173–74, 209; influence on
    environmental views, 35; integral view
    contrasted, 37; irrationality of, 89;
    logic of, 135–36; mechanisms of, 136;
    pitfalls of, 106; population paradigms,
    134–36, 143; population-resource
    balance views, 109; public action
    retardation by, 11; reasons for, 11,
    89–90; rejectionist, 10, 32, 76, 90–94,
    209; self-defeating nature of, 11;
    tendency toward, 89, 99, 106; tenet
    valuation, 97; types of, 31–33, 76
paradigms, 4, 20, 36n5; development of,
    59; tenets in, 5. See also social theory
    paradigms
Parsons, Talcott, 27, 33
Pearce, David, 93, 167, 172, 173
Peet, Richard, 82
Pepper, David, 82, 189, 201
Perelman, Michael, 128
Perez, C., 66
personal environmentalism, 11, 194–96,
    204
pessimism, 2, 108, 120, 207; ideology and,
    143
Pestel, Eduard, 153
Place, Francis, 122
plants, domestication of, 51, 64, 74n9
pluralist paradigm. See individualist
    paradigm
Polanyi, Karl, 20
polemics, 4; on environmentalism, 200;
    internal, 7, 12n4, 77; within
    managerial paradigm, 85
policy, 8; environmental, 200; as hunger
    cause, 139; inadequacy, 106; on
    population growth, 134, 135;
    reform/change, 89, 97, 98, 107n6, 161,
    212; role of, 99
policy making, 3, 82
political ecology, 80, 81–82, 107n4;
    antigrowth view in, 164
political economy, 21

Political Economy Research Center, 169
political ideology. *See* ideology
political orientation, 4
political science, 5, 21; conceptual
    categories, 9, 30–31 (*see also* political
    spectrum); sociology and, 28
political spectrum, 6, 15;
    environmentalism on (*see*
    environmentalism); label distortion,
    30–31; Malthusian debate and, 122;
    social theory paradigm alignment on,
    21, 22, 28–31, 208
politics, 45; culture and, 97; in ideology,
    3–4, 15
pollutants, 161, 214
Poncelet, Eric C., 202
population: affluence and, 61; class and,
    62–64; concentration of, 45; culture
    and, 63, 66; environmental impact of,
    10 (*see also* population growth); excess,
    118–20, 128 (*see also* population-
    resource balance); human evolution
    and, 38, 40–41; interactions with other
    social theory variables, 63, 72, 73;
    power and, 63, 65; reduction, 134;
    stabilization number, 110; support
    capacity, 108; technology and, 61–62
Population Action International, 124, 133
population catastrophism, 117–18, 119;
    agreement with, 124, 126; neo-
    Malthusian view, 128, 132
population growth, 3, 13–14, 49, 50;
    absolute numbers, 139, 143; beneficial,
    132, 133; capitalism and, 126–28;
    causes of, 133; control of, 2;
    deleterious, 65, 121, 133, 138;
    demographic transition (*see*
    demographic transition); in developing
    countries, 48, 56, 113, 143;
    environmental change and, 47–48; in
    last century, 149; poverty and, 118–19,
    122 (*see also* poverty); processes of,
    141; projections, 109–10, 114, 134;
    pulses, 48, 50; rate, 117, 118, 122, 139,
    214; reversal, 55, 132–33; solutions to,
    134; synergistic interactions fostering,

59; unequal rates of, 48; war and, 132;
    working-class decisions, 126. *See also*
    fertility rates
population paradigms, 10; antecedents of,
    108–9, 117–21; changes in, 134–35;
    contemporary, 121–25; dominant, 122,
    125–34, 143; exemplary statements,
    129–31; integration models, 140–43;
    integration of, 136–40; polarization,
    134; tenet acceptance, 138
population planning, 124, 127, 138;
    opposition to, 3; by poor, 118, 122,
    126
population-resource balance, 10, 109–17,
    138; achieving, 134; biological limits,
    121; contemporary views, 121–25; data
    sources, 109; dominant paradigms,
    125–34; equity needs, 134, 135,
    136–37; Malthusian theories, 118;
    neo-Malthusian views, 128, 132, 135;
    paradigm isolation and, 143;
    population-food equation, 108,
    113–14; problem resolution methods,
    125; theoretical models, 140–43; views
    of, 108–9
Porter, Gareth, 104
postmodernism, 19
poststructuralism, 82
poverty, 9, 55, 138; aid restraint theory,
    118–19, 124; alleviation, 150, 183;
    causes of, 77, 119, 125, 128; economic
    growth for reducing, 177, 178, 180;
    environmental destruction and, 69, 77,
    157; fertility rates and, 125, 133, 139;
    food purchasing power, 113, 134, 139,
    143; Malthusian theories, 118–19;
    relation to wealth, 69–70, 73;
    resolution of, 54, 134
power, 9; affluence and, 63, 65;
    association with center, 108; class and,
    59; culture and, 60; environmental
    change and, 44–46, 209; human
    evolution and, 40–41; interactions
    with other social theory variables, 63,
    72, 73; population and, 63, 65;
    relations, 181; as social theory

variable, 37, 38; sources of, 24; of state, 65, 209; technology and, 63, 65–66
power relationships, 24
preconceptions, 2
presuppositions, 16
privilege, maintenance of, 46
production: attention to, 205; forces of, 21; means of, 21, 43; modes of (see modes of production); relations of, 21, 22, 23
production function equations, 154
production process, 153, 161; content decrease, 158; reform of, 162
profit, 23, 64, 166; conversion of, 70–71; increasing, 78
progress, indefinite, 67. See also sustainable development
pronatalism, 127. See also anti-Malthusianism
property rights, 106, 119, 169
Prugh, Thomas, 104

race, 18
radicalism, 9
radioactive waste, 58
rain, acid, 56, 58
rational choice theory, 27–28
rationalism, 47
rationalization, 23, 66, 84, 181; world-level, 192
Reagan, Ronald, 3
reductionism, 34–35
reforestation, 56
regime building, 82, 84, 107n5
regulatory environmentalism, 193
relations of production, 21, 22; oppression in, 23
religious ideology, 18
representation, empiricist models of, 19
resource limitations, 137, 141; existence of, 172; overcoming, 170
resources, 132–33; constraints on use, 88, 89, 141, 153; consumption of (see consumption); demand on, 56, 59, 77; dependence on, 1; depletion, 70, 118, 214; distribution, 121, 150; EKC

relationship, 161; endowments of, 185n4; exploitation of, 70, 213; management of, 86; net primary productivity, 57; overconsumption (see overconsumption); in production process, 153, 158; productivity of, 158; renewable, 156; services from, 160; substitutes, 132, 153, 154–55; technology to transform, 51. See also environment
responsibility, individual, 85, 98
Ricardo, David, 118, 119
right/conservative, 29–30, 30–31; anti-Malthusianism, 108, 126, 128; corporate environmentalism, 11; culture association with, 108; deep ecology and, 191; economic growth debate position, 152; individualist anti-Malthusianism, 136; individualist paradigm alignment with, 28, 35; progrowth stance, 11
risk, 67, 190
Ritzer, George, 33
Robbins, Richard H., 60
Roberts, Geoffrey, 28
Roberts, J. Timmons, 161
Roemer, John, 23
Ross, Eric B., 125
Rothenberg, David, 86, 104, 172
Ruth, Matthias, 159
Ruttan, Vernon, 117
Ryan, Alan, 211

Sachs, Wolfgang, 80, 90, 99, 103; on environmental diplomacy, 172; managerialism and, 175; on power relations, 181; on overconsumption, 164
Sage, Colin, 141
Salter cycle, 181
Sarkar, Saral, 81, 82, 93, 122
scarcity, 141–42, 213; emerging, 10
Schmidheiny, Stephan, 193–94
Schmookler, Andrew Bard, 60, 65
Schnaiberg, Allan, 77, 93, 94, 181, 198
Schor, Juliet B., 159, 172

Schroeder, R. A., 81
Schurman, Rachel, 125, 133
Schwartz, Herman M., 66
scientific method, 47
sea level, 57
Seabrook, Jeremy, 80
Selden, Thomas M., 160
self-interest, 27, 47, 88, 89
September 11, 2001 terrorist attacks, 18
Serageldin, Ismail, 116
serfs. *See* feudalism
Sessions, George, 86, 93, 104, 172
Shafik, Nemat, 160
ships, sail, 52
Shiva, Vandana, 103
Simmons, I. G., 51
Simon, Julian, 3, 121, 134, 170; anti-
    Malthusianism, 126, 132; on *Limits to
    Growth* report, 152
Simonis, Udo, 162
slavery, 39, 43, 59–60, 213–14; emergence
    of, 64
Smelser, Neil, 27
Smil, Vaclav, 51, 53
Smith, Adam, 27
social change, variables in, 38
social ecology, 7, 80, 81
social evolution, 37–38; early farming
    phase, 38, 40–41, 46, 48; early urban
    phase, 38, 40–41, 48; environmental
    outcomes, 39, 41–42, 56–58, 69; high
    energy phase, 38, 40–41, 48; outcome
    synergies, 68–72; phases of, 38–39,
    40–42; population growth and, 62;
    primeval phase, 38, 39, 40–41, 46, 48;
    social outcomes, 41–42, 54–56;
    socioeconomic, 3, 9, 40–42; variables,
    38
social outcomes: environment's effect on,
    70; linkage to environmental
    outcomes, 9, 68–72
social problems, causes of, 23–24, 26
social representations, shared, 14
social science: managerial/environmental
    theorizing, 85; objectivity in, 25
social structure: culture and, 25;
    determinants, 22, 24, 27

social theory, 5–7, 20–21, 35n2;
    capitalism in, 15; classical, 34–35;
    definition, 20; interactions among
    variables, 58–68; political ideology in,
    14; uses of, 24; variables of, 37, 38
social theory paradigms, 4–5, 21, 22;
    classical, 6; conflicts among, 7, 8, 90,
    97–98; cross-boundary work, 98;
    disparities within, 77; dominance
    patterns, 126; in economic growth
    debate, 163–72; environmental, 6,
    77–89; in environmentalism, 198–201;
    importance of, 6–7; incompatibilities
    among, 5, 6, 8, 33, 35, 99; individual
    insufficiency of, 98, 210;
    integration/merger of (*see* paradigm
    integration); isolation of (*see* paradigm
    isolation); objectives of, 98; political
    spectrum and (*see* political spectrum);
    population paradigms and, 121–25;
    position softening in, 175; prime
    mover in, 89, 93, 96, 99, 135; prime
    mover thinking, 138, 139, 183, 209,
    210; reductionism in, 34–35; strengths
    and weaknesses of, 211–13; tenet
    valuation, 90, 94, 99, 106, 135, 175;
    tenets of, 11–12, 31, 35, 208; "third
    way," 210–11; for understanding, 208;
    variables in, 37
social-environmental synergies, 68
socialism, 80. *See also* communism
societal processes, 25
socioeconomic evolution, 3, 9, 40–42
sociological theory, 6–7, 20
sociology, 25, 28
solar energy, 53, 54
Solow, Robert, 153, 154, 167
Song, Daqing, 160
Sonnenfeld, David A., 162
Southwick, Charles H., 51
Soviet Union, collapse of, 18
Spaargaren, Gert, 182
stakeholder partnerships, 188, 194, 201,
    210
state, 212; capitalism and, 45, 198;
    development of, 44–46, 59, 66;
    economic growth and, 45, 46, 164;

elites and, 46; environmental action levels, 192; free market view of, 94; ideology and, 60; instrumental view of, 98; in liberalism, 28–29; national, 45; opposition to, 81, 139; power of, 65, 209; responsibility for environmental problems, 82, 99; role in environmental matters, 187, 189 (*see also* state environmentalism); role in capitalist society, 15, 23–24; roles of, 46, 104, 180, 213; social complexity needed for, 45. *See also* power

state environmentalism, 11, 188, 189, 190, 192–93; instrumental goals in, 196; motivations for, 198, 204

statism, 192

Stern, David I., 161

Stiglitz, Joseph E., 153, 154, 167

Stockdale, Jerry, 157

Stokke, Olav, 94

Stott, Philip, 82

strategic environmentalism, 193

stratification. *See* class

Stretton, Hugh, 80

structural scarcity, 142

structural transformation, 181

structuralism, 27, 81

substatism, 192

Sullivan, Sian, 82

Sun, J. W., 159

suprastatism, 192

Suri, Vivek, 161

sustainable development, 78, 156–57, 183; class paradigm view of, 80, 99; ecological modernization theory and, 181; free market environmentalism view of, 88–89; middle-ground position re, 155; opposition to, 169, 200; paradigm integration in, 157; proponents, 166, 167, 213; theoretical core, 82; weak versus strong, 155, 166, 167

Switzer, Jacqueline Vaughn, 200

synergies, 58–72; negative, 59, 61, 73

Taliban, 18

Taylor, Peter J., 196

technology: affluence and, 62; for agricultural productivity increases, 116, 134; biotechnology, 116–17; class and, 64–65; climate amelioration by, 74n10; culture and, 63, 67; development, 3, 53; development incentives, 61, 64; economic growth limits and, 152–53; environmental change and, 51–54; environmental impact of, 10; as environmental problem cause, 94; as environmental problem solution, 8, 94, 107n6, 162, 181, 212; human evolution and, 38; innovation, 64, 66, 121, 162, 180, 213; interactions with other social theory variables, 63, 72, 73; policy change and, 107n6; population and, 61–62; power and, 63, 65–66

terrorism, 18, 58

thermodynamics, laws of, 154, 172

Thomas, Vinod, 180

throughput growth, 148, 214; critiques of, 164; income growth distinguished, 156, 183; reducing, 158, 184

Tilly, Charles, 59

Tokar, Brian, 198

topsoil, 57

Torras, Mariano, 162

trade, 66

trade unions, 18

training, 26. *See also* education

truth, 14, 16; absolute, 19

Turner, Bryan, 25

Turner, R. Kerry, 155

UNCED (United Nations Commission on Environment and Development), 167

unemployment, 119

unions, 18

United Nations Commission on Environment and Development (UNCED), 167

United Nations Commission on Sustainable Development, 201

United Nations Development Programme, 149

urbanization, 15, 25, 66; early population growth and, 118; early urban phase, 45

U.S. Agency for International
Development (USAID), 84, 202
USAID. *See* U.S. Agency for
International Development

value: creation of, 23; energy theories of,
185n6; surplus, 23
values, 15, 46; cultural, 31; distorted, 106;
of Enlightenment, 47; in
functionalism, 27; individual, 26,
36n8; overconsumption and, 213;
revolution, 172; traditional, 86;
universalizing, 16, 32; Western, 60, 88
van Dijk, Teun A., 14, 15, 16
Velázquez, Margarita, 139
views, contradictory, 3. *See also* paradigm
integration; social theory paradigms
violence, 18; scarcity and, 142; state
control of, 45, 59
voluntary simplicity, 47

wage laborers, 43, 119, 214
Wallerstein, Immanuel, 23, 80, 90, 94,
198
Walley, Noah, 194
war, 59, 62; population growth and, 132;
reasons for, 65; state power and, 65,
209
war on terrorism, 18
water: availability of, 57, 115; quality, 56,
58, 160; use increases, 57
water wheels, 52
Wattenberg, Ben J., 127, 132
Watts, Michael, 81, 82
wealth, 9; generation of, 39; relation to
poverty, 69–70, 73. *See also* affluence

Weaver, James H., 173
Weber, Max, 5, 24; intellectual legacy of,
20, 89; Marx's theories and, 33; on
state development, 66
Wernick, Iddo K., 158
westernization, 67, 86
Whitehead, Bradley, 194
Wiener, Anthony, 153
Wiley, Norbert, 33
windmills, 52
Woolard, Ed, 193
World Bank, 70, 82, 121; on elite power
abuse, 179; food redistribution, 139;
NGO funding, 202; poverty-
environment linkage, 157; progrowth
view, 167; publications, 156–58, 160;
WCD and, 203; WWF collaboration,
202
World Commission on Dams, 203
World Commission on Environment and
Development, 69, 84, 156–57, 167
World Conservation Union, 203
World Resources Institute, 84
world society theory, 192
world systems theory, 80
World Wide Fund for Nature, 202
worldviews, 36n7: of disenfranchised, 34;
paradigm founders, 89; revision of,
136; shaping of, 14. *See also* social
theory paradigms
Worldwatch Institute, 1–2, 84, 124, 166
Wright, Erik Olin, 23

Young, Oran R., 93

Zeitlin, Irving M., 20

~

About the Author

William D. Sunderlin spent his early years in Washington, D.C., Brussels, Belgium, and New York City. After finishing his undergraduate degree at Williams College in 1976, he worked with the Syracuse Peace Council for eight years on various activist causes, including opposition to the construction of nuclear power plants in New York State and opposition to the U.S. war against Nicaragua. From 1984 through 1992 he was in graduate school in the Department of Rural Sociology at Cornell University. He produced a master's thesis on agricultural cooperatives in Nicaragua and a doctoral dissertation on the Java Social Forestry Program in Indonesia. In 1993 he conducted research on fishing and resource decline at the International Center for Living Aquatic Resources Management (ICLARM) in the Philippines. From 1994 to the present he has been a scientist at the Center for International Forestry Research (CIFOR) in Bogor, Indonesia. At CIFOR he has done research on the underlying causes of tropical deforestation, population growth, macroeconomic Dutch disease, the effects of economic crises, and the use of forest resources for poverty alleviation. He can be contacted at w.sunderlin@cgiar.org.